THE DEVIANCE PROCESS

SECOND EDITION

The Deviance Process

SECOND EDITION

Erdwin H. Pfuhl, Jr.
Arizona State University

Wadsworth Publishing Company
Belmont, California
A Division of Wadsworth, Inc.

Sociology Editor: Sheryl Fullerton

Production Services Coordinator: Jerilyn Emori

Production: Cece Munson
   The Cooper Company: Publication Services

Interior Designer: John Odam

Manuscript Editor: Carol Dondrea

Cover Designer: John Edeen

Print Buyer: Ruth Cole

Printed in the United States of America

   2 3 4 5 6 7 8 9 10—90 89 88 87

ISBN 0-534-05892-2

**Library of Congress Cataloging-in-
Publication Data**

Pfuhl, Erwin H., Jr.
   The deviance process.

   Bibliography: p.
   Includes indexes.
   1. Deviant behavior.   2. Stigma (Social
psychology)
I. Title.
HM291.P485   1986   302.5'42   85-15799
ISBN 0-534-05892-2

To My Family

Acknowledgments

Acknowledgment is made to the following publishers and individuals for permission to reprint quotations:

Howard S. Becker. *Outsiders: Studies in the Sociology of Deviance.* Copyright © 1973 by Howard S. Becker. Copyright © 1963 by The Free Press. Reprinted with permission of The Free Press, a Division of Macmillan, Inc.

Brendan Behan. *Borstal Boy.* Copyright © 1958, 1959 by Brendan Behan. Reprinted with permission of Alfred A. Knopf, Inc. and Hutchinson Publishing Group, Ltd.

Claude Brown. *Manchild in the Promised Land.* Copyright © 1965 Claude Brown. Reprinted with permission of Macmillan Publishing Company.

Jack D. Douglas and Paul K. Rasmussen, with Carol Ann Flanagan. *The Nude Beach.* Copyright © 1977. Reprinted with permission of Sage Publications, Inc.

Charles E. Frazier. *Theoretical Approaches to Deviance: An Evaluation.* Charles E. Merrill Publishing Company, 1976. Reprinted with permission of Charles E. Frazier.

Erving Goffman. *Stigma: Notes on the Management of Spoiled Identity.* © 1963 by Prentice-Hall, Inc. Reprinted with permission of Prentice-Hall, Inc.

Jerry Jacobs. *Deviance: Field Studies and Self-Disclosures.* Mayfield Publishing Company (formerly National Press Books), 1974. Reprinted with permission of Jerry Jacobs.

Merle Miller. "What It Means to Be a Homosexual." *New York Times Magazine,* January 17 and October 10, 1971. Reprinted with permission of Merle Miller.

Barbara Ponse. "Secrecy in the Lesbian World." *Urban Life,* Vol. 5, No. 3, October 1976. Copyright © 1976. Reprinted with permission of Sage Publications, Inc.

Joseph Sataloff. *Hearing Loss, 2nd ed.* J. B. Lippincott Company, 1980. Reprinted with permission of J. B. Lippincott Company.

Charlotte Green Schwartz. "The Stigma of Mental Illness." *Journal of Rehabilitation,* Vol. 22, July/August 1956. Reprinted with permission of the National Rehabilitation Association.

Frank Tannenbaum. *Crime and the Community.* Originally published by Ginn and Company, 1938. Reprinted with permission of Columbia University Press.

W. Clinton Terry III and David F. Luckenbill. "Investigating Criminal Homicides: Police Work in Reporting and Solving Murders." In W. B. Sanders and H. C. Daudistel (eds.), *The Criminal Justice Process.* Praeger Publishers, 1976. Reprinted with permission of W. Clinton Terry III and David F. Luckenbill.

Frederic M. Thrasher. *The Gang.* The University of Chicago Press, 1936. Reprinted with permission of The University of Chicago Press.

Preface

As with the first edition of *The Deviance Process,* the purpose of this brief text is to offer students a perspective for studying deviance that will help them make sense of their everyday lives. In this second edition of *The Deviance Process,* a number of theoretical considerations carried in the first edition have been deleted, while other matters have been expanded and made more understandable. Overall, the examples used explicate elements of the theoretical model used. Further, examples of aspects of the deviance process have been updated, now drawing on more contemporary events as well as new research.

The perspective used in this text is called the Paradigm of Definition and includes elements of interactionist and phenomenological sociology. It is a view that perceives deviance (and its opposite, respectability) as a human creation resulting from people interacting with one another and that reflects the meaning they assign to one another and to patterns of behavior. It is a view that regards deviance as the outcome of the antagonisms, contradictions, and conflicts in society. It is a perspective that gives serious attention to people's explanations for their actions. Above all, it is a view that rejects the notion that deviance is the "essence" of things.

To avoid the impression that there is something about certain conditions and behaviors—an essential or inherent element—that makes them deviant calls for a perspective that allows for flexibility. That is, making sense of the deviance-creating process (such as how behaviors get banned by law and how laws are enforced with varying degrees of emphasis) calls for a morally relativistic position. We do not live in an absolutistic world; in dealing with the affairs of everyday life, each of us behaves as a relativist. This approach is consistent with the fact that we live in a society marked by internal differences of every conceivable sort; it is a heterogeneous society wherein few things remain sacred and unquestioned, where rules seldom go unchallenged, and where behavioral styles are revised regularly. No valid consideration of deviance can ignore these differences and dynamics. The approach used here focuses on these very things and weaves them into the larger explanatory framework.

Examining deviance in this way also requires that it be studied in political terms, that is, as a fundamental part of the business of making and enforcing public rules. Although other theoretical approaches to the study of deviance do not necessarily preclude discussion of the politics of deviance, neither are they known to promote it. In the present instance, however, deviance is expressly viewed as an outgrowth of making, enforcing, and administering social policy—that is, the business of politics.

Studying deviance as an ongoing aspect of collective life means we must examine it as a series of events and actions occurring over time. Accordingly, materials in this book are arranged sequentially, following the events or stages that make up the deviance process. Categories or types of deviation—obesity, blindness, mental illness, drug use, prostitution, homosexuality, and so on—are subordinate to the study of the process and are used only to highlight select aspects of it.

Given a sequential orientation, the book is organized to provide an overview of the deviance process. The first chapter, Studying Deviance, introduces students to the assumptions, about society, people, behavior, and so on, on which the interactionist and phenomenological approaches rest and which will be employed throughout the volume. Taken together, these approaches and assumptions are called the Paradigm of Definition.

Chapter 2, Breaking Rules, presents an explanation of rule breaking that is consistent with the relevant aspects of the Paradigm of Definition. Chapter 3, Counting Deviants, examines official statistics on deviance (such as police and FBI statistics on crime), focusing especially on how they are created, whether or not they are biased, and what meanings can be given to them. Chapter 4, Banning Behavior, is an excursion into the sociology of law. Here we examine how select patterns of behavior come to be defined as deviant. The roles of moral entrepreneurs and the media are stressed. Deviance also includes the official identification and public labeling of a select number of rule breakers. The activities of social agencies involved in this aspect of the deviance process are examined in Chapter 5, Creating Deviants. In Chapter 6, Consequences of Stigma, we discuss the theory behind the concern over labeling people deviant, and give consideration to the personal and social consequences experienced by people who are identified as deviant. Special attention is given to the idea of deviance amplification and the evidence bearing on the validity of that idea. Lastly, in keeping with theoretical considerations established at the outset, Chapter 7, Managing Stigma, focuses on the individual and collective ways people seek to manage or deal with having been stigmatized. We conclude with a brief Epilogue, focusing on deviance as an ever-changing, yet enduring aspect of collective life.

In each chapter critical terms are italicized and a working definition is provided. A more complete definition of terms is provided in the glossary at the back of the book.

Finally, no one writes a book alone. I owe a hugh debt of gratitude to many people who, in various ways, have assisted in this effort. Included, of course, are those from whom I have borrowed ideas and information; their names are listed in the index. More direct has been the support and valuable suggestions provided by David O. Friedrichs, University of Scranton; Trudy Knicely Henson, University of South Caroline; Craig B. Little, State University of New York College at Cortland; Armand L. Mauss, Washington State University; and David A. Nordlie, Bemidji State University. A special thanks is also in order for my former students, Bryce T. Johnson, Southern Oregon State College, and Richard L. Schuster, Virginia Polytechnic Institute and State University, who have added much to the satisfactions of my academic life. For their contribution by way of being good listeners and offering timely and constructive ideas, I acknowledge the support and assistance of my good friends and colleagues David L. Altheide, Ronald A. Hardert, John M. Johnson, Richard H. Nagasawa, and Robert P. Snow.

But getting out a book involves more than authoring. Thus, I wish to give a special thanks to Sheryl Fullerton, my editor, as well as to the many other people at Wadsworth who helped make this a pleasurable experience; to Debbie Sult who, with great skill, typed the entire manuscript; and to Cece Munson of The Cooper Company who answered all my letters and phone calls without complaint and expertly shepherded the manuscript through the maze called "production."

Lastly, I thank my best friend, companion, and wife, Joan. After 32 years she continues to listen, provide the needed "boosts," and make life a joy.

Erdwin H. Pfuhl, Jr.

Contents

The Deviance Process

SECOND EDITION

1 Studying Deviance

Introduction

Public interest in rule breakers and their behavior runs high in our society. Collectively, Americans spend millions of hours each week watching fictional and nonfictional TV presentations of a wide variety of such people.[1] As a result of its popularity, this programming has become a prime source of network profit. In fact, what would we do for "entertainment" without this element of popular culture? Such interest is also reflected in the press and other news media, where information about crime and other morally objectionable behavior is given equal coverage to news of international events, business and the economy, art, theater, music, and sports. Clearly, rule breaking is well established in our society as both an attention getter and a money maker. It may be that nothing else is so capable of titillating the masses while at the same time leaving them horrified.

To be sure, people's interest in deviance is often more than recreational. For example, students sometimes enroll in deviant behavior courses because they anticipate a vicarious thrill from examining accounts of the lives of "whores, hoods, and homos." Sometimes interest stems from having been victimized by rule breakers. Perhaps their automobile has been stolen, or they have had a fender crunched by a "hit-and-run" motorist; perhaps their residence has been burglarized or vandalized; or they or a family member or friend has

been assaulted. Or, their interest may be based on F.B.I. reports that crime and deviance are among the nation's most serious problems. On the other hand, people's interest may stem from their own participation in socially discreditable and proscribed forms of behavior: smoking pot or using cocaine or other outlawed substances, engaging in publicly disavowed sexual behavior, fudging on income tax, petty (or grand) theft, and the like, ad infinitum. After all, it has been said that ours is a nation of law breakers, and someone must be doing the kinds of things authorities say go on (Wallerstein and Wyle, 1947; Short and Nye, 1958; Murphy, Shirley, and Witmer, 1946; Robin, 1969; Gold, 1966 and 1970).

Whatever the reason for our interest and however widespread it is in our society, not all forms of rule breaking elicit the same response. Sometimes the action evokes a smile or chuckle, as when we learn that some San Francisco call girls accept payment for services by credit card. Other incidents leave us with a "chill," as when we read that a college professor at Edward Walters College has been shot and killed by a student angered over a poor grade. Other incidents might leave us a bit puzzled, as when we read in the press that a 60-year-old man cut his honeymoon short when he discovered that his new "bride" was a man undergoing treatment in preparation for a sex-change operation. Other people may be dismayed and wonder "where will it all end" when they learn that a Roman Catholic priest, the Vatican's fourth-ranking diplomat at the United Nations, was arrested for allegedly smuggling Italian art treasures into the United States; or that a former Florida Supreme Court Justice was arrested for allegedly conspiring to import and distribute over five tons of marijuana; or that the Church of Jesus Christ of

---

[1]Between 1953 and 1977 the percentage of time devoted to crime and law enforcement shows during the prime television viewing hours grew from a low of 7% (1953) to a high of 39% (1975). Immediately thereafter the proportion declined to about 30% (Dominick, 1978: 114), where it tends to hover.

Latter-day Saints is charged with "flagrant violation of the Sherman Antitrust Act through its corporate business subsidiaries." Finally, we may suppose that many people cheered while others screamed "book burners" and charged "censorship" when they learned that a group of three mothers in a small Arizona town launched an effort to strip the junior high school's library shelves of books discussing menstruation, masturbation, training bras, teen-age sexuality, and other things the parents defined as morally objectionable. In short, rule breaking and associated events take incredibly diverse forms and get an equally mixed response.

These and similar situations, anecdotal in nature and perhaps interesting in their own right, major and minor, funny and deadly serious, immediate and abstract, could be listed indefinitely. However, these anecdotal materials are to the sociology of deviance what the tip is to the iceberg; by themselves they are only a small part of what sociologists mean when they speak of deviance. Sociological interest runs far deeper and encompasses much more. It involves identifying common elements among many behaviors and conditions regarded as deviant, arranging these things in categories, and investigating a host of related personal and social elements. Let's talk about how sociologists study deviance.

In doing their work, sociologists have been guided by a variety of theoretical mental "pictures" or models. As one sociologist put it:

Each sociologist carries in his head one or more "models" of society and man which greatly influence what he looks for, what he sees, and what he does with his observations by way of fitting them, along with other facts, into a larger scheme of explanation. In this respect the sociologist is no different from any other scientist. Every scientist holds some general conception of the realm in which he is working, some mental picture of "how it is put together and how it works." (Barber, 1973:2)

Models, then, guide investigations and are intended to help us understand our world. However, at the same time they promote understanding, models also impose limitations. These reflect the assumptions about people, society, behavior, and other things on which models rest. Given these assumptions, models may "illuminate" some aspects of the human condition but leave others in "shadow." While a model may open one avenue of exploration, it simultaneously blocks other possible avenues. The implications of this are far-reaching, extending into areas beyond the scope of this volume. However, an appreciation of the approach used in this book calls for a brief examination of its origins and assumptions, and the consequences of applying it to the study of deviance.

It is important to note that the model used in this book, like all models, rests on answers to such questions as "what should be studied, what questions should be asked, how they should be asked, and what rules should be followed in interpreting the answers obtained" (Ritzer, 1975:7). Moreover, the answers to these questions rest on the several elements or assumptions comprising the model, including a philosophical base, a notion of the methods to be used to study the subject matter, beliefs about the nature of reality, people, and society, and, finally, a perspective on the basis of human behavior. How the particular model used here, called the Paradigm of Definition, treats these matters will be considered at some length.

The Paradigm of Definition

As noted, models, or paradigms, differ in their fundamental conception of the subject matter under study and in how it should be investigated. In the following paragraphs, the unique elements of the Paradigm of Definition will be presented, along with the implications of each element. These elements are shown in abbreviated form in Table 1-1.

Philosophical Base

Many words and phrases used in everyday conversation reveal that people customarily believe that a reality exists above and beyond their conscious awareness. For example, people are often heard to talk about the world "as it is" or about things "as they are." And a

TABLE 1-1
Paradigmatic Distinctions

	PHILOSOPHICAL BASE	NATURE OF REALITY	METHOD OF STUDY	NATURE OF SOCIETY	HUMAN NATURE IN SOCIETY	BASIS OF BEHAVIOR
PARADIGM OF DEFINITION	Nominalism Reality is essentially mental	A human contruction Socially constructed	Systematic observation Social emergent Investigate social basis of reality construction	Changing Internally conflictful Constraint and coercion	An active and adaptive agent An interactive organism Humanistic	Reasons The meanings people create and assign to things Voluntaristic and purposive Indeterminate social causation

common expression is "tell it like it is." The same customary belief seems to underlie the popular expression "let the facts speak for themselves." Although few of us have ever heard a fact speak, all these common expressions seem to rest on the assumption that there are basic meanings associated with things and that these meanings have a vitality independent of any person or group of persons.

In contrast to this taken-for-granted assumption, the philosophical base of the Paradigm of Definition leads us in a different direction, one we may understand by a brief "side trip." Let us begin this trip by suggesting that musical notes and colors do not exist as tones or light beams floating about in the atmosphere. "A flat," or the name of any other specific musical tone, has no existence outside people's minds. To be sure, audible vibrations of various frequencies occur in nature, as when a hammer strikes a taut wire in a piano. Similarly, light waves of differing frequency occur in nature, as may be seen in the phenomenon of a rainbow. But designating the audible vibrations by such names as "A flat," "C sharp," or "F," and identifying different light waves by names like "red" are *acts of mind*. By acts of mind we mean that terms like "B flat" and "red" are *mental constructs,* concepts and words that people create and use to identify things perceived as having elements in common and that are, therefore, classified together. Most important for our purpose is the idea that *names do not exist outside the human mind* and should not be confused with the *things* they symbolize. A map is not the terrain to which it refers. Things and names are not the same.

Further, *things may be named in whatever way people wish.* In the case of musical notes and colors, the name "A flat" may just as well have been applied to the vibrations known as "C sharp" and the word "red" could just as well have been assigned to the light waves identified as "blue." What is important is that there be agreement among people as to the name used to refer to specific things. For example, regardless of the name, it is important that the keynote of the normal or natural major scale be referred to in some consistent way.

However, the specific symbol used to refer to that tone, C, is arbitrary.

This position regarding musical notes and light waves is referred to as a *nominalistic* position and may be useful in helping people make sense of issues involving morality and immorality—that is, deviance. Unlike other paradigms that suggest "reality is 'out there,' " nominalism suggests that "realities are achieved only when they can be imagined and labeled" (Inciardi, 1978:7). Using the same argument we used in talking about the names of audible vibrations and light waves, we may say that while behaviors such as selling sexual favors, ingesting mood-altering chemicals, and so on occur, names like "misconduct," "crime," or "deviance" do not exist outside the human mind. That is, *deviance does not exist until something is designated deviant.* Moreover, nominalism frees us from such ideas as that there are universal essences, that things have inherent meaning, or that meaning exists independent of people's consciousness. Alternatively, nominalism suggests that qualities such as moral and immoral, and deviant and nondeviant are human constructions (concepts) imposed on things and reflecting people's attitude toward them. An appreciation of this calls for a brief examination of the nature of reality according to the Paradigm of Definition.

Nature of Reality

As we noted in speaking about the philosophical base of our model, some people are concerned with apprehending the world "as it is." But what is the nature of that world? For those concerned with the world "as it is" it is a world consisting of things that are *objective*—that is, independent of the mind (consciousness) of the observer—and that operate whether or not people are aware of them (Zukav, 1979:29). Further, those concerned with the world "as it is" are likely to assume that the real (tangible) things populating this world have inherent meanings or *essences,* that is, core properties (sometimes including a moral element) that are permanent and unchangeable, and that these are the things scientists (social and otherwise) should study.

However, there is another view of reality,

one more consistent with nominalism. We may appreciate this alternate view of reality by recounting the tale of three baseball umpires, each of whom is seeking to describe how he approaches his work (Henshel and Silverman, 1975:26). The first umpire says, "I call them as they are!" The second umpire says, "I call them as I see them!" The third umpire says, "They're nothing until I call them!" This tale points to three major Western approaches to knowledge. The first umpire apparently regards knowledge as objective and independent of mind, and himself as the impartial reporter of things "as they are." The second umpire's position represents the view that people mediate knowledge of the real world. Accordingly, the nature of the real world must be approached in terms of the categories of thought people create and through which information about the world is filtered and interpreted. Finally, the third umpire represents the nominalist or social constructionist perspective. Accordingly, conceptions such as "strikes" and "balls" have no meaning except that given them by the observer. "Strikes" and "balls" are acts of mind. Because this is the position to be used in this book, let us expand on these matters and link the tale of the three umpires to the issues of ontology and epistemology.

Ontology is concerned with the nature of the world: what it is and how we come to know it. In studying the nature of reality, we ask: What is the real world like? The first umpire is inclined to the view that the "real" world is validly described as one that operates according to the laws or principles of logical systems "discovered" by people. And, consistent with traditional Western thought, the first umpire intimates that human reason is the principal instrument and final authority in the search for truth.

The second umpire is far less assured in responding to the ontological question. This umpire implies that people's consciousness must be considered in any evaluation of the validity of their descriptions of the "real" world. This leads to the third umpire and the social definition paradigm.

Unlike the two preceding cases, the third umpire (and the Paradigm of Definition) sug-

gests that there is no such thing as a "real" or objective world consisting of things that have essences. People deal with all manner of things in their environment. However, the way they define and respond to these things reflects their own perception of them rather than the thing's "essence." In short, as the last umpire implies, *the world to which people respond is whatever they perceive it to be. Beauty and ugliness, morality and immorality, deviance and nondeviance represent states of mind resulting from the assignment of meaning to things.* In accepting this position one is led to conclude that the world to which people respond is *a world without essential meaning.* Rather, the meanings to which people respond are of their own making. Reality is a social construction; it is whatever people say it is. In response to the ontological question, then, the Paradigm of Definition leads to the conclusion that the world has no objective character. As the wag says, there are no dirty words, only dirty minds. Further, as the following cartoon indicates, the appearance of the world can be very different, depending on one's perspective. Thus, the question What is truth? or What is reality? may be answered in an infinite variety of ways.

Epistemology raises different, but related, questions: How do people know about the world? How certain is our knowledge of the world? If the only world about which people have knowledge is one to which they have assigned meaning—that is, if reality is socially created—it follows that they are unlikely to have knowledge of an external, objective world. Further, even if there is an external, objective world independent of human consciousness, people are unlikely to apprehend it because they are "encapsulated" by a world of socially constructed meanings. If people never confront the hypothesized "real" world, can they ever have knowledge of its properties (Quinney, 1970a:138)? If they cannot have this knowledge, people are left with an awareness only of things to which they have given meaning; the issue of whether or not an objective world exists may then be dismissed. On the other hand, to understand a socially created reality and the basis of the meanings people assign to things, we must look to people themselves. We must examine the stuff of their everyday life, their social experience. This is the position to be followed in this book. It is a position consistent with the Paradigm of Definition and has an important bearing on the method of study, which we turn to next.

Method of Study

Americans and other Western peoples have long had a love affair with science, tending to regard the scientific method as the proper way to study the human condition. This generally favorable orientation toward use of the scientific method rests on a set of postulates with which people are less familiar. These postulates, called the canons (rules) of the scientific method, are taken-for-granted beliefs—that is, beliefs that are assumed to be valid but that are fundamentally unproven and unprovable. These canons are as follows: (1) The world exists, (2) the world is knowable, (3) the world is knowable through our senses, and (4) the elements comprising the world are related to one another in terms of cause and effect (Goode and Hatt, 1952:20).

As an extension of these postulates, scientific work customarily places heavy emphasis on positivism and empiricism, two intimately related doctrines. *Positivism* suggests that scientific questions must be answerable by means of empirical (observable) data. In turn, *empiricism* is the belief that knowledge (or "evidence" in scientific work) should be directly or indirectly observable through the senses—touch, sight, taste, hearing, smell—under specifiable and repeatable conditions. Thus, whether measuring

Used by permission of Johnny Hart and News Group Chicago, Inc.

the speed of a runner, whom we may observe directly, or measuring the effect of subatomic phenomena, which may be done only indirectly by noting a track on a photographic plate or the movement of a needle on a meter, and so on, empirical data are knowable through the senses. Methods of study based on this orientation are known as empirical (Zukav, 1979:20).

Finally, consistent with an emphasis on positivism and empiricism, scientific methods involve the analysis of *variables* (any phenomenon that can change, be measured directly or indirectly, or be quantified) to determine their objective character and to discover how they influence one another *in nature.* Such analysis is wholly consistent with the idea that "the world exists" and that the purpose of investigation (social or otherwise) is to reveal the nature of the world "as it is." The emphasis on the study of "things in nature" rests on the idea that knowledge (including natural law principles, truth, and so on) has an absolute foundation, is independent of and external to the knower (remember the first umpire?), and is not determined by anything outside itself. The knowing person is passive so far as "shaping" that knowledge is concerned (Brown, 1977:89).

In contrast with this orientation, the Paradigm of Definition and the nominalist perspective suggest that the canons of the scientific method and related beliefs are no more than *concepts,* that is ideas developed and used by people in an effort to introduce order to a world that is without essential order. For example, a taken-for-granted belief in our society is that broken homes cause delinquency. Is it in the objective nature of things that broken homes cause delinquency? That is, does disruption of family have an authoritative and conclusive effect on the moral behavior of its members? Many people also believe it is in the nature of things that violence in the media increases crime, that social change *necessarily* leads to a reduction in social control, and/or that "imbalances" in the social structure cause deviant behavior. In sharp contrast, the Paradigm of Definition suggests that these cause-and-effect statements reflect sociologists' and

others' perceptions rather than conditions existing in an objective world. If these linkages of causes and effects are human constructions (rather than properties of a "real" world), is there an alternative to the traditional notion of cause and effect whereby we may order the elements of a socially constructed reality? Let's briefly explore this question.

Sociological research has traditionally been dominated by *variable analysis* (Blumer, 1956). This means that much sociological research has consisted of examining human groups as if they consisted only of variables and their relationships. For example, as previous comments suggest, a relationship is assumed to exist between deviance (a *dependent variable;* a phenomenon whose value or magnitude is influenced by other phenomena), on the one hand; and broken homes, violence in the media, and social structural conditions (the *independent variables;* phenomena capable of effecting change in the value or magnitude of a dependent variable), on the other. Thus, much research rests on the prior assumption that a causal relation exists between these things. This is done by contending that A causes B if (1) they occur together in the way the hypothesis predicts, or (2) A occurs prior to B, or (3) B occurs simultaneously with A. In practical terms this means that phenomena occurring together are likely to be regarded in cause–effect terms. That is, *by embracing the concept of cause, one is inclined to perceive causal relationships.* For example, if higher delinquency rates seem to occur in areas with more broken homes, not only are these factors likely to be perceived as related, but the latter is prone to be viewed as a cause of the former. Alternative interpretations to cause and effect tend to be precluded because things that exist in an allegedly real world are believed to be objectively united that way. Alternative ways of ordering the universe are ignored (Kotarba, 1975).

Continuing with the example of the broken home and delinquency, research studies using large samples of official delinquents have shown that between 30 percent and 60 percent of them come from broken homes. This means, conversely, that between 40 and 70 percent of official delinquent's homes are intact. At best, concordance at that level provides weak support for the "broken homes cause delinquency" hypothesis. But this relationship is even weaker when careful matching of delinquents and nondelinquents is attempted (Smith, 1955:307). Despite weak data and questionable research methods (Wilkinson, 1974:734), the causal importance of broken homes on delinquency continues to be accepted in varying degrees. Weak statistical relationships have led some researchers to expand the meaning of the concept "broken homes" to include homes broken not only physically by death or divorce, but psychologically as well; that is, they have expanded the concept to include homes in which the relationships between parents and children are "disturbed" in some way (Bordua, 1962). Investigation has also focused on the relative effects of different types of broken homes (death vs. divorce, mother absent vs. father absent), on the relative influence of broken homes on male vs. female children, and on comparisons of the effect of broken vs. reconstituted homes (Cavan, 1969; Nye, 1958; Perry and Pfuhl, 1963; Toby, 1957). Rarely, however, has consideration been given to the idea that the presumed link between these variables is a consequence of (1) the meaning of the broken homes (however defined) among police, juvenile court personnel, and other officials and (2) the long-range influence of these meanings on social policy or policies that produce statistics supportive of the "broken homes cause delinquency" thesis.

For example, to what extent has the relationship between broken homes and delinquency been a result of differential treatment given such youngsters by police and juvenile court? Are victims more prone to report offenses committed by juveniles from broken than unbroken homes? Is the absence of a parent taken as an indication of lax parental control necessitating official intervention? Are children from unbroken homes more likely to be released by police with a warning, while their counterparts from broken homes are more likely to become subject to official processing (Smith, 1955:309)? Questions of this sort are

critical; they hypothesize that variations in officials' response patterns rest on their *definition of the situation* rather than on the objective and constraining influences of home conditions on young people's behavior. The statistical relationship, then, does not necessarily reflect a causal relationship. Rather, the statistical relationship is an outgrowth of the intervening process of defining (Blumer, 1956:686). Let's explore this intervening process just a bit further.

Karen Wilkinson (1974) has suggested that the importance attached to the influence of the broken home on delinquency has varied markedly over the course of this century. Between 1900 and 1932 there was widespread acceptance and support of the idea that broken homes caused children to misbehave. However, acceptance rested less on irrefutable evidence (actually, the strength of the evidence was weak) than on the bias of the sociologists of that time. This bias included an implicit belief in the indispensable role of the family in society and a high evaluation of the family as an institution. Because of the way they defined the family, they perceived (defined) negatively whatever seemed to threaten it or to be a departure from an ideal conception of it. Instability in the family or divorce were so defined. The link in the belief that broken homes cause delinquency was provided by those persons who, in addition to having strong valuational roots in the family, became involved in the "child saving" movement of the late nineteenth and early twentieth centuries (Platt, 1969). The interests of those reformers led them to define the broken home as incapable of socializing children properly—a task, they felt, that demanded the attention of a pair of stable parents. Inadequate socialization was felt to lead to maladaptation or delinquency on the part of the child (Rubington and Weinberg, 1977:22).

Between the years 1933 and 1950 emphasis on the role of the broken family as a cause of delinquency declined greatly. However, that change in emphasis rested less on empirical evidence than on (1) sociologists' declining interest in the family as an institution; (2) an increased tolerance and acceptance among sociologists of urban social conditions—including divorce and family instability; (3) changes in the roles of women such that family-related matters became less important whereas satisfactions derived from extrafamilial sources (such as employment) became more important; and (4) the increasing sophistication of sociologists' research methods and their rejection of the "value judgments" of their predecessors (Wilkinson, 1974:732–733). In sum, this change in emphasis demonstrates that the alleged relationship between variables does not necessarily reflect an immutable condition found to exist in nature, in some objective reality. Quite the contrary; the presumed relationship between variables appears to be a consequence of general cultural and ideological factors influencing the meanings assigned to the family by these generations of sociologists. In short, the change in emphasis is a definitional matter.

The essential implication of this observation is that human beings do not respond to things as they are (in an objective sense), but to their definition of them. For example, research in delinquency has shown that police often employ offender's speech patterns, grooming, dress, and general demeanor as cues—that is, as hints or intimations—of the character of the offenders. These cues have no objective meaning; they have only the meaning police assign to them. Yet, on the basis of these things police make inferences about the youth's character and respond accordingly. Further, research reveals that police assess the seriousness of youths' delinquent conduct on the basis of whether the youths are perceived to be "contrite about the infraction, respectful to officers, and fearful of the sanctions that might be employed against them" (Piliavin and Briar, 1964:210–211). Such youths are considered salvageable. On the other hand, youths who are seen as unruly, stubborn, nonchalant, or "cool" are defined as "tough guys" or "punks" who deserve severe sanctions. On the basis of the belief that certain groups, especially blacks, are more disposed to the latter traits, police become sensitized to and concen-

trate their energies on policing such youths. As one police official commented:

They (Negroes) have no regard for the law or for the police. They just don't seem to give a damn. Few of them are interested in school or getting ahead. The girls start having illegitimate kids before they are sixteen years old and the boys are always "out for kicks." Furthermore, many of these kids try to run you down. They say the damnedest things to you and they seem to have absolutely no respect for you as an adult. I admit I am prejudiced now, but frankly I don't think I was when I began police work (Piliavin and Briar, 1964:212).

The role of these symbolically meaningful cues will be further examined when we consider rates of deviance and the process of labeling rule breakers.

Failure to consider the role of defining as an integral part of the perceived relation between variables has produced a sociology in which the very things that should be under investigation (the social basis of meaning) are taken for granted. We have a sociology in which the common sense meanings of things are replaced by those of the sociologist. As Howard Becker has noted:

We often turn collective activity—people doing things together—into abstract nouns whose connection to people doing things together is tenuous. We then typically lose interest in the more mundane things people are actually doing. We ignore what we see because it is not abstract, and chase after the invisible "forces" and "conditions" we have learned to think sociology is all about (1973:190).

Not the least of the forces and conditions pursued by generations of sociologists are the illusive "causes" whose presumed "effects" so trouble us.

The alternative to studying social life in terms of cause–effect relations is to base concepts and principles of human behavior on careful and systematic observation of the social world as it is constructed and experienced in the course of everyday life. This way of pursuing science, following the Paradigm of Definition, calls for relinquishing the idea that things have intrinsic and fixed meanings. It calls for examination of the social origins of meaning, how meanings are applied to things in the environment, the consequences of applying these meanings, and, finally, how meanings change. The remaining chapters of this volume will deal with these issues.

Nature of Society

Traditionally, sociologists have attached great importance to the notion of society and have tried to describe and account for it. In this effort, many scholars have tended to emphasize, above all else, the assumed orderly nature of society. In this sense, *order* means that society is characterized by stability, internal harmony, and value agreement (consensus) among the bulk of its members. Stated differently, for these scholars, society is another name for group life, for people interacting in a wide variety of situations for varying periods of time, and doing so according to rules, norms, and expectations with which they are *assumed* to be in agreement. Patterns of interaction, then, are said to be repetitive, for the most part, and predictable. The roles people play (in family, in business and professions, in play, and so forth) are regarded as largely harmonious or congruent with one another. Moreover, people are assumed to agree among themselves, for the most part, about the propriety of existing norms, rules, and expectations. The consensus and conformity that is taken as an index of the essential orderliness of society, then, is regarded as rooted in nature (Piven, 1981:490) and part of the objective or real world. The essence of society is held to be orderliness.

However widespread, this notion of the essential orderliness of society is questioned by some sociologists; they ask if this explanation is the most valid way to explain social order. Is society validly described when it is characterized as an oasis of conformity and consensus, with value disagreement being the exception? Or is it equally, if not more validly described by the suggestion that a principal characteristic of heterogeneous society is the relative lack of value consensus? And is apparent conformity based less on value agreement than on the effect of coercion? Is society an arena of ongoing conflict over what is right, proper, moral, and so on? These questions reflect two ways of viewing society. Called the

consensus and the conflict perspectives, each deserves brief examination.

As we've seen, the *consensus perspective* proposes that the various age, sex, occupational, racial, ethnic, and other groupings share (imperfectly, to be sure) a set of core values and meanings. These values are said to transcend the basic social groupings (Williams, 1960:397ff), and are the basis of some durable relation among these segments of society. Because they share these values, it is claimed, these various groups form a meaningful whole, that is, society. Further, the notion of consensus suggests that each part of the social system makes a contribution to the maintenance and stability of the whole. In short, value consensus is said to underlie social structure (Dahrendorf, 1959:161).

The consensus perspective also implies that deviance is a "foreign" element. That is, deviance arises either as a result of unintended conditions that are alien to the ongoing social system (such as an unintended blocking of people's opportunities to achieve legitimate goals) or as a consequence of groups embracing values and interests that are contrary to those of "right-minded" citizens—all of whom are assumed to agree on a single moral code. Out of this model come corrective suggestions calling either for social change—that is, social engineering—or, more frequently, the rehabilitation of the offender, meaning that the offender's values ought to be brought into harmony with the values of those who are "right-minded." Fundamentally, however, there is assumed to be a single, relatively dominant moral code to which the bulk of the population subscribes.

An alternative view is called the *conflict perspective*. Point for point this perspective is in sharp contrast to the consensus perspective. First, rather than perceiving society as in a condition of stability, it is seen as in a condition of constant change; social change is omnipresent. This means that the elements comprising the social system have no lasting relationship with one another. Second, rather than being well integrated with one another as a result of shared values, segments of society are in conflict. For example, the fact that we divide ourselves into groups embracing different, if not mutually exclusive beliefs, norms, values, ideologies, and interests (for example, Catholic, Protestant, Jew, atheist, and agnostic) is evidence not of consensus, but of disagreement and conflict. Similarly, workers and employers, consumers and producers or distributors, voters and elected representatives, and innumerable other interest groups reflect varying degrees of conflict. There is generation conflict, as well as that based on racial and gender differences. Third, the factor of change being everywhere and constant means that each element of the social system contributes not to the persistence but to the disintegration of the whole as it exists at any point in time. Society is dynamic and ever changing, with each of its elements contributing to the instability and flux of the whole.

Given this position, there is no basis for assuming the existence of a set of values regarding which one may find consensus *and in terms of which people's everyday actions are organized.* To be sure, instances of widespread public agreement may be found wherein consensus appears to prevail. For example, on a very abstract or general level we would certainly find widespread support for values such as justice, equality, progress, and the like (Williams, 1960). However, the various age, race, socioeconomic, or sex groups in society are often in conflict with one another (and even among themselves) as to the specific and situational meaning of each of these values. For example, historically whites and blacks surely have disagreed on the meaning of justice, just as many men and women currently disagree sharply over the practical meaning of equality.

In the context of everyday life such general and abstract ideas as "fair play," "justice," "decency," and other values take on meaning relative to specific situations. Thus, while most people may subscribe to a general morality on the *public* level, the *private* morality that influences our everyday life consists of *situated moral meanings,* that is interpretations of abstract morals applied to concrete situations (Douglas, 1970:20). For example, in terms of public (abstract) morality such things as rape and murder are, doubtless, widely condemned

in our society. However, as we will note later, not every "commonsense" behavioral instance that reasonably fits legal definitions of these things comes to be so defined. Everyday life clearly shows that the *meanings of things, moral and otherwise, have a contextual base.* We will return to this point shortly.

Finally, the values and interests that prevail at any point in time, relative to any specific issue, do so as a result of coercion rather than consensus. For example, regardless of the outcome of present social conflicts over such issues as abortion, homosexuality, use of mood-altering drugs, and pornography, the views that "win" will do so as a result of public and official condemnation and/or suppression of the opposite viewpoint by force or the threat of force. As such, it is invalid to suggest that representatives of "losing" interests conform on the basis of consensus. Similarly, do all young people who register for the draft do so because they like war or subscribe to prevailing public policy? Does the fast-driving motorist slow down at the sight of a police car because he or she suddenly arrives at the position of consensus with public law? Some do, but many others do so because of their reluctance to test the authority of the state. Rather clearly, in innumerable everyday situations, behavior rests on the unequal distribution and use of political power among various interest groups and individuals, and the related decisions people make. In short, rather than resting on consensus, the conflict perspective (included in the Paradigm of Definition employed in this book) suggests that "every society rests on constraints of some of its members by others" (Chambliss, 1973a:3). Indeed, as Ralf Dahrendorf suggests, any heterogeneous society is marked by conflict; in turn, conflict presupposes disagreement and dissensus concerning values (1964:215). Surely ours is a society in conflict. We will return to this and related issues in the pages to follow.

Human Nature in Society

Consistent with their belief in an essentially orderly society, some scholars have tended to view people as basically conforming creatures. As Dennis Wrong (1961) notes, traditional sociology adopted an "oversocialized" conception of people. That is, people were seen as basically conforming creatures guided by a superego or conscience. Conscience, in turn, has been defined as a consequence of people having been *socialized,* that is, having had the values, rules, and expectations of society "built into" them. People behave in the "right way" largely because they have been "programmed" that way. The values, rules, and expectations are believed to have a constraining influence on people. It is apparent, then, that the notion of people as "essentially conforming" harmonizes with a conception of society as "essentially orderly."

These models of people and of society have been particularly stressed in the study of rule-violating behavior. Thus, rule breaking has been traditionally regarded as statistically exceptional—exceptional because people are assumed ordinarily to be striving for normative conformity, a conformity reflecting their socialization and the existence of value agreement (consensus). Departure from these norms often has been explained as the result of some imperfection in what is otherwise an essentially integrated and harmonious social system, or a fault among the persons violating the norms.

As with the nature of society, however, not all students of society share so mechanistic a view of humankind; they ask whether it is valid to contend that people are largely what external forces such as "society" and "socialization" have made them. In contrast with the oversocialized conception of people, the Paradigm of Definition suggests that the nature of people is not validly described by the metaphor of a billiard ball or a hockey puck. People are not propelled willy-nilly by external forces. To avoid those metaphors, Richard Quinney has proposed a *humanistic* conception of humankind. This conception suggests that people are "capable of considering alternative actions, of breaking from the established order" (Quinney, 1970b:13). This is a view of people that stresses their awareness of self, the active part they play in shaping their own lives, and their ability to make evaluations and judgments. This conception regards people as

conscious beings who *interact* with elements in their environment on the basis of the meanings they assign to them. Instead of seeing people as *reactive* entities, the Paradigm of Definition perceives them as *interactive.* This leads to a consideration of the basis of behavior.

Basis of Behavior

As noted in the discussion of the method of study, some sociological models suggest that elements comprising the real world are related to one another in terms of cause and effect. *Causes* are things that make other things (including behavior) happen. Nothing happens without a cause, and every effect ultimately becomes the cause of a future effect. The cause–effect chain is regarded as uninterrupted. Things do not "just happen"; everything happens for a reason (has a cause) and the scientist's task is to provide a rational explanation for why things happen (Babbie, 1979:41).

In explaining behavior, scholars of this persuasion tend to rely on a more or less deterministic model of behavior, one that contrasts sharply with what is sometimes called a free-will explanation. Free-will explanations suggest that people act as a result of their own willpower, uninfluenced by external forces. *Determinism,* however, suggests that we behave as a result of "forces and factors in the world that [we] cannot control and may not even recognize" (Babbie, 1979:424) but that are necessary to the occurrence of the behavior. As mentioned earlier, people are perceived to be influenced by constraining forces.

Finally, deterministic forces (variables) are held to operate impersonally. They are the features of the real world that take no heed of the individual inhabitants, and go blindly on their way, part of the world "as it is." Thus, poverty and broken homes, two factors often cited as causes of crime and delinquency, are often regarded as deterministic and impersonal influences on people's behavior.

As we might suspect, however, the Paradigm of Definition provides an alternative accounting for human behavior. If we are to perceive people as conscious beings and interactive agents, our notions of the basis of human behavior must change accordingly. That is, if human behavior (deviant or otherwise) is the action of conscious beings, it becomes explicable in terms of the choices people make, in terms of reasons rather than constraining forces (Brown, 1977:84). These reasons are to be found in the meanings people create and apply to things in the world around them. Reasons serve to explain the actions of those engaged in both rule-breaking *and* non–rule-breaking behavior. *In both cases people are behaving in ways meaningful to them.* Thus, while other models seek causes in the form of external and constraining forces, the Paradigm of Definition seeks explanations based on people's perception of their situation and on their values and meanings. That is, the Paradigm of Definition introduces the notion of *indeterminate social causation* as an alternative to the idea of determinism.

That people behave on the basis of meanings rather than external constraining forces may be seen in any number of events making up everyday life. For example, many students reading these lines are probably doing so because they think familiarity with the material has a bearing on some goal they have chosen to pursue. That is, they are behaving on the basis of *intention*—a goal or goals they have decided to seek. Or, some students may be kept from reading these lines by a phone call from a friend. They may welcome the phone call, first, because they *define* reading this material as tedious and, second, because they regard the phone call as an *excuse.* That is, the phone call permits them to avoid doing what students are expected to do without accepting full responsibility for their actions (Scott and Lyman, 1968). Finally, some students may be reading this material for the second or third time because they have a pending exam on the material and either wish to avoid getting a low grade or wish to get a high grade. Here we have people who are goal-oriented acting on the basis of their *awareness* of the consequences of their actions vis-à-vis their goals. This example, as well as innumerable others, demonstrates that people act on the basis of interpretations, definitions, and intentions. Moreover, we may note the meaningfulness of actors' conduct by examining their *motives,* that is, the

meanings that make people's behavior seem suitable and justifiable in their own terms (Weber, 1962:39). If behavior rests on motives, it is not necessary to resort to deterministic forces to explain it. Again, the Paradigm of Definition involves an indeterminist position; human behavior is voluntaristic and purposive. It is based on situationally based reasons rather than on external constraining forces.

To summarize briefly, this text proposes to analyze the phenomenon of deviance by employing the Paradigm of Definition. Accordingly, it is necessary, first, to view reality as a set of human or social constructions, consisting of the meanings people create and assign to things. Being a social product, it may be referred to as *social reality.* Second, this paradigm calls for the use of *social causation* rather than causality defined in a deterministic/constraining sense. By social causation we mean the *relationships people perceive to exist* between things and in terms of which they respond. Again, these presumed relations are social constructions. Third, the Paradigm of Definition calls on us to view people as active agents rather than as passive agents acting without conscious purpose. As active agents, people are the creators of their own reality as well as the beings who are influenced by it. Related to this is a fourth major element of this model, namely, that reason, choice, judgments, and intention become the bases of behavior. Finally, this model proposes that society be viewed as an arena of conflict and change rather than as one of consensus and stability. With these preliminaries in mind, let us turn to a more concentrated examination of the idea of social reality, how it is constructed, and how socially constructed meanings apply to the study of deviance.

Constructing Social Reality

The term *social reality* refers to the meanings (definitions, conceptions, and typifications) people assign to things in their environment and in terms of which they seek to introduce order to their world. *Order* refers to the regularization of behavior and human relationships to the point that social life is possible. Unlike forms of social life that are governed by instinct, humans develop and maintain order through learning. Order exists when people learn successfully to predict one another's behavior and, hence, become able to direct their own actions vis-à-vis others so as to achieve at least a minimum level of need satisfaction. That is, order occurs when people share meanings of their own and others' behavior as well as of things in their environment. Such order is a product of people interacting with one another in terms of socially created and shared meanings.

The construction of these meanings is an elemental aspect of our daily lives—so elemental, in fact, that few people are even aware they are engaged in the process. Nonetheless, as we deal with one another, often under new and strange conditions, and as we confront unique situations—that is, as we face circumstances calling for decisions and some mode of adaptation—we are "writing the script" for subsequent actions. So, too, are others. Out of these efforts come socially constructed and shared meanings.

Acceptance of this view of reality and behavior is sometimes blocked because we lack a sense of a social order that is based on socially constructed knowledge. Rather, most people define reality as an objective thing existing "out there" to be discovered, not constructed (Holzner, 1972:14). At least that is what everyday, commonsense experience would lead most people to conclude. For example, as children, we are introduced to a set of beliefs, meanings, definitions, values, rules, understandings, and the like, that appear to be permanent. More often than not, these things are presented to us as "the way things are." This seems to be the case in matters of socializing new family members, and in orienting those entering a new environment: young children to school, recruits to the armed forces, new members to the club, new inmates ("fish") to a prison, and so on.

As a result of the usual way people are introduced to these groups, it is difficult to regard their respective realities as social or human

constructions. How is it, then, that what is presented to each new generation as firm, reliable, seemingly objective knowledge can be reconciled with the view that reality is socially constructed? How does the subjective come to be perceived as objective? One answer lies in the processes of externalization, objectivation, and internalization (Berger and Luckmann, 1967). By these processes, an illusion is created that reality is external to people, independent of human consciousness, absolute in character, and ontologically certain and orderly. Let's briefly explore these processes.

Externalization

The first step in transforming subjective meanings into seemingly objective knowledge is *externalization,* that is, the overt expression of subjective meanings, understandings, definitions, and so on through speech and other forms of communication. At the risk of oversimplification, we may begin by noting that people do engage in solitary activity and that much of their solitary activity is *habitual;* that is, it occurs repeatedly without benefit of conscious reflection. People engage in a variety of daily routines of this sort—brushing teeth, combing hair, and dressing to name a few—all of which provide satisfaction. But note, the satisfactory outcome of such activity is not dependent on people sharing the meanings of these acts with others. There is no need to communicate to others "how" or "why" I brush my teeth or put on my clothes in the way I do. Because the utility or satisfaction of these acts is not enhanced by sharing this information with others, the meanings underlying them tend to remain subjective. They are unspoken.

But not all human activity is solitary. People are social animals, engaging in a wide variety of behaviors in concert with others. To move from the level of solitary activity to that of pair relationships (the smallest group and the most limited form of social interaction) requires coordination if order is to be achieved. That is, whether two people wish to build a log cabin, cook a meal, make love, or whatever, the outcome of their effort will likely be enhanced if they share their respective subjective meanings, preferences, and definitions with each other. As examples, does one have a preference for building log cabins using the Norwegian method rather than some other method, for beef steak over pork chops, or for "his thighs outside" as compared to the "woman above, across his thighs" as a coital posture? "Preference" refers to how and why people wish to have things done as they do. Given these preferences, sharing them may be expected to promote people's goals, if only because sharing reduces the likelihood of chaos through misunderstanding. This exchange of meanings, preferences, techniques, and the like may be referred to as *externalization*.

In interaction at the pair level, externalization may, but need not, be elaborate. At a minimum, coordinated and orderly interrelations may be achieved by the language of gesture. That is, bodily movements and facial expressions, demonstrative of acceptance or rejection, approval or disapproval, agreement or disagreement, and so on, may be sufficient for many purposes. For example, men seeking homosexual contact with strangers in *tearooms* (public restrooms where impersonal homosexual encounters occur) effectively convey to one another their interest in sexual relations by means of various forms of "signaling." Included are: engaging in pseudomasturbation in view of others, eye contact, beckoning hand and head motions, and foot tapping (Humphreys, 1970:63–64; Delph, 1978:83–89). In other cases some form of verbalization is required, as when one person seeks to tell another "how" to do something. But whether gestural or verbal, at the level of pair relationships this communication may be informal.

In sum, then, *as a first step* in establishing enduring, sometimes highly complex, interdependent activity, private and subjective meanings must be externalized and shared. However, the need that two or three persons have to communicate with one another in order to act in concert is minor in contrast with that need among larger collectivities such as people in workplaces, schools, neighborhoods, and entire communities. Consequently, as

group size increases, the techniques of communicating this shared information become more formalized. This observation leads to a consideration of objectivation.

Objectivation

Objectivation refers to "the process by which externalized products of human activity attain the character of objectivity" (Berger and Luckmann, 1967:60), that is, how human creations come to appear to be independent of people. This process may be understood by noting that as group size increases, so does the variety and complexity of the relationships among group members. In turn, this gives rise to a need for more elaborate efforts to achieve order. Ways need to be found to introduce new members to standard group definitions and practices. Formulae for coordinated activity in large groups must now be established. There are two noteworthy elements involved.

First, in large groups, efficient and rapid methods must be found to introduce new members to the collectivity and integrate their activities with those of others. "Introducing" in this context involves providing novice members with information about "what" and "how" things are to be done, and "why" things are done as they are. That is, prescriptions and proscriptions are linked with rationales and justifications. For example, prisons develop inmate rule books, information concerning the "how" and "why" of inmate conduct in prison. In the armed forces this type of information is called a "code of conduct," while among sorority members it is called "standards." For members of some religious groups this knowledge appears as doctrinal summaries called catechism.

Such statements of rules, expectations, and so on, are examples of externalized and objectivated information concerning what is and is not defined as correct action, and what must be known by people in order to get along when engaged in routine activity (Berger and Luckmann, 1967:42). It is on the basis of such shared knowledge, called *recipe knowledge*, that social order is possible. What is most important to note is that this knowledge consists of socially (humanly) created definitions and expectations and their supporting rationales.

A second and vital element of objectivation involves *giving names* to the things and activities to which new group members must be introduced. By naming things we *reify* them. That is, what was initially subjective and personal is given objective and social quality. To use an earlier example, while there may be audible vibrations in nature to which we give the name "A flat," "A flat" does not exist in nature. Yet we commonly find people who fail to make this distinction—in fact, who give little thought to the distinction between names and things. For example, it is possible for someone to take another person's property without his or her permission. For one losing property in that way, the event is a substantive matter, possibly of great importance. However, giving the name "theft" to that behavior reifies it. *Reification* involves "elevating" a symbol for a thing (for example the word used to refer to the thing) to the level of the thing itself. When this happens, the meaning assigned to the *thing* tends to be transferred or projected to the *name* of the thing. Thereby, the name and the thing become indistinguishable so far as people's reactions are concerned (Kaplan, 1964:61; Berger and Luckmann, 1967:89ff). Without people being consciously aware of it, names may take on an existence of their own. The name and the meanings assigned to it are what people respond to.

Examples of reification are abundant. Take the case of "ghosts" and "goblins" and other "scary" things that allegedly populate a supposed "spirit world." Despite the lack of apparent substance or a tangible and objective referent for these terms, some people act as if such things were part of an objective world. Thus, people are often as fearful of and as horrified by a word and the images it connotes as they are by the substantive matter to which it refers. Further, many people take great precautions against criminal victimization, their concern reflecting the meaning they assign to "rising crime rates" and "horror stories" concerning crime. Such statistics and stories are symbols, but they may be invested with many of the properties of the thing itself. And we

may note that some people become quite sexually stimulated by looking at pictures, reading so-called "dirty" stories, or watching soft or hard core pornographic films, none of which are other than symbolic representations.

In public life, too, names often take on an importance independent of relevant substantive matters. For example, during the 1979–1980 conflict between Iran and the United States, residents of Iran Street in a small Arizona community reportedly felt "ashamed" to have that be the name of their street. Despite the fact that nothing connected with the physical character of the street (a mere two blocks long) had changed, people came to define the street as an undesirable place to live and petitioned for a name change. The city council agreed with the petitioners and the name was changed to Intrepid. And in Colorado, where license plates using a three-letter prefix system recently went into use, more than 180,000 license plates were rejected on the assumption that certain three-letter combinations would prove suggestive or objectionable to motorists. Included were such prefixes as B-U-G, B-U-N, B-V-D, C-A-D, G-A-Y, G-O-D, H-O-G, H-O-R, J-A-P, J-E-W, M-E-X, S-A-D, S-E-X, S-O-B, and Y-E-S, to name a few. These examples involve the human creation and assignment of meaning to things (in these cases, words) that are without essential or objective meaning. In transmitting these meanings to others, especially in formalized ways, the illusion is created that the knowledge is independent of its creators. Were it not for the fact that order and regularization of behavior requires some degree of communication and that communication calls for sharing perceptions through verbalization and naming, these meanings would remain private and subjective, as they were when they originated. However, the sense that this knowledge is objective is promoted, too, by internalization. Let's turn to that aspect of constructing reality.

Internalization

Internalization is the process whereby select elements of prevailing recipe knowledge are learned and become part of one's self. By participating in the activities of family, school, church, workplace, and so on, people are introduced to the institutions of society. As used here, *institutions* refer to the "commonly accepted and established ways of doing things" (Scott, 1972:18) that are *presented* to people. Such knowledge is presented to most people as a set of nonnegotiable rules and expectations. Parents and employers, for example, don't usually discuss the propriety of rules with their children or employees, or debate with them about the circumstances under which some exception to the rule will be tolerated. If the rule says "don't pick your nose" or "be on time," it tends to be uttered without exceptions or equivocation. These rules are not presented as merely *one way* of doing things; they are presented as the *only way* of doing them. And, often as not, challenges to the rule are met with a response that strongly suggests that "that is the way things are." Further, when children or workers compare their situation with that of others, they are likely to discover that, in just about the same nonnegotiable way, the others were introduced to some very similar rules. In short, being introduced to *seemingly* absolute, universal, and nonnegotiable rules regarding "how things are" promotes the sense that the basis of recipe knowledge is objective. The sense of finality that is attached to the rules encourages a belief in their objectivity.

Much the same sense of finality, objectivity, and, perhaps, absoluteness, is promoted when persons in authority transmit rules and meanings to others. In doing this, rule givers reinforce their own acceptance of this externalized and objectivated knowledge. This is particularly so when, in the face of a challenge to a rule, one is called on to provide a justification for it. Thus, when "eat your vegetables" is met with resistance, a possible countermove by the parent may be "they are good for you." As a result of seemingly endless repetitions (externalizations), the rule giver or socializer comes to accept the knowledge as objective. Much like the first umpire, the parent or other rule giver/interpreter comes to perceive himself or herself as the more or less impartial reporter of "things as they are." Jointly then, the rule giver and receiver internalize this objecti-

vated material, and as a result of this internalization process, the *meanings become shared or common.* That is, as the reinforced understandings of the rule giver come to be internalized by the other, the understandings become reciprocal; in that way, actors become "fused" and at least a minimally acceptable degree of social order is possible.[2]

The social order that is created by these means is not limited to integrating interpersonal relations. On a far grander scale, we create meanings that on a theoretical level consolidate all institutionalized activity into one coherent whole. These meanings or integrative ideas are referred to as the *symbolic universe*. The symbolic universe consists of ideas that provide a transcendent orderliness to our world. All things come to have a place in "the scheme of things" and a place is provided for everything. We create meanings about how the abstraction "family" harmonizes with an equally abstract notion called "the economy," how the "economy" and "education" complement one another, and how all is unified into a coherent whole referred to as "one nation under God." Birth, our own as well as that of our ancestors and descendants, death, and all in between are incorporated into one meaningful, ongoing process and assigned a place in the cosmos. These integrative ideas, constructed by people, externalized, objectified, and internalized, appear in everyday life as mythologies, cosmologies, theologies, and similar constructions (Berger and Luckmann, 1967:92ff). In sum, just as individuals become "fused" as a result of acquiring shared understandings, so do entire societies become united with the "natural order of things" by means of creating a symbolic universe.

---

[2]In noting that people internalize these meanings and rules, that understandings become shared, and that one's self and others thereby become "fused," we do not mean to imply, as does the concept of the "oversocialized man," that people are being "programmed" or otherwise rendered incapable of exercising judgment, making decisions, choices, and so on, and acting upon them. We are saying only that people "inherit" meanings and understandings; they are equally capable of changing them, challenging them, and acting in ways contrary to them. Internalization does not reduce people to the level of automatons (see Piven, 1981:496).

To summarize briefly, we have examined three elements involved in the social construction of reality: externalization, objectivation, and internalization. By these processes, which are simultaneous and endless aspects of everyday life (1) people transmit subjectively created meanings and understandings to others; (2) in being transmitted, these understandings take on the appearance of objectivity and become reified and divorced from their source; and (3) these now seemingly independent meanings become internalized and a subjective part of the actor. To the extent these understandings are shared, they become the means whereby social order is established. What was initially a human creation appears to be suprahuman (Berger and Luckmann, 1967:89). People come to identify with and be influenced by their own creation. What people create becomes part of them through internalization. Thus, as Berger and Luckmann state: "Society is a human product. Society is an objective reality. Man is a social product" (1967:61).

Multiple Realities and Problematic Meanings

Having explored the general idea that reality is a social construction, let's try to refine this notion to take into account our earlier skepticism concerning value consensus and the suggestion that society is an arena of conflict. The implication of these positions is that conflict rests on the existence of not one but a variety of realities. In short, the meanings that comprise reality are plural and often are linked to the situation in which they arise. Let's explore this general issue of multiple realities and problematic meanings.

At the outset it should be recognized that social reality is not all of a kind. This is particularly so in heterogeneous, urban industrial societies. However legitimate some versions of reality may be, and no matter how much lip service is paid to official or public morality, experience serves to challenge and weaken our convictions regarding the unity and absoluteness of social reality. For example, during their early years children are introduced to the "right way" of doing things and to the "why" of them. They may be taught to go to school, develop effective study habits, obey their parents, show regard for others, and so on. Each of these do's and don'ts, pre- and proscriptions for behavior, is supported by some justification, a *legitimation*. These legitimations seek to provide either instrumental (utilitarian) or spiritual justification for the rule. Moreover, these rules are presented in nonnegotiable form. Often this means that the rules are given the status of *moral absolutes*, that is, universal standards applying everywhere and at all times. The consequence of this is a sense of moral certainty and unity. However, as ontologically certain as the world of our childhood may have seemed, experience is likely to have revealed there is little basis for believing in its unity and absolute nature.

The initial sense of certainty and unity may well survive until we move beyond the sheltering effect of home, which is often a morally homogeneous environment. As horizons broaden, however, we are exposed to different, sometimes conflicting and mutually exclusive realities. As children move from home to neighborhood, from neighborhood to school, and on to other progressively larger and more complex social situations, they are introduced to a variety of different and sometimes conflicting social realities and subuniverses of meaning. They encounter beliefs and meanings reflecting differences in age, sex, religion, social class, occupation, and ethnicity. Taught tolerance at home, they soon learn it is an abstraction quite often more spoken about than practiced. Weaned on the idea of human equality, they are faced with evidence that some people are regarded as being more equal than others. Taught to respect the nation's leaders, they find them standing before the bar of justice. In these and countless other ways, we are exposed to events and conditions reflecting markedly different meanings. Many of these different constructions of reality challenge the validity and universality of our own. The world we once thought of as a place of moral unity and certainty becomes one of contradictions. In short, we are exposed to multiple realities. As a consequence, we sometimes are left in a state of confusion, not knowing what is true or who to believe.

Our initial sense of stability and unity also founders on the rocks of contextually based meanings. Moral absolutes begin to appear to be anything but absolute. We are told that killing violates a divine sense of morality, that it violates the natural order of things and is therefore proscribed in the Ten Commandments. Yet, it is all too apparent that the applicability of that code varies with the context. Thus, it is one thing to oppose killing, but not to the extent that it precludes war. Similarly, while "thou shall not kill" is the rule, a killer may avoid conviction and public condemnation by successfully pleading self-defense. We encounter people who oppose the death penalty while simultaneously advocating more liberal abortion laws. Apparently, though war, the death penalty, and abortion interfere with the life process, that interference has different meaning depending on the context in which it occurs.

To cite another example, let's consider the issue of whether public nudity is moral or immoral. Early training in a society that associates public nudity with sexuality may lead one to condemn such behavior or, at least, view it with concern and apprehension. But what if the nudity referred to is that of a model in a drawing, painting, or art anatomy class? Does the same general association of nudity and sexuality apply in that specific situation? For many people, given the situation or context in which the nudity occurs, the general condemnation (that is, the general meaning) of nudity is withheld. Thus, morality is seen to be situationally based.

Situational variation in moral meaning is also found in the case of several symptoms of psychiatric disorder. Depending on the context in which they occur and the social position of the person exhibiting them, these symptoms may or may not be defined as evidence of mental illness (Scheff, 1966:34). Daydreaming or engaging in reverie, hallucinating, and talking to "spirits" are such symptoms. None of these have explicit rules against them; nor do we have explicit labels for people who do these things. Indeed, in our society we have "holy persons" who have been elevated to high status on the basis of their professed ability to experience revelations, have visions, or otherwise bridge the gap between this world and the hereafter. Joseph Smith, founder of the Church of Jesus Christ of Latter-day Saints, and Mary Baker Eddy, founder of Christian Science, are cases in point (Brodie, 1945; Powell, 1940). When these activities are engaged in by such persons, a favorable definition is fairly certain; yet if engaged in by one not held to be competent in such matters, or if engaged in under circumstances defined as inappropriate, the same behavior may serve as evidence of mental illness.

The contextual basis of meaning may also be noted in how people react to events that comprise everyday life. In a study of persons with visible physical (war-related) injuries (White, Wright, and Dembo, 1948), men were asked how they perceived others' curiosity, questions about, or attempts to discuss their injury. One important factor influencing the reaction of the injured men was the situational context of the discussion about the injury. Fundamentally, if questioning or discussion of the injury seemed to the injured person to grow out of the context, that is, if it "came up naturally" as part of a broader conversation, it was more likely to be defined as acceptable. If, however, questioning occurred "out of the blue," or if it were seen by the injured person as an unwarranted intrusion on his privacy, the questioning was regarded as morally offensive. Such instances included "off the wall" questions from total strangers. In short, like many other things people deal with, absolute meanings are abstractions and may well have little use in helping us understand how people are likely to behave in specific situations. Most important is the idea that the meanings we assign to things and events are problematic or uncertain. They are part of the "script writing" it was earlier suggested all people engage in.

Evidence of the situational and problematic nature of meaning may also be noted in our everyday language. For example, politicians frequently send up "trial balloons" to see how their constituency will respond to a legislative proposal or other action. If meanings were clear, unequivocal, and absolute, no metaphorical balloons would be needed. Likewise, if meanings were unproblematic, we wouldn't have to "play it by ear" or "fly by the seat of our pants." We would behave on the basis of more certain understandings. Lest these popular expressions be understood to reflect the actor's ignorance rather than the problematic nature of meaning, we may point to things regarded as "blessings in disguise." How can a thing be a beneficent gift at one time and a malediction at another unless it be that meanings are situational and, hence, problematic? It would seem that the uncertainty and ambiguity of meaning (rather than ignorance) underlies each of these phrases.

To summarize briefly, the absence of moral certainty precludes the idea that socially constructed reality is a unitary whole, that it is all of a kind. Social reality is multiple rather than singular. These several realities often are more contradictory than consistent, more in conflict than in harmony. Consistent moral definitions of things may be said to exist only in the abstract. As they apply to concrete events, these definitions are highly variable, fluctuating from one setting or context to another. It is out of the conflict between the elements of social reality and variable moral meanings of things that deviance emerges. Indeed, deviance (connoting the assignment of moral meaning) is part of social reality. Let's turn now to a consideration of deviance as social reality.

Deviance as Social Reality

By extension of the principles already presented, we may regard deviance as a concept reflecting the socially constructed negative moral meanings attached to select behaviors (for example, crime, suicide, and mental illness) and personal attributes (for example, obesity, physical handicaps, and disfigurement). In one sense, then, deviance is a social creation. Deviance is the name given to those conditions that run counter to the moral meanings possessed by some groups. Between the thing held to be deviant and the assignment of the label are moral meanings. As a social crea-

tion, then, deviance is an expression of moral meaning.

But what is meant by the term *moral meanings?* Though subject to extensive philosophical scrutiny, the meaning of the term *moral* remains terribly abstract and seemingly unrelated to our daily affairs. Yet people do have a commonsense understanding of things as being moral, respectable, virtuous, and right. The everyday meaning of these terms is perhaps best known by their opposite, with which they are linked (Douglas, 1970:3–4). In terms of such opposites we can best know our sense of morality (what is right) by pointing out what we consider wrong. Thus, many people believe abortion is wrong because it is right that pregnancies come to full term; that it is wrong to steal because people have a right to hold and dispose of their own property. Left-handedness is wrong only in relation to right-handedness. In short, goodness is relative to evil, morality relative to immorality.

Although for most of us morality may be understood in terms of these dualities, it is still possible to differentiate between moral meanings and meaning in general. As a class, moral meanings are recognizable by the fact that their violation may result in the violator being defined as a socially unacceptable person. That is, moral meanings are identifiable (may be inferred) by the reaction that *may* result from their violation. The qualifier "may" is inserted on the grounds that not every violation results in public rejection of the violator. For example, violation of criminal law is punishable, but not every known violator is punished. Nonetheless, it remains true that violation of moral meanings carries the threat of punishment and public condemnation of the violator.

Defining rule violators as socially unacceptable persons also means that such persons may be subject to a public transformation of their character. As Howard Becker states: "When a rule is enforced, the person who is supposed to have broken it may be seen as a special kind of person, one who cannot be trusted to live by the rules agreed upon by the group. He is regarded as an outsider" (1973:1). Rule breakers, then, may be defined as qualitatively different from others.

Investigation of public conceptions of deviants reveals that people construct and assign stereotypic character traits to different types of deviant actors. Adulterers are perceived to be insecure, lonely, self-interested, passionate, and irresponsible. Homosexuals are perceived to be effeminate, lacking self-control, secretive, sensual, and sensitive (Simmons, 1969:29). Each category of deviant has an assigned set of negatively valued character traits.

As these examples show, expressions of rule violators' unacceptability—of their being outsiders—take various forms. They may be declared criminal, mentally ill, or heretics. The attachment of these labels, however, is not simply a consequence of a person's behavior (alleged or otherwise). Labels reflect the moral sense of the labelers. Deviance, then, is an expression of moral meaning and an integral part of social reality.

Defining Deviance

We began this chapter with several examples of rule-violating behavior. Deviance is commonly defined in such terms; *deviance* and *deviant* are terms used generically to refer to conditions and people that depart from a norm or a rule (Hoult, 1969:105). Clearly, the referent of the term goes beyond the matter of crime and criminal behavior. To be sure, crime and criminality contravene legal rules and may therefore be regarded as deviant. Deviance, however, also includes noncriminal departures from norms such as those involved in mental illness, alcoholism, homosexuality, or physical disablement, to name a few. However adequate legal definitions may be for some purposes, our consideration of the Paradigm of Definition should make it clear that these definitions are insufficient to convey the full range and complexity of the *phenomenon of deviance*. This is particularly apparent when we note that deviance and deviants are outgrowths of the social construction of reality, an outgrowth of the processes of creating and assigning moral meaning.

Viewed from the perspective of the Paradigm of Definition, how shall we define deviance and deviant? Basically, *deviance* refers to behavior and conditions that people so define. The basis of such definitions is the definer's interests, which are felt to be jeopardized or threatened in some way by these acts or conditions. As we will see later, when such concerns are linked with power and given legitimacy, the label of deviance may be assigned. *Deviant,* on the other hand, is the label attached to persons or groups defined as violators of moral rules; the term reflects the discreditable character usually attributed to them. In turn, on the basis of this *presumed* discreditability, such people tend to be assigned to a lower level position in the status hierarchy. *Deviant,* then, is also a status assumed by some people who are identified as rule breakers.

Such definitions are deceptively simple. An understanding and appreciation of the dynamics of the phenomenon of deviance calls for a grasp of more than definitions taken out of context. This phenomenon is best apprehended as a complex social process, a process we will explore in depth in the chapters to follow. In doing so, we will begin with a consideration of how and why people engage in behavior known to be proscribed, behavior that puts them in a position to be declared an "outsider."

Another important matter in studying deviance is official rates of deviance and how such rates are constructed. Because these rates are held to constitute "knowledge" of how deviance is distributed in society, and because these statistics are often regarded as evidence of the objective existence of deviation, it is important to examine how they are compiled and how they are influenced by the problematics and uncertainties associated with defining people and conditions as deviant. Consistent with the Paradigm of Definition, Chapter 3 examines the problematics of these statistics with the view to determining whether or not they may be regarded as valid. In Chapter 4, we examine the process of banning, how moral meaning comes to be assigned to behavior. Understanding that process calls for an investigation of the sociological basis of law. Chapter 5 explores the work of rule-enforcing groups, official agencies having the authority to assign the formal label "deviant" to actors. In conjunction with this, we examine how people seek to negotiate, moderate, or otherwise resist being labeled. Try though they may, not everyone is able to resist being labeled. In Chapter 6, then, we give extended consideration to the social psychological effects and the social consequences of being labeled—of being stigmatized. Viewing people as interactive agents, however, suggests that people may not simply accept and resign themselves to a degraded social status. Many people seek to manage their stigma. The variety of forms this effort may take on an individual and a collective level is treated in Chapter 7.

Though these aspects of the phenomenon of deviance do not exhaust the matter, they do suggest that it is far too complex to be defined in simple terms. It is perhaps valid, then, to say that this entire volume is devoted to defining deviance—perceived as an ongoing social process that is seemingly without end.

Summary

This chapter has been concerned with providing a theoretical foundation for the study of deviance. It has done so by presenting the assumptions of the model or paradigm we will use to guide our investigation.

In contrast with other approaches, the model to be used in this volume rests on philosophical nominalism. Its major thrust is to help people understand the process by which they introduce order into their world, a process called the social construction of reality. It is by this means that people create and assign meanings to things, reify these meanings, and then apprehend them as if they were objectively real. Included among these socially constructed and reified meanings are the moral meanings that underlie deviance. Deviance, then, is a product of the complex, ongoing effort whereby people seek to create social order; deviance is part of that social order. Accordingly, behaviors are deviant not because of some moral essence but as a result of human activity.

In contrast with other models, the definition model seeks no information about the supposed inherent meanings of an alleged objective or real world. Indeed, this approach questions whether such a world exists. And, according to this model, even if one does exist, it is of no consequence since the meanings to which people respond are those of their own making.

Thus, we proceed to examine deviance in an interactional framework, investigating how rule breakers and others interact to shape the direction and outcome of the deviance-producing process. Interactionally, then, who defines behavior as deviant? How do they do this? How do individuals labeled deviant respond to that definition? And with what consequences? By these and other questions, which will be considered at length, it is clear that the Paradigm of Definition calls for more than an investigation of the deviant actor—no matter how extensive that investigation may be.

With these considerations in mind, let us begin to examine the deviance process in detail.

2 Breaking Rules

Introduction

In the first chapter we set down the assumptions and examined the implications of the general perspective to be used throughout this book. In the present chapter we employ that perspective to explain rule-breaking behavior. Specifically, we employ an interactionist orientation, a point of view consistent with assumptions of the definitional model regarding human nature in society and the basis of behavior. In contrast with competing perspectives, the interactionist orientation contends that human behavior is a matter of volition. In the negative, this means behavior is neither a result of genetic predisposition nor a matter of mechanical responses resulting from anticipated rewards. Indeed, social action, it is contended, is not well understood as a consequence of any alleged determinative influence. Stated positively, interactionism holds that behavior is based on people's choices, decisions, judgments, and reasons, and that these are created, maintained, and/or changed in a nexus of social relations. Behavior reflects the meanings people give to things in their environment. Viewed as the authors of these meanings, people are self-ordaining. These are the ideas that are employed and expanded upon in the pages to follow. Let us now begin our analysis of the basis of rule-breaking behavior.

People, Effective Environment, and Behavior

We begin by placing people in context—that is, in an environment the meaning of which varies from person to person and from one time to another. Two concerns to be dealt with are (1) what is meant by environment and (2) how does environment relate to individual behavior. We explore these concerns simultaneously.

Commonly in sociological work the term *environment* is used to refer to an ill-defined set of mysterious and obscure "external physical and sociocultural elements," or to "one's physical surroundings," or, finally, to one's "milieu." Further, it is sometimes intimated that the elements comprising the environment have a fixed character, influencing people in similar and determinate ways. In contrast to this, we shall use the term *effective environment,* referring to those *objects people experience*—that is, objects perceived by people to have relevance to the events that comprise their lives (Meltzer, 1967:16–17). Unlike the idea that environment includes everything, *effective environment* consists of the highly individualized experiences one has with a limited set of objects and the meanings people give to these experiences and objects. The precise objects comprising one's effective environment—the external elements one experiences—depend on the person's activities. As people's activities change, so does their effective environment. As activity changes, people experience different objects. However, it is also true that the same external object may be assigned different meaning. As Meltzer notes, chalk may be variously defined as a writing instrument or a missile (1967:17). For a child, a stone may be a thing to be admired at one moment and a thing to throw at another moment. Depending on the actor's mood, or on whether he or she has had a good or bad day "at the office," his or her spouse may be an enjoyable companion or a pain in the neck. There are many other practical examples. However, the important thing is that people respond to chalk, stones, spouses, and all other elements in their effective environment on the basis of assigned and variable meanings. Clearly, then, whatever relationship exists between environment and people's behavior, the *actor plays the role of mediator*. Effective environment is a social construction. We may conclude, then, that the relation between effective environment and behavior is largely indeterminate, extremely individual, and highly situational (Meltzer, 1967:17).

As a word of caution, and to preclude carrying these observations too far, we should note that the individualized nature of effective environment does not rule out the existence of *shared meanings*. As our earlier comments on externalization, objectivation, and internalization indicated, people arrive at common interpretations, definitions, and understandings by means of communication. Thus, however personalized our effective environment may be, the meanings on which it rests are transmittable and shareable. As such, the concept of effective environment does not preclude coordinated or social action.

Biography, Affinity, and Willingness

In addition to the concept of effective environment, our explanation of rule-breaking calls for examination of the concepts of biography and affinity. As a general proposition, it is contended that the basis of a person's involvement in *any pattern* of behavior is a manifestation of his or her unique and continually changing biography and the consequent accumulation of meanings. Because biography is experienced in the context of an effective environment, it, too, defies highly detailed description. Further, because a person's biography is never final and always subject to redefinition, specification of its relation to behavior can never be definitive. However, it is on the basis of biography that people acquire a greater or lesser affinity for particular patterns of behavior. As such, the concepts of biography and affinity require exploration.

Nothing mysterious is meant by the notion of *biography*. Literally, it refers to the events and their meanings (the effective environment) that make up a person's life. Biography consists of the infinitely variable circumstances and events, as well as their changing meanings, that constitute: the "career" of people growing up in a ghetto or on a farm; being accepted or ostracized by one's peers; being male or female; being black, Indian, Oriental, or white; being poor, comfortable, or wealthy; being considered attractive or unattractive; and so on. These individually unique and incredibly varied experiences and meanings are part of what it means to be situated in a complex social structure. People are situated simultaneously in many "places"—that is, in terms of such factors as race, sex, religion, socioeconomic status, and age, among others. Being situated in these "places" means that people who are similarly situated will experience *roughly* similar events, while those located in different "places" within the social structure are likely to have correspondingly different experiences. People occupying different niches in the social structure experience widely differing life situations, and each of us occupies many different niches. As a result, people have very different and extremely complex biographies.

It is important to recognize that biography, as used here, has no final form. A person has no definitive biography. *Biography is constantly in the making; it is constantly being added to and "remade" as a result of every unique experience and each new situation.* Unique experiences today make tomorrow's biography different from yesterday's. Thus, the precise events comprising biography can never be fully grasped and must be understood retrospectively, often in terms of each situation in which the actor finds him- or herself. Further, and most important, the finality of biography, its supposedly definitive character, is precluded because it is always subject to redefinition. That is, as we've seen, our effective environment consists not of events per se, but of the meanings we assign to them. Because these definitions/meanings are subject to change, our biography is always open to redefinition as seems appropriate/necessary in terms of the situation in which we find ourselves. We redefine aspects of our biography; by redefining and giving it new meaning, we change biography on a symbolic level. That is, select aspects of our biography and their meanings may be effectively extinguished and replaced by different meanings.

24

Because of this, and while biography is relevant to an understanding of human behavior, no determinative or definitive statement can be made about the consequences of past experiences for present or future actions.

Affinity may also be interpreted literally. The experiences comprising our biography leave us with a *general orientation* that may range from an extreme affinity (or attraction) to a marked aversion (or antipathy) toward any pattern of behavior. That is, experience may result in a *general disposition* (positive or negative) toward any subsequent behavior pattern. More particularly, our affinity–aversion consists of the meanings or definitions we have developed that are pertinent to any *general pattern* of behavior. Future behavior will be influenced (albeit imperfectly) by these meanings. *Affinity,* then, is comprised of the meanings consistent with being favorably disposed toward any particular course of action.

To say that affinity consists of a favorable disposition toward a pattern of behavior means that we are *open* or *willing* to engage in such actions; we are free to enter into such activity. Willing, in this sense, is not to be equated with determinism. Nor is willingness to be confused with the notion of free will. Quite often the term *free will* is taken to mean that people exercise choice without regard for external or situational considerations. That is, "will" is free of context. As employed here, however, being *willing* means that we make choices, exercise options, and so on, but we do so *in context* (Matza, 1969:116). That context consists of everyday conditions (elements of effective environment) faced by us all, including the opportunity to engage in rule-breaking behavior.

Willingness or openness, then, must be understood in terms of the *general meanings* applied by a person to a particular kind of behavior seen *in the abstract.* Whether or not we behave consistently with those meanings rests on a decision that must be made in context. That is, even though *in general* we may be willing and open to engaging in some pattern of behavior, it remains problematic whether we will decide to engage in that behavior *at any specific time.* For example, many students are likely quite open to using alcohol, marijuana, or other controlled substances (a general condition), yet decline the opportunity to use them at specific times, such as just before going to class or taking a major exam. The meaning (definition) of the exam, together with their sense of the consequence of using mood-altering substances at such a time, the meaning of the classroom as a particular place, and perhaps several other things, combine to form the context in which use of these substances seems inappropriate. Likewise, many married people are open to swinging (extramarital sexual relationships); however, it strains credibility to suggest they actually engage in such relations at each and every opportunity. Nor do people cheat, exceed the speed limit, or break other rules at every opportunity—despite their being willing to do so under *some circumstances.* To repeat, then, acquired affinities or aversions may be regarded only as general conditions; they are not determinants of all future actions.

Willingness to engage in rule-violating behavior and subsequent decision making also needs to be understood in terms of actors' "self" conception. That is, just as experience provides us with meanings of objects in the environment, so, too, does it leave us with a definition of self, that is, with a *self-concept.* Just as our definition of things helps shape our responses to them, so does the meaning we have of self influence our willingness to engage in this or that behavior. Do we define ourselves as the type of person who would engage, even experiment, in the behavior in question? Does the idea of self as a participant leave us disgusted, mildly intrigued, pleasurably excited, or strongly attracted? How we define self vis-à-vis engaging in a particular act strongly influences our decision to participate. What is most important is that participation is not determined by external forces. Rather, the meanings we have of self permit *self-ordination* (Matza, 1969:112). How we respond to the opportunity to engage in rule-breaking behavior, then, reflects our definition of it viewed in context and whether we perceive participation to be consistent with our self-concept. In the final analysis, rule breaking reflects our choices, decisions, and goals.

In summary, we suggest that on the basis of both experience in an effective environment and a constantly developing biography, at any point in time people are more or less attracted to particular patterns of behavior; and that affinity–aversion is based on the meanings and understandings they have of the behavior. Such meanings are never final; they are prone to change as a result of the ongoing experiences that comprise biography. Further, an affinity is not a determinative condition; that is, it does not dictate or shape all subsequent behavior. It is no more than a general condition leading one to be favorably disposed to some kinds of rule breaking under some conditions. Thus, based on biography, people learn that rule breaking is "possible, permissible, rationalizable and even valued within a particular context" (Pfohl, 1985:274). When faced with the opportunity to engage in any particular form of rule breaking, people are either willing or unwilling, open or closed, to varying degrees. However, being open or closed is not an irreversible condition. In the last analysis "to do or not to do" is a matter of individual choice that rests on decisions made in context. As we will see, specific decisions may or may not be consistent with our general affinity-aversion. In short, there is a "bit of the beast" in all of us. Whether this "beast" is displayed depends on the meanings we assign to situations in which we find ourselves. But let's cast these notions in the context of everyday experience.

Willingness and Everyday Life

That experience may promote an affinity for a lifestyle others regard as deviant has been noted by Wallace (1965) in his study of recruits to skid row. The biography of the majority of men coming to skid row left them with no "fixed place" in society. Working as lumberjacks, migrant farm workers, or serving in the military required them to be absent from home for long periods of time. As a result, they were not practiced in living with members of their family—parents, spouse, or children. Family life and its associated values were given low priority by these men. Frequently enough, these men were not accepted back

into their families. In short, biography leads some men to define home as an irrelevant and/or unpleasant place (Wallace, 1965:166).

Supplementing this experience were the job-related contacts and associations some men had with skid row men. Interacting intimately with skid rowers over prolonged periods exposed these men to that subculture; they became aware that an alternative lifestyle exists.

It is at this point . . . that an unsatisfactory home situation becomes relevant in explaining a man's move to skid row. If before he left home he was at constant odds with his family, he may be less inclined than ever to "put up with it"—now that he knows another way of life complete with a few friends is open to him. Problems at home plus the weakening of family ties brought about by his absence reinforce his sense of isolation, push him further adrift, and he'll sever the few remaining roots he has in the respectable society. The skid row way of life—a life without care, worry, and responsibility, a life with friends, drink, and plenty of time in which to enjoy them—begins to look better and better. (Wallace, 1965:167)

In short, given the character of their biography and pertinent definitions, it is understandable why these men have an affinity for skid row living and are willing to exchange one lifestyle for another.

Unique experiences and meanings associated with occupation also help to explain lesbian activity among striptease dancers. "Specifically, conditions supportive of homosexual behavior in the stripping occupation can be classified as follows: (1) isolation from affective [emotionally significant] social relationships, (2) unsatisfactory relationships with males, and (3) an opportunity structure allowing a wide range of sexual behavior" (McCaghy and Skipper, 1969:266). Absence of affective ties may be a consequence of marital problems and/or the job-related difficulties strippers have establishing relationships of trust with others. Working at odd hours and touring from city to city leads to loneliness. Further, the males with whom strippers have the most frequent contact comprise their audience: unattached men they frequently characterize as "degenerate" because of their tendency to engage in exhibitionism and masturbation during the stripper's performance. Add to this the warm reception strippers are likely to receive from those who frequent gay bars where they may go for relaxation, and the presence of lesbians among the strippers is explained. En toto, this complex of biographical factors, elements of which promote a negative definition of relationships with men and a positive definition of relationships with women, are wholly consistent with the actor's willingness to enter into a lesbian relation.

Consider, too, the following lines from the autobiography of a female heroin user regarding her introduction to "smack."

I learned [about] smack from a boyfriend. . . . I met the guy on a farm in Oregon. . . . Because of a fortuitous combination of circumstances I ended up back here in school, the guy followed, did about a year [in jail], and got out, with the intention of turning middle-class. He and I and a buddy of his . . . used to go around together a couple of nights a week, usually not doing much except getting loaded—smoking marijuana or maybe dropping reds or rainbows—none of which I much liked except that it was a rather different social activity.

Then the buddy got a girlfriend who was a hype from way back. . . . I never knew anyone who took so much dope. All she cared about was getting loaded and that's all she ever did. My boyfriend and I often dropped by their pad. . . . One night they had just bought some smack and offered us some. My boyfriend demurred but I said "hell, yes, I want some," just because that's about the only thing I'd never done. Everyone was rather surprised at *my willingness*. . . . (Anonymous, 1974:60–61. Emphasis added.)

In this case, as in so many others, the opportunity to use heroin was a chance affair. However, the company this girl kept, her previous experiences, and the circumstances under which she had the opportunity to try heroin and other drugs—all elements of biography and effective environment—may be considered to have continuity with the use of drugs. But *none of these factors may be regarded as decisive or compelling*. In the final analysis, her use of heroin was volitional. It was a matter of choice. She was willing.

The role of choice and willingness may also be noted in the case of a black youth nicknamed Goat, a member of the Van Dykes, a Chicago fighting gang. When Goat was 12 years old, his family moved from California to an area of Chicago where access to school playgrounds, public parks, movie houses, street corners, and so on, was controlled by gangs. Two weeks after his arrival, while on the way to the store, he was confronted by ten members of the Braves (another gang) who beat him up and took his money. Goat had to make a decision. He knew only that he needed protection in order to live in the neighborhood.

So I asked a cat how do I become a member of the Van Dykes . . . and he say you gotta fight one of the baddest cats in the club and even if you lose, long as you give a good thumpin', you can become a member.

I went home and thought about it. Do I fight this dude and become a member or do I just don't fight him and become a rebel? Then I thought that rebels can't go to the show, can't go to the beach, can't go to house parties, can't have no girlfriends and walk the street. I went back and said "OK, Jack, I'll thump one of the tough cats." (Dawley, 1973:23)

Finally, we may examine the decision-making process leading some young blacks to enter pimping as a way of making a living. In studying the biographies of pimps, Christina and Richard Milner (1972) found the early life and effective environment of many of these men included being exposed to the ubiquitousness of sex and to hustling as a way of life, and led them to define formal education as largely unrewarding and irrelevant to their existence (Milner, 1972:137–138). Yet in no case are these factors compelling. Rather, they are situational elements that influenced the perception these men had of pimping and other, alternative ways of making a living. Observation led them to conclude that despite its hazards, pimping pays more handsomely than "chump jobs" such as being a delivery boy as a youth or, later in life, occupying some "straight" job. Some men become willing in high school when they encounter a girl who will trick for them, or perhaps because they have an uncle who is a pimp. Some others get turned out after they have been married and had children, been in the Service, and tried working to support their wives. They are disillusioned with what society offers them because . . . they have tried living "straight" as adults and found the experience not only wanting but emasculating. (Milner, 1972:142)

Willingness and the Support of Others

In addition to the reasons discussed in the preceding sections, a person's initial willingness to participate in deviance may be promoted by the support and encouragement he or she receives from others, particularly trusted others such as friends. In his study of drug use, Erich Goode (1972:40) identifies three ways friends may influence a person to engage in proscribed behavior (in this case, smoking marijuana). First, friends may serve as examples, thereby making the behavior seem acceptable. If friends are doing it, perhaps it can't be so bad. "Doing it" is "in." (And logically, to refrain is to be "square.") Second, friends are often a source of justification for the behavior. They provide a rationale—a reason, a foundation—for the behavior. Third, with particular relevance to behaviors that depend on the use of "facilitating substances" (such as drug use), friends may make such substances available. In these ways, the contribution of friends is crucial and, in some cases, quite indispensable.

As we noted earlier, willingness is not an "all or nothing" condition. Many people are ambivalent, their openness being limited by a sense of caution and reticence. Such ambivalence and reticence may be dissipated, at least temporarily, by friends and others. Thus, the support and encouragement of others often helps people manage their reluctance, overcome the influence of negative definitions and attitudes, or strengthen a mild affinity. For example, Weinberg (1981a:292) notes the importance of interpersonal relations in helping people overcome their reluctance to participate in nudism and nudist camp activities. One of Weinberg's female interviewees, commenting about her ambivalence over participating in nudism, remarked as follows:

[Whether or not I would go to a nudist camp would] depend on who asked me. If a friend, I probably would have gone. . . . If an acquaintance, I wouldn't have been interested. . . . If it was someone you like or had confidence in, you'd go

along with it. If you didn't think they were morally upright you probably wouldn't have anything to do with it. (1981a:293)

Weinberg further notes that over three-fourths (78 percent) of his female interviewees became interested in and were introduced to nudism through their husbands, parents, or in-laws. Only 20 percent became interested through impersonal sources such as magazines or motion pictures (1981a:292).[1]

Similarly, in studying spouse swapping, Charles Varni found that, initially, women typically perceived mate swapping with revulsion. This reaction was followed by the husband's efforts to alter his wife's definition of mate swapping. This involved a "convincing" or "coercing" process that, at least, brought the wife to the point of being willing to experiment in this behavior (1972:511–512).

The support and encouragement of friends and acquaintances is also apparent in the introduction of people to the nude beach scene. Referring to "nude beach seductions," or ways people are encouraged to take off their clothes in public when they are reluctant, Douglas and Rasmussen (1977:74) indicate these "seduction" attempts frequently involve the subtle pressure put on girls ("nude beach virgins") by their boyfriends, as well as the friendly persuasion of boys by girls. To be sure, the effect of these efforts varies but, again, they frequently bring the novice to the point of experimentation.

In addition, the support provided by others enables some people to perceive rule breakers as "people like themselves," people who are not different in any appreciable way. For many people it is important that their involvement in questionable behavior be compatible with a moral self-image. Support of trusted others allows people to overcome the reluctance that

[1]Interestingly, in Weinberg's sample, fewer men had their interest aroused by other persons (33 percent) than by the media (59 percent). This is consistent with what is known about males being more responsive than females to such stimuli, and with the general biographical experiences of males in our society, particularly their greater exposure to material that might be defined as pornographic. Again, then, these data support the alternative perspective presented here.

may arise when they try to combine a moral conception of self, on the one hand, with participation in morally questionable behavior, on the other. If the behavior is engaged in by "people like themselves," that is, by moral people, perhaps the behavior isn't so bad after all. This same support also permits us to overcome objections that rest on stereotyped definitions of "people like that." Again, Weinberg reports that prenudist attitudes of nudists consisted of such stereotypes. One respondent commented, "I thought . . . [nudism] was a cult—a nut-eating, berry-chewing bunch of vegetarians, doing calisthenics all day, a gymno-physical society. I thought they were carrying health to an extreme, being egomaniacs about their body" (1981a:292). Another informant remarked, "I'm afraid I had the prevailing notion that [nudist camps] were undignified, untidy places populated (a) by the very poor, and (b) by languishing bleached blondes, and (c) by greasy, leering bachelors" (1981a:292). To the extent they exist, such attitudes need to be somewhat dissipated or resolved in order for a person to be willing to engage in morally questionable behavior.

In addition, would-be rule breakers often must grapple with what it may mean to engage in behavior that, in public terms, is shameful. Here, too, the role of others may be critical. For example, in examining middle-class women's entry into prostitution, Douglas (1977) concludes that these women do not "fall" into whoredom. Rather, the entry process is protracted, and during this period the possibilities are thought about and discussed.

They think about it and generally talk about it with similar friends—testing out the idea and its fateful shame implications. They are all intellectually convinced that sexual freedom and so on are good ideas, but their bodies at this stage are still saying something different—almost a dread of being shamefully ostracized from society, that is, stigmatized. (Douglas, 1977:66)

To the extent these women discuss their concerns with "insiders" (such as liberated women who support sexual freedom, or women who are either thinking about entering prostitution or have already done so), it can be demonstrated that shame is manageable or, if not,

that at least it can be hidden. "This connection with the insider is often crucial. The person who is already inside has already overcome most of the fear of shame and may feel pride by now. They provide evidence that shame can be overcome or avoided, or . . . they act as if there is no such thing" (Douglas, 1977:66–67).

As a final consideration bearing on the relationship between others and one's willingness, let's turn to the issue of *commitment,* that is, the "pledge" or bond we may have with other persons (such as family) and a related dedication to a course of action (Johnson, 1973:397; Becker, 1960). In general, willingness may be influenced by our behavioral commitment to conformity. Stated differently, willingness is often balanced against the actor's anticipation of the possible consequences of engaging in punishable behavior. A decision to engage in conduct that has some probability of punishment calls for consideration of the material and social consequences—punishments—should we be discovered. Included here are the consequences of discovery on preserving our public image, maintaining relationships with valued others, and on the ability to maintain our present statuses or achieve desired statuses in the future (Briar and Piliavin, 1965:39). In short, each of us possesses innumerable interests to which we attach varying degrees of importance. Behavior consistent with one interest is often considered in terms of the consequences it may have for our other interests. A person with a high commitment to law-abiding behavior is therefore less likely to engage in rule breaking than a person lacking such commitment. Thus, commitment entails an appreciation of the factors that encourage us to continue to pursue a line or course of action—in this case, conformity—as opposed to the consequences we may anticipate as a result of discontinuing that action line.

As an example of the constraining aspect of commitments, especially the anticipated "costs" of engaging in proscribed behavior, some sexually inactive college women have indicated that their decision to be inactive rests on their parents' expectation that they avoid such involvement. These women's sense of commitment to their parents—that is, a wish to avoid hurting them by violating their trust and to avoid the costs of damaging a valued relationship—is a major element in their thinking. A similar set of constraints based on commitments was found by Rossman (1976:180) in his study of homosexual pederasts. Among the constraining factors cited by pederasts who choose to refrain from actual sexual encounters are (1) a concern for the feelings of and a desire not to hurt family and friends and (2) a reluctance to do things the discovery of which would destroy their lives, especially (but not only) in a professional sense.

Willingness and Neutralizing Constraints

People's willingness to break rules is often restricted by internalized beliefs and ethical systems. However, such restraints are unlikely to serve as permanent or insurmountable barriers to engaging in banned behavior. Thus, everyday experience and systematic research reveal the ease with which people may profess their commitment to the values of legitimate society while violating them behaviorally.

Serving to resolve this apparent contradiction between "saying and doing" are several *techniques of neutralization* (Sykes and Matza, 1957), devices that allow a person to preserve his or her conception of self as a "moral" person while simultaneously engaging in proscribed behavior. That is, a person may subscribe to a moral code while simultaneously violating its prescriptions. Using these techniques of neutralization before engaging in deviant behavior makes it possible for a person to avoid the self-disapproval that may result from violating internalized proscriptive norms. These are devices that release us from the moral bind of our value commitments. There are five of these techniques. We will consider each briefly.

One technique of neutralization is called *denial of responsibility*. When asked why she engaged in systematic theft, a teenage girl replied that she had no other choice: Jobs just weren't available, and she had to have clothes and wanted to have some fun, and her unemployed parents didn't have the money to provide these things. Accordingly, she felt compelled to steal. That assertion contains the basic element of denial of responsibility; that is, the actor professes to have no control over his or her actions, to be driven to act by external forces, or to be a "billiard ball." This assertion is contained in the popular notion that poverty is a "cause" of such behavior. Other "causes" sometimes enlisted to account for rule breaking include poor home conditions, alcoholic parents, bad companions, and the like. Given the operation of these elements, the impact of which is felt to be beyond their ability to resist, people see themselves as essentially blameless: "More acted upon than acting" (Sykes and Matza, 1957:667).

A second technique of neutralization, *denial of injury*, rests on the morality of consequences. That is, the claim is made that whether or not a person's actions may be properly referred to as deviant or immoral depends on the injury or harm that results from those acts. Cases reflecting a "denial of injury" are abundant. For some people, fistfights are a customary means of resolving interpersonal problems even though such fights are legally definable as assault. Adopting the former perspective precludes the latter—including the sometimes harmful consequences resulting from assault. In similar fashion, auto theft is defined as "borrowing" and vandalism is defined as "mischief" or a "prank" (Sykes and Matza, 1957:667). Obviously, "fistfighting," "borrowing," "mischief," and "pranks" refer to behaviors that involve no serious injury to person or harm to property.

A third technique is *denial of the victim*. For example, a young man reported that he shoplifted from a major national retail chain store because of the store's policy toward its customers. According to the young man's perception of that policy—that it was "legalized theft"—he defined his thefts as what the company deserved. The company "had it coming." Similarly, "straights" often justify "gay bashing"—that is, beating up homosexuals—by claiming that homosexuals deserve to be assaulted. In both these cases responsibility for the rule-violating behavior is accepted and injury admitted. Indeed, acknowledgment of these elements is necessary to a denial of the victim. However, as these examples indicate, the victim is converted into a legitimate target and the actor becomes a "moral avenger." The rule violator becomes a modern-day Robin Hood, dealing out deserved rewards to "evildoers."

In researching the behavior of "unwed fathers" (Pfuhl, 1978), the author encountered a man who, unknowingly, had steadily dated a woman engaged to marry someone else. Upon discovering this, the man was infuriated and set out to "punish" the woman by getting her pregnant. Consistent with the tactic of "denial of the victim," the man became the offended "avenger" and the woman the "transgressor." He states:

I found out about the two of them and played the dumb routine. At the time I thought she was a virgin. . . . She was pretty religiously hung up. . . . She was anti-abortion, anti-sex, and she was kind of a tease—letting you go just so far and then clamming up and saying she had a headache and wanted to go home. And at first I thought she was just hanging on, but then I found out about this other guy. So then I just began trying a little harder . . . so I could get to her. She misled me to think that I was the only one for her . . . it wasn't just that she didn't tell me about this. That was what offended me so much. I didn't like being used this way. She was Miss Socialite, and I was supposed to escort her around, pay her way here and there, and all the time she was tight with this other guy. (Taped interview)

Asked how he felt when he learned she was pregnant, he replied:

I was happy about the predicament she was in and that if everyone found out it would put the damper on the angelic front she was putting up. I wouldn't have been happy had the circumstances been different. I had finally gotten to this girl after she had made a monkey out of me. (Taped interview)

A fourth pattern of neutralization, *condemnation of condemners,* centers on those who disapprove, reject, or condemn the rule breaker on the basis of his or her actions. In this case violators reject such persons—they "reject the rejector" (Sykes and Matza, 1957:668). For example, prison inmates are often heard to make morally condemning remarks regarding police, prosecutors, and judges. To have been rejected or condemned by such "morally reprehensible" people is defined as an honor by some convicts. Further, the alleged immorality of one's condemners is often said to be far greater than one's own. Thus, attention is focused on the condemners rather than on the deviant, and the behavior of the condemners is seen as the more reprehensible. The utility of this technique lies in redirecting the negative sanctions and condemnation from the rule breaker to the rule enforcer.

The final technique of neutralization, *appeal to higher loyalties,* is commonly encountered as a form of *role conflict;* that is, people are faced with competing demands as a consequence of role inconsistency. In the vernacular, people claim to be "caught between a rock and a hard place." Disentangling themselves necessarily entails violation of one set of demands or expectations. The expectations (expressed as rules) that are violated are defined as being of lesser importance. Their constraining influence is thus reduced.

The popularity of this technique is readily apparent. Perhaps the best known example is young people experiencing conflict between peer group and family expectations. Another example is the appeal to "secular necessities" that people use to justify violating religious codes of conduct. In a study of "religious deviants," Dunford and Kunz (1973) report that Mormons violating their church's rule against Sunday shopping neutralized the rule by citing such things as their need to purchase medicine for a sick family member, or the need to obtain food for unexpected guests—such needs taking precedence over the moral norm. In this way an appeal to a higher loyalty aids in resolving a conflict in roles.

Contracultural Values

Our comments on the need to neutralize value commitments rest on the assumption that people are committed to the legitimate institutional system and are in agreement with its values. However, experience demonstrates that such an assumption is not always warranted and may not be taken for granted. That is, not all people who violate public rules do so *in spite of* their subscribing to these same rules. Given the pluralistic value system in heterogenous societies, it is quite plausible that many rule violations reflect the actor's rejection of the conventional and his or her advocacy of a contrary perspective. Several examples may be cited.

First, since the 1960s people have become increasingly aware of events called political violence and terrorism, the work of a diverse array of organizations such as the Baader–Meinhof group in Germany, the Weather Underground and the Armed Forces of National Liberation for Puerto Rico (FALN) in the United States, and the Irish Republican Army in Northern Ireland, to name a few. Referred to as *terrorism*—that is, "the deliberate and systematic use or threat of violence against . . . human targets . . . whereby the immediate victims . . . cannot dissociate themselves from the conflict" (Schmid and de Graaf, 1982:15)—these frightening and distressing actions are often interpreted as a result of some psychopathology. A more valid explanation, we suggest, rests on the perceptions, beliefs, ideology, and values of these actors, as well as on their bitter opposition to the values represented by the status quo (Wilkinson, 1977:93–102). In short, the terrorist's efforts are most readily understood as matters of religious and secular dispute and "have as their objective the destruction of the society's system of power, changes of policy by means of violence, or the forceful removal of those exercising power in the system" (Sykes, 1972:413; Rapoport and Alexander, 1982).

A second example of rule breaking based on values other than those of the legitimate institutional system is *civil disobedience*—that is, carefully chosen and limited behavior known to be illegal and openly engaged in for the express purpose of promoting limited social change (Bay, 1967:166). Embracing this principle and the practical goals upon which it rests means one is unlikely to be constrained by rules that derive their legitimacy from the very system one wishes to change. For example, in April 1968, Philip Berrigan, a former Catholic priest, and three other persons (the so-called Baltimore Four) went on trial for interfering with the military draft as an act against the war in Vietnam (Berrigan, 1971). For Berrigan and

his associates, that act was simultaneously an expression of their profound Christian beliefs and their consequent opposition to the war in Vietnam, as well as a rejection of the values and interests that sustained and justified America's presence in Vietnam. More recently, Phillip Berrigan, his brother Daniel, and six other people, were apprehended when they entered the General Electric nuclear weapon assembly plant at King of Prussia, Pa. Their purpose was to express their idealism and Christian pacifism, and their continuing opposition to activities, based on legitimate values, that they regard as "crimes against God and humanity" (*Arizona Republic*, 1980a). Such behavior in our society is not unique. Though less well publicized, numerous groups openly violate public law as an expression of opposition to dominant public policy on such issues as use of nuclear energy, disposal of hazardous wastes, transportation and use of nuclear weapons, and defiling the environment, to name a few.

In each of the instances mentioned, the actor's commitment is to values contrary to those of the dominant social order. These alternative values have been referred to as *contracultural* or *countervalues* (Yinger, 1965:231). These are terms applied to values perceived by some to threaten the interests of dominant groups and legitimate normative order. These values are often held to be deviant (Glaser, 1971:15–19).

Finally, people may break rules without needing to secure "release" from moral rules if they define the behavior involved as *amoral*, that is, behavior about which they feel no sense of wrongfulness since they define it as outside the realm of morality. Often, behaviors with a negative moral meaning undergo a change in public definition, largely due to social change and the dynamics of moral meanings (Sykes, 1972:415). Behavior once publicly regarded as immoral and taboo becomes widely practiced, and rules once zealously enforced tend to be ignored. A case in point is divorce, once regarded as a shameful event but currently accepted (though in some quarters with alarm) with few if any moral connotations. For a substantial segment of the population, adultery, abortion, and the use of some psychotropic drugs (for example, marijuana and cocaine) fall into this category.

A Cautionary Note

At this point a cautionary word on the general issue of willingness and commitment is in order. First, people's occasional willingness to break rules should not be perceived as an exclusive condition. As most people's biographies affirm, rule breaking is most often an episodic thing, a momentary digression. Likewise, people are not committed exclusively either to legitimate or to nonlegitimate values. Such dualisms lack validity. Few persons, including the most dedicated delinquent, engage in rule-violating behavior at each and *every* opportunity (Short and Strodtbeck, 1965:265). "Severely disturbed" mental patients conform to most rules most of the time. And even among the most dedicated professional offenders, violation of law is occasional. Further, those who violate some rules stand foursquare in support of others. Thus, among hardened offenders the child molester is held in extremely low esteem. Rather than being unique, similar observations may be made of anyone. Realistically, most people conform to the bulk of our legitimated values most of the time.

Second, for most people, release from moral constraint is situation-specific and short lived, and must be renewed from time to time. This episodic release, as the term implies, is an event that stands out or apart from other customary conditions. Thus, willingness to engage in one form of rule breaking at one time cannot necessarily be generalized to other forms, or to that form at other times. For example, evidence suggests that as age increases, as people's responsibilities change, as opportunities diversify, and so on, so do their options, commitments, self-conception, and, hence, their behavior (Brown, et al., 1974). In other instances people simultaneously live a public life of normality and a secret life of rule breaking (Bensman and Lilienfeld, 1979:60–61). Thus, William Chambliss (1978:72) notes that "in Seattle one of the city's leading jewelers served simultaneously as a financier for large [illegal] drug transactions and as a fence

for stolen jewelry." Finally, it is no surprise that people defined as "radical hippies" in the 1960s become sedate middle-class businesspeople in the 1970s and 1980s, or that Abbie Hoffman, outspoken leader of the radical left in the 1960s and early 1970s, should finally tire of the role of fugitive, establish himself as a respectable citizen, become a successful author, and finally turn himself in to the legal authorities.

Summarizing to this point, "being willing," as used here, refers simply to a person's *availability* for participation in some form of rule breaking. A person who is willing is merely a *potential* rule breaker. Whether or not he or she does in fact break a rule is yet highly problematic, dependent upon a number of conditions. Among these are the person's commitments, the encouragement provided by others, and the degree to which the person embraces countercultural values. However, when all is said and done, a person's involvement in rule-breaking conduct continues to be a matter over which the actor has control. That is, people who stand at this juncture make decisions as to whether they should remain on the periphery, become more involved, or withdraw completely. Let's examine these decisions and how they are made.

Turning On—Turning Off

Having once engaged in rule breaking, the actor must decide whether or not to persist in it. The outcome of this decision-making effort rests on whether or not the person's experience with deviance (part of an ever-changing biography) results in being *turned on* or *turned off* (Matza, 1969:177ff). One meaning of the term *turned on* involves familiarity with a thing as a consequence of experience rather than abstract knowledge (Partridge, 1970:1484). In this sense, being "turned on" is not synonymous with "being hooked" or with having an indelible commitment to the behavior. Simply, experience renders a person at least minimally knowledgeable. Through experience he or she comes to associate with others who are engaged in the same behavior and through them becomes more knowledgeable, skilled, or sophisticated in the behavior. On the basis of that knowledge the actor decides that continuing in the behavior either is or is not appropriate for him or her. In the context in which it is experienced, the actor is able to make reasoned choices and decisions.

One consequence of experience is that people may have second thoughts about their actions that lead to a decision to refrain from further involvement. It may lead to people being "turned off." As an example, the initial experience some people have with psychotropic drugs almost precludes anything but future abstinence. Consider the following results of snorting heroin for the first time. After the initial "rush,"

My guts felt like they were going to come out. Everything was bursting out all at once, and there was nothing I could do. It was my stomach and my brain. My stomach was pulling my brain down into it, and my brain was going to pull my guts out and into my head. . . . And then it seemed like everything in me all of a sudden just came out, and I vomited. . . . I was dying, . . . I threw up, and I threw up. It seemed like I threw up a million times. I felt that if I threw up one more time, my stomach was just going to break all open; and still I threw up. I prayed and I prayed. . . . After a while I was too sick to care. . . . I was sick about two days after that. I didn't even want a reefer. I didn't want anything, anything, that was like a high. I started drinking some of Dad's liquor after that, but I was scared of those dry highs. Anyway, that was the big letdown with horse . . . The horse had turned out to be a real drag. (Brown, 1966:111–112)

In other instances, rule breaking may result in the actor being overcome with problems of conscience and remorse. Thus, one Chicago purse thief felt constrained to attach a note of apology to his booty expressing his "deepest sympathy" to the victim and hoping the owner of the purse wasn't caused any loss or harm; the purse was then left where it would be found and, hopefully, returned to its owner (*Arizona Republic,* 1982a). In another instance, New York's Waldorf Astoria Hotel reported that during calendar 1980 it received more than $30,000 worth of silver table service from persons who had, as long as 65 years before, acquired it by pilfering. That 1980 was a peak year for returning the "pilferware" has been attributed to the then rapid rise in the price of silver. Apparently the change in price led people to redefine their earlier thefts. What had been an insignificant matter came to be one imbued with guilt and shame (Tonge, 1980).

These examples all indicate that for a variety of reasons some actors are led to change their definition of the behavior in question. In short, they become "turned off" and unwilling, and what was once viewed as an enticing novelty, a moderately tolerable possibility, or perhaps a long shot, comes to be rejected. Unlike the decision to experiment, which was made in the abstract, rejection rests on experience. To be sure, the decision to reject may not be indelible. Additionally, experience may refresh or renew the actor's commitment to a prior reality (Matza, 1969:112). For example, Douglas and Rasmussen relate the case of Kay, a young, pretty Kansas schoolteacher whose introduction to the nude beach was with an experienced friend, Diana. At the time of the initial suggestion that they go to the beach, Kay "thought it sounded great and decided to go nude publicly for the first time in her adult life" (1977:77). Upon arrival at the beach, Diana immediately stripped and encouraged Kay to join her. Despite every gentle encouragement from her friend and other acquaintances, Kay ended the day fully clothed, crying "I can't."

Obviously, these experiences do not always leave actors in a state of distress. Often enough, the satisfaction of the initial experience promotes a decision to persist. For example, Octavio Rodriguez reports the following concerning his encounter with heroin:

I adapted to it very well, probably because I was having a hard time trying to establish relationships with people—I couldn't get to know people very well . . . but I discovered that if you were a junkie in my neighborhood people really didn't expect too much from you. That was an easy way out: if I became a heroin addict, I wouldn't have to try to meet people and people would leave me alone. . . . Well, anyway, heroin sort of satisfied my feelings of frustration, and I really became quite involved in it—as a user mostly. (1974:84)

On the basis of positive or utilitarian experiences, then, people may get "turned on" in a second and related sense; that is, they may be "converted" to the behavior. From experience they know (at least to a limited degree) the positive and negative features of the deviation. It is no longer an abstraction. It is now part of their biography. Through experience the actor is able to revise or supplement former meanings attached to the behavior. Nudism, for example, once taboo, may become invested with "good purposes" such as healthy bodies and minds cleansed of distorted sex curiosities (Weinberg, 1981b:336ff). A similar "conversion" was noted by Varni in his study of mate swapping. Though they characteristically approached spouse swapping with anxiety, apprehension, and misgiving, many wives reported

The main effect of the first swinging experience was to greatly reduce the level of anxiety . . . and thus provide a climate in which the experience could be evaluated in a more "objective" light. If anything, the experience was anticlimactic in relation to the woman's expectations. The typical response was that it was not such a big deal after all. Many women made guardedly positive remarks such as "Well, it wasn't as bad as I thought it would be," or "I might try it again." (Varni, 1972:512)

Varni also reports that if the initial swinging experience is not traumatic, a couple is likely to try it again. On the basis of the knowledge provided by the first experience, and its tendency to reduce anxiety and apprehension, people usually report the second experience to be more enjoyable. Such a reaction, of course, rests on the condition that no unmanageable or threatening situations arise to alter the definition of the experience. "This second experience, if it proves to be nonthreatening—and especially if it is enjoyable—is usually the clincher in that it validates the nonuniqueness of the first experience" (1972:513). On that basis (and that of subsequent nontroubling experiences), the actor is proceeding toward acquiring a new set of moral meanings—a "new" social reality.

Experiences of this sort are legion; they are the stuff of everyday life. On the basis of just such experiences we validate and reinforce, or question, revise, and reject, our conceptions of things in our environment. In the context of deviance, it is these experiences that enable people to make decisions regarding the appropriateness of their behavior in light of self-attitudes and their position in society. It is out of this experience that the once "willing but reticent," now "turned on" actor, builds a revised social reality. This is a learning experience in which the actor "gives up" one social reality and "takes on" another (Varni, 1972:510).

Throughout this learning process, however, the actor is in a position of control and authority over his or her actions (Matza, 1969:123). As such, explanations of conduct based on "pressures" by others or "capitulating" to external or immutable forces are seen as invalid. Although people perceive themselves as objects, they are actually actors, doing the acting. People perceive themselves as sometime rule breakers in the context of their various social positions. They contemplate the possibility of social rejection should their rule breaking be made a public issue, and they mediate and resolve any conflict between their rule breaking and other commitments. In short, people perceive themselves in a *relational sense,* that is, in relation to many other things. On the basis of such perceptions and their assigned meaning, people make the decision to pursue or not to pursue a course of rule-breaking behavior (Matza, 1969:122). As noted earlier, *deviation is self-ordained.*

The Question of Motives

It has been indicated that rule-violating behavior is volitional and based on reasons. Among these reasons are *motives* or motivation, the "complex of meaning which appears to the individual involved . . . to be sufficient reason for his conduct" (Weber, 1962:39). In short, among other things, the decision to pursue a deviant course of action rests on the actor's motivation. Stated differently, deviant conduct is intentional and meaningful activity. Our concern now is with various foundations of that intent.

One motive for rule-breaking behavior is people's desire to break with the established order (Quinney, 1965:122). This is the case with several forms of delinquent and criminal behavior as well as with mass protest. One classic expression of this pattern of motivation is the more than 250 slave revolts and conspiracies engaged in by blacks during the time of American slavery (Aptheker, 1943:162). To black slaves, these uprisings were cases of "carrying the fight to the enemy" and were based on the hope of obtaining personal freedom as well as destroying that "peculiar institution" (Franklin, 1956:208). Black antipathy to the established order did not, of course, cease in 1865. As W. Haywood Burns (1963) makes clear, the "voices of Negro protest" were never silenced in our society and became particularly strident after the end of World War II.

Another group in our society that has engaged in mass protest is women. The history of women in America bears great similarity to both the condition and the protest efforts of blacks (Kirkpatrick, 1955:158–160; Hardert et al., 1977:Chapter 9). The history of the feminist movement reveals innumerable cases demonstrating the degree to which women's protest has been considered deviant, particularly by those occupying positions of authority in the established order. So much does the activity of some contemporary feminist groups violate institutionalized expectations (the established order) that the topic of "militant women" has been included in some topically oriented works on deviance (Bell, 1976). At least one recent volume focuses on the devaluation of women in general, and on the negative labeling of feminist women who are perceived to be in violation of traditional gender norms (Schur, 1984). Other examples of domestic protest seen as deviance include student protests of the 1960s and 1970s, and the gay liberation movement.

Not all forms of protest regarded as deviant are of the mass type. Turning again to the history of slavery in America, we find numerous examples demonstrating that much black protest against the established order, a reaction against subordination, took an individual and private form. Included among these efforts were

Loafing on the job, feigning illness in the fields and on the auction block, and engaging in . . . sabotage. The slave was so hard on the farming tools that special ones were developed for him. He drove the animals with a cruelty that suggested revenge, and . . . was . . . ruthless in his destruction of the crops. . . . He burned forests, barns, and homes. . . . [Finally] self-mutilation and suicide were popular forms of resistance to slavery. (Franklin, 1956:206)

As viewed by the slave owner, self-mutilation and suicide constituted destruction of property. Equally individualized are such contemporary forms of protest as shoplifting, destruction of telephone equipment, and, at least on one occasion, an airplane hijacking by persons seeking to redress what they regarded as grievances stemming from having to deal with impersonal, unresponsive, and unregenerate bureaucratic systems.

Another pattern of protest against elements of the established order is civil disobedience. As noted in our consideration of countercultural values, civil disobedience is engaged in for the express purpose of promoting social change. On a grander scale, revolutionary activity has the same essential purpose.

Delinquent behavior, too, is sometimes engaged in as an expression of hostility toward and rejection of persons and agencies representing what some young people regard as onerous. Eloquently symbolic of this hostility and contempt is the incident, related by Albert Cohen (1955:23), of the student who defecated on the teacher's desk.

A second motivation for rule-violating behavior involves immediate, tangible, and utilitarian goals. Theft sometimes reflects this motivational base. For example, a student who engaged in systematic theft while employed as a route salesman for a wholesale bakery put the matter this way. Too frequently and for a variety of reasons, the difference between the cost of the merchandise consigned to him and what he was required to pay the bakery for it left him "short."

Being a novice, . . . I came up short all too often. The amounts were usually small, but they added up. A dollar or two a day devastated my budget. Even more inconvenient was an occasional major (to me) shortage—$5–$10. I would have to settle all the shortages on the weekly payday. When I would go home with the remains of my check and tell my wife how much I had left, she gave me the practical advice "Either stop coming up short or get another job." She wasn't recommending stealing. She was recommending that I change jobs. I checked the job market and found no practical alternatives. There was no real wrestling with conscience. It was more the feeling of agony, of being substantially short again with my stomach knotting up and muttering a vow. "Shit, this is going to happen to me again." There were no trips to the Garden of Gethsemane in making the decision to steal; they came later. There was just an awareness of what to do and then doing it. (Unpublished paper)

Just as meanings linked to immediate, practical matters influenced this person's decision to steal to supplement his income, so, too, do situational conditions influence women in their decision to obtain an abortion. In a study of the motivations of women receiving abortions (Steinhoff, Smith, and Diamond, 1971:3), it was found that 36 percent wanted an abortion because they were not married. Other reasons cited were inability to afford having a child at the time, the belief that a child would interfere with educational goals, that occupational or other activity would be disturbed, or that the woman was too young to have a baby. These reasons reflect women's perception of the personal situation in which they found themselves. The bulk of the women claiming to be "too young" were, in fact, under 20 years of age. Of those who claimed they already had too many children, 50 percent already had given birth to four or more children. Over half of those citing educational goals as the reason had some college training and, apparently, were desirous of advancing their education.

Henslin's (1971:116–118) study of criminal abortion also reveals the relationship of situational factors to women's decisions to undergo an abortion. Regardless of marital status, Henslin's subjects defined their pregnancy as a dilemma that could be resolved by abortion. In the case of an unmarried woman, the man did not want to (or would not) marry her; a married woman's marriage would be unduly strained financially by the birth; and a divorced woman anticipated that giving birth would create insoluble problems with her former husband regarding custody of their children

(compare with Manning, 1971a). To the extent that it is regarded as deviant, then, the motives for abortion often rest on personalized, situationally based circumstances.

A third pattern of motivation is the recreational—the general idea that rule-violating behavior is fun. There appears to be a tendency to regard a variety of deviant and delinquent acts as sport or play (Sykes, 1972:411; Richards, Berk, and Forster, 1979). The idea of deviance as fun has long been recognized. Thrasher noted that "going robbing" was a common recreational diversion among gang boys (1963:269). Tannenbaum, too, early recognized the play element in rule-violating behavior. He noted that

In the beginning the definition of the situation by the young delinquent may be in the form of play, adventure, excitement, interest, mischief, fun. Breaking windows, annoying people, running around porches, climbing over roofs, stealing from pushcarts, playing truant—all are items of play, adventure, excitement. (1938:17)

And who would deny that a great deal of so-called sex delinquency is pleasurable.

More contemporary expressions of recreational deviance include the construction and operation of complex gadgetry in order to "beat" the phone company out of the cost of long-distance phone calls, interfering with national poll samples, rerouting mail, and tampering with radio and television broadcasts (Toffler, 1970:289–290). Toffler suggests that these diversionary forms of deviance are likely to increase in the future with the development of *antisocial leisure cults,* "organized groups of people who will disrupt the working of society not for material gain, but for the sheer sport of 'beating the system' " (1970:289). As social definitions of leisure change, suggests Toffler, the inclusion of socially disruptive forms of behavior under the heading of "fun" is a distinct possibility.

Other expressions of breaking rules for "fun" include the use of mood-altering substances. Erich Goode (1972:172) suggests that at least the "honeymoon phase" of heroin use is based on a desire for its highly touted euphoria and pleasure. In the case of marijuana, intermittent and moderate users, probably the largest proportion of users, employ marijuana as a "social relaxant" to facilitate social interaction, just as others use alcohol (Geller and Boas, 1969:65). Particularly important in this respect is the widely held belief that marijuana use enhances the enjoyment and appreciation of shared activities such as music, art, films, and food (National Commission on Marihuana and Drug Abuse, 1972:37). Thus, marijuana smoking has become the focal point of much social and recreational activity.

Lastly, to refer to some rule-breaking behavior as "fun" or recreational is not to trivialize it. These remarks do not mean that recreational rule breaking—for example, most delinquency—is "whimsical or inconsequential, or that its sole purpose is entertainment. . . . Play serves a number of purposes, and can help refine skills, technique and awareness of social rules that are useful in a variety of contexts. Popular types of delinquency . . . have similar potential" (Richards, Berk, and Forster, 1979:183). We suggest only that a substantial portion of rule-breaking behavior, and perhaps most of delinquency, has its origins in matters that are far from representing social and individual pathology. Rule-breaking behavior is human behavior.

Rule Breaking as "Negotiated" Events

As a final element in our consideration of the interactional nature of rule breaking, let's consider the emergence of some proscribed behavior as a consequence of how people define their immediate situation and how they perceive themselves in relation to other persons who are part of the immediate situation. Unlike the preceding comments, in what follows our focus is on how people's motivations arise sequentially in the context of an ongoing social relationship. That is, a person's motives do not always arise well in advance of the action they are associated with. Rather, some *motives may emerge in the course of the action itself,* largely as a consequence of the perceived nature of the interaction between one's self and others. Viewed sequentially and as an emergent of interaction, some proscribed behavior may

properly be said to be "negotiated" by the actors involved. Let's examine this idea in relation to two patterns of offense: homicide and burglary.

As the result of an intensive study of 70 murder cases, David Luckenbill concludes that in every situation the death may be viewed as the culmination of *situated* transactions, that is, "a chain of interactions between two or more individuals that lasts the time they find themselves in one another's physical presence" (1977:177). These transactions are carried out in a wide variety of settings (bars, automobiles, parties, people's homes, dances, and so on) and between persons representing a wide array of relationships (spouses, friends, co-workers, acquaintances, and strangers). What is critical is the dynamics of these situated activities.

Luckenbill contends that such acts are frequently the result of an intense period of interaction between persons, one of whom eventually assumes the role of victim and the other the role of offender, the ultimate determination of these positions being entirely problematic. Each of the parties is a contributor to the final outcome of the event.

Quite often these events are "character contests" in which (1) one person says or does something to another that (2) is perceived by the other person to be a disparagement, insult, or other affront to his or her self-image. This is accompanied by (3) a retaliatory move by the offended person consisting either of a verbal or physical challenge, or a direct physical retaliation resulting in the death of the original offender. If the third step is limited to a challenge by the offended person, the initial offender is now in a position that marks a possible fourth stage of the transaction: He or she must now "either stand up to the challenge and demonstrate strength of character, or apologize, discontinue the inappropriate conduct, or flee the situation" (Luckenbill, 1977:182). Any response other than the first of these, a demonstration of character, constitutes a loss of face—an abandonment of the self-image that the person has claimed for himself or herself in that situation.

To avoid a loss of face and a demonstration of weakness, many people at this point tacitly arrive at a definition of the situation as one wherein violence is a suitable means of resolving the problem. At this point the probability that violence will occur is enhanced.

In establishing a shared definition, a "working agreement," it becomes incontrovertible that both parties are active contributors to homicide as a situated transaction. Who ultimately becomes the victim and who the offender is quite problematic. Becoming a victim or an offender is a consequence of situationally based conditions. The action of each party is shaped by the action of the other and by the desire to save face, demonstrate character, and develop or preserve a reputation. In short, the homicidal outcome is a result of an interaction rather than the consequence of an aggressive offender imposing his or her will on a passive victim (Luckenbill, 1977:185–186). Homicide often is a joint enterprise, situationally based, problematic, and reflective of people's existential condition.

A second example of how the motivation to engage in proscribed behavior may be "negotiated" and emerge out of interpersonal relations viewed sequentially involves the case of three college students who decide to rob a post office. As we pick up the situation, the students are in conversation.

The conversation began with a remark about the numerous recent bank failures in the state, probably stimulated by one of us glancing at a map of the state. It then shifted to discussion of a local bank that had closed its doors the day before. Tom, who worked at the post-office occasionally as special mail clerk, happened to mention that a sack containing a large amount of money had been received at the post-office that afternoon, consigned to a local bank that feared a run.

The conversation then turned to the careless way in which the money was handled at the office—a plain canvas sack thrown into an open safe. We discussed the ease with which a thief could get into the building and steal the money. Tom drew a plan showing the desk at which the only clerk worked and the location of the only gun in the office. At first the conversation was entirely confined to how easily criminals might manage to steal the money.

Somehow it shifted to a personal basis: as to how easily we might get the money. This shift came so naturally that even the next morning we were unable to decide when and by whom the first vital remark had been made.

A possible plan was discussed as to how we might steal the package. Tom could go to the office and gain admittance on the pretense of looking for an important letter. Then Art and I, masked and armed, could rush in, tie Tom and the clerk, and make off with the package. We had lost sight of the fact that the package contained money. We were simply discussing the possibility of playing an exciting prank with no thought of actually committing it. We had played many harmless pranks and had discussed them in much the same way before; but the knowledge that there was danger in this prank made it a subject to linger over.

After about an hour and a half of talk, I started to take off my shoes. As I unlaced them, I thought of how it looked as if I were the one to kill our interesting project. I foolishly said something to the effect that if Tom was going down town, I thought I would write a letter that was already overdue. Tom was anxiously awaiting a letter that should be in that night. He suggested that I go down also as it was a very decent night. I consented and Art decided to join us. I sat down and wrote the letter—meanwhile we continued our talk about the money package.

My letter finished, something seemed to change. We found further inaction impossible: we had either to rob the post-office or go to bed. Tom brought out his two guns; I hunted up a couple of regular plain handkerchiefs, and Art added some rope to the assortment. At the time we were still individually and collectively playing a game with ourselves. Each of us expected one of the other two to give the thing the horse laugh and suggest going to bed and letting the letters wait till morning. But it seemed that we forgot everything—our position in school, our families and friends, the danger to us and to our folks. Our only thought was to carry out that prank. We all made our preparations more or less mechanically. Our minds were in a daze.

Putting on our regular overcoats and caps, we left the rooms quietly. On the way down town we passed the night patrolman without any really serious qualms. Tom entered the post-office as was his usual custom, being a sub-clerk, and Art and I crept up to the rear door. Tom appeared at a window with his hat, a signal that there were no reasons why our plan would not be effective. At the door, in full illumination of a light, we arranged our handkerchiefs over our faces and took our guns out of our pockets. We were ready.

"Have you enough guts to go through with this thing?" I asked, turning to Art, who was behind me.

"If you have," he answered.

Frankly I felt that I had gone far enough, but for some unknown reason I did not throw out a remark that would have ended it all then and there. And Art didn't. He later said that he was just too scared to suggest anything. We were both, it seems, in a sort of daze.

Tom opened the door and we followed our plan out to the end. There was no active resistance by the regular night man.

Then after we left the office with thousands of dollars in our hands we did not realize all that it meant. Our first words were not about getting the money. They were about the fact that our prank (and it was still that to us) had been successful. When we reached our rooms, having hidden the money in an abandoned dredger, the seriousness of the thing began to penetrate our minds. For an hour or so we lay quietly and finally settled on a plan that seemed safe in returning the money without making our identity known. Then I went to sleep." (Thrasher, 1936:300–303)

In the preceding examples of homicide and robbery, it seems clear that the parties to these events exhibit little, if any, of what lawyers would identify as "malice aforethought." Indeed, it may validly be said that if not opposed to these acts, the participants were at least reluctant. This is most evident in the case of the robbery. In spite of such reluctance, however, the behaviors and their motivational base emerge as a consequence of group activity. The "stuff" of the motivation includes an unwillingness by the young men to lose status with their peers by refusing to go along with the developing plan. As a result, each of them kept his doubts, misgivings, and fears to himself. By maintaining silence and going along with the scheme, a "mutual deception" was created, an illusion of daring from which none of these young men felt they could escape. There arose a condition of "group motivation" in which "each member is behaving in accordance with the same interpretation of what is expected of him—whether or not this is in accord with his own wishes and regardless of the

correctness of the interpretation" (Korn and McCorkle, 1959:339). In short, each of these students was acting in terms of his interpretation of the others' expectations rather than on the basis of a desire to rob or a commitment to rule breaking per se.

Continued demonstration of the practical and/or situational bases of people's perceptions, definitions, and motives seems unnecessary. Escape—from boredom, a "bad" home situation, or poverty—is one possible motivating factor. Expressing hostility and contempt, striving for political or social change, seeking recreation, seeking to make a living or just trying to "keep one's head above water," seeking to preserve a threatened self-image, or "keeping faith" with one's peers are all motivating factors, factors that help people make sense of their rule-violating behavior.

Not the least important consequence of recognizing these varied grounds for behavior is that they permit an understanding of deviance in nonmoral terms. To examine rule breaking from these alternative perspectives opens doors to analysis and understanding that more traditional perspectives are unlikely to reveal. Acknowledgment of these considerations throws light into corners where, largely, only darkness has prevailed (Polsky, 1967:101; Letkemann, 1973: Chapter 1). Finally, perhaps it is sufficient to conclude by noting again that an understanding of why people behave as they do is best acquired by examining reasons rather than so-called determinative causes, and that, as such, human behavior is unpredictable and uncertain. In the final analysis these reasons are best known to the actor. To consider the actor's sense of reality and the situational basis of behavior is consistent with the model employed in this volume.

A Final Word, or, Are There No Exceptions?

To avoid being doctrinaire, let's once more consider the plausibility of the idea that rule breaking is volitional and a result of individual choices. The interactionist explanation proposes that our actions generally rest on an active, deliberate, and conscious series of choices, and are situationally rooted. Thus, while behaviors may be established and practiced by others, the actor's involvement is a consequence of decision making rather than simply association with supportive meanings. The question to be considered now is whether such an explanation may be regarded as the only plausible account.

The interactionist perspective suggests that a person's biography provides a foundation for subsequent behavior; through biography a person acquires meanings that render him or her willing or unwilling to experiment with deviance. These meanings are fundamental to the decision-making process. It should be clear that the decision making referred to presupposes some degree of intellectual and social-psychological maturation—at least to a degree that would permit the actor to make informed choices and decisions.

However reasonable these contentions may be when considering the behavior of persons who have at least reached early adolescence, they seem inappropriate when considering children's involvement in rule-breaking behavior. A case in point is "tiny-doping" (Adler and Adler; 1978), which refers to the use of marijuana by children between the ages of 0 and 8 years who have been introduced to marijuana smoking by their parents.

Given their age, lack of adult capabilities, and the absence of a well-developed sense of self, the "tiny-doper" represents a case in which it is somewhat inappropriate to contend that all actors become involved in deviance on the basis of more or less informed choices. Some children are introduced to marijuana smoking (at least to marijuana smoke) while still diapered toddlers as a consequence of being taken to gatherings where their parents and other adults smoke pot. Clearly, this involvement reflects neither decision making nor self-reflection on the part of the child. Prior to 1½ years of age, children are passive subjects; they simply breathe air that is sometimes filled with marijuana smoke. The drug's effects are apparent, however, as this exposure tends to have a calming effect on the child. Between the ages of 1½ and 3 years, youngsters become

more aware of their surroundings and are free to watch adult behavior, imitate these behaviors, and "play" with marijuana and its paraphernalia (and sometimes try imitatively to smoke the marijuana). However ineffective their efforts to smoke at this age—that is, to inhale the smoke, retain it, and so on—the breathing of marijuana smoke–filled air continues, sometimes augmented by a mother or father exhaling a lung full of pot smoke directly into the mouth of the eager youngster.

Around age 3 or 4 inhalation is often achieved, as is a more sophisticated appreciation of the use to which roach clips and other paraphernalia are put. By age 4 or 5 children acquire at least a vague social sense regarding pot smoking. Rapidly becoming more sophisticated, youngsters of age 7 or 8 differentiate users from nonusers (who is and isn't cool) and who should and should not know about their pot smoking. In short, by age 7 children have learned the rudiments of the legal and moral public meanings of marijuana smoking as well as the private meanings shared by their immediate family and parents' friends. Moreover, as a direct result of the various stratagems employed by the parents, children learn to distinguish between situations when these different meanings are operative. Overall, however, from a state of total innocence to one of active and knowledgeable participation, the tiny-doper's involvement rests on intergenerational transmission in which children are passive agents.

In summary, from their earliest years these children are exposed to (associate with) meanings supportive of marijuana use. Pot smoking is normative in their families. It is learned in a process of interaction within intimate personal groups. It is a pattern of behavior engaged in by the child's *orientational others,* such as the child's parents—the ones from whom he or she learns vocabulary, basic concepts and categories, and general recipe knowledge (Kuhn, 1967:181). By parental "instruction" children are explicitly or implicitly introduced to the legal and moral meanings of pot smoking. Taken together, these elements lead to the conclusion that tiny-doping rests on normal socialization and in critical respects reflects an expression of affiliation and indoctrination (Matza, 1969:101ff).

A second instance in which the applicability of an interactionist model may be questionable is that of homosexuality. Thus, the question frequently asked is "Why are some people homosexual and others heterosexual?" In the view of some contemporary students of sexuality, the idea that a person's *primary sexual identity* is learned is an illusion created by Sigmund Freud and perpetuated by many others (including social scientists) following in his footsteps (Whitam, 1975). By primary sexual identity is meant the gut-level feelings about the objects of sexual attraction—be they male, female, or both—that people have in the privacy of their sexual fantasies. This primary identity is not to be equated with sex roles, sex norms, or sex-related behavior. Restricting our concern, then, to fundamental sexual inclination, there is increasing cross-cultural evidence suggesting that sexual preference originates in early childhood and substantially predates people's knowledge about sex. Data also suggest that a homosexual orientation is not an outgrowth of "disturbed" parent–child relations, is not determined by aspects of the social structure (such as family configurations or social class), is ahistorical, and transcends culture. In short, homosexuality, it is suggested, "is not learned, but rather emerges" (Whitam, 1975:5). As such, homosexuality should not be perceived as a role, either achieved or ascribed. Roles are cultural elements, while homosexuality is an orientation that likely gives rise to a particular sex role (Whitam, 1977a:2; 1977b). Finally, Whitam suggests, homosexuality as an orientation should not be confused with the concept of role since children who experience this orientation are neither socialized to it in the traditional sense, nor do they choose it on some rational bases (1977a).

The foregoing examples strongly indicate that there are instances to which our interactionist explanation of rule breaking seems not to apply. However, rather than nullifying that explanation, the cases presented supplement it. That supplement is welcomed rather than resisted since it serves to reinforce the fundamental dictum that nothing so complex and varied as human behavior may be accounted for by a single explanation. Nor is it unreasonable to contend that assumptions that apply to the bulk of the population may not be applicable to all. What is essential is that our accounts be faithful to the phenomena. Only then may they be regarded as valid representations of the world as seen and experienced by people (Matza, 1969:25).

Summary
In this chapter we have examined an interactionist explanation for people's involvement in rule-breaking behavior, an explanation meeting the assumptions of the paradigm of definition. On the basis of available evidence we conclude that involvement in much proscribed behavior is a consequence of a variety of elements comprising one's biography, elements and meanings of which are constantly changing and subject to situational influences (Schur, 1973:136; Matza, 1964; Lemert, 1967a:40). Finally, consideration was given to the cases of the "tiny-doper," which reflects indoctrination of rather passive subjects to marijuana smoking, and of homosexuality, which, it has been suggested, is an "emergent" that predates learning. Rather than nullify the interactionist perspective, however, these exceptional cases point up the complexity of human behavior and the need, at our present level of knowledge, to recognize the existence of more than one explanation of events, as well as the need to avoid a doctrinaire position.

Having sought to explain individual conduct, consideration must also be given to the statistical distribution of deviant behavior in time and space. It is to this second aspect of rule breaking that we now turn.

3 Counting Deviants

Introduction

In Chapter 2 we considered the question of why people break rules. Our attention was therefore focused on individuals per se. Our interest in the phenomenon of deviance is not limited to that question, however. A second concern of great importance is how the incidence of rule-breaking behavior is distributed among different segments of the population (age groups, social classes, sex, race, ethnic groups, and so on), how that distribution is expressed in statistical terms or rates, how variations in rates relate to other social conditions, how these rates are developed (the rate-producing process), and, finally, what the uses or consequences of these rates are. In the present chapter our attention will be focused on these and related matters. Before turning to these issues, however, two questions deserve attention: (1) Precisely what is meant by the term *rates* and (2) why study rates when our concern is with individual behavior?

The Meaning of Rates

The term *rates* refers to a type of ratio, a way of relating the size of one number to that of another. Official rates of deviance, such as official police or Federal Bureau of Investigation statistics on crime, or a city or county health department's rate on suicide, are numerical expressions of how the known frequency of the behavior (one number) relates to units of population (expressed by a second number). For example, the F.B.I. Uniform Crime Reports (1985:42) estimates there were 84,233 forcible rapes committed in this country in 1984. Taken out of context, that is, without giving simultaneous consideration to the size of the population among whom these rapes occurred—that number is relatively meaning-less. Converting that number to a rate or ratio, however, provides a meaningful statement of the extensiveness of the phenomenon. Thus, given the total estimated U.S. population for that year (236,158,000), the estimated rate of rape was 35.7 per 100,000 persons; here we have the size of one number in contrast with the size of another. By establishing rates of deviance for known segments of the population—for example, women or men; blacks, whites, or Indians; juveniles or adults; metropolitan areas, cities, or rural areas—it is felt that changes in the volume and character of criminal behavior may be determined relative to the size of these different categories. For example, while the overall rate of rape in this country in 1984 was 35.7, the rate per 100,000 for metropolitan statistical areas was 41.1, for cities it was 20.9, and for rural areas it was 17.0. These figures should make it clear that rates are based on a context within which their relevance may be judged. As such they are regarded as more meaningful than raw numbers, that is, figures that lack a contextual reference point.

Studying Rates

Turning to the second question, there are several reasons for considering rates of deviance. First, they are a means whereby we can objectify the phenomenon of deviance. As we noted in Chapter 1, deviance involves the assignment of subjective meanings to events; creating deviance is a matter of naming. Further, by naming things it becomes possible to reify them, that is, give objective character to things that are fundamentally subjective. The amassing of statistics on a variety of forms of rule-breaking behavior exemplifies the process of objectivation and reification. To the degree that people take the apparent meaning of official statistics for granted, the nature and consequences of objectivation remain obscured. Thus, people tend either to ignore or forget that the designation (naming) of an act as deviant is a complex social process involving the official assignment of meaning and names to acts, and assigning the named acts to socially created categories of things. Further, people tend to overlook the idea that whether a given act is defined and categorized as deviant is problematic and may not be taken for granted. Thus, like the umpire who "calls them as they are," citizens commonly perceive official crime statistics and other official data as an indication of the "way things are," as valid and faithful representations of the world "as it is." In reaching this conclusion, people inadvertently and uncritically promote the objectivation and reification of various forms of deviance. The "gap" between things or events, on the one hand, and names, on the other, is ignored; to all intents and purposes the "map becomes the terrain." Stated differently, these uncritical assumptions invite the conclusion that deviance is a "real" phenomenon, part of an allegedly objective world. In circular fashion, the numeric data that prompt this conclusion become the basis of its validation.

Such an orientation is inconsistent with elements of the Paradigm of Definition and the idea that reality is a social construction. To be fully aware of the implications of referring to official data as social constructions calls for an examination of many things that influence the process of assigning meanings to things that are ultimately incorporated into these official data. A substantial portion of this chapter will address these matters.

A second reason for examining rates is that these statistics are *official;* that is, they are produced and disseminated by public (ranging from municipal to federal levels) and publicly approved agencies charged with the responsibility of dealing with deviants. The production and dissemination of these data by control agencies is consistent with the legal definitions that prevail in our society. As we will see, many forms of deviance have been defined in law. Thus, the *official* designation of a form of

behavior as deviant is an act of the state. As a consequence,

most forms of deviance today cannot be said to exist until they are legally (officially) defined in concrete cases. That is, crime, suicide, and so on, exist only when the legal procedures have "certified" them. . . . Basically, then, most forms of deviance today are constructed by official action and by law. (Douglas, 1971a:68)

Recognition of this is critical since, quite clearly, not all behavior that might reasonably fit the official criteria of deviance comes to the attention of officials and not all behavior that fits the criteria and comes to their attention is defined as deviant. Whether any instance of rule breaking is defined as deviant is problematic and subject to the influence of a variety of conditions. When considering explanations of deviance based on these official data, then, it is essential that we be aware of the manner in which rates are constructed. Again, the meaning of these statistics cannot be taken for granted.

As an extension of their "official" character, these data and their apparent meaning are often used as the basis for formulating and/or giving legitimacy to public policy. They are used, for example, as the basis for writing legislation as well as for allocating resources to fight crime or combat other social ills. Given the cost (however measured) of such policies, citizens might be well served by an understanding of the process by which these data are constructed (Pfuhl, 1983).

A third reason for considering official statistics arises from the use made of them by sociologists and others seeking to explain deviant conduct. Several generations of sociologists have built and/or relied on theories of deviance that utilize these official sources. For example, in 1897 Emile Durkheim published his classic study of suicide, which he based on suicide statistics from several European countries (Durkheim, 1951). Since that time students of suicide have consistently relied on official data (Schmid, 1928; Cavan, 1928; Powell, 1958; Gibbs and Martin, 1964; Maris, 1969). Students of crime have similarly relied on officially created statistics. In 1833 Andre-Michel Guerry published his essay on French "moral statistics," a work regarded as the first "scientific criminology" (Vold & Bernard, 1979:167). By 1929, in the United States, standardized (uniform) offense categories of criminal law violations had been established and were being employed by the Federal Bureau of Investigation in reporting national crime data (Barnes and Teeters, 1951:52). The establishment of these standardized categories allowed for comparison of crime rates between cities and states at various points in time, as well as for the establishment of "trends in crime." Most important, however, and despite criticism of these figures for their biases and other deficiencies, sociologists came to accept these data for the purpose of establishing and testing theory (Douglas, 1971a:67–68). It follows that the value or merit of theories based on and tested by these data is hinged to their adequacy. Thus, a first step in judging the adequacy of some theories is an appreciation of their statistical foundation. Again, then, a critical examination of rates is in order.

With these several bases for studying rates in mind, let's turn to an examination of these statistics, how they are constructed, and what factors contribute to their variation.

Official Statistics as Social Constructions

Official statistics on crime and other forms of deviant conduct have long been accepted by authorities, scholars, and laypeople as relatively valid measures of "moral phenomena." That acceptance rests, in part, on the abiding belief in the Western world that enumeration is the "cornerstone of knowledge." Recall that in Chapter 1 we discussed epistemology, the basis or method by which one claims to know things. In the Western world it has been a commonsense assumption (an epistemological assumption) that "one knows something only when it has been counted" (Douglas, 1967:163). Similarly, in a half (but only half) facetious way, scholars have been heard to say "If you can't count it, it's not worth knowing."

Counting things certainly has advantages.

Perhaps the greatest of these is that numerical information is readily systematized; that is, it may be arranged in columns and rows, or tables, so as to "display" some supposed interrelationship, and may then be proffered as rational knowledge. Operations of that sort derive a great deal of their respectability and acceptability from the trust and faith the Western world has long had in the methods of the physical sciences. On such grounds, the numerical information accumulated by nineteenth-century "moral statisticians" (such as Lambert-Adolphe-Jacques Quetelet and Andre-Michel Guerry) was regarded as "rational knowledge" and became the basis for establishing and administering social policies designed to curb immoral behavior (Douglas, 1971b:52). In the hands of these *moral statisticians* (persons dedicated to the statistical analysis of moral phenomena), data of this sort were used to "prove" the existence of *dangerous classes*, that is, segments of society believed to contribute most to crime and social disorder and commonly referred to as parasites, criminals, nomads, barbarians, strangers, and savages.

Such "proof" as moral statisticians provided, of course, was consistent with popular opinion of that day, particularly the upper-class view that a well-ordered society existed only when people, especially the lower classes, were engaged in honest and steady work (Radzinowicz, 1966:38–39). By assigning to the data of the moral statistician the objectivity and rationality assigned to the data of the physical sciences, unquestionable "proof" became available of the *objective* existence of the "dangerous classes." At least the claims were not questioned: "What could be more certain than ideas and findings based on the ultimate criteria of scientific methods and knowledge? . . . Who could deny the truth of a finding or an explanation obviously based on the forms of science?" (Douglas, 1971b:53). Knowledge, thereby, was advanced by the "magick of number" (Douglas, 1971a:43).

Numbers, then, seem to many people to have a validity of their own, a validity that is all but unquestionable, and many people stand in awe of them, however mythical they may be. A practical example will show how even mythical numbers have vitality. Based on information provided by official agencies and their representatives, it is common for knowledgeable people to claim that the amount of property stolen and violent crime engaged in by heroin addicts far exceeds their proportion in the total criminal population (whatever that may be). Thus, in the late 1960s and early 1970s it was claimed that about half of all New York City's property crime was committed by drug addicts and that they annually stole property valued at between $2 and $5 *billion*. That is, the claim was made that an addict population estimated to number about 100,000 persons with a drug habit that, on average, then cost about $30 per day to support, needed more than $1 billion to support it. Because fencing stolen property was assumed to yield no more than 25 percent of its retail value, addicts had to steal more than $5 billion worth of property to pay for their drugs. At least that is what many people argued.

Though widely believed, the preceding claims were based on questionable and unproven assumptions, including the size of the addict population, the cost of maintaining a habit, and the methods addicts used to acquire that money. In an effort to examine these claims, Singer (1971) began by asking if the preceding figures could possibly be correct. By determining the total value of all reported stolen property, whether stolen by addicts or nonaddicts, and assuming that the value of property stolen by addicts must be less than the total, Singer concluded that such figures could not possibly be accurate. Singer further suggests that even if we assume (fallaciously) that addicts are responsible for *all* thefts from homes and from persons, and are credited with *all* the shoplifting in New York City, and even if we allowed for "fudge factors," the value of property stolen by addicts in one year could not be estimated at more than $330 million. Thus, while a third of a billion dollars is a lot of property, it is very much less than the figure of $2 to $5 billion that had been widely and uncritically accepted (Singer, 1971:5–6).

Neither Singer's analysis nor this discussion

are intended to make light of drug-related crime. Indeed, based on a study of the crimes engaged in by heroin addicts in Miami over a 12-month period, Inciardi (1979:324) reported that the average male addict committed some 337 offenses, 80.5 percent of which were to support a drug habit. However, violent crimes such as robbery and assault, and property crimes such as thefts accounted for only 32.6 percent of the offenses committed by these people. On the other hand, victimless crimes (procuring, drug sales, gambling, and loan sharking) and alcohol offenses accounted for 62.9 percent of the reported offenses. In fact, over 50 percent of the reported offenses involved drug sales. What emerges from this analysis is that the image of drug addicts as highly predatory creatures, skulking about ready to pounce on innocent and unsuspecting passersby, and engaged in the most heinous offenses, seems quite false.[1] To be sure, addicts commit a great many offenses, but the overwhelming bulk of them are of the victimless sort. Moreover, and finally, claims concerning the extensiveness of loss due to property crimes by addicts seem at the least farfetched, if not downright preposterous. Nonetheless—and this is the major point—such claims continue to have "vitality," another example of the "magick of number" (U.S. Dept. of Justice, 1983:3).

Given an aura of respectability that is derived from science, official statistical data tend to have their validity and moral implications taken for granted. However, in taking the meaning of these official statistics for granted and by assuming they refer to objective conditions, sociologists, public officials, and laypeople have failed to recognize that official statistics are an example of how subjective

---

[1]Though it is taken for granted that "drug addiction causes crime," there is no supporting evidence. Rather, the crimes engaged in by addicts are regarded by many authorities as "secondary crimes," that is, offenses engaged in by addicts in order to pay the inflated cost of blackmarket drugs, whose inflated cost is a result of their having been outlawed. There is no evidence that the crimes of addicts are a consequence of the drugs or their addicting effect per se. For an examination of the myth that "drug addiction causes crime," see Pepinsky and Jesilow, 1984:95ff.

meanings are converted into symbols of objective reality, in this case an official reality. That is, we have noted that things and acts have no inherent meaning, but must await the meaning assigned them by people. Official statistics represent the meanings assigned to things by a group of officials to whom such responsibility has been assigned. Official statistics reflect officials' interpretations of acts. Further, the data become an objectivation and a reification of some person's definition of an act. As such, in the first instance, official statistics on any kind of crime, mental illness, suicide, and so on represent a *typification*—that is, the way people classify and characterize things on the basis of their perception of them, and the consequent actions of officials (Buckner, 1978:313ff). Thus, the relationship between official statistics and the actual volume of rule-breaking behavior is problematic.

Moreover, "from their very beginnings official statistics were policy oriented and determined primarily by the political goals of the officials" (Douglas, 1971a:49). Douglas notes that seventeenth- and eighteenth-century officials used statistics on the number of persons confined and the reasons for their confinement to demonstrate that they were doing their job to contain or fight immorality; the statistics were a way of showing that the officials were performing their duty (Douglas, 1071a:49). In addition, these data could be used as a rational basis for allocating monies and other resources to control immorality. What was true of seventeenth- and eighteenth-century church officials is true of a variety of officials in twentieth-century United States. For example, *clearance rates* (a statistic representing the proportion of crimes known to the police which they have solved and for which an offender has been arrested) have long been used by police departments to promote an image of police efficiency. Some authorities regard the clearance rate as the most important index of police performance (Skolnick, 1966:167). Similarly, official crime statistics are used by police for purposes of self-justification, organizational survival, and improvement of community relations (Manning, 1971b:175). By raising or lowering statistics police departments seek

either to validate their claims for additional budget allocations or to demonstrate the efficiency with which they do their job. As one officer told the author in conversation,

Pretty regularly people call in saying they think their car is stolen. We check the report out and after a little checking we locate the car in some great big shopping mall parking lot where the owner left it. They just forgot where they parked and called us. They are real embarrassed. But it don't matter. We just list the thing as another stolen auto we recovered. It makes us look pretty good.

Rather clearly, then, clearance rates, as well as crime rates, may be (and are) inflated or otherwise "adjusted" figures (Sutherland and Cressey, 1978:30).

The danger and consequences of assuming that these "adjusted" figures are valid and objective measures of crime may well be obvious. Yet the conditions leading to bias in official statistics deserve extended examination.

The Problem of Bias

The term *bias,* when applied to social science research data, refers to a condition whereby the faults in these data are such that conclusions drawn from them are systematically distorted. According to some observers, these errors of bias creep into social science data as a result of "carelessness, incompetence, or poor judgment" (Thomlinson, 1965:70). In the case of official data, however, far from being inadvertent, bias often appears to be a matter of design or, at the very least, a reflection of the operation and organization of social control agencies.

To understand how official statistics become warped, we must recognize that there is no necessary or consistent relationship between the *actual volume of offender behavior* and statistical indices of that behavior. That is, statistical rates may vary (increase or decrease) without any corresponding change in the actual volume of the behavior to which they refer. This is because, as we have noted, *statistical rates reflect official action; they are social constructions.* They are created by official agencies (police departments, psychiatric hospitals, public health facilities, coroners' offices, courts, drug and alcohol rehabilitation centers, prisons, and so on) whose task is managing one or another form of deviance. These agencies, and only these, have the legal authority to decide when a specific act shall be designated as deviant. It is these agencies that assign the *official* moral meaning to behavior coming to their attention. As we have noted, given the role of the state in defining deviance, it is readily apparent that official action is critical in shaping the statistical record.

However, official agencies do not exist in a vacuum. To appreciate the complexity of the process of biasing official statistics, the operation of official agencies must be viewed in context. Several factors deserve consideration.

Underreporting. Before officials can construct a statistical record, information must come to their attention. Bearing very heavily on the content of the statistical record is the fact that not all behavior that might reasonably fit the official criteria of rule breaking is brought to the attention of official agencies. A survey of criminal victims in three Washington, D.C., police precincts reported that

for certain specific offenses against individuals the number of offenses reported to the survey per thousand residents 18 years of age or over ranged, depending on the offense, from 3 to 10 times *more* than the number contained in police statistics. (President's Commission on Law Enforcement and Administration of Justice, 1967a:21)

Victim survey data for the entire nation revealed an amount of crime against persons almost twice that shown in the F.B.I. Uniform Crime Reports (based on police department data), and the volume of crime against property was revealed at more than double the Uniform Crime Report figures (President's Commission on Law Enforcement and Administration of Justice, 1967a:21). In another victim survey 2077 incidents were discovered that reasonably fit legal definitions of crime. Of those 2077 cases, 1059 (51 percent) had not been reported to police and, hence, were not part of the official crime statistics (Ennis, 1967:49).

Data reported by Ennis have been supplemented by more extensive and recent information. National crime surveys in many U.S. cities reveal that in the area of personal crime (including crime against persons and property), the percent of victimizations reported to police range from a low of 25 percent (Houston, Texas) to a high of 42 percent (Washington, D.C.). Household offense (burglary, household larceny, and auto theft) reports range between 36 percent (Houston) and 50 percent (Boston and Washington, D.C.). Crimes against commercial establishments (burglary and robbery) are reported most often, ranging from 72 percent in Houston and New Orleans to 85 percent in Cincinnati (U.S. Department of Justice, 1975).

It is estimated that perhaps only half of all acts that satisfy the legal criteria of crimes become part of the official record. This does not mean that only 50 percent of the incidents definable as murder, robbery, or burglary and so on, come to the attention of the police. The extent to which behavior of a specific type is reported to police is highly variable. For example, in 1979, the overall reporting rate for violent crimes in the United States was 45 percent; for the personal crimes of theft the reporting rate was 25 percent, and for total household crimes the rate was 36 percent (U.S. Dept. of Justice, 1981b:15). Incidents definable as murder and auto theft are, perhaps, the most fully reported; well over 90 percent of all completed auto thefts were reported to the police in Buffalo and New Orleans in 1973 (U.S. Dept. of Justice, 1975). Far lower in rate of reporting is consumer fraud; because it occurs covertly, it is a low visibility offense and is seldom even detected by victims (Ennis, 1967:42). Further, the rate at which citizens report crime to police varies with their perception of the seriousness of the incident and the age of the victim. Thus, as the value of stolen property rises, so, too, does the rate at which such thefts are reported. On the other hand, young people aged 12 through 19 are less prone to report crimes than any other age group (U.S. Dept. of Justice, 1981b:15).

Why officials lack more complete information is believed to be largely a result of underreporting of incidents by victims and others. As Table 3–1 reveals, the reasons for this

TABLE 3-1
Reasons for Not Notifying Police Among Those Not Reporting Incident

REASONS FOR NOT NOTIFYING POLICE	MENTIONED AT ALL	MOST IMPORTANT
1. Did not want to take time	13%	6%
2. Did not want to harm offender	12	7
3. Afraid of reprisal	5	2
4. Was private, not criminal, affair	41	26
5. Police couldn't do anything about matter	58	36
6. Police wouldn't want to be bothered	28	8
7. Didn't know how or if they should notify police	6	1
8. Too confused or upset to notify police	6	2
9. Not sure if real offenders would be caught	31	12
10. Fear of insurance cancellation	1	0
Total	(1,017)	100%
N		(906)

SOURCE: P. H. Ennis, *Criminal Victimization in the United States: A Report of a National Survey* (Washington, D.C.: U.S. Government Printing Office, 1967), p. 44.

underreporting are numerous. Moreover, as Figures 3–1 and 3–2 indicate, the reasons for nonreporting are the same whether one is concerned with personal crimes or household crimes.

Beyond the "garden variety" crimes dealt with in victim surveys are the far more frequent *crimes without victims*—those involving "willing exchanges of strongly desired (though legally proscribed) goods or services" (Schur, 1979:451). Homosexual relations between consenting adults, drug addiction, gambling, sale of pornographic materials, prostitution, and other forms of socially proscribed sexual behavior are included under this heading. Given the fact that these goods and services are sought by people and that there are no victims in the usual sense of that term, we would expect few complaints. That expectation is confirmed. How much of this behavior occurs that would reasonably fit legal definitions is unknown. It is not implausible to assume, however, that the amount coming to the attention of authorities is no more than the tip of the iceberg (Rossman, 1976:11–13). In any case, official statistics on rule breaking are not

likely to provide a valid index of the actual volume of these behaviors.

In addition to the standard crimes without victims, there is a wide variety of low-visibility offenses that has traditionally received relatively little mention in the press and has only occasionally been dealt with by authorities. These behaviors include male prostitution, sexual fetishisms, sadomasochism, pederasty, and incest. Regarding incest, no accurate figures exist on its frequency. Several reasons may be noted for its underrepresentation in official data. First, the matter is usually a closely guarded secret. Second, sometimes it is a consensual relationship, reflecting strong affection between partners. Third, cases of incest often involve young girls under the authority of dominant adult males, who therefore are not free to report the condition. Fourth, if the fault or culpability is shared by both parties, the reason to avoid reporting the matter is doubly strong. Fifth, reporting may be avoided to prevent the negative consequences of losing an adult (male or female) member of the family through arrest and imprisonment (Hughes, 1964:325–326).

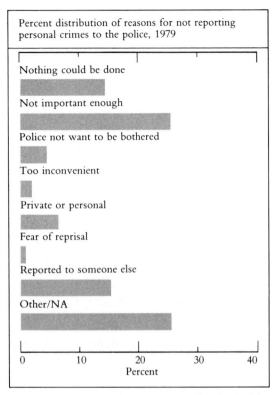

Percent distribution of reasons for not reporting personal crimes to the police, 1979

Nothing could be done

Not important enough

Police not want to be bothered

Too inconvenient

Private or personal

Fear of reprisal

Reported to someone else

Other/NA

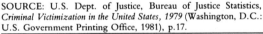

SOURCE: U.S. Dept. of Justice, Bureau of Justice Statistics, *Criminal Victimization in the United States, 1979* (Washington, D.C.: U.S. Government Printing Office, 1981), p.17.

FIGURE 3–1

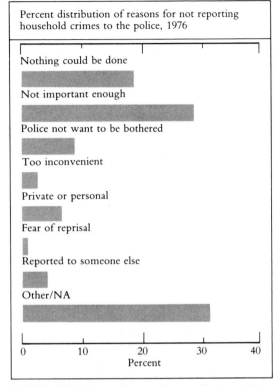

Percent distribution of reasons for not reporting household crimes to the police, 1976

Nothing could be done

Not important enough

Police not want to be bothered

Too inconvenient

Private or personal

Fear of reprisal

Reported to someone else

Other/NA

SOURCE; U.S. Dept. of Justice, Bureau of Justice Statistics, *Criminal Victimization in the United States, 1979* (Washington, D.C.: U.S. Government Printing Office, 1981), p.17.

FIGURE 3–2

Because some of these behaviors (for example, pederasty) have received so little official attention in the past, a relatively modest increase in the number of known cases can represent a sizable *proportional* increase in official rates. What is most important to note is that an increase in known cases does not necessarily reflect an increase in the actual frequency of these behaviors. All that may be involved is a change in perception. This change in rate is seen in the instance of "child sexual abuse" or pedophilia. According to the American Humane Association, cases of child sexual abuse rose 700 percent between 1976 and 1982 (*Phoenix Gazette*, 1984a). However, there seems to be no evidence that adults are cur-

rently engaging in such behavior to a significantly greater degree than ever before. Thus, in the absence of some supposed "causal factor" that arose after the mid-1970s, we are inclined to conclude that the *rate increase* is more a result of increased levels of visibility and higher incidences of reporting than of changes in offender behavior.

The problem of undercounting is by no means limited to criminal behavior. Examples may also be noted in cases of mental illness and child battering. Regarding the former, we have little or no confidence that official rates of mental illness accurately reflect the actual incidence of these conditions. Psychiatric *nosology* (a branch of medical science dealing with the classification of disease) has led to the belief that qualitatively different categories of mental and personality disorders do exist in fact and that persons either do or do not display the unique symptoms from which the existence of these "diseases" may be inferred (Taber et al., 1969:351). That is, there are those who contend that personality disorders, schizophrenia, and neuroses are on the same existential level as malaria, tuberculosis, or a kidney disorder (Movahedi, 1975:313).

Despite these diagnostic claims, many psychiatrists recognize that practitioner's ability to diagnose

mental illnesses is at a quite primitive level, particularly in regard to its most important problems— schizophrenia, depression, and the various neuroses. Depression and schizophrenia are better studied than the neuroses, probably largely because they are more reliably diagnosable, though *they leave much to be desired in this area. Diagnosis of neuroses is far from reliable, that is, reproducible by equally qualified diagnosticians.* (Lemkau and Crocetti, 1967:228. Emphasis added.)

Some observers attribute these diagnostic difficulties to insufficient contact between patient and physician prior to diagnosis; a dearth of psychiatrists trained in research methodology, which would sensitize them to the importance of classificatory criteria; and a general disinterest among psychiatrists in problems of classifying illness (Clausen, 1976:113). Given these conditions, it is not surprising that psychiatrists have different diagnostic practices and sometimes arrive at grossly different diagnoses. In turn, these varying practices lead to the contention that most large differences in hospital admission diagnoses are the result of diagnostic practices rather than of real differences in the incidence of clinical symptoms (Schwab and Schwab, 1973:69).

The problem with mental health rates does not rest solely on the diagnostic idiosyncrasies of the medical profession, however. In addition, it has been recognized that "treatment rates [of mental illness] vary with the availability of facilities and with public attitudes toward their use . . . [therefore] treated rates do not tell us much about . . . the occurrence and distribution of true rates of disorder" (Dohren-

wend, 1975:366). Over 40 years ago Faris and Dunham (1939:162) recognized a related condition when they noted that mental hospital admission rates among higher income groups may be artificially low because of a tendency among such people to have family members treated at home or otherwise avoid their inclusion in official statistics. The result was a bias, an overestimate of the incidence of mental illness among the lower class relative to the upper classes.

The concern registered by Faris and Dunham rests on the fundamental issue of how official rates of these disorders may be influenced by such factors as when people seek help with emotional and mental problems, when and under what circumstances people come to define the bizarre or threatening behavior of others as mental illness, and when and under what circumstances people are defined as mentally ill. Since such matters rest only on the meanings attributed to persons and their behavior by actors and others operating in varying situational contexts, any assessment of the accuracy of rates of mental disorder must reckon with the highly subjective and situational basis of these meanings. Let's consider an example.

That the diagnosis of mental illness rests on subjective and situational elements may be seen in the work of Rosenhan (1973), who employed one psychology graduate student, a pediatrician, a housewife, a psychiatrist, a painter, and three psychologists to act as pseudopatients complaining of hearing voices that used words such as "empty," "hollow," and "thud." These people were voluntarily admitted to 12 different mental hospitals. "Beyond alleging the symptoms and falsifying name, vocation, and employment, no further alterations of person, history, or circumstances were made" (1973:251). During hospitalization none of these people behaved differently than they did ordinarily and none complained of persistent "symptoms"; indeed, following admission to the hospital most told attending psychiatrists that they "felt fine" and were experiencing no further symptoms. Nonetheless, 11 of the pseudopatients were diagnosed as schizophrenic and 1 as manic depressive. Finally, upon discharge, the "disease condition" of these pseudopatients was listed as being "in remission" (1973:252).

The question raised by Rosenhan is why the attending psychiatrists were unable to detect sanity among these pseudopatients on admission or later, during hospitalization, when they displayed it? The answer, Rosenhan suggests, lies in the way physicians, including psychiatrists, perceive the patient population—that is, they "are more inclined to call a healthy person sick . . . than a sick person healthy" (1973:252). To determine if psychiatrists might also be inclined to label "sick" people healthy, Rosenhan conducted a second experiment in which psychiatrists were led to believe a portion of the patients to be received in a three-month period would be pseudopatients; the staff was asked to rate these patients as to whether they were genuine or not. In fact, none of the patients admitted in the three-month period were pseudopatients. Nonetheless, the rate of diagnostic error (the rate at which genuine patients were labeled sane by one or more staff members) was so high that Rosenhan concluded that "any diagnostic process that lends itself so readily to massive errors cannot be a very reliable one" (1973:252).

The implication of Rosenhan's findings for the validity of official statistics on mental illness seems obvious. That is, based on roughly equivalent circumstances, rates of mental illness have broadly similar characteristics to rates of crime. As in the case of crime, a substantial but *unknown and unknowable* proportion of the behavioral episodes that fit standard categories of mental illness never get reported to those with the authority to assign that designation. Further, not all cases coming to their attention are defined by psychiatrists in terms of standard psychiatric classification. On such grounds it is perhaps no overstatement to suggest that, like crime rates, the validity of statistics on mental illness may not be taken for granted.

As a final example of underreporting, let us turn to *child abuse,* which is defined as the deliberate inflicting of painful (sometimes fatal) injuries and indignities upon children by parents. Prior to the early 1960s, few cases of child abuse were reported or recorded in this country and even fewer cases were defined as deviant (Pfohl, 1977:311). At that time, however, the number of cases of child abuse that were observed and recorded began to rise, not only in the United States but in other nations as well (Fontana, 1973:27). Rather than being a function of an increase in the "true" incidence of child abuse, this change in statistics stemmed from reporting differences generated by the child-abuse reporting movement (Pfohl, 1977:319). That is, current and rising statistics on child abuse do not reflect any known substantive change in parental abuse of children. Instead, the current rate increase reflects increasing responsiveness by observers to an already existing, age-old phenomenon. This responsiveness is a manifestation of a change in meaning regarding the limits of parents' authority in imposing physical or corporal punishment on their children. This change, finally, is the outgrowth of an effort by a number of interested groups: the medical profession, especially pediatric radiologists; social welfare organizations such as the Children's Division of the American Humane Association; governmental agencies; and the media.

Despite the relatively precipitous rise in rates of child abuse over the past several years, official data on child abuse have still extremely limited validity. Thus, writing in 1973 Fontana noted that

The means to accurately pinpoint the incidence of abuse are not yet at our disposal. . . . It is difficult to estimate the number of children being physically abused or neglected in the course of a year. We do not even know how many cases of child maltreatment are *reported* across the nation; we do not know how many reported cases refer to neglect, how many to abandonment, how many to sexual abuse. We do not know how many cases go *unreported*, although we cannot help suspecting that what we see is only the tip of the iceberg. (1973:34)

It is apparent, then, that official statistics covering a variety of phenomena rarely, if ever, provide a valid picture of the actual volume of rule breaking in society. Invariably, these data underrepresent the incidence of such acts. Variation in rates, rather than reflecting a change in the "real" incidence of these behaviors, more often is a consequence of a change in the awareness (sensitivity) of persons reporting these phenomena and in the organizational apparatus established to compile and maintain such records. In no sense may the validity of these statistics be taken for granted.

Defining Rule Breaking. Another major reason why official records of rule breaking are biased is that a number of factors influence people's (witnesses, victims, and authorities) definition of the behavior. For example, while commonsense understandings may suggest that all forcible rapes are equally serious, such is not the case. On the basis of research, Rossi, et al. (1974) report that the perceived seriousness of such an act varies considerably depending on the circumstances surrounding its commission. For example, people were asked to rank 140 crimes (including four different forcible rape situations) in terms of perceived seriousness. The results were: A rank of 4 was given to a forcible rape occurring after a home break-in, a rank of 13 to a forcible rape of a stranger in a park, a rank of 21 to a forcible rape of a neighbor, and a rank of 62 to a forcible rape of a former spouse (1974:228). To the degree that the reporting of offenses varies with its perceived degree of seriousness (among other things), we may assume that these situationally different rapes are likely to be represented differently in official statistics (Sellin, 1951:497; Pfuhl, 1983).

Problems in definition influence official statistics in other ways, too. As noted, not all behavior coming to the attention of rule enforcers and that reasonably satisfy official criteria of deviance are so defined. For example, though a "commonsense" case of rape may occur, police may label it *unfounded;* that is, the case may be declared to have no factual basis. That does not mean the victim was not subjected to forced sexual intimacy, possibly intercourse; rather, it is a technical-legal term bearing on the prosecutability of the case. Thus, most unfounded rape complaints result from at least one of the following "flaws":

1. evidence that the victim was intoxicated;
2. delay in reporting by the victim;
3. lack of physical condition supporting the allegation;
4. refusal [of victim] to submit to a medical examination;
5. the previous relationship of the victim and the offender; and
6. the use of a weapon without accompanying battery.
(LeGrand, 1973:928)

Such factors represent conditions that substantially reduce the probability of obtaining a conviction against the alleged assailant. On that basis, no "official" recognition is given the case; not the least result of this is a bias in rape statistics as an index of proscribed behavior. However, unfounding is not restricted to rape cases.

Similar to unfounding is the tactic of *defounding,* wherein acts that satisfy the legal criteria of a felony are redefined as misdemeanors (Lundman, 1980:65). For example, acts that satisfy the legal definition of felonious burglary are classified as "breaking and entering," a misdemeanor. The result is a reduction in the *official* incidence of burglary. The biasing influence of these redefinitions on official data is readily apparent.

Similar biasing of official data occurs because of the way police assign a criminal definition to people's behavior. Research among youth (Piliavin and Briar, 1964) reveals that in managing police–citizen encounters that may lead to arrest, police respond not simply to the "objective" and legal criteria related to the suspect's actions. Rather, the decision to arrest often rests on the inferences the officers make about the suspect's character. These inferences, in turn, stem from the police officer's definition of cues that are unrelated to the alleged offense but that emerge during the course of the police-citizen encounter. Included among these cues are the suspect's age, group affiliation, race, dress, general grooming, and, most important, the youth's general demeanor. An older youth known to be a member of an outlaw gang, a black youth, a youth wearing a black jacket and soiled blue jeans, or one who behaves toward the police in a way defined as "disrespectful" is more likely to be seen as a case calling for arrest and formalization. On the other hand, a youth who displays cues characteristic of persons perceived to be essentially law-abiding tends to be defined and responded to in a different manner. The consequences for biasing official data need no elaboration.

Another factor influencing official data is the private conceptions and typifications found among rule enforcers. For example, research has shown that the moral beliefs and stereotypic definitions a police officer has about offenders, whether a police officer is politically liberal, conservative, or reactionary, and how an officer categorizes various groups are all things likely to influence his or her definitions of and reactions to people's behavior. A study of police recruits reports that young officers tend to categorize people in depersonalized terms. For example, police recruits see people as "either law-abiding or not. Radical students were spoiled. Liberal politicians were subversive. Blacks were criminally inclined. Intentions had no place in law enforcement, especially if the [offender] belonged to a major outgroup" (Harris, 1973:127). Categorizing of that sort is felt to promote intolerance on the part of police toward representatives of some groups while serving to provide a kind of immunity for others. Differential enforcement results. In turn, differential enforcement (a kind of official action) helps produce biased data.

Examples of how categorization and stereotyping relate to differential rule enforcement and distorted statistics is contained in Chambliss and Nagasawa's (1969) study comparing self-reported and official arrest rates of white, black, and Japanese-American youth in Seattle, Washington. These researchers found that police consistently overestimated the involvement of black youth in delinquency and underestimated the involvement of white and Japanese-American youth. These incorrect estimates were based on prevailing stereotypes of the involvement of these youth in unlawful behavior, stereotypes that led police to take action against members of these groups that was disproportionate to their acknowledged involvement in rule-breaking behavior. Thus, while almost identical proportions of black and white youth (52 and 53 percent, respectively) admitted to being highly involved in delinquency, only 11 percent of the white youth were arrested, while 36 percent of the black youth had been arrested. Lastly, while 36 percent of the Japanese youth admitted being highly involved in delinquency, only 2 percent had been arrested.

Similar biases were noted among department store detectives contacted in Cameron's (1964) study of shoplifters. While only 6.5 percent of the arrested shoplifters were black, they accounted for 24 percent of all prosecutions. Further, while only 10.9 percent of non-blacks were charged with larceny, charges were brought against 58 percent of the blacks. Finally, though only 8.8 percent of the apprehended white women were formally charged with larceny, 42 percent of the black women shoplifters were formally charged. Cameron concludes that "decisions as to which people will be released with an admonition and which people will be formally charged with larceny . . . *reflect the biases and prejudices of* [store security] *staffs*" (1964:136. Emphasis added.).

Suicide is another instance in which official data are likely to be subject to systematic bias. For example, given the relatively stronger condemnation of suicide among Roman Catholics and Mormons than among people of other religions, we would expect a greater effort by members of these religions to hide the occurrence of suicide. For this and perhaps other reasons, we may expect that among various subgroups there will be a variable rate of attempted concealment of suicide. Thus Douglas has hypothesized that "the rate of attempted concealment will vary directly with the degree of negative moral judgment associated with the act of suicide and with the degree of negative sanctions believed to be imposed for violations of moral judgments" (1967:208). Douglas further suggests that concealment will likely vary in terms of the degree to which the suicide victim is involved in supportive social relations and according to the social status of the deceased (1967:209).

Biasing statistics on suicide is also promoted

by the post hoc or "after the fact" definition of suicides. For example, suicide has been defined as self-imposed extinction by methods the deceased knows will result in death. Thus, *knowledge* possessed by the deceased and the *role played by the deceased in his or her own death* are two critical elements influencing the decision to legally and officially declare a death as suicide. The obvious indeterminateness of these elements suggests how equivocal will be the assigning of official meaning to suspected suicides. At one extreme is the clear case of the person who has long talked of suicide, and who, after leaving a note indicating his or her suicidal intentions, proceeds to take an overdose of sleeping pills. At the other extreme is the instance of a body found floating in some body of water. Did he or she jump, or fall, or get pushed into the water? From a bridge or boat? In the absence of notes or other hard evidence to answer these questions, the labeling of unattended deaths as suicide (or murder or an accident) may rest on circumstantial evidence. In any event, the open-ended nature of what evidence may exist, and its ambiguous character, may result in the introduction of error in official data (Douglas, 1967:185–190).

The case of suicide provides another example of how official data may be in error and lead to invalid conclusions. Authorities are becoming increasingly interested in *autoerotic fatalities*—that is, accidental "deaths occurring in the course of autoerotic activities [masturbation] in which a potentially injurious [and life-threatening] agent [for example, asphyxia] was used to heighten sexual arousal" (Hazelwood, Dietz and Burgess, 1983:ix). Many of these fatalities appear to the unsuspecting eye to be the result of suicide. This is particularly true if persons finding the deceased's body remove evidence of autoerotic activity prior to notifying authorities of the death. Such cover-ups are not uncommon since a substantial proportion of these deaths occur among teenage males; being sexually motivated deaths, parents or others are often inclined to engineer a cover-up to avoid the anticipated social stigma (Brody, 1984:17).

If such cover-ups and the resulting misclassification of these deaths was occasional and

random, their biasing effect on official data might be disregarded. However, knowledgeable authorities suspect (though on speculative grounds) as many as 500 to 1000 autoerotic deaths occur each year in this country; most of these are alleged to be misdiagnosed or, if accurately identified, are likely to be misclassified as other than autoerotic deaths since, for most coroners, no such official category of death exists (Hazelwood, Dietz and Burgess, 1983:59; Brody, 1984:20). We might reasonably assume such deaths would be listed as suicide by hanging, strangulation, or suffocation. Let's look briefly at official data on such suicides among males aged 15 through 19, and 20 through 24 years of age, and how such data may be distorted by the mistaken inclusion of *accidental* autoerotic deaths among reports of deaths assumed to have been *purposive* (as suicide is).

However speculative, the above estimates of the number of autoerotic deaths suggest that between 9 and 19 percent of the 5115 official suicides among males between age 15 and 24 in 1978 could be wrongly classified.[2] To avoid overstating the case, however, let's limit our argument to the lower estimate of 500 autoerotic deaths per year, and assume that 66 percent of these 500 deaths (330 cases) were misclassified as suicide by hanging, strangulation, or suffocation. The official number of deaths by those means for males aged 15–24 in 1978 was 797 (National Center for Health Statistics, 1982:1–246 and 1–247). Could it be that 41 percent (330/797) of these deaths were of the autoerotic type? It's possible! Finally, let's carry our speculation one step further. Official data for 1978 indicate that there were 301 suicides among males aged 15–19 years by hanging, strangulation, or suffocation. Is it possible that 41 percent (123) of these cases are matters of misclassification? Again, it's possible!

These remarks clearly are based on some speculative data. For that reason, any conclusions drawn from them should be regarded as conjectural. In the spirit of conjecture, however, we may suggest that it takes little or no

---

[2]The 9 percent figure is derived from 500/5115; the 19 percent figure from 1000/5115.

effort to see that an error in official data of the above magnitude, if corrected in line with what we may come to know about autoerotic deaths, would lead to a significant revision of official data on suicide among teenage and young adult males and, in turn, to a revision of some current thinking about suicide being the second-ranked cause of death among teenagers (*Arizona Republic,* 1984b).

The importance of ambiguity as a factor in classifying behavior may be further demonstrated by examining police work where homicide may be involved. On the basis of careful observation of police investigative methods, Terry and Luckenbill (1976) conclude that homicide detectives tend to divide cases into one of two classes: *walk-throughs,* those in which there is little or no ambiguity as to the legal classification of a case, and *whodunits,* cases in which the nature of the events that transpired are problematic (crime, or accident, or suicide) and, hence, subject to variable interpretation and labeling. Characteristic of the walk-through type is the case in which a person responsible for the death of another calls the police, informs them of what has happened, and then awaits their arrival and his or her arrest. In such a case the identity of the victim and the offender, the nature of their relationship, and some plausible explanation of the act and what prompted it are all rather readily available. In sharp contrast is the whodunit investigation, wherein the identity of the deceased, the identity of the assailant (if, indeed, there is sufficient evidence to justify referring to the deceased as a victim), the events leading to the death, and other possibly relevant information is lacking. In such a case the nature of the event (and how it should be classified and treated) becomes a matter of social construction. For example,

Detectives entered the scene of an apparent suicide. They found a "suicide note" written in the victim's own hand; her relatives and a close friend related that she had been very depressed the previous few weeks over her family affairs; the room was locked from the inside; she was found slumped on her bed with a pump-action shotgun wedged between her legs. The victim was dead, the top of her head splattered against the ceiling.

Closer examination of the scene gave investigators cause to consider the possibility that there had been another person who either assisted in the suicide or killed the victim. Of primary importance in this regard was the observation that the breach of the pump-action shotgun was open and the shell casing in the wastebasket on the other side of the room.

By testing the victim's shotgun as the victim would have had to use it in order to have shot herself—that is, with the gun stock on the ground and light pressure applied to the slide—it was discovered that a shell would indeed eject from the chamber. That the casing landed in the wastebasket was held to be pure happenstance. Consequently, the case's designation changed from "possible suicide" to "suicide." (Terry and Luckenbill, 1976:85)

In this case the initial classification was "possible suicide," reflecting an element of ambiguity or uncertainty that could only be resolved by careful investigation. The essential point, however, is that meanings and the classification of cases are far from certain and may, in an unknown number of incidents, result in misclassification. This is because detectives, no less than other officials, are

not neutral observers of unambiguous events. They are active agents. Their activities determine whether a set of events will be placed within the criminal-homicide column or seen as instances of suicide or natural death. . . . To assume, therefore, that statistical data accurately represent the universe of criminal homicides overlooks both the ambiguous and perplexed, albeit reasonable, nature of investigations and the probable inaccuracy in the reports of homicides. In the light of these difficulties, the thought must at least be entertained that official documents reflect only those homicides that are readily visible and capable of being investigated. Thus, murders committed by urban ghetto dwellers of the lower socioeconomic and racially disadvantaged classes are heavily overrepresented in the official statistics. (Terry and Luckenbill, 1976:92–93)

Let's talk a bit about the matter of visibility.

Visibility. Contributing to the biasing of official statistics is the fact that lifestyle and circumstances make some segments of the population (especially the less affluent) more subject to observation than others, and their involvement in rule-breaking incidents more likely to be observed and recorded (Bensman and Lilienfeld, 1979:31). This is particularly the case for persons on welfare, ADC mothers, and others whose lives, as part of the price of obtaining public assistance, are subject to sometimes microscopic scrutiny. Such visibility increases the opportunity for authorities to become aware of behavior definable as rule violating. For example, regarding the relationship of poverty to the discovery of victims of statutory rape, Skolnick and Woodworth report that

the largest single source of [statutory rape] reports is from the family support division (40%). At the time of the study ADC aid could be given to a mother only if her real property was worth less than $5,000 and her personal property less than $600. One social worker reported that most applicants possessed no real property; those who had originally owned such property had exhausted its value prior to applying for aid. Thus, statutory rape is punished mainly among the poor who become visible by applying for maternity aid from welfare authorities. (1967:109)

While the life conditions of some people increase the visibility of their rule breaking, the life conditions of others have a reverse effect. For example, it is reported that between 1 and 2 percent of physicians in the United States are addicted to chemical substances: alcohol, drugs, or both. If so, this is a rate of addiction between 30 and 100 times that assumed to exist in the general population (depending on what estimate one accepts). Public and official recognition of this has been nil, however, due to physicians' ability to obtain drugs within the context of their normal medical routine and, thereby, conceal their drug dependency. Treatment, too, serves to obscure physicians' addiction in that errant doctors are assured complete anonymity during treatment and rehabilitation, and are afforded the support of their professional colleagues (*Arizona Republic,* 1982b and 1983a; Grosswirth, 1982).

The influence of life conditions on the visibility of rule-breaking behavior is further demonstrated by the increasing reliance of people on insurance to cover property losses. Because claims against insurance companies for property lost through theft must be validated by the insured filing a report of the theft with po-

lice, the official data on theft are increased. Such increase, however, may not be assumed to reflect a simple increase in offender behavior. A statistical increase does not necessarily mean a "real" increase.

The distortions due to variable perception and differential law enforcement have never been more noticeable than in research based on the technique of "reported behavior" (Short and Nye, 1958). Developed in the mid-1950s, this technique has been used in a substantial amount of research and has revealed systematic evidence that official statistics, especially those on delinquency, provide a distorted picture of the actual pattern and distribution of offender behavior (Short and Nye, 1958: Dentler and Monroe, 1961; Clark and Wenninger, 1962; Akers, 1964; Gold, 1966 and 1970; Williams and Gold, 1972). Using an anonymously administered questionnaire designed to measure the range and frequency of involvement in delinquent behavior, Short and Nye compared responses of high school students in three western and three midwestern communities with responses from a western training school group (adjudicated delinquents). From this comparison they concluded that delinquency is distributed far more evenly in the general population than official statistical data would suggest. These conclusions have been further confirmed by Ronald Akers in a retest of the original Short–Nye investigation. Akers reported "no significant differences in delinquent behavior by socioeconomic status, and analysis revealed no correlation between the two variables" (1964:38). Finally, on the basis of an extensive interview study among over 500 randomly selected Flint, Michigan, teenagers, Martin Gold concluded that official data, which indicated a ratio of 5 lower-class youngsters to 1 higher-status youth, are selective and incomplete. Gold suggests that if the most highly delinquent youth were dealt with in a complete and unselective manner, the ratio of lower-status–to–higher-status youth would be closer to 1.5:1, a clear indication of a more even distribution of rule-violating behavior than is ordinarily acknowledged (1966:44).

More recently Williams and Gold (1972) studied the differences between self-reported and official delinquency rates among a national sample of 847 boys and girls, age 13 through 16. In conducting this research Williams and Gold examined boys' and girls' admitted (self-reported) delinquencies as well as whether or not they were caught by police; if caught, whether or not a record was made of their offense; and, if they had an official or quasi-official record, whether or not they had been declared delinquent by the court. On the basis of this extensive investigation, Williams and Gold conclude that actual delinquency is not at all accurately reflected in official records (1972:226). Indeed, official records often amplify (that is, overstate) and present a distorted picture of the actual delinquency engaged in by some youth. These authors state that "both delinquent behavior and official delinquency are important phenomena deserving attention, but they are not by any means the same thing. Measures of one . . . are far from . . . [identical] with measures of the other" (1972:227). This study, then, confirms the general conclusion reported by Gold (1966) on the basis of the study of a single city.

As we have noted, one area of distortion in official data on rule-violating behavior involves the underrepresentation of violations by upper-status persons. This distortion does not result simply from police and other officials focusing attention on lower social status groups. Equally involved is an active tendency to underplay violations of higher-status persons. Ordinarily, police and others simply withhold negative judgment of influential persons or groups in deference to the moral meanings generally assigned to these people. On the basis of the assumed positive qualities of residents of "better" neighborhoods, police tend not to perceive them as potential or actual violators. Rule violations committed by these people have a low level of *social-psychological visibility;* that is, authorities are disinclined to perceive or officially define these behaviors as intentional violations. It is more likely that they will be defined as "exceptions" and dealt with as informally as possible (Westley, 1970:97–98).

A most graphic instance demonstrating this and the seeming subordination of police to the power-wielding capacity of upper-status groups is the case, stumbled on by a cub newspaper reporter, of the intentional shooting of a member of one of Long Island, New York's wealthiest families by his wife. All newspaper coverage of the event was immediately suppressed, and within hours of the murder the physical evidence was removed never to be seen again. Witnesses to events associated with the death were never permitted to be heard in public. At an inquest held five days after the death, it was officially established that the wife was awakened when she thought she heard burglars, went to investigate, and, because she was groggy with sleep, accidentally shot her husband. The death was officially declared an accident (Chambliss, 1975:259–261).[3] Rather clearly, the elements of murder are not always defined that way.

The definitions authorities assign to behavior is also influenced by the necessity, particularly of police, to rely on citizen complaints to initiate the rule-enforcing process. Basically, police pursue law enforcement in either of two ways. They may perform in a *proactive* manner—that is, discover rule-violating behavior on the basis of extensive patrol and search operations—or they may operate on a *reactive* basis by relying on citizen complaints to initiate the law enforcement process (Reiss and Bordua, 1967:25). To the extent that police operate on a reactive basis, the construction of official statistical records will in some measure reflect the moral meanings, prejudices, and stereotypes of the complainant. For example, the greater awareness people have of being victimized by burglary or auto theft (as contrasted with being victimized by consumer fraud) the more prone they will be to report blue-collar types of crime. Obviously, then, regardless of the actual frequency of blue-collar vs. white-collar offenses, selective reporting will

[3]For a case displaying remarkable similarity, see "The Shooting of the Century," *Life,* November 14, 1955, pp. 34–45, about the shooting death of New York socialite William Woodward. Revealed in this article are the rather mysterious but never fully explained deaths of several other socially prominent persons.

result in the inflation of statistics on one type and the deflation of statistics on the other.

Further, the ordinary citizen, like police recruits and store detectives, is prone to stereotype various categories of deviant actors. Complainants respond in terms of these stereotypes and are prepared to perceive (define) and report offenders who fit their stereotypes. The popular social construction of crime and deviance in this country suggests that offenders are more likely to be male than female, black than white, and lower class than upper or middle class. Given this construction, we would expect complaints to be more frequently lodged against lower-class black males than against more affluent white females. And this expectation is indeed supported by the data collected in Cameron's (1964) study of the disposition of shoplifters and by a study of how corporations respond to employee thieves (Robin, 1970). For example, *holding the dollar value of the theft constant,* comparison of publicly exposed and prosecuted employee thieves revealed that significantly more men (60 percent) were prosecuted than women (47 percent) and significantly more lower-status employees (cleaners, servicemen, and stock workers) were prosecuted than were higher-status workers (executives, salespersons, and white-collar workers). Of the former group, 73 percent were exposed and prosecuted, compared with 50 percent of the latter. Robin concludes "that the offenders with whom the enforcers can more easily identify are treated more sympathetically—and what better way to express such identification and empathy . . . than by not exposing him publicly" (1970:129).

In another instance of "selective perception," some observers indicate that the label of "child abuser" is less likely to be assigned by physicians to parents of battered children "if the diagnostician and possible abuser share similar characteristics, especially socioeconomic status, particularly where the injury is not serious or manifestly a consequence of maltreatment" (Newberger and Bourne, 1978:601). As we will note again later, this selectivity reflects a tacit rule in labeling people

deviant: "The greater the social distance between the [labeler] and the person singled out for [labeling] the . . . more quickly it may be applied" (Rubington and Weinberg, 1973:8). As a fundamental characteristic of rule enforcing, including labeling, such selectivity has an ultimate effect on official statistics: It renders them unreliable as measures of the actual volume of offender behavior.

Organizational Interests Our discussion thus far clearly notes that how behavior is defined and rules are enforced is highly problematic, and suggests that full enforcement of law is nonexistent. It is nonexistent, first, because it is physically impossible in an open society where the legitimate activities of police and other rule enforcers are restricted by *procedural law,* that is, rules governing the administration, enforcement, and so on of substantive law (Vago, 1981:10). A second reason for less than full enforcement—one that is more relevant to our concern for official statistics—is that police bureaucracies are linked with one another and with other agencies in a network of interdependent relations and reciprocal obligations, many of which serve to limit police involvement in cases of rule violating. Thus, universities, businesses, and other organizations frequently themselves deal with rule violators in their midst, despite the fact that the offenses committed by students, employees, and so on are violations of law. To the extent that police stand "in the wings" in such matters, such cases do not get included in official statistical records (Box, 1981:162; Hills, 1982). Finally, full enforcement is nonexistent because laws are enforced in ways that maximize organizational rewards and minimize organizational strain (Chambliss, 1969:86; Chambliss and Seidman, 1971:100–101). That is, people are arrested, tried, sentenced, hospitalized, declared mentally ill, have their deaths declared suicides, and so on, in inverse ratio to the trouble such official actions and declarations may bring to the respective agency. Let's explore this more fully.

Maximizing rewards and minimizing trouble is a principal element in many bureaucratic organizations. To appreciate how this element is related to official statistics, it is necessary to note that rule enforcers operate in a context of *value pluralism*. That is, as we've noted, there is no single set of values and moral meanings to which the entire population subscribes; social reality is multiple. To be sure, there are some behavior patterns regarding which there exists overwhelming public moral consensus, but even in the case of apparent murder we may note times when the seemingly appropriate meaning is withheld. Further, though most people subscribe to the ideal of "law and order," the practical meaning of that term for one group is not shared by others. We should also note that a substantial variety of behaviors, particularly "crimes without victims," are subject to very different meanings and serve as the basis for significant social conflict. Examples of this conflict include the current controversies over abortion, decriminalization of possession of marijuana for personal use, and the definition of pornography. Each of these conflicts is rooted in a condition of value pluralism.

Pluralism influences law enforcement in that no matter how they perform their assigned tasks, rule enforcers will likely be damned by some and praised by others, because in a pluralistic society rule enforcers will inevitably interfere with some group's interests. Enforcing rules that contravene a group's interests will promote opposition and antagonisms.[4] In order to maximize rewards and minimize strain, then, rule enforcers may be expected to exercise discretion in performing their duties. In the case of police, laws are more likely to be enforced when doing so is either independent of strains or when enforcement is likely to bring positive recognition. However, when

enforcement is likely to promote strains, discretionary *nonenforcement* is most probable. Discretionary nonenforcement is sometimes the most rewarding course of action.

These issues raise the question of how rule enforcers know whether enforcement or nonenforcement is the most judicious course in any given situation. Certainly, they do not know these things in any definitive sense, but there are situational factors and rules of thumb that help provide them with answers. Included is the knowledge that power in our society is differentially distributed. The police, for example, must deal with persons occupying lower-, middle-, as well as upper-class socioeconomic positions. These people differ not only in values and interests, but they have differing degrees of power—degrees of ability to impose strain on police should their interests be threatened by them. Full enforcement directed against powerful segments of the community is likely to produce criticism, and, perhaps, influence the resources of the rule-enforcing body.

Allocation of resources is another element influencing the enforcer's decisions on how and when to exercise discretion. Like many service organizations, rule-enforcing bodies seldom, if ever, produce their own resources (Chambliss and Seidman, 1971:266). They are dependent on others—legislative assemblies, city councils, executive bodies—for operating funds, personnel allocations, and salary and benefit increases, among other things. Astute rule enforcers do not operate in ignorance or disregard of their dependent position and do not "bite the hand that feeds them." Among other things, that means they will select and respond to their clientele with care; they will respond to persons and groups on the basis of their potential for making trouble for the organization. Disregard for the practical implications of the distribution of power and their dependent status may have politically disadvantageous consequences for the offending organization.

Let's relate these matters to official statistics. For the reasons cited, rule-enforcing bodies exercise discretion. That is, practical considera-

---

[4]Among cases resulting in much public controversy over the propriety of law enforcement methods, ABSCAM stands near the top of the list. Of major importance to some critics was whether or not FBI methods constituted entrapment. The methods used led *Washington Post* correspondent William Raspberry to ask "what is the point of using . . . subterfuge to *create* a crook: to talk a congressman, reporter or housewife into criminal activity that had never crossed his or her mind? . . . Why induce crime?" (*Arizona Republic*, 1980b).

tions influence organizational action and bring about a substitution of informal goals for the formal goals on which the organization is based (Etzioni, 1964:10–11; Chambliss and Seidman, (1971:266). Previously we noted that official statistics were records of official actions. That is, the number of people arrested, convicted, or imprisoned reflects actions engaged in by officials. How many official suicides are recorded in a county reflects the action of the county coroner. Because these actions are to some extent discretionary, the statistics they generate are biased in particular directions. Discretion is not exercised randomly; it is systematic and has a discernible pattern. Groups with power and the ability to make problems for the organization are dealt with in ways different from those who lack power. An awareness that official data are influenced by organizational discretion, by a concern for minimizing trouble, and that agency actions are sometimes influenced by stereotypes and other factors, all lead to the conclusion that such data should be interpreted with caution.

As we have seen, arrest statistics indicate an overinvolvement of poor, blacks, and youth in crime; however, the apparent meaning of these data ought not be taken for granted. Let's reverse the situation and ask if the relatively low rate of arrest and conviction of white-collar offenders may be taken at face value; do the data mean that men of business are really men of virtue? In his study of white-collar crime, Edwin Sutherland (1956) investigated 980 adverse legal decisions against corporations. These decisions were based on cases of fraudulent advertising, violation of labor laws, violation of antitrust laws, embezzlement, and violation of trust by corporate officials. *Each case involved violation of criminal law.* However, only 159 (16.2 percent) of these decisions were made by criminal courts. Decisions for 786 of these criminal law violations were handled by civil courts or by commissions. It seems quite apparent that examination of conviction statistics (a record of criminal court actions) would not yield valid information about the unlawful activity of corporate groups and their representatives. Getting at the meaning of these and other official statistics necessitates careful examination of the rates and the rate-producing process.

That the meaning of statistics on crimes known to the police and arrest statistics may not be taken for granted is also indicated by the fact that these data are sometimes consciously manipulated by police in order to promote organizational interests. For example, rather than these data reflecting genuine increases and decreases in unlawful behavior, Rosett and Cressey (1976) contend that they have been juggled to satisfy federal regulations regarding the distribution of financial grants. Rosett and Cressey comment:

The artificial nature of these statistics became evident when the federal government modified its law enforcement grant policy, which had been to give financial aid to cities with high crime rates. The new policy gave large grants in proportion to the reduction of the crime rate in target cities. A city no longer would receive extra money because its crime rate was high, but if the rate went down, it would be granted more money for police equipment and services. This amounted to thinly concealed bribery of police departments to make "the crime problem" go away statistically, and impressive results were obtained. (1976:177)

In a substantial proportion of cases official data may be found to be self-serving (Weis and Milakovich, 1974:33). Police departments are not, of course, the only organizations that use statistics for self-serving purposes. Organizations using official data for those purposes extend to the highest levels of national government and include the White House and executive agencies such as the Bureau of Narcotics and Dangerous Drugs (B.N.D.D). Thus, in 1971 President Richard Nixon sought emergency powers (including no-knock warrants, pretrial detention, wiretaps, and unorthodox strike forces) to deal with what was hailed in the media as an "uncontrollable heroin epidemic" that "will surely in time destroy us" (Epstein, 1977:51–52). Rather than being the result of increased numbers and activity among heroin traffickers, this "epidemic" was a social construction, the work of B.N.D.D.

statisticians and White House strategists, manufactured in an effort to create sufficient concern and fear to win public support for the White House's "war on crime." Information supplied to the media in support of the claim that the nation was in the throes of an epidemic purported that "the number of addict-users [in the nation] had increased from 68,000 in 1969 to 315,000 in 1970 to 559,000 in 1971" (Epstein, 1977:52). These data—representing an eightfold increase in the number of addicts in the short span of two to three years—were produced simply by applying a "new formula" to old (1969) figures. Of course, such prodigious increases may also produce a sort of backlash, which, in this case, was soon feared. When it became apparent that this "increase" in addicts had occurred *under the Nixon administration,* which was hardly consistent with that administration's goal, all statements emanating from the B.N.D.D. had, thereafter, to be cleared by White House staffers (Epstein, 1977:52).

Lastly, we may refer to the ever-expanding use of undercover agents by police and the tendency of such agents to play the role of *agents provocateurs,* in which officers not only penetrate organizations of offenders, but sometimes provide the necessary opportunities for others to engage in crime, for example, through ABSCAM and other "sting" operations (Marx, 1980:430). Though these efforts were intended to make police more efficient and improve their public image, they seem also to have some unintended consequences which, in turn, influence official crime statistics. Thus, it had been suggested that more than 25 percent of the complaints filed against New York City police officers stem from the actions of people posing as police.

In 1979 more than 1200 crimes by police impersonators were reported in New York City, almost double the figure for 1973. Several thousand police impersonators are known to have operated in New York City in recent years. The phenomenon is likely much more widespread than official statistics indicate, since those victimized are hesitant to report it. In cities *where police undercover work is minimal, impersonation and other criminal activity stemming from it are rare.* (Marx, 1980:422. Emphasis added).

Additionally, it must be noted that *agents provocateurs* who, by definition, lead others to commit illegal acts, contribute to the amount of crime and violence police are intended to control (Marx, 1974a:3; 1974b:405 and 429). The implication of these police methods for official statistics is apparent; even though not all cases of officer impersonation or covertly facilitated crime gets recorded, those cases that do get recorded contribute to a counterfeit record of crime, a record, paradoxically, reflecting the contrivances of rule enforcers intended to promote the unlawful acts of others. Never has it been more true that official records are, in the first instance, records of officials' actions.

Summary

In this chapter we focused attention on the matter of counting deviants and related issues. The importance of this issue rests on the uses of official statistics for formulating public policy and for building and testing theories of deviance, and on the way enumeration contributes to the objectivation and reification of the phenomenon of deviance. Underlying these uses and consequences of statistical data is the implicit acceptance of their adequacy or validity, that is, that they measure what they claim to measure. The fundamental question under examination, then, is whether or not official statistics on deviance are a faithful representation of rule-breaking behavior. To examine this question several elements were considered in terms of their influence on the rate-producing process and the rates themselves, including the matter of underreporting; the definitions of deviance among witnesses, victims, and officials; the relative visibility of some forms of rule breaking and the rule breaking of some segments of the population; and organizational interests. On the basis of this examination we may conclude that official records of deviance are not an adequate or faithful representation of some supposedly objective world; being social constructions they are subject to systematic biasing and should not have their apparent meaning taken for granted.

The implications of this conclusion, however, are not limited simply to such questions as whether it is true or false that middle- and upper-income groups engage in unlawful or deviant behavior, or whether whites and blacks engage in objectively similar or different patterns of rule breaking, or whether police and other agencies manipulate official data for organizational advantage. Rather, the more crucial question is whether the materials and analysis presented here are sufficient to challenge the validity of explanations of deviance and/or the social policies based on these data? For example, are these data sufficiently suspect to question the deeply rooted belief that delinquency, crime, and deviance are functions of lower-class living and a response to the frustrations of ambition? Are they sufficiently biased to challenge the long-standing idea that the "real" danger posed by criminals is so-called street crime and that it is against such miscreants that the bulk of our social control efforts must be directed? Our analysis suggests they are. In short, contentions and policies based on these data are likely to be flawed.

Based on our analysis we conclude that juvenile court records, police arrest statistics, and the records of correctional institutions, mental hospitals, coroner's offices, and other official agencies are highly suspect when used to explain alleged objective differences in the distribution of deviance in society. However, official data may be adequate for research on the operation of agencies that compile them since they are, in the first place, indices of agency operations. In that sense, they may be used to study *official* delinquency, *official* crime, *official* deviance. As an index of *delinquency, crime,* and *deviance* in the general population, however, they are inadequate.

4 Banning Behavior

Introduction

Repeatedly over the previous chapters we have been reminded that deviance is what people define it to be, that it is a social construction, and that in modern industrial societies the official designation of behavior as deviant is a state function. In this and subsequent chapters we examine this aspect of the deviance process and related matters. We begin by noting that the deviance-creating process consists of several identifiable sub-elements. Three of these are seen when "a group, community, or society (1) interpret behavior as deviant, (2) define persons who so behave as . . . deviant, and (3) accord them the treatment considered appropriate to such deviants" (Kitsuse, 1962:248). A fourth, analytically distinct element of the process occurs when groups of people who have been labeled deviant—homosexuals, the disabled, and some prostitutes, among others—take collective action to promote a change in the public and official meaning of their alleged deviation. In terms of everyday life, then, the deviance process includes the assignment of moral meaning to behavior and to people, the way labeled individuals or groups resist or otherwise manage those assigned meanings, the consequences people experience as a result of being labeled, and, finally, the way in which assigned moral meanings may be changed.

These sub-elements of the deviance process are consistent with the position established in Chapter 1—namely, that deviance is a social construction that involves assigning moral meaning to things and people, and acting on those assigned meanings. If deviance is a consequence of people's interpretation of things, rather than an inherent part of things "as they are," how are these interpretations arrived at?

How do private and subjective meanings become public and objective rules of behavior, violations of which are punishable by the state? How, in the course of everyday affairs, do things get defined as immoral? The present chapter is concerned with these questions, all of which focus on the first and most basic sub-element of the deviance process: *banning* or imbuing an activity with guilt and proscribing it as bad, evil, wrong, or immoral (Matza, 1969:146).

The Deviance-Making Enterprise

The process of constructing and applying moral meanings may be understood as a moral enterprise (Becker, 1973:162). The term *enterprise* used in this sense means that creating moral meanings is an undertaking of major proportions calling for considerable management and initiative. It does not occur without conscious human intervention. The business of deviance making is an enterprise in two senses. First, it consists of rule making (without which there could be no deviant behavior), and second, it entails rule enforcing, that is, applying rules to some specific group of people. These activities are the work of two subtypes of moral entrepreneur: *rule creators* and *rule enforcers*.[1] For the present we will focus on the work of the rule creator.

Many individuals play the role of rule creator. However, the term is most appropriately

---

[1]The distinction between rule creators and rule enforcers is analytic. In the actual process of deviance the same individuals and groups that are instrumental in the creation of rules may be equally active in their enforcement. For example, police departments may suggest legislation to municipal and state authorities, as well as enforce the ensuing laws.

applied to groups of people joined together by shared concerns who wish to have public policy reflect their interests. Thus, in 1977 Anita Bryant embarked on a crusade against homosexuality and other forms of sexual behavior she regarded as deviant. However, Anita Bryant is more properly seen as a symbol or representative of (and perhaps a spokesperson for) a far larger collectivity—people who fear homosexuality and sexual deviation. In short, rule creators are similar to *interest groups* in that they are organized on the basis of shared and distinctive interests among the members. When groups try to convert their interests into public law or some other facet of public policy, they may be identified as *pressure groups* (Hoult, 1969:169, 247).

In terms of creating deviance, the existence of these groups in heterogeneous societies like ours is extremely important; their existence ensures a constant supply of deviance and deviants. As indicated previously, social reality is multiple. Thus, in societies like ours there exist all manner of distinctive belief systems. These belief systems are the stuff of varying and often conflicting social realities; out of this conflict (ultimately) comes deviance. Howard Becker comments:

Social rules are the creation of specific social groups. Modern societies are not simply organizations in which everyone agrees on what the rules are and how they are to be applied in specific situations. They are, instead, highly differentiated along social class lines. These groups need not and, in fact, often do not share the same rules. The problems they face in dealing with their environment, the history and traditions they carry with them, all lead to the evolution of different sets of rules. Insofar as the rules of various groups conflict and contradict one another, there will be disagreement about the kind of behavior that is proper in any given situation. (1973:15)

Rule-creating groups, then, are a product of moral heterogeneity. The belief that the interests of various groups are mutually exclusive, together with an almost unlimited variety of interest groups, makes it inevitable that the goals and purposes of some will purposely or accidentally encroach upon the interests of others. But even when no direct encroachment

occurs, a heterogeneous and highly impersonal society like ours is characterized by one group perceiving threats in, and feeling fearful, distrustful, and suspicious of, the behavior of another group (Lofland, 1969:13).

That such emotions play a prominent role in initiating the work of the moral entrepreneur is noted in Sutherland's research on the diffusion of sexual psychopath laws (Sutherland, 1950a). Sutherland concluded that these laws are established because of the fear aroused by the occurrence of sex crimes in a community. Because these events are sometimes subject to extensive amplification by the news media, the perceived danger and fear resulting from them may be sufficient to give rise to collective efforts to seek relief. In seeking relief, interest groups may be transformed into rule-creating assemblages. In broad terms, then, the work of the rule creator begins with dissatisfaction over some existing or anticipated condition in society and leads to an effort to correct or prevent it. Let's expand on these matters.

Awareness

The work of the rule creator is much like that of the manufacturer. Both seek to invest a thing with new form—to bring something to pass. In manufacturing, this involves making finished consumer goods out of raw materials. In rule creating it involves giving new form to moral meanings—making them into new rules. In a very literal sense, moral entrepreneurs are *creators of new moralities*.

New moralities are created slowly, however. The creation process begins with *awareness*, a condition wherein "some person or group [defines] . . . objective conditions as problematic, posing a danger or containing the seeds of some future difficulties" (Becker, 1966:12). This defining procedure occurs long before the time rules are created and is a necessary precondition of that later development. When it does occur, the process of rule creating may begin.[2]

[2]Awareness and the assigning of problematic meaning to objective conditions does not inevitably lead to the creation of new moral rules. However, as a precondition of rule making, it may be said to be necessary without being sufficient.

Ostensibly, the goal of the rule creator is to correct conditions experienced as problems or to forestall anticipated problems. On a relatively limited scale, these kinds of perceptions and rule-creating efforts occur when, in support of their respective interests, parents set down rules for their children, school administrators establish rules for students when they are on school grounds, and employers regulate the general business demeanor of their employees. In each case the rule makers seek to correct or prevent conditions they think interfere with their interests. The rule creators we will deal with operate on a far grander scale, although they use the same principle. These people seek to translate private interests into public law and, at least in theory, have the rules apply to everyone. Making deviance is therefore an aspect of making public policy. Making deviance is an act of politics.

Practical Examples. In working to promote a change in social policy, moral entrepreneurs may advocate returning to an earlier social condition (a conservative or reactionary orientation) or they may seek a progressive form of change. Whatever is advocated, the rule creator defines the perceived condition(s) and those who engage in them as a threat to his or her values and/or interests. Examples are legion.

In Denver, Colorado, Lorraine Jacques is reported to have begun a grass-roots movement to counter the ultra-conservative religious and political teachings of Rev. Jerry Falwell, whom she perceives as a "pulpit tyrant" who "hides behind a facade of religion" (*Arizona Republic,* 1981a). In Cincinnati, Ohio, prompted by a priest friend, Charles H. Keating, Jr., a lawyer, began a one-man crusade against pornography. Incorporated in 1958, Keating's organization is called the Citizens for Decency Through Law; at one time the CDL boasted chapters in 300 American cities (*Arizona Republic,* 1983b). Keating became a member of the President's Commission on Obscenity and authored a dissent from the majority report of that Commission. In that dissent against the majority recommendation to repeal several federal and state pornography statutes, Keating referred to such recommendations as "presumptuous" and "the advocacy of moral anarchy," and saw the retention of legislative control as necessary for the continued stability and progress of the nation (Commission on Obscenity and Pornography, 1970:578ff). Finally, across the nation are several diverse interest groups opposed to cigarette smoking. Included are several agencies of the federal government (Public Health Service, the National Clearing House for Smoking and Health, the Civil Aeronautics Board, the Federal Trade Commission, and the Interstate Commerce Commission) as well as many citizen groups such as Action on Smoking and Health (ASH), GASP (Group Against Smokers Pollution), NIC (National Interagency Council on Smoking), the American Cancer Society, the American Heart Association, and the American Lung Association. These and other interest groups—each in its own way—seek an end to smoking (at least in public places) and constitute the core of the antismoking crusade (Markle and Troyer, 1979). Quite clearly, the central issue is health—the health of smokers and nonsmokers alike.

In each of these examples, the problem situation arises when something of great value is perceived to be threatened. On these grounds, *anything* could be regarded as deviant. Like beauty, deviance is in the eye of the beholder. What is and is not regarded as loathsome, threatening, fearsome, and so on, depends on the perspective of the definer. The property of menacing or nonmenacing conditions, then, is not an inherent or essential property of things (or acts); it is a moral definition assigned to them. In the final analysis, these definitions may be as much (or more) a reflection of the definer's condition as they are of the behavior in question.

Resolving Distress: Instrumental and Symbolic Goals

In addition to a sense of distress or dissatisfaction, moral entrepreneurs are moved by the lack of available means to solve their problem. This lack is noted by the very term *creator.* Rules do not exist, or existing rules are felt to be inadequate to end the threatening condition.

If formal rules do exist, there may be no agencies—police, welfare, medical, and the like—to whom the distressed group may turn for relief. These two conditions, a sense of distress and a lack of ready means for its resolution, underlie the efforts of the moral entrepreneur. They serve as the stimuli to create new rules, alter existing rules, or in some other way set things right.

In seeking to resolve distress, moral entrepreneurs may work toward *instrumental* or *symbolic* goals (Gusfield, 1967). Instrumental goals involve having the law directly influence people's actions. The essential element of the instrumental function of law is enforcement since, without it, such laws have little effect. As we have seen, resolution of the moral entrepreneur's concerns often calls for controlling the behavior of people seen as a threat. As an example, a group of women in southern California founded a movement to put an initiative on the ballot to tighten sex crime laws. These women, parents of several young male murder victims, call their movement the Voting Initiative Concerning Tougher Imprisonment of Molesters and Sex Offenders. They state that "the laws don't have to be the way they are. We can make the courts protect us if we change the laws so they can't let these idiots out to prey on us and our children" (*Arizona Republic,* 1980c). Their hope is to make it more difficult for convicted sex offenders to be released from prison.

Seeking relief by way of the instrumental function of law does not always involve seeking new rules or laws. Equally important is defending existing rules that are perceived to be under attack. The dissent by Charles H. Keating, Jr., referred to earlier, is a case in point. Another example is the stand of pro-life (anti-abortion) groups in this country, who have banded together to resist liberalization of abortion policy and existing law, even to the point of advocating amending the U.S. Constitution to prevent such change.

Finally, crusaders occasionally pursue their interests by *opposing* enforcement of the law; that is, they advocate nonenforcement. For example, representatives of agribusinesses that rely on illegal Mexican aliens ("wetbacks") as a source of cheap labor sometimes seek to block enforcement of immigration laws, especially during harvest time, when the presence of large numbers of such workers is consistent with agricultural interests. After harvest, however, a different interest arises and more aggressive enforcement is called for to get rid of a group that has now become a liability (Bustamante, 1972). Instrumental use of law, then, reflects the rule creators' perceptions of their needs and interests.

At other times moral entrepreneurs have recourse to the law for its symbolic effect. Seen in a conflict perspective and in the context of a heterogeneous society, the *symbolic effect of law* lies in its ability to give legitimacy to some interest groups and deny it to others (Gusfield, 1967:178). Thus, the law is seen as a symbol of the interests and values of a particular group; interests represented in the law are thereby given a legitimacy—a position of superiority—that is denied to opposing values and interests. Further, although they may not be enforced, the mere passage of such laws reflects the distribution of power in a political area. Moreover, to have the interests of one's own group reflected in the law may be taken as a measure of the stature of that group in the local scheme of things. Concern over the issues of social power and status was noted by Gusfield in his comments regarding middle-class Yankee resistance to modifying gambling laws in Boston. Gusfield notes:

The threat to the middle class in the increased political power of Cornerville [a lower-class area] is not that the Cornerville resident will gamble more; he already does gamble with great frequency. The threat is that the law will come to accept the morality of gambling and treat it as a legitimate business. If this happens, Boston is no longer a city dominated by middle-class Yankees but becomes one dominated by lower class immigrants. . . . The maintenance of a norm which defines gambling as deviant behavior thus symbolizes the maintenance of Yankee social and political superiority. Its disappearance as a public commitment would symbolize the loss of that superiority. (Gusfield, 1967:181–182)

Concern for the legitimating (hence, symbolic) function of the law has also been noted with respect to the Catholic Church's position on homosexuality. As Simpson notes, "In addition to its clear position that homosexuality is patently inadmissible, the Catholic Church has another reason to oppress homosexuals: in order to maintain its status as a "moral leader." It must fight any change in attitude toward the church-state laws on homosexuality . . . or it will lose its 'moral' credibility" (Simpson, 1977:60–61).

A similar attitude exists among some crusaders and legislators for whom the absence of a law against something is equal to an official endorsement of the thing (Blaustein and Ferguson, 1957:110–111). This is known as the *declaratory argument*, according to which the repeal of a prohibitory law is seen as a public declaration that the conduct at issue is no longer considered morally wrong. Thus, it is feared that without a law against it, incest may become acceptable to people (Sklar, 1979:75). Or that, without laws restricting obscene or pornographic materials, people will come to define such materials as acceptable. The validity of such arguments has been challenged by the findings of a number of research studies (Walker and Argyle, 1964; Berkowitz and Walker, 1967). Nonetheless, opinion persists in some quarters that repeal of or failure to enforce laws against marijuana, prostitution, abortion, gambling, pornographic literature, and other things will be defined as an official endorsement of them. That is, the absence of a law against something is equated with its official approval. In turn, such approval is regarded as an inducement for people to engage in the questionable behavior. This contention fails to distinguiish between legal rules and *conduct norms,* the definitions people have of behavior that reflect their biography and that stand apart from the law (Sellin, 1962:7).

On occasion, it seems, the effort to create rules and expand the scope of deviance stems neither from moral concerns of an instrumental or symbolic sort nor from the existence of distressing conditions as ordinarily understood. Such effort also may arise as a result of threatening conditions faced by formal organizations. For example, the Narcotics Division of the Internal Revenue Bureau in the years immediately following passage of the Harrison (narcotics) Act in 1914 found itself severely restricted in its field of operations. Thus, the Narcotics Division strove for growth and expansion, normal tendencies among most bureaucratic organizations. It was hampered in this, however, by an apathetic public and an unresponsive Congress. To bring about change

> the Division launched a two-pronged campaign: (1) a barrage of reports and newspaper articles which generated a substantial outcry against narcotics use, and (2) a series of Division-sponsored test cases in the courts which resulted in a reinterpretation of the Harrison Act and substantially broadened powers for the Narcotics Division. Thus the Division attained its goals by altering a weakly held public value regarding narcotics use from neutrality or slight oppositon to strong opposition, and by persuading the courts that it should have increased powers. (Dickson, 1968:149)

Although it is subject to different interpretations (Galliher and Walker, 1977; Becker, 1973; Reasons, 1974), some scholars maintain that a similar campaign was waged by the Bureau of Narcotics in the 1930s in an effort to win passage of the Marijuana Tax Act (1937). It is alleged that this was another attempt by the Bureau to rescue itself from the organizational perils of a decreasing budget and reduced power — this time by heightening public awareness of the "dangers" of marijuana use. It also has been argued that the involvement and zeal of some federal agencies in the antismoking crusade is linked with their organizational need for "survival, role definition and power" (Nuehring and Markle, 1974:522). What is most important is that these cases reflect the sometimes problematic intention of rule creators.

Holy Crusades. These comments do not preclude the idea that moral entrepreneurs are often moved by a sincere and unwavering belief that their expressed views and interests are correct and that they oppose things they regard as absolutely evil—evil at all times and places. As noted, belief in the objectivity of moral meanings is an important element in the social construction of reality. Some moral entrepreneurs are so convinced of the objective rightness of their position that their efforts take on elements of a *holy crusade*. That is, the rightness of their cause is no longer defended (if it ever was) on rational, empirical, or this-worldly bases, but is supported by scriptural and other references to supernatural entities, divine command, and the "natural moral order." An example of this type of moral entrepreneur is John Brown of antislavery fame, who felt he had a divine mission to take vengeance against proslavery forces and effect the freedom of all enslaved blacks. Carry Nation, noted prohibitionist, was also a holy crusader. Fancying herself a messiah of sorts, standing six feet tall and weighing about 175 pounds, dressed in black and white clothing of a somewhat religious nature, and often assisted by hymn-singing women, "she would march into a saloon and proceed to sing, pray, hurl biblical-sounding vituperations at the 'rummies' present, and smash bar fixtures and stock with a hatchet" (*Encyclopaedia Brittanica,* 1974:207; also see Taylor, 1966).

Similarly, Anthony Comstock, noted for his lifelong fight against pornographic and salacious art and literature, is felt to have been "possessed of a curious, vague, sense of sin" and a "determination to exorcise sin from the whole of the . . . environment" (*Dictionary of American Biography,* 1930:330). So pronounced was Comstock's dedication that it led to the coining of the terms *comstockery,* referring to the zealous purging of society of so-called obscene materials, and *comstock* for those who are so engaged. On the latter, Robert Haney comments:

The comstocks are not merely people with intellectual theories who might be convinced by more persuasive theories; nor are they pragmatists who will be guided by the balance of power among pressure groups. Many of them are so emotionally involved in the condemnation of what they find objectionable that they find rational arguments irrelevant. They *must* suppress what is offensive in order to stabilize their own tremulous values and consciences. Panic rules them and they cannot be calmed by discussions of legal rights, literary integrity, or artistic merit. (1960:176–177)

A more recent example of a holy crusade was Anita Bryant's campaign against equal rights laws for homosexuals. Likening herself to Carry Nation, Bryant saw America at a moral crossroads: one path leading to a Sodom and Gomorrah, the other to a life of biblically defined moral virtue. She and her crusade were in the vanguard of those taking the latter course (*Playboy,* 1978). Similarly, in San Francisco an organization calling itself In God We Trust, Inc., was established in 1981 to conduct a $3 million campaign against homosexuality through the mass media. Taking its "authority" from Scripture, spokespersons for this group refer to San Francisco as "the Sodom and Gomorrah of the United States and the armpit of this perverted [homophile] movement" (*Arizona Republic,* 1981b). The ultimate goal, it is said, is to minister to homosexuals and get them to stop sinning.

Whether religiously inspired or not, the moral reform sought by many rule creators is often prompted by humanitarian impulses. An example is the American temperance movement. As Gusfield tells us, during the nineteenth century this movement

was part of a general effort toward the improvement of the worth of the human being through improved morality as well as economic conditions. The mixture of the religious, the equalitarian, and the humanitarian was an outstanding facet of the moral reformism of many movements. (1955:222–223)

The plight of the poor and women, of farmers and workers, of slaves and prison inmates, among others, concerned these reformers. Inspired by their humanitarian concerns and reinforced by notions of *noblesse oblige* and stewardship, members of the predominantly middle- and upper-class Women's Christian Temperance Union marched forth in the nineteenth century to solve the drinking problem of less fortunate folk—the lower class (Gusfield, 1955:225–226).

A Cautionary Note
A word of caution is in order. In our earlier discussion of the nature of social reality we noted that there is no external reality, no objective meanings, to which people respond. There are only shared, socially constructed meanings. Applying that observation to ban-

ning, we are reminded that the "reality" of the threat underlying banning is as much a social product as any other aspect of reality. The threat need not be validated in objective terms; there need be no spilling of blood for one to fear for one's personal safety. In short, the threat may be a thing of the mind up to and including "ghostys and ghoulys and things that go 'bump' in the night." But the threat may be a "thing of the mind" in a special sense.

A *perceived* threat can be as important for moral entrepreneurs as an objectively validated one. Indeed, objective conditions have no necessary bearing on the matter. Objectively similar behaviors may be defined and responded to in totally different ways. For example, Chambliss informs us of a situation in which an upper-middle-class white gang and a lower-class white gang attending the same high school and engaging in roughly the same type and frequency of delinquent behavior, were subject to quite opposite responses from police and citizen groups. Despite being involved in a greater number of delinquent acts, the Saints (upper middle class) avoided being stopped by police. Indeed, the "townspeople never perceived the Saints' high level of delinquency. The Saints were good boys who just went in for an occasional prank" (1973b:27). On the other hand, and despite their equally episodic involvement in delinquent forms of behavior, the Roughnecks (lower class) were subject to a very different perception: "everyone agreed that the not-so-well-dressed, not-so-well-mannered, not-so-rich boys were heading for trouble" (1973b:27).

The different perceptions people had of the Saints and the Roughnecks were not based on objective differences in the gangs' behavior. Rather, they stemmed from and reflected the perceptions of police and citizens. That is, the "visibility" of the Roughnecks and the relative "obscurity" of the Saints reflected the definitions people had of these boys. Indeed, citizens and police were prepared to "see" the delinquency of one group and the innocent pranks of the other.

To the degree that perceptions rather than objective conditions influence (bias) the re-

sponse of moral entrepreneurs, these definitions may be regarded as *self-fulfilling prophecies.* That is, people may react to a prophecy (a definition) in ways that bring about its validation (Merton, 1957). In the study reported, the behavior engaged in by the Saints was perceived as a prank or some other transitory, nonthreatening form of behavior. When the same behavior was engaged in by lower-class youth like the Roughnecks, the probability of its being defined as persistent delinquency rose. The consequent differences in official response are reflected in arrest statistics—official data that provide "validation" of the accuracy of the original prophecy (definition). In short, the meanings of behavior are problematic. Nonetheless, as W. I. Thomas suggested long ago, *when people define situations as real, they are real in their consequences.*

In summary, moral entrepreneurs or rule creators are those who seek to alter the content of rules, establish new rules, or influence the enforcement of existing rules. They are initially moved by what are perceived to be real or anticipated threats that others pose to their interests, goals, and values. Their motives range from that of the self-seeking bootlegger who, fearing a decline in business, sanctimoniously opposes repeal of prohibition, to the genuine self-sacrifice of an Anthony Comstock, a John Brown, or a Carry Nation.

Moral Conversion

In and of themselves, the perceptions, fears, and interests of moral entrepreneurs are never sufficient to bring about the desired change. The "awareness" that originates with the crusader must be disseminated to and accepted by a significantly broader segment of the community. Achieving this may require the rule creator to (1) overcome the effect of contrary realities (remember, reality is multiple) and/or (2) convert persons who are neutral on the issue into supporting partisans. This means that to achieve the desired goal the moral entrepreneur may have to alter a variety of perceptual and cognitive structures.

To begin with, most people will probably have little or no interest in the crusader's views and, at best, be barely cognizant of the troubling condition. Among those who are aware of the troubling condition, there may be a variety of views. Some may regard the matter as a passing event; these people may be said to have *optimized* the condition. Other people may have *neutralized* it; that is, they may have accommodated themselves to it and no longer define it as deviant. Others may have *normalized* the matter to the point where they perceive it as "normal though unusual." In contrast to these cognitive structures, the would-be rule creator *pessimizes* the situation in that the evil vested in the matter is so great that it may not be tolerated (Rubington and Weinberg, 1981:29). In short, moral entrepreneurs must work to bring these individual and collective perceptions into line with their own pessimistic definition.

If rule creators succeed in changing people's perceptions to any significant degree, they may look forward to a change in public policy consistent with their interests. In order to bring about individual and collective "moral conversion," then, awareness must be extended to others. The scope of this effort may vary, but creating the desired moral environment requires it. Another term for this is *legitimacy*: the achievement of a public, legal, and authorized status. In itself, achieving legitimacy is part of the process of constructing an *official* reality—of changing the official or public moral meanings of things and altering the applicable rules.

Legitimacy is a critical need. To be effective in any ultimate sense, rule makers must appeal to people's sense of propriety. When rules are approved by members of the public, they are likely to be obeyed, and those who violate them will likely be sanctioned. This means that people tend to follow both rules they think are proper and rule makers they think have a right to rule. That is, people tend to follow rules and rule makers they think have legitimacy. This tendency has been referred to as the *rule of law*.

The phrase [rule of law] is useful to describe the willingness of a people to accept and order their behavior according to the rules and procedures which are prescribed by political and social institutions . . . and enforced, when necessary, either by

those bodies or by other institutions such as governors, police, and courts. The "rule of law" expresses the idea that people recognize the legitimacy of the law as a means of ordering and controlling the behavior of *all* people in a society, the governors and the governed, the rich and the poor, the contented and the discontented. (National Commission on the Causes and Prevention of Violence, 1970:8–9)

Achieving this legitimacy is part of the enterprise of deviance.

To have rules established that will have legitimacy requires the transformation of *personal troubles* into *public issues*. C. Wright Mills distinguishes between troubles and issues as follows:

Troubles occur within the character of the individual and within the range of his immediate relations with others; they have to do with his self and with those limited areas of social life of which he is directly and personally aware. . . . A trouble is a private matter; values cherished by an individual are felt by him to be threatened. . . . *Issues* have to do with matters that transcend these local environments of the individual and the range of his inner life. They have to do with the institutions of an historical society as a whole, with the ways various milieus overlap and interpenetrate to form the larger structure of social and historical life. An issue is a public matter: some value cherished by publics is felt to be threatened. (1959:8–9)

What is important about the distinction between troubles and issues is how the former is amplified to the point that it comes to be defined as the later. This change in definition comes about largely as a result of moral entrepreneurs' seeking to raise people's levels of consciousness and win adherents to their perspective. This is accomplished by the repeated portrayal (for example, via the media) of disturbing conditions as public events. This was noted by Sutherland (1950a) in his study of the diffusion of sexual psychopath laws. Following the occurrence of a few sex crimes that are disseminated through the mass media, members of the community become agitated; the public interest is aroused. "The attention of the community is focused on sex crimes and people in the most varied situations envisage dangers and see the need of and possibility for their control'' (1950a:144). To facilitate this transformation, horror stories involving one or a relatively small number of people are played upon in the media and used to symbolize the "experience" of the masses. In modern parlance, such cases are "hyped" by the media to the point that what began as a private trouble of great concern to a relatively few individuals and families becomes a matter for public concern (Johnson and Bohon-Bustamente, 1982:11). That is, what began as essentially private matters are rendered "experience" for great numbers of people (Molotch and Lester, 1974:103). By the dissemination of these events and their assigned meanings, social awareness is heightened and moral conversion promoted. Let's explore these elements and their relationship to mass media.

Mass Media and Visibility

To disseminate meanings and effect conversion requires that the moral entrepreneur's views be given a high degree of visibility; claims to legitimacy hang in the balance. Thus, visibility and the opportunity to broadcast the entrepreneur's views is extremely critical. Prior to the advent of modern mass communication techniques, particularly the electronic media, dissemination of a perspective to a nation of millions was a monumental task. This was the case in nineteenth-century China when moral entrepreneurs sought to eliminate the centuries-old custom of binding the feet of young Chinese girls. The goal was to convert an erotic custom long held in esteem to one regarded with disdain and to have rules established banning the practice. One method used to circulate the desired meaning and challenge the customary definitions was poetry and song. These were designed to appeal to the emotions. One popular poem, written by a natural-footed poetess, was as follows:

Three-inch bowed shoes were non-existent in ages before, And Great Kuanyin has two bare feet for one to adore. I don't know when this custom began; It must have been started by a despicable man. (Levy, 1966:68)

In addition, essays and tracts extolling the virtues of the unbound foot, and addressed to the masses, were widely circulated. Adding to the impact of these efforts was the influence of posters, placards, slogans, and critical catchwords. These things were widely distributed. Being easily recalled and repeatable, they became highly popular. Some examples:

One pair of bound feet, but two cisterns of tears.

or,

Once feet are bound so small,
Such effort to do any work at all!

and

Once feet to a sharp point are bound,
The woman's cries to Heaven resound. (Levy, 1966:86)

To be sure, such efforts were centered largely in urban areas and their immediate surroundings—places easily reached by existing means of communication—yet these efforts contributed greatly to the eventual emancipation of the female Chinese foot.

Like their nineteenth-century counterpart, today's moral crusaders also face the task of achieving visibility by bringing their message before large audiences. However, through use of the mass media contemporary moral entrepreneurs are sometimes provided a degree of visibility unavailable to crusaders of earlier times. Daily and Sunday newspaper circulation in the United States runs between 55 and 60 million (*World Almanac and Book of Facts*, 1983:429). Combined paid subscriptions to three leading weekly newsmagazines—wherein the claims of crusaders are very likely to appear—reached almost 10 million in 1981 (*World Almanac and Book of Facts*, 1983:430). Further, as of January 1984, 83.8 million U.S. households were estimated to own at least one television set and 55% of these households had multiple sets, thus making this medium accessible to more than 220 million people (*Nielsen Report*, 1984:3–4). It is in such terms that the word *visibility* must be understood.

The initial problem faced by the moral entrepreneur is whether or not the media will concern themselves with the issue. In this sense it is essential to recall that establishing a public definition of a thing as a problem involves the interaction of various interest groups. Not the least influential of these are the media themselves and the interest groups with whom media officials identify. Thus, access to the media often requires negotiation between media and other interest groups, on the one hand, and the moral entrepreneur, on the other. In deference to their own interests and those of the groups with whom they identify, media officials authoritatively protect access to these many organs. As such they may promote one social reality at the expense of others. All parties to a conflict may regard their positions as valid, but not all views will have equal access to the media. Some may have no access at all; they may be systematically and purposely excluded.

Information supporting the interests of one group may be excluded because it is perceived as incompatible with the interests of media officials and other significant interest groups. Further, for practical reasons associated with the management of the news business, information vital to the goals and interests of crusaders may be seen in opposite terms by newsworkers (Althiede, 1976:112ff). Exclusion, of course, does not mean groups are without recourse. "News" is as important to the newsworkers as it is to the newsmaker (crusader). That fact makes it possible for moral entrepreneurs to use various strategies to gain access to the media. Let's turn to some of these.

Managing the Media. Simple visibility via the media, though necessary, is not sufficient to bring about legitimacy. Equally important is *how* the media present the issue. And, depending on how this is handled, the legitimacy of the entrepreneur's claim may be enhanced or diminished. Of particular relevance is the sequence in which the pros and cons of an issue are presented, the amount of coverage given an issue, and the orientations of those reporting the "facts." By altering these elements, the constructed image of an issue may be changed and the desired definition (meaning) affected. Through variations in visual and auditory stimuli it is possible to increase or decrease the likelihood that a potential audience will perceive a situation as consistent with or contrary

to recognized standards or principles. For example,

Among . . . ways in which the media influence legitimacy is the pointed inclusion or exclusion of certain ostensibly critical pieces of factual information. Thus, if a news article reports that a study has shown deafening noise levels in a residential area near an airport, a reporter, or an editor, may make a point of interviewing a resident who does not mind the noise. Or if the community group has asked an expert to represent them at a hearing, a delegitimizing point may be made merely by giving the information that the expert does not live in the affected area. Legitimacy may be created, in a similar manner, by following up a press conference, e.g., about rising unemployment, with man-on-the-street interviews at the lines in front of a state unemployment compensation office. (Ross and Staines, 1972:22)

Other ways of influencing legitimacy include using emotionally loaded words or, in the case of television, emotionally loaded visual images, and selectively linking a cause with or disassociating it from existing positive social values. This may also be accomplished by using cartoons, especially those dealing with moral issues such as crime. *Polemic cartoons,* those that minimize humor and maximize the message, may be especially useful in that the message, whether direct or indirect, tends to be over simplified, short, pungent, and easily remembered. In some respects, such cartoons are little different from the slogans, catchwords, and posters of an earlier time (Hess and Mariner, 1975).

Douglas and Rasmussen illustrate several of these points in their description of the efforts of a group of nude bathers to resist attempts by beachfront property owners to have their behavior declared unlawful (to delegitimize it). The effort was substantially aided by the nature of television news coverage. "The nude bathers got a great press, especially great TV coverage, partly because they carefully controlled what was presented, . . . and partly because almost all of the newsmen and women who covered the beach were favorable to its existence before and after coverage" (1977:199). These researchers also note that the politically astute moral entrepreneur (which is the role the nude bathers were playing) uses any prior information concerning the ideological predispositions of media personnel:

Most of the feature news coverage of the nude beach can be seen in the major filming and airing done by one of the network affiliates. The . . . reporter in charge of this programming had done a small program on Cliff Beach earlier, so it was known by the beach organizers that he was basically sympathetic or, at least, libertarian about the whole thing. They [the nude bathing advocates] had decided at one of their meetings that they should try to get some more favorable coverage on the beach and that the reporter was the man to approach. They got hold of him and arranged to let him have an exclusive on their side of the story if he'd do it. (Douglas and Rasmussen, 1977:200)

Manipulating the media to further enhance their legitimacy, some members of the nude bathing group (The Committee to Save Eden Beach) collected trash that lay strewn about the beach and arranged it neatly in sacks. When the sacks were filmed by the TV camera operators, the general scene of cleanliness provided an image connoting the nude bathers' ecological awareness and sensitivity to "nature." Though nude bathing is hardly an ecological issue, the two interests were shown to be at least compatible, thereby forestalling opposition from ecology groups.

Skillful manipulation of camera operators also helped the group avoid display of possibly damaging materials: nude males with erections, the sexual parts of voluptuous females, or any of the casual or heavy sex (heterosexual or homosexual) that occasionally occurs on the beaches. On the other hand, film of "a lovely young nude mother with long, flowing blonde hair, bending over her toddler in the shallow water, with the sun a little behind her to produce a sparkling halo effect on film . . . and . . . no pubis shot to get it banned by the censor" (Douglas and Rasmussen, 1977:201) greatly enhanced the image desired by nude bathers; no direct link was made between nude bathing and orgiastic sex, and nudity and motherhood were shown to be quite compatible.

In much the same way, the binding of Chinese girls' feet was linked to select values. Of significance was the effort of the antifootbinding group to define the practice as contrary to the laws of nature as well as a symbol of the oppression and punishment undeservedly heaped upon women. Footbinding was proclaimed to be an evil crippler of women, a condition that intensified the misery of the poor, raised the infanticide rate, made women dependent and reduced their effectiveness as mothers and homemakers, and reduced their intellectual activities (Levy, 1966:77–78). Continued binding of the female foot was also defined as an obstruction to China's entry into the mainstream of world commerce and the modern age. As this economic goal increased in favor, footbinding, symbolic of cultural stagnation, lost favor (Levy, 1966:76–77). Finally, the unbound female foot came to be associated with the liberation of Chinese women in general.

In the case of both nude bathing and footbinding, then, the association of the moral entrepreneur's position or goal with other major values—ecology, motherhood, infanticide, poverty, economic growth, national prestige—of both a positive and negative sort proved critical in the effort to win support of others or to preclude effective opposition.

In addition to aligning their own cause with positive values, moral entrepreneurs try to associate the opposition with negative values. In this way the moral entrepreneur tries to denigrate opponents, and success in this effort ensures at least a relative increase in one's own moral legitimacy. Thus, in the case of nude bathers vs. beachfront property owners, efforts were made to have the property owners defined as people wanting to control public beaches for their private use. Among people living in increasingly densely populated urban areas, such an image can have a negative effect, as it did in this case. So, too, did the image of property owners as reactionaries seeking to repress the enthusiasm and freedom of youth. Skillful use of these themes, together with the nude bathers' upstaging of the property owners by airing their own views earlier and more extensively, so damaged the position of the property owners that they abandoned their effort to present their position through the media, choosing instead to work privately through local governmental functionaries and the courts (Douglas and Rasmussen, 1977:204–205).

A Cautionary Note. Because it is easy to overstate the impact of the mass media on their audience, a word of caution is in order. Rarely do the media convert "puritans" into "hedonists," and rarely are members of an audience transformed in any substantial ideological way by the media. The media by themselves are not able to construct social reality. Nonetheless, the way information is presented, particularly the way the variables mentioned earlier are manipulated, may readily give credibility to one set of meanings at the expense of alternatives. As Shaw (1969:126) notes, in a heterogeneous society, *public* expression of morality on any issue reflects a range of attitudes, and these attitudes have a modality. By careful engineering, media officials may present an issue so as to place it within or beyond the limits of that modality. Thus, Altheide correctly notes that a medium "molds public events" (1976:27). Molding the event (rather than the audience) means that conditions are assigned a definition/meaning consistent with or contrary to the moral entrepreneur's sense of prevailing public morality. In a similar way, while selectively presenting "facts," the media may support or discredit perspectives, ideologies, and behaviors. Further, the simple act of withholding contrary perspectives or information may add to (or detract from) the legitimacy or credibility of publicized meanings. The importance of this effort is seen in that "not only is a symbolic environment created within the society, but personal actions take their referent from that environment. Indeed, the construction of a conceptual reality is also the creation of a social reality of actions and events" (Quinney, 1975:262). Taken together, these matters are all part of what makes deviance an "enterprise."

Obtaining Respectability: Alliances, Testimonials, and Endorsements

To promote their legitimacy, rule creators may use means other than manipulating the media. Of great importance to moral entrepreneurs is their public image. For example, they prefer an image of humanitarianism to one of self-seeking. To increase their acceptability, they may seek prestige and respectability from others who may be enlisted in their cause. Obtaining this respectability serves to (1) enhance the moral stature of the proposed goal of the crusader and (2) further reduces any question of the legitimacy of the crusading group itself. Overall, respectability promotes the goal of moral conversion. We'll explore this issue in detail.

Alliances. One method of achieving prestige and respectability is to "borrow" it from publicly acknowledged moral leaders—for example, the charismatic types. In this respect, moral crusaders often seek to establish alliances or otherwise affiliate themselves with significant persons or groups. Such alliances sometimes result in great promotional benefits, the examples of which are abundant.

Perhaps the most common expression of "borrowing" respectability by affiliation is the use of notables' names on the letterhead stationery of special interest groups. On a more organizationally sophisticated level is the creation of *coalitions,* temporary alliances between groups for the limited purpose of achieving a specific goal. For example, the Religious Coalition for Abortion Rights (RCAR) represents 23 Protestant and Jewish religious groups. Established in 1976, the RCAR is a response to the anti-abortion rights campaign of the National Conference of Catholic Bishops. Members of the RCAR hold the view that the abortion controversy is fueled by religious beliefs, whereas the right of abortion is actuallly a matter of privacy and personal freedom guaranteed by the U.S. Constitution. Operating as a unit, these 23 groups, with support from substantial numbers of their respective memberships, seek a level of legitimacy, respectability, and influence on lawmaking bodies that would be unavailable to them as single entities, and that collectively may be sufficient to counter the influence and authoritative position of the National Conference of Catholic Bishops (*Unitarian Universalist World,* 1976:1–2).

The antifootbinding crusade in nineteenth-century China was substantially aided by the authority and respectability of Christian missionaries who sternly discouraged the practice among their followers, even to the point of accepting only persons with unbound feet as members of the church (Levy, 1966:75). In still another instance, Edwin Sutherland (1950a:142ff) described the association between psychiatrists and groups seeking enactment of sexual psychopath laws. Given their publicly acknowledged expertise and usually unquestioned authority on the "mental pathology" underlying sex crimes, the instrumental role of psychiatrists in that movement is hardly surprising. However, Sutherland notes, too, that passage of these laws is consistent with and promotes the professional interests of psychiatrists. Finally, the benefits of affiliation may be seen in the case of the antismoking crusade. In this instance, the very existence of some groups (for example, Action on Smoking and Health) is alleged to depend on the antismoking activity of several other groups. Among the latter are the American Cancer Society, the American Heart Association, and insurance companies, all of whom maintain quite respectable and legitimate images (Nuehring and Markle, 1974:522). Each of these cases reminds us that creating deviance (like constructing reality in general) is an interactional process, the behavior of the principals being influenced to a large extent by their self-interest.

Testimonials and Endorsements. Moral entrepreneurs may also seek to enhance their image and that of their "cause" by the use of testimonials and endorsements. In Arizona, for example, where copper mining and smelting has been a leading and influential industry, conflict once centered about the ecological consequences of these activities. An innovation in the battle involved the mine association hiring a well-known and highly popular professional athlete to do spot TV ads supporting mining, extolling the industry's contribution to the state (taxes plus primary and secondary payrolls), and praising its costly effort to curb all ecologically questionable practices. The athlete's lack of expertise in mining and ecology was compensated for by his popularity and his posing in the ads as a concerned citizen who was "just trying to get the facts," a position with which many confused but concerned citizens could readily identify. In this way the mine association's goals were pursued and perhaps promoted by, first, the status-conferring function of the media, second, having their activities linked to the economic vitality of the entire state and, finally, the support of esteemed persons in the local area.

In some instances moral entrepreneurs have less need of outside endorsement. This is particularly so when the crusader already has a public image that provides credibility and legitimacy and that may be used to heighten the visibility of the crusade. Such appears to have been the case when Anita Bryant launched her campaign against a Dade County, Florida, ordinance forbidding discrimination against homosexuals in jobs and housing. Miss Bryant's public image, a consequence of her long-term role as a TV personality promoting Florida orange juice and enhanced by her status as a "born-again Christian," undoubtedly gave added impetus to her effort. Not the least consequence of that effort was her ability to attract the attention of national media, and to amplify a local issue, placing it in a more global perspective (Hacker, 1977; *National Observer,* 1977).

Legitimacy and prestige (to say nothing of visibility) may be further enhanced by endorsement of a crusade by public officials. As self-proclaimed defenders of their constituent's views, officials may be expected to be aware of the limits of public morality. Endorsement of a position by officials, then, may be taken as prima facie evidence of its legitimacy. Causes based on contrary views are thereby denied some legitimacy, and the goal of moral conversion is promoted. Efforts by administrators of philanthropic goals to have their programs endorsed by public officials are neither wasted nor accidental.

In addition, endorsement by officials may be expected to promote dissemination via the media and, simultaneously, to limit the opposition's access to the media. According to William Wilde's analysis of news organizations, "News is what officials say and do. The more sensational the more newsworthy. Even . . . outrageous charges go unanalyzed. Unsubstantiated statements go unquestioned. They are given the status of news as the media prints them without further comment or analysis" (Wilde, 1969:186). Furthermore, the public official preempts the opposition by controlling and engineering the flow of information to the media and by making his or her comments appear to be official pronouncements. In this way they overwhelm and delegitimize alternative perspectives. After all, such public figures are among the "officially accredited definers of reality" (Berger and Luckmann, 1967:97). Thus, news is what officials say and do, regardless of how meaningless those words and actions are.

Examples of the ability of public officials to influence the content of, as well as the interpretation placed on, information carried by the media is well documented. For example,

In 1971 President Nixon's bitter anti-busing statement was circulated to millions . . . by newspapers, radio and television. But it went almost unnoticed that the very next day the school superintendent of Harrisburg, Pa. (Dr. D.H. Porter), refuted the Nixon position point by point, in an account of the actual experience of that city.

This was a classic demonstration of the extent to which the American press—print and electronic—merely react to the statements of important officials rather than trying to make an independent judgment on the facts. Mr. Nixon's distortions were trumpeted in headlines, because he is President; the facts put forward by Dr. David H. Porter were ignored, because he was not "newsworthy" enough. (Wicker, 1971)

In 1976, then Secretary of State Henry A. Kissinger seems also to have used his official position to defuse and reduce the impact of the information being revealed by the House Select Committee on Intelligence's investigation of covert aspects of American foreign policy. Among the obstacles Kissinger is alleged to have placed in the path of the Committee was his "leaking" to the press embarrassing stories about the Committee (Latham, 1976:70). By embarrassing the Committee and its Chairman, Congressman Otis Pike, Kissinger caused the Committee's work to become at least as suspect as the very activities it was investigating.

Such efforts by public officials are often aided by the media's use of the tactic of *advocacy journalism*. By this tactic the traditional roles of "critical questioner" and "investigative journalist" are exchanged for that of "advocate." With advocacy journalism comes the tendency for media to boost "good causes" without developing a comparable tendency to attack "bad causes" (Ross and Staines, 1972:24). By definition, this tactic promotes the conclusion that whatever is presented by the media is "good."

Finally, acquiring the support of respected and prestigious figures may enhance the image of the moral entrepreneur's goals by reason of *transfer of authority* (Lowry and Rankin, 1969:254). As a result of this process, ideas achieve increased legitimacy because their author is associated with admired or respected others, such as esteemed professionals, public figures, and the like. Social psychological experiments reveal that attitude change (which is what banning may require) is likely to increase if the communicator of a new idea is identified as a member of a prestigious group; if he or she is, then the entire group is likely to be regarded as in support of the idea (Secord and Backman, 1964:128). Studies also reveal that negatively labeled proposals have less chance of acceptance than those with liked or prestigious labels attached, even when the substance of the proposal is the same (Newcomb, 1950:235–239). Thus, in this country the identification of a proposal as communistic is very likely to bring about its rejection. On the other hand, if the same proposal is defined as being good for the community, its acceptance is more probable.

Myth Making

We have noted that banning involves (1) bringing the views of the moral crusader to the attention of the community, (2) having them endorsed and legitimized by public officials and others in positions of authority and respectability, and (3) avoiding the detractive effort of the opposition. Acceptance of the moralist's view, however, does not depend solely on the appeal of abstract statements and claims. As noted in discussing the media, it is necessary for these views to be made part of the public morality, the morality shared by those to whom the appeal is made. The crusader's position must appear compatible with others' thoughts, feelings, values, interests, and fears. The morality to be created must be woven into the fabric of the reality already possessed by the crusader's listeners. To achieve this unification, moral entrepreneurs may employ myth.

As used here, *myths* refer to elements within the belief system that people share and in terms of which they explain, interpret, and justify the affairs of everyday life (Kasen, 1980:132). Ordinarily, myths contribute to the legitimation of the established institutional order. As such, they are objectivations, part of what was earlier (see Chapter 1) referred to as the symbolic universe (Berger and Luckmann, 1967:92–104).

In addition to explaining elements of the institutional and legitimate order, myths also explain problematic events—the kinds of things that concern moral entrepreneurs. Such myths are often *etiologic;* that is, they deal with the supposed causes of the troubling phenomenon. They may also concern the "evildoer"; myths often portray such persons or groups as people opposed to the legitimate values of the community, as people who seek to undermine the vitality of fundamental moral precepts and institutions. Three such myths are those of white slavery, the dope fiend, and the Mafia.

White Slavery. The term *white slave,* or *white slavery,* derives from the Mann Act (also known as the White Slave Act), which was passed by Congress in 1910 to halt the interstate and foreign transportation of women for immoral purposes—that is, for purposes of prostitution. The Act itself was the culmination of a period of marked public agitation over the immorality of prostitution, particularly the stereotype of prostitution. Evolving out of the literature generated by this public agitation was the myth of white slavery (Reasons, 1970:5).

According to the myth of white slavery "prostitution was . . . a consequence of a class of merchants of flesh who obtained innocent, unsophisticated girls of foreign extraction, often underage, by false pretense, drugs and coercion" (Reasons, 1970:5; Feldman, 1967). In this myth, behaviors and people are explicitly cast in opposition to premarital chastity, the purity of womanhood, and the sancity of home and hearth. The public morality dominant during the late 1890s and early 1900s, reserved its most severe condemnation for anyone believed to systematically violate these values, especially for profit. This myth, generated and spread by countless muckrakers and other moralists who published antiprostitution books and tracts, played an important part in incorporating the aims of reformers into public policy—in linking the "new" and the existing moralities. This was a vital element in a vigorous campaign to eliminate prostitution.

The "Dope Fiend" Mythology. Myth has also been employed in the effort to establish prohibitions against addictive drugs. In this myth, termed the "dope fiend" mythology by Alfred Lindesmith (1940), the alleged deviant is cast as a totally discreditable person whose behavior is without redeeming virtue. Consistent with the stereotype that addicts are criminals independent of narcotic drug law violations, the myth provides materials (anecdotes, stories, and so on) supporting a variety of labels used to refer to addicts: *dope-crazed killer, dope fiend rapist, moral degenerate, thief,* and *liar* are a few such terms. The myth also alleges that addicts have a "positive mania" to convert others to drug addiction. And it points out the insidiousness of drugs. The use of drugs, even of a mild sort, is said to result in an inevitable progression to the use of stronger drugs and that over time there is a need to enlarge the dose gradually. Finally, drug use is hailed as a certain path to moral degeneracy, debauchery, and the like. This supposedly irreversible process has been referred to as "the path to demoralization and despair" (Horton and Leslie, 1965:565; also see Inciardi, 1974).

Many of these same values, supplemented by visual imagery, appeared in motion pictures of the 1930s and 1940s such as "Tell Your Children" (also known as "Reefer Madness"), "Marijuana," and "Assassin of Youth." In the first of these, Bill and his sweetheart Mary, a "model young couple" symbolizing the innocence of high school youth, fall victim to the blandishments of two unscrupulous drug peddlers and the evil effects of marijuana. Under the spell of the drug, the unsuspecting Bill becomes a moral weakling and allows himself to be seduced by the evil addict, Blanche. Mary and her younger brother Jimmy are also caught up in the debauchery; Mary is accidentally shot and killed. As befits peddlers of the "insidious weed," one is killed and the other is judged insane; their female accomplice, Blanche, commits suicide. The once innocent Bill survives, but his life is wrecked. Thus, the various ways in which marijuana destroys the lives of all who have contact with it are graphically illustrated; debauchery, crime, murder, and suicide await the unsuspecting (*Look,* 1938). Today these films are advertised and perceived by the general public as camp art. Interestingly, however, the same message was regarded as objective truth by an earlier generation. Such are the dynamics of social reality.

The values stressed in these films also find expression elsewhere, though perhaps not in so dramatic a fashion. For example, Stuart L. Hills has noted that the Federal Bureau of Narcotics relied on several American values in its effort to secure passage of the Marijuana Tax Act of 1937.

In its publicity campaign, the bureau could appeal to a number of traditional societal values . . . it could emphasize humanitarian values as well as those stressing the importance of self control, by portraying the bureau's efforts as preventing persons from becoming "enslaved" to drugs and protecting them from their own weakness. It could fur-

ther appeal to the values of the "Protestant ethic," which disdains "ecstasy" and pleasure when deliberately sought as ends in themselves rather than as by-products of achievement and work. (Hills, 1971:70)

Using the term *ideology,* Sutherland found similar materials in popular literature being used to support formulation and passage of sexual psychopath laws. Contained in the ideology were several ideas: (1) Women and children were in grave and immediate danger at the hands of "crazed psychopaths"; (2) such offenses were committed most often by "degenerates" and "sex psychopaths" who (3) are unable to control themselves because of their mental condition; (4) this mental state renders them identifiable as potential offenders; (5) nonetheless, these offenders should be punished and never be free to inflict harm on others, (6) at least not until they are fully cured; and (7) the care and treatment of these people should be the concern of psychiatrists, the professionals best equipped to deal with them (1950b:543-544). However, Sutherland contended that, on the basis of evidence, each of these ideas was factually false or questionable.

Myth of the Mafia. A final example of myth is the case of the *Mafia,* a term commonly used to refer to several highly organized "families," largely of Italian-American ancestry, alleged to be responsible for the origin and persistence of such organized unlawful activities as drug trafficking, gambling, prostitution, and labor racketeering, among others (President's Commission on Law Enforcement and Administration of Justice, 1967a and 1967b; Cressey, 1969). Contrary to this view, some scholars allege that evidence substantiating this taken-for-granted, official view is lacking (Smith, 1975 and 1976). A more valid perspective, it is suggested, is the view that the Mafia is a social construction spawned over a period of some 80 years by several interest groups operating as moral entrepreneurs. Uppermost among these is the Federal Narcotics Bureau which, after World War II, allegedly needed such a "threat" to the national well-being to avoid being eclipsed in status and organizational advantage by the FBI's efforts at that time to combat what was held to be an internal Communist conspiracy. Equally, if not more, important was the Federal Narcotics Bureau's need to explain its inability to stem the flow of illegal narcotics into the country (Smith, 1976:85). Both these needs were somewhat satisfied by rekindling a then-dormant idea that such crimes in this country were the work of an "alien conspiracy." This is a theme that, in one form or another, had been (and continues to be) used to account for otherwise unexplained events perceived to be threatening to the social stability of the nation and to a variety of publicly legitimate values and interests (note the element of alien conspiracy also in the myth of white slavery).

Ultimately supported by the news media and the entertainment industry (movies, television, and literature), as well as being validated by several congressional investigating committees, the spectacular testimony of Joseph Valachi in 1963, and the prestigious President's Commission on Law Enforcement and the Administration of Justice in 1967, the idea of the Mafia has now become thoroughly reified in the American consciousness. As a consequence

it is no longer possible to say with certainty that there is or is not an organization called Mafia. . . . After a quarter of a century of having been labeled as mafiosi, a sense of group identification and acceptance of the label would have occurred to a number of Italian-Americans even if there had been no basis for it previously. . . . One could argue, then, that if there was a Mafia today, it would owe its existence to the efforts of the Federal Narcotics Bureau and their legal and commercial disciples. (Smith, 1976:86)

Myth vs. Truth. Sutherland's contention concerning the falsity of ideas about sex offenders and Smith's contentions concerning the Mafia as a social construction raise a critical issue concerning ideology and myth. The content of these myths is often attacked on the grounds that they have limited validity or that they distort reality (viewed as an objective condition). For example, there likely are cases wherein unsuspecting women have been drawn into prostitution by deception, and cases of persons becoming involved in systematic law violations after becoming addicted to drugs. That is, there are cases that conform to and afford some validation of select elements of these myths. But so, too, can we find cases reflecting a quite different set of conditions. Some women are recruited to prostitution on wholly rational (for example, economic) grounds (Fairfield, 1959). Such was the case of a university student who entered prostitution quite voluntarily. For her, the income earned by prostitution far exceeded what she could earn otherwise and made the difference between a student life free of financial worries and one that was economically marginal (Williams, 1974:1).

Turning to the "dope fiend" mythology, qualified observers note that a substantial number of practicing physicians are drug addicts (Hessler, 1974:146–147). In 1967 the Federal Bureau of Narcotics estimated the incidence of addiction among U.S. physicians at about 1 in every 867 doctors but only 1 in every 3228 for the general population (*American Druggist,* 1968). Others have placed the rate of physician addiction as high as 2.5 percent (Hessler, 1974:147). Despite this, it is maintained, most addicted physicians fulfill their professional and community obligations without undue difficulty. Indeed, in that regard, some researchers have reported addict physicians to be more successful than the average nonaddict physician (Winick, 1964:264; Hessler, 1974:150).

Finally, there is no question that some persons involved in drug trafficking and other forms of syndicated crime are of Italian-American ancestry. Likewise, there is no question of the existence of a phenomenon called *mafia*—that is, the use of unauthorized violence as a means of social control—and the existence of persons called *mafiosi,* who engage in such violence, in Sicily where many American Mafia members are said to have their roots (Blok, 1974:xiv). However, it is a quantum leap from that acknowledgement to the contention that an international conspiracy is responsible for major crime in the United States and that control over such criminality is frustrated by this alien conspiracy and especially by the code of silence, *omerta,* by which its members are bound.

Resolution of what appear to be contradictions between myth and fact is often of concern to those who seek an objective truth. However, from the perspective of the social definition model, these efforts to resolve "contradictions" are somewhat misleading in that they obscure the point that myths and the specific charges they contain are dimensions of meaning. What is regarded as "invalid" and a "distortion of reality" by one group is likely to be an expression of another group's sense of reality. What is needed is not the substitution of one construction of reality for another; that is, we don't need the social scientist's construction of reality, for example, replacing that of the crusader. Rather, as David Matza (1969) states, it is incumbent on students of society to take an "appreciational" stance. This means one must be sensitive to the experience and values of those involved in the situation, the moral crusader as well as others. This calls for a faithful rendering of the phenomenon. To "appreciate" in this sense does not require the social scientist to agree with any particular perspective, but to understand, "to comprehend and to illuminate the subject's view and to interpret the world *as it appears to him*" (Matza, 1969:25).

An appreciational perspective helps us to see that notions of "validity" and "distortion" have little to do with the utility of these myths. In this regard, it is important to recall that the deviance process involves defining behavior and actors as discreditable. The aim is to incriminate, to discredit, to control, and to stigmatize, perhaps for symbolic reasons or perhaps to legitimize "treatment" of the alleged deviant. At the banning stage of the process, efforts to validate factually the characterizations of the deviant actor and his or her behavior are unnecessary. If any justification for incrimination is needed, it is provided by the *meaning attributed to the rule breaker's behavior.* The perceived immorality of the behavior leads one to define the actor as a discreditable person. As we shall note later, to engage in deviance means one is devious; that is, one's

behavior justifies the assigning of appropriate character traits to the actor (Matza, 1969:157). The assigned characterizations serve also to justify existing (read: "appropriate") treatment. In other words, these myths justify (1) the proposed moral environment, (2) the distribution of authority, (3) the proposed disposition of the deviant, and (4) the moral superiority of the nondeviant (crusader). In this regard, myths serve the same symbolic purpose as rules in general.

One final example of this is found in the media, wherein images are arranged and presented so as to "fit" an acceptable world view and a prior existing set of meanings (social reality). Decades ago Berelson and Salter (1946) noted the consistent distinction in characterization between fictional heroes and villains. Heroes were consistently white, Anglo-Saxon, Protestant types, while villians, fools, and other denigrative roles were played by minority group members and foreigners. Such imagery fits well in a world view in which virtue is held to be the exclusive property of the politically dominant group, while all other groups are defined as subordinate. Such imagery neatly divides the world into "good guys" and "bad guys." Further, such images and myths are constructed to support the claim that "what is is right," or to otherwise support the claim of the moral entrepreneur. To the degree that the validity of these myths and images is taken for granted and acted upon, our public life is shaped by them. Myths *may* therefore be self-validating. They serve to legitimate the institutional activities called for by the moral entrepreneur. They are another important part of the symbolic universe.

These images and meanings are not born full-blown. Rather, they are the consequence of the accumulation of countless individual utterances, definitions, and meanings, each of which is originally private and subjective and many of which may have been purposive misrepresentations and distortions (Inciardi, 1978:14). Rather than being a consciously sought goal, the myth is constructed of highly specific meanings reflecting the perceptions and interpretations of people who are strategically located (such as those who have access to the media) so as to influence "official" reality.[3] This accumulation results in a kind of "semantic amalgamation," whereby utterances that bear reasonable similarity are lumped together. By stages, people create subuniverses of meaning (Berger and Luckmann, 1967:85ff), whose elements (myths) take on the autonomous character of the larger bodies of meaning. As a result of increasing abstraction and autonomy, the "knowledge" involved—for example, that whoring is never voluntary, that addiction to drugs precludes legitimate role play, or that the Mafia survives on the basis of a code of silence called "omerta" (Bell, 1962:138-141; Anderson 1968:369ff)—becomes separated from the social conditions out of which it develops. This knowledge takes on a "life of its own" and very often is regarded as an accurate, valid reflection of "what's out there." It is reified, becoming objective and independent of individual consciousness. As noted earlier, the meaning and definitions we attach to things tend to move from a subjective to an objective status. Myth making reflects this tendency.

Power

A crucial element in the banning process is power. As noted earlier, deviance is indissolubly bound to politics. That is, deviance entails making and enforcing public policy. In an attempt to influence the content of public policy, moral entrepreneurs seek to translate their values and interests into rules (laws) that may be applied to the population at large. However, having one's definition of reality declared "official" does not occur without power, particularly the power to influence the legal (rule-

making) process. An appreciation of this aspect of banning calls for an examination of the role of power and of the authority of the state in the rule-making enterprise.[4]

Attempts to control the behavior of others are widespread in any society. Most of this effort is confined to informal techniques of control: gossip, ridicule, ostracism, and various corporal punishments. These techniques have proven highly effective under specific circumstances, such as in a small, homogeneous community, neighborhood, or family setting where primary-group relationships prevail. But in a highly impersonal, urban society, where members' contacts are limited in time and lack depth, and where pluralism prevails, the informal and individualized application of labels and other control techniques is not generally effective in curbing offensive behavior. For that reason, to be effective, moral crusaders must ultimately have recourse to the state, where the "signification of deviance becomes a specialized and protected function. . . . The main substance of that state function is the authorized ordaining of activities and persons as deviant, thus making them suitable objects of surveillance and control" (Matza, 1969:145). Access to this state apparatus may be achieved either by direct exercise of power by the moral entrepreneur or on the basis of one's ability to influence those who do have power—influence them to act in accord with the crusader's goals. Power, then, requires careful attention.

Power, Law, and Deviance. The final transformation of values and interests into rules, and their enforcement and administration, is the responsibility of public officials, including police, prosecuting attorneys, court judges, and legislators, as well as various standing and ad hoc administrative agencies such as the Federal Communications Commission, the Securities

---

[3]As a case in point, it is now conceded that the events comprising what is known as Watergate were not unique in American political life. What led to the *public event* known as Watergate, including the meanings assigned to its components, was the work of the media. Thus, in the hands of several media personalities, conceptually discrete events were linked and given the name "Watergate." As Altheide has noted, "Nixon fell from power because the news perspective transformed the series of events known as Watergate into a whole, which was then used as evidence of corruption and immorality" (Altheide, 1976:159).

[4]We must distinguish between *power* and *authority*, the latter being a publicly acknowledged *right* to assert control over others. Authority is what distinguishes the passage of prohibition laws by a legislative assembly from the tavern-busting behavior of a Carry Nation.

Exchange Commission, and the Federal Aeronautics Administration. These agencies engage in the deviance-making enterprise when they regulate some specialized activity, when they decide which proscribed acts shall be labeled deviant, and when they decide how zealously rules will be enforced and to which groups the rules will apply. Variation in these activities—in the formulation, enforcement, and administration of law—has led to law being defined as "an instrument for furthering the interests of certain groups within society" (Shaskolsky, 1973:295).

Contrary to the idea that law is a human expression of some divine command or that law serves the purposes of an abstraction like "justice," law is an expression of the values and interests of groups able to influence the actions of the legal role players mentioned. In a politically dynamic, pluralistic society such as ours, the class, ethnic, occupational, cultural, or other interest groups that win the day in the political marketplace are those with the greatest power. In short, banning behavior is a result of the interaction between legal functionaries and the representatives of interests, with power being the critical variable (Piven, 1981:501).

Working with these same factors, Richard Quinney (1969) formulated an interest theory of law consisting of four propositions. First, Quinney defined law as the "creation and interpretation of specialized rules in a politically organized society [the state]" (1969:26). By this definition, law is a "way of doing something," it is a kind of action (Quinney 1970b:36–37). Law is not simply a means of social control. And it is not limited to an abstract body of rules contained in statute books. Rather, *law is a process*. It is an integral part of society in that it arises from the dynamic character of society, in which interest groups compete and conflict with one another for public and official favor. Likewise, once created, law influences these interactions; it is a factor that groups must consider when dealing with one another. Law provides at least the rough boundaries of legitimate group interaction. Most important,

law is one of the methods in which *public policy* is formulated and administered for governing the lives and activities of the inhabitants of the state. As an act of politics, law does not represent the norms and values of all persons in the society. Legal decisions, rather, incorporate the interests of only some persons. Whenever a law is created or interpreted, the values of some are necessarily assured and the values of others are either ignored or negated. (Quinney 1969:27)

The making and interpreting of laws are acts of politics. This is the *politicality of law*.

Second, Quinney, noted that "politically organized society is based on an interest structure" (1969:27). By this he meant that the state (a politically organized society) is influenced by the interests of certain constituent groups—specifically, those who are equipped to command. This led to his third proposition: "The interest structure of politically organized society is characterized by unequal distribution of power and by conflict" (Quinney, 1969:28). This means that not all segments of society are equally well situated or equipped to command—to have their interests incorporated into public policy. They do not all have equal amounts of or access to power. Since interest groups have differing amounts of power and conflict with one another, power and conflict become critical factors in the politics of deviance. It is out of the interplay of such differentially situated and equipped groups that public policy emerges. Quinney's fourth proposition is that "law is formulated and administered within the interest structure of a politically organized society" (1969:29). This proposition follows from the fact that it is the groups with the greatest power that are able to influence policy makers. We thus come full circle: Law is a way of doing something—it is a way of controlling segments of the society who threaten dominant interest groups. In answer to the question "Which groups have the ability to create deviance?" one is inclined to answer "Those with the clout!"

The idea that law is a means of control deserves further comment. As used here, "control" refers not only to the direct control of some groups by others, as, for example, by exerting coercive force upon people and the exercise of violence. "Law as control" also refers to the legitimizing capacity of the law, a position consistent with our earlier distinction between the instrumental and symbolic purpose of law. As Turk (1976:281) notes, "Those definitions . . . given legal expression or approval are thereby given the support of what is not only one of the most prestigious cultural structures, but also that structure most directly supported by the apparatus of political control." In short, by having power, groups are better able to employ the dignity of law to legitimize their interests at the expense of others.

Defining Power. Given these considerations and the model of society within which we are working, how may we define *power?* Basically, power is "The production of intended effects by some men on other men" (Wrong, 1968:676). Closely related to force, prestige, influence, and similar concepts, *power* is a general term referring to a variety of means whereby people seek to control the behavior of others. Consistent with our dynamic model of society, the distribution among groups of the ability to control others is variable and ever changing. That is, power does not rest exclusively in the hands of some and not at all in others. *Power is bilateral or multilateral and power relations are asymmetrical* (Wrong, 1968:673; 1979:chapter 1). That is, at any instant in time several groups and/or individuals may be classified as power holders or power subjects. Thus, in the context of everyday life, such designations as "power holder" and "power subject" may distort actual conditions. Everyday life reveals that in specific instances and areas of interaction power is relative, a matter of degree rather than an "all or nothing" condition. Consequently, in the course of enduring social relations and interaction, superordinate and subordinate positions are far from permanent. Those who wield power in one situated activity (or *scope*) or at one time period may be quite subordinate in other scopes or at other times. For example, labor unions control hiring while employers control the place and time of work. In short, the model employed here is

one of *intercursive power.* "Intercursive power exists where the power of each party in a relationship is countervailed by that of the other, with procedures for bargaining or joint decision making governing their relations when matters affecting the goals and interests of both are involved" (Wrong, 1968:674).

That power is bilateral/multilateral and asymmetrical is revealed in Pamela Roby's (1969) investigation of the effort to revise the New York State Penal Law on prostitution. To accomplish this task the legislature's Penal Law and Criminal Code Revision Committee labored for four years to produce a workable statute. Subsequently, public hearings were held concerning the Committee's proposed revisions. Testimony during the hearings and the outcome of the hearings make it apparent that several individuals and interest groups sought to influence the writing and enforcement of this law. Included among them were the following: the Chief Magistrate of New York City, who had long been concerned over the issue of prostitution and the law; the American Social Health Association, whose interest stemmed from its concern over controlling venereal disease; representatives of hotels and other businesses whose profits were felt to be influenced by enforcement policy; the New York Commission on the United Nations Secretariat, which was concerned about foreign diplomats and businessmen being arrested as patrons of prostitutes; civil liberties groups who were concerned that the revised statutes and enforcement practices could infringe the civil liberties of prostitutes, patrons, or others; the mayor, who wished to relieve the pressure he was receiving from several discontented groups in New York City; and the police department, which wanted the revised statute to be so worded as to make their enforcement task easier (Roby, 1969:104–107). To be sure, not all these persons and groups were equally influential in having their interests reflected in the law. However, their variable influence is consistent with the power model we have adopted—that is, one in which groups exert limited rather than comprehensive influence. Moreover, revealing a multilateral tendency, some sections of the revised law reflected the interests of some groups, while other sections bore the stamp of other groups, and no single group exerted its power over all others. Influence was negotiated in an ongoing series of interacts. Taken together, these several features are consistent with an intercursive power model.

Placed in the perspective of "deviance as politics," then, power is a vital element in the struggle (conflict) among interest groups. It is a struggle that involves simultaneous movements to impose restraints, on the one hand, and to limit, resist, or escape control, on the other.

These remarks concerning power prompt additional questions: What is the basis of the moral crusaders' power? How do they wield power? What tactics do they employ? Let's turn to these questions.

Bases of Power. Becker (1973:149) notes that rule-creating groups derive power from (1) the legitimacy of their moral position and (2) the generally superior socioeconomic position of their membership. Regarding the first of these, a certain degree of power stems from the fact that the moral entrepreneur pursues ends that many people are reluctant to oppose publicly. To do so, it is feared, would result in their being publicly discredited as immoral. As every politician knows, it pays to stand four-square for "motherhood and apple pie." The reverse of this principle is that public figures, especially officials, do not ordinarily take a stand in support of morally questionable behaviors—even when they are convinced of the "victimless" nature of these behaviors and the pointlessness of legal proscription. And, if asked, the chances are great that public figures will lend at least minimal support to movements to eradicate publicly discreditable behaviors. (It is a virtual certainty that discredited behavior will be opposed.) A case in point was the effort of a city council member to bring about more vigorous enforcement of anti-prostitution ordinances in her city. Publicly, this council member received little support (largely, one suspects, because the buildings housing the brothels were owned by and pro-

vided a handsome income for wealthy and influential people in the town). Privately, she was criticized for stirring up an issue that had lain dormant for years and about which the public seemed unconcerned. Frustrated beyond endurance, the woman finally resorted to confronting her foot-dragging colleagues on the street and elsewhere announcing she was establishing a committee to legalize prostitution and intended to nominate them for membership. Needless to say, among the city council members private criticism diminished and public support for the original proposal increased.

Similarly, members of the "smut detail" of a southwestern city police department publicly called on all state legislators to spend one full day viewing pornographic movies and magazines. Said one officer, "Without the legislators having first-hand knowledge of the type of filth being peddled in our communities, it is difficult to convince many of them of the need for stronger laws and penalties in this area" (Schwartz, 1976:1). For their part, members of the legislature declined the invitation. Nonetheless, this was an astute move by police. What legislator, having been exposed to pornography in this way, could then fail to support such restrictive legislation? In short, exposing a legislator to pornographic material under these publicized circumstances would be almost certain to secure his or her support for controlling legislation.

The point is that the goals of moral crusaders are presented so as to appear consistent with the public morality to which all "right-minded" people are expected to subscribe. This is a consequence of the legitimacy of that version of morality. Privately, the same people who support that public morality may behave in a markedly different way, as, for example, when a safecracker was contacted by a minister offering to provide the combination to his church's safe (which contained a sizable portion of the proceeds of a successful fundraising effort) if the safecracker would agree to split the loot with him. Thus, while public and private morality may sometimes differ radically, the public moral position of the moral entrepreneur is often (if not always) unassailable. This forestalls public opposition and promotes public support.

The second source of power Becker mentions is the superior socioeconomic position occupied by many crusaders and their followers. As noted earlier, a number of humanitarian reform movements are conducted by middle- and upper-class persons ostensibly for the benefit of the poorer classes. Their humanitarian quality and the fact that upper-class people are recruited to lend their names to the crusade (how could they refuse?) lead to a kind of "halo effect." The use of testimonials, mentioned earlier, is an illustration of this. Testimonial support is often necessary to offset the inherent limitations of having one's moral position supported only by obscure or unknown persons. In circular fashion then, unassailability of the crusader's perspective promotes its support by significant public figures, while support by significant public figures contributes to its unassailability.

Wielding Power. Given the factors on which power rests, moral entrepreneurial groups may pursue their goals in a variety of ways. Operating as *pressure groups,* these entities have been found to use any means that will maximize goal achievement and minimize costs (Turner, 1958). One way of achieving the desired goal is to establish a formal group and work to expand membership in order to increase the group's political strength. As group membership increases so, too, does the probability that members will engage in direct political activity: letter writing, soliciting funds (with which to engage in costly advertising or launch an expensive media blitz), applying direct pressure on public figures, seeking to influence the media, phone campaigns, and so on. The core leadership of interest groups finds it easier, of course, to enlist members in these activities if the leadership's legitimacy and integrity have been secured by means discussed earlier.

Another tactic used by interest groups is to establish *coalitions*—that is, formal or informal, covert or overt cooperative relations with other groups for limited periods of time and for the pursuit of limited goals. To the degree that they do not compromise the discrete interests of either group (Carmichael and Hamilton, 1967:58ff), these affiliations may be mutually advantageous. Thus, legislation proposed by one group may be seen to have advantages for another group, leading to the latter's support of the proposal.

Examples of coalitions among interest groups seeking change in the "moral climate" are abundant. Among black civil rights groups, coalitions have been established between militants and moderates, as well as between representatives of religious, labor, and libertarian groups (Bennett, 1965:162). In the early 1970s it appeared there would emerge a strong coalition among the gay liberation movement, Third World freedom groups, women's liberation groups, and black liberation groups (Humphreys, 1972:161). The group In God We Trust, Inc., mentioned earlier, is a coalition whose goal it is to rid San Francisco of homosexuals. As might be suspected from its fundamentalistic tone, this organization represents a coalition of fundamentalist church groups (*Arizona Republic,* 1981b). A last example is the coalition of 17 Protestant denominations and 200 Roman Catholic orders, called the Interfaith Center on Corporate Responsibility, that "will use church stockholdings to pressure utility companies to stop funding a $20 million nuclear-industry advertising campaign" (*Arizona Republic,* 1984c).

Unlike these examples, some coalitions are covert and their activities legally questionable. Such was the case regarding the alleged coalition between the Roman Catholic Church and the New York State Right to Life Committee (NYSRTL), groups well known for their mutual opposition to liberalizing abortion law. In this case the Roman Catholic Church, like all tax-exempt, tax-deductible organizations, is forbidden by the U.S. Internal Revenue Code from engaging in any political campaign on behalf of any candidate for public office. The same code also places restrictions on the political activity of the NYSRTL, itself a tax-exempt body. Contrary to these restrictions, it was alleged, the "NYSRTL, with fund raising assistance from the church, . . . directly intervened in scores of New York political races, both local and statewide" (Norton and Stokes,

1977:12). Not the least of the charges against the church was its alleged collection and contribution of $155,000 toward the election of James Buckley to the U.S. Senate.

The contribution an organization may make to a moral crusade may not always involve direct or material support; sometimes it may be quite indirect—perhaps a consequence of the group's philosophical and ideological positions. An example of this occurred when the Roman Catholic Bishop of the diocese of San Diego, California, issued an order denying elected lay church offices and sacraments to any member of the National Organization for Women or of any pro-abortion group (*Arizona Republic*, 1975). By this order, the church not only denigrated one group and perspective, but implicitly gave its approval to its opposite. In still other cases, coalitions are agreed to by support groups simply for the supposed utility (for example, of improving the organization's image) of affiliating with a publicly unassailable proposal. Thus, police agencies have commonly enlisted in the crusade against child abuse by affiliating with child-saving organizations (Hazlett, 1976).

In addition, interest groups are known to focus attention directly on legislators in an effort to promote their own and frustrate other's attempts to shape public policy. Highly trained professional lobbyists, equipped with secretarial services, research personnel, and press agents are readily available in every capital city in the nation to testify before legislative committees or represent their client's interests whenever possible. Not the least influential aspect of the lobbyists' job is to impress on legislators their client's ability to reward or punish the legislator and so help or hinder his or her career (Turner, 1958:66). For example, one of the best-known lobbies in the nation is the National Rifle Association (NRA). Operating with a budget of $10 million annually and a membership of about one million, the NRA has thus far been able to successfully blunt any effort to pass national gun control legislation calling for licensing and registration of guns or their owners. On the list of NRA victims is the influential National Council on Crime and Delinquency and the late Senator Thomas

Dodd, who was defeated for reelection in 1970, in part, because of NRA opposition (Halverson, 1975:18).

In another example, it is alleged that a U.S. Senate resolution calling for a full-scale public investigation of the disappearance of James R. Hoffa in 1975 was effectively stalled because of "high-pressure lobbying" by officials of the Teamsters union. "The day after the resolution was introduced . . . Mr. [Frank E.] Fitzsimmons [Teamster president] sent telegrams to every member of the Senate urging 'opposition to this resolution because the present law contains ample means for protecting working people' " (Frutig, 1975:50). Members of Congress, as well as Justice and Labor Department officials were contacted in a similar manner to get them to stop "harrassing the union."

An appreciation of the extent of the pressure placed on legislators by lobbyists and others representing special interests may be seen in the report by Common Cause that the 80 freshmen congressional representatives elected to the U.S House of Representatives in 1982 received a total of $7.4 million during the 1982 campaign. This amounts to a contribution of $92,500 per representative. Added to that sum are monies made available to these officials by political action groups and others following their election. Inclusion of such funds raises this average to $111,250 for the campaign period and the first six months they were in office (*Arizona Republic*, 1983d).

In addition to the legislature, lobbyists also seek to influence the executive and judicial branches of government. Thus, pressure is directed at the president and governors as well as the heads of agencies and cabinet officers who regulate and rule on the basis of executive authority. For example, in 1982 President Reagan was urged by the National Federation for Decency (a federation of religious, political, business, and educational people) to press for enforcement of obscenity laws and to establish a Pornography Awareness Week (*Arizona Republic*, 1982d). Similarly, environmentalist groups and representatives of extractive industries (Sierra Club, Friends of the Earth, the mining and forestry industries) pursued their respective interests when they sought to influence the president in his choice of a successor to Secretary of the Interior Rogers C.B. Morton. And in 1941, famed black leader A. Philip Randolph, on the basis of his threat of a march on Washington by 10,000 disgruntled unemployed black workers, was instrumental in bringing about President Franklin Roosevelt's issuance of Executive Order No. 8802, which established the wartime Fair Employment Committe, a forerunner to the Fair Employment Practices Committee (Bennett, 1965: chapter III).

Efforts to exert pressure and influence decisions of the judiciary tend to be less blatant than those on the legislative and executive branches. Yet no astute moral entrepreneur would ignore the fact that policy formulation involves all branches and levels of government. In the case of courts, then, the cause of the moral entrepreneur often calls for initiating litigation. The importance of this effort is reflected in the fact that several national organizations maintain permanent legal staffs whose function includes becoming directly involved in *test cases,* court cases in which the decision is likely to influence or control the decision of future cases resting on similar points of law (Vose, 1958:20ff). The National Association for the Advancement of Colored People, the American Liberty League, the National Consumers League, and the American Civil Liberties Union are just a few of the groups involved in such efforts.

Beyond the use of these socially approved methods, powerful interest groups in our society have always sought to compromise the integrity of the courts. As Charles R. Ashman (1973) has noted, some of our judges are the "finest that money can buy." To the extent that deviance involves moral and legal issues frequently resolved in the courts, it should be no surprise that judges historically have been targets for those wishing to control the outcome of criminal and civil cases at both the trial court and appellate court levels (Krisberg, 1975:35ff). For example, in 1971, U.S. Court of Appeals Justice (and former governor of Illinois) Otto Kerner was indicted by a federal grand jury for "accepting bribes—purchasing race track stock at virtually giveaway prices

[buying at 40 cents and selling ten months later at $2 per share—a 500 percent increase] in exchange for seeing that certain race track owners received favorable treatment in the assignment of racing dates" (Ashman, 1973:203). In a somewhat more complex case, Chief Justice Roy J. Solfisburg, Jr., and Justice Ray I. Klingbiel, both of the Illinois Supreme Court, resigned their positions because of the pressure of investigations into some questionable behavior on their part. It was alleged that these justices were "paid off" for having approved dismissal of an indictment (on a technicality) against Theodore Isaacs, an organizer of the Civic Center Bank and Trust Company of Chicago. Isaacs was charged with collusion and conspiracy in the handling of state contracts. For their approval of the motion for dismissal of the indictment, it is alleged, Justices Solfisburg and Klingbiel were offered stock in the Civic Center Bank at below market price and were given "gift" certificates of stock in the Civic Center Bank. These transactions occurred after oral arguments were heard but before Isaacs' indictment was dismissed. The case was terminated upon the resignation (with full pension) of these justices (Ashman, 1973:195ff).

Such tactics are undoubtedly employed by a large number of organizations in this country and have become a standard feature of the American political scene. In utilizing these tactics, those who share the dominant symbols of wealth, property, status, and the like have an obvious advantage (Gable, 1958). But what of groups for whom these indices of power are unavailable and who may embrace a different sense of reality? Given a bilateral and intercursive power model, what can be said of the power-wielding tactics of the "have nots"?

One of the most noted orchestrators and solidifiers of latent influence among less privileged groups in this country was Saul Alinsky. What Alinsky lacked in polish he made up for in effectiveness; where others sought for style and sophistication, Alinsky focused on the pragmatic. As such, he once listed 13 principles that organizations, even tiny ones, could use in formulating operational tactics to influence private and public policy makers. In listing these principles, Alinsky notes that money and people have traditionally been the sources of power. Lacking the former, he maintained, the poor had to use their numbers—flesh and blood—to achieve their goals. His suggestions reflect this point.

1. Power is not only what you have but what the enemy thinks you have.
2. Never go outside the experience of your people.
3. Wherever possible go outside the experience of the enemy.
4. Make the enemy live up to their own book of rules.
5. Ridicule is man's most potent weapon.
6. A good tactic is one that your people enjoy.
7. A tactic that drags on too long becomes a drag.
8. Keep the pressure on.
9. The threat is usually more terrifying than the thing itself.
10. The major premise for tactics is the development of operations that will maintain a constant pressure upon the opposition.
11. If you push a negative hard and deep enough it will break through into its counterside.
12. The price of a successful attack is a constructive alternative.
13. Pick the target, freeze it, personalize it, and polarize it (Alinsky, 1972:127–130).

This is not the place to discuss the efficacy of Alinsky's principles. Suffice it to say that their use helped make it possible for the black minority of Rochester, New York, to secure concessions from Eastman Kodak of that city, and for the Woodlawn Organization of Chicago to force municipal authorities to support programs beneficial to its ghetto residents—that is, to serve black interests (Alinsky, 1972:140–144).

In summary, then, a wide variety of tactics are employed by interest groups wielding power. No one knows precisely how effective these tactics and principles are since few researchers have directly addressed the question of how much influence pressure groups actually exert on rule-making bodies. One might guess, however, that the continued use of these tactics is the best possible evidence of their effectiveness. On that basis we conclude that power is indeed bilateral and intercursive.

Summary

In this chapter we focused attention on the process of banning, whereby behavior is officially defined as evil, bad, immoral, and wrong, and is proscribed. This process is part of the larger deviance-construction enterprise and involves the work of those moral entrepreneurs called rule creators; these are groups of persons that have common interests and that are organized to have their interests translated into public policy. Another variety of moral entrepreneur is one who defends the existing network of rules rather than seeking to create new rules. Overall, the interests pursued by these groups and persons may be narrow or broad, humanitarian or self-serving, and may have sacred or secular inspiration. The action of the moral entrepreneur may be a response to real or anticipated threats to the group's interests. In either event, the effort to ban reflects the intention to impose meaning on conditions in the world.

The banning process has been examined in terms of its several elements. Among these is "awareness," defined as the perception by "some person or group of an objective set of conditions as problematic." A second element is moral conversion, during which an effort is made to convert what is a personal trouble into a public issue. This transformation entails the dissemination of meanings and their acceptance by others as plausible and legitimate. Meanings that are initially private and subjective are transformed into public and objective beliefs. Achieving this transformation calls for making the entrepreneur's meanings visible. To achieve widespread visibility in our society necessitates use of the mass media. Access to the media, however, is far from universal, and the visibility it affords must be engineered by a variety of techniques.

Moral conversion and legitimacy are influenced by other factors as well. Included are the prestige and respectability that may be acquired when the moral entrepreneur selectively identifies with publicly important persons or groups. Testimonials and endorsements, to say nothing of organizational alliances, are seen to promote the cause of the moral crusader.

Out of these efforts there may emerge an image or set of meanings regarding the problematic event. Called myths, these meanings seek to harmonize the claims of the moral crusader with the legitimate dominant values of the community. Simultaneously, the troubling behavior is displayed as running counter to dominant norms, values, and interests.

In modern society, the conversion of any given set of beliefs into public law—thereby to control people against their will—calls for the exercise of power. Because the impersonal and pluralistic nature of our society prevents effective use of informal social control techniques, the moral entrepreneur must rely on the state, whose function it is to designate activities and persons as deviant. Access to state functionaries varies, as do the principles and tactics used by moral entrepreneurs to influence the actions of these state functionaries. The successful outcome of such effort is that public policy is shaped by interest groups. The law is shown to be a means whereby the interests of some groups may be secured at the expense of others. In the final analysis "the chance that a group will get community support for its definition of . . . deviance depends on its relative power position. The greater the group's size, resources, efficiency, unity, articulateness, prestige, coordination with other groups, and access to the mass media and to decision makers, the more likely it is to get its preferred norms legitimated" (Davis, 1976:54). Lastly, the public meanings of allegedly deviant behaviors may be seen to be those shared by select segments of society.

Moral meaning, then, is negotiable and problematic, part of our socially constructed reality. It is expressed in the public rules intended to guide our lives. Expressing values and interests as rules is the "creation," the "new morality," of which we spoke at the beginning of this chapter.

5 Creating Deviants

Introduction

In Chapter 4 we noted that the deviance process consists of several phases, and we talked about one of these: banning. In this chapter we examine the second phase: how some rule breakers come to be defined, classified, and dealt with as deviants—that is, how deviants are "created." But first, a few preliminary considerations must be introduced.

First, we consider how an "innocent" actor assumes the status of deviant. Examination of the facts of everyday life reveals the need to distinguish between those who break rules and those who get tagged as deviant. By no means are they the same; indeed, the bulk of those who break formal or informal rules are never confronted or charged with violations. Essentially, then, we are concerned with a relatively small segment of the rule-breaking population. Nonetheless, this is an important segment, as many who occupy the status of deviant will likely attest. The importance of understanding this phase of the deviance process, then, is not a matter of numbers; rather, its importance lies in the changes in the quality of people's lives that may result from being so labeled. The importance of this will become clearer as our analysis proceeds.

Second, in shifting our attention from making and breaking rules to assigning people to the status of deviant, it is necessary to call attention to the difference between "simultaneous" and "sequential" approaches to studying deviance. Becker suggests that students of deviance have most often employed a *simultaneous model,* one that assumes that all the factors producing deviance (that is, its causes) are operative at the same time and call for "variable analysis." *Sequential models,* on the other hand, rest on the idea that "all causes do not op-

erate at the same time, . . . that patterns of behavior develop in orderly sequence" (Becker, 1973:23).

The orientation we are using to understand deviance is based on the ideas of sequence and process. Thus, the phenomenon of deviance is not exhausted with the development of individual behavior. Understanding the deviance process involves far more than seeking answers to the question of why people break rules. Indeed, according to some observers, the most important aspects of the deviance process, those having the most lasting consequences, come *after* rule-violating acts become known to people in positions of authority who have the capacity to apply the label of "deviant" to the actor (Lemert, 1951:75–79; Becker, 1973:31–36).

In stressing the sequential nature of the deviance process, these observers have emphasized the importance of *career deviance,* referring to the stages through which people pass in developing a deviant identity and coming to occupy the status of deviant. These stages include (1) being publicly identified as a deviant, (2) being excluded on that basis from participation in a variety of nondeviant activities, (3) coming to regard oneself as a deviant, and (4) managing one's deviant identity, including phasing out involvement in rule breaking, and/or seeking to promote a change in the official and public meaning of that type of rule breaking. To perceive deviance in this way, to consider it as a process influencing a person's social position and self-regarding attitudes, calls for an examination of an interactive process between individuals and groups.

A major *initial* outcome of this interactive process is that some rule breakers assume the status of deviant. In focusing on the informal and formal aspects of a person's induction into that status, we examine how a person's identity is changed from that of a moral person to that of a person regarded as "essentially" deviant, that is, immoral or "defective"—a person whose being is deviant. In focusing on being deviant, we consider the relationship between deviant actors, on the one hand, and social control agencies, on the other (Lemert, 1967a:44–46). We begin with an examination of the status of deviant.

The Status of Deviant

When referring to the status of deviant, we are focusing on the fact that people identified as rule breakers are often set apart from others; that is, they are differentiated from those who are regarded as morally acceptable and, on the basis of that presumed difference, awarded a position (a social status) that is reserved for persons officially defined as objectionable. However, there are two bases on which people may be classified as objectionable and assigned the status of deviant. One basis is people's behavior or deviant action; the second basis is the traits people display that others regard as objectionable. The first case we refer to as being deviant by *achievement;* the second case we refer to as being deviant by *ascription.* Each of these calls for brief examination.

Deviant as an Achieved Status

Being deviant by achievement means that people occupy this position because they engage in behavior that is banned. That is, being assigned this status rests on the public meaning of the actor's performance. A wide variety of deviations fall into this category, including the following: (1) those who engage in acts destructive of another's property or injurious to their person (such as murder and assault), (2) people who demand and/or consume unlawful goods and services and those who provide them (users of illicit drugs, prostitutes and customers of prostitutes, drug pushers and pimps, to name a few), (3) those whose behavior (public drunkenness and nudity, for example) offends another's sense of propriety, and (4) people whose beliefs challenge legitimated

ideologies—as a sect may challenge the beliefs of an orthodox religious group (Glaser, 1971: chapter 1). In each case some overt action (or suspicion thereof), some performance by the actor, underlies the assignment to a deviant status. In the case of achieved status, then, *people's deviant status is based on the meaning of their behavior.*

Deviant as an Ascribed Status

Being deviant by ascription, on the other hand, refers to the assignment of status on the basis of some quality the person is assumed to possess that is defined as a departure from expectations, and that may result in sanctions being imposed. These "offensive" qualities include any number of overt conditions: left-handedness in a society where right-handedness is preeminent and its opposite the subject of centuries-old prejudices (Hertz, 1960; *Time,* 1974:85); being short in a nation stressing height (Sagarin, 1969:196ff); being obese in a society where weight watching has become a religious exercise (Millman, 1980; Chernin, 1981); being an amputee or spastic, or being otherwise physically disabled in a society stressing athletic and physical prowess (Clark, 1978; Cleland, 1982); being blind or deaf in a society dominated by sighted and hearing people (Scott, 1969; Higgins, 1980). These and other conditions may arouse feelings of fear, loathing, and a sense that the deviant is in some way inferior to normals—inferior physically, psychologically, emotionally, or morally (Scott, 1969:24). Such conditions become *stigma,* signs or attributes that are deeply discrediting (Goffman, 1963:3). In contrast with those whose deviance is a matter of performance, *the deviation of these people rests on the meaning of their being.*

Primary and Secondary Deviants

In addition to considering the status of deviant as a matter of achievement or ascription, we need to examine people's entry into a deviant status in sequential terms. In order to examine this process sequentially, sociologists have employed two relevant concepts: primary deviant and secondary deviant (Lemert, 1951:75–76; 1967a:40ff). The concept of *primary deviant* refers to those persons whose deviation is "rationalized or otherwise dealt with [by the rule breaker] as functions of a socially acceptable role" (Lemert, 1951:75). That is, a person's deviation is incidental to the balance of his or her life and the socially approved statuses he or she occupies. Similar to the concept of primary deviant is Becker's *secret deviant* (1973:20): a person whose rule-violating conduct is publicly (that is, officially) neither recognized nor responded to as such. It is the privacy of the deviation that the concepts of primary and secret deviant have in common.

But not all people are able to keep their transgressions secret. In many cases the signs of deviance—drug addiction, disablement, blindness, obesity—may not be effectively hidden. As a consequence, it is felt, such conditions may become a central aspect of the person's life. This means the deviation may take on great importance (in contrast with its incidental nature among primary deviants), and many other nondeviant aspects of life (such as a job or role as student) may become subordinate to the deviant condition. If this occurs, the person may be said to be a secondary deviant (Lemert, 1951:75–76; 1967a:17–18, Chapter 3). Similar to the notion of secondary deviant is Becker's concept of the *pure deviant* (Becker, 1973:20): a person who has broken the rules and is perceived by others to have done so. According to Lemert, secondary deviants are responded to primarily as rule breakers. Ordinary statuses (being someone's child, a spouse, a worker) tend to be obscured because people often focus attention almost exclusively on the deviant behavior or condition. It is the *attention of others and the actor's response to that attention* that are central to the concept of secondary deviance. Thus, Lemert defines *secondary deviation* as "a special class of socially defined responses which people [deviants] make to problems created by the social reaction to their deviance" (Lemert, 1967a:40). Consistent with the felt need to adjust to others' behavior, the secondary deviant "is a person whose life and identity are organized around the facts of deviance" (Lemert, 1967a:41). In short, the principal distinction between primary and secondary deviation lies

in the salience of the person's rule-violating behavior.[1]

Master and Auxiliary Status Traits

To say a person's deviance takes on saliency means that it takes precedence over and supersedes most other status positions. It is as if self and others became blinded to every aspect of a person's social being except for the deviant aspect. As we will later note in greater detail, a person's identity (at least his or her public identity) may come to be recognized solely as that of deviant. *A person comes to represent the thing described.* The priority of this identity over that of a nondeviant has been commented on by Everett C. Hughes (1945) and Howard Becker (1973).

Hughes makes the distinction between *master and auxiliary status traits*. Master status refers to those statuses that obscure and take precedence over others. The master status "tends to overpower, in most crucial situations, any other characteristics which might run counter to it" (Hughes, 1945:357). Becker, too, indicates that deviance tends to be a master status. "One receives the status [of deviant] as a result of breaking a rule, and the identification proves to be more important than most others. One will be identified as a deviant first, before other identifications are made" (Becker, 1973:33).

Closely linked to a master status is "a complex of auxiliary characteristics which come to be expected of its incumbents" (Hughes, 1945:353). Thus, priests (master status) are expected to be men (auxiliary trait), physicians (master status) are expected to be male, white, and Protestant (auxiliary traits), and nurses (master status) are expected to be women (auxiliary trait). Similarly, there are auxiliary traits associated with particular deviant master statuses. Homosexuals (master status) tend to be regarded as sexually abnormal, effeminate, insecure, and sensitive (auxiliary traits), while

---

[1]Although this is likely the most notable distinction between primary and secondary deviance, there is reason to qualify it as a universally applicable distinction. Of major importance in positing the need for qualification is the process of symbolic labeling, which we deal with in Chapter 6.

people who use marijuana have been regarded, among other things, as escapist, hedonistic, insecure, frustrated, weak minded, and dangerous (Simmons, 1969:29). Thus, master statuses and their auxiliary traits reflect a marked tendency toward *moral congruence*. That is, almost invariably, statuses and their accompanying auxiliary traits tend to be morally consistent. In the common scheme of things, then, traits associated with deviant statuses carry a negative valuation. On the other hand, positively valued statuses are linked with positive or morally neutral traits. Further, morally negative statuses and positive traits are often regarded as mutually exclusive, and vice versa. As an example, many people have marked difficulty resolving the "contradiction" between the statuses of "athlete" and "homosexual," especially if the athlete is a professional football player (Garner and Smith, 1977), and experience cognitive "discomfort" when seeking to reconcile other seemingly mutually exclusive statuses—for example macho jack hammer operator and transvestite.[2] By linking these master statuses and their auxiliary traits, the public image of the deviant actor comes to be that of one who is *generally deviant;* that is, deviance becomes the dominant element of the person's public self (Becker, 1973:34). *The person is regarded as essentially deviant* and is dealt with as such.

The idea that a person is essentially deviant brings us back to the concept of secondary deviant. That is, being perceived and reacted to by others as exclusively deviant may well create problems for the person so treated—problems associated with being stigmatized, punished, segregated from society, or otherwise being made the object of social control. Such concerns are felt to be central to the life of some deviants. Their involvement in deviance is therefore often regarded as qualitatively different from that of the primary deviant. For

the primary deviant, rule breaking is hypothesized both as subordinate to a person's legitimate roles and statuses and as having relatively few personal and social implications. For the secondary deviant, however, the deviation and ensuing moral problems are alleged to become central in terms of both self–other relations and one's conception of self. Thus, according to theory, the secondary deviant's life tends to revolve about the fact of his or her rule breaking.

However central a person's deviance may be, evidence indicates that involvement in deviance is not mutually exclusive of legitimate role playing. Not only is this true in the case of the primary deviant (which includes almost everyone at some time or other), but it applies as well to the secondary deviant—for example, people who make their living by means of rule-violating behavior. In their study of black pimps, the Milners discovered that relationships between pimps and their parents and other family members persist, often with only minimal difficulty (Milner and Milner, 1972:130ff). Further, Klockars notes that the role of professional fence is not incompatible with that of straight businessperson (Klockars, 1974:77–78). Rossman (1976:198) relates cases indicating that participation in *pederasty*—that is, the sexual involvement of men with young boys, including anal intercourse—is fully compatible with socially acceptable roles and relationships. Fathers who engage in incest with their daughters often are, in other respects, the model of the proper husband and father (Justice and Justice, 1979:60–61; *Phoenix Gazette,* 1984b). Finally, Humphreys reminds us that a substantial proportion of the men he studied who engaged in homosexual acts in public places (that is, "tearooms") were married and living with their spouses, and engaged in a wide variety of wholly legitimate occupations (Humphreys, 1970: chapter 6). These examples demonstrate that, despite popular perceptions and the tendency to categorize people in mutually exclusive terms, deviant and nondeviant roles are far from incompatible. Indeed, as the case of the professional fence suggests, legitimate and deviant roles may be interdependent and, hence, difficult to separate. However, this

[2]Interestingly, it is through humor that people are helped to resolve the "contradictions" and otherwise come to grips with the restrictions humans impose on themselves by the way in which they categorize people, behavior, and other aspects of their world. See: *Playboy,* May 1979, p. 238.

in no way denies that such people may experience problems related to the deviation.

In Chapter 6 we will consider at length the problems experienced by deviants as a consequence of their status. At the same time, we will examine some refinements of the distinctions we have drawn between primary and secondary deviance. At this point, it is important to begin considering the formal process by which a person takes on the public status of deviant.

Institutionalizing Deviance

Bureaucratization

Once behavior is banned, it becomes subject to control by public law. That is consistent with our earlier contention that banning involves the conversion of private meanings into public laws that, at least in theory, apply to all persons falling under the jurisdiction of the state. The responsibility for processing deviants becomes the task of official agencies—either public or publicly approved. That is, new organizations may be established or existing organizations assigned the task of enforcing the rules. In some cases a new department may be created within existing organizations. As examples, we may note the creation of private groups (that is, nongovernmental) such as homes, treatment and recreational centers, and similar organizations. These groups often receive official endorsement and public legitimation as "deviance-processing" agencies. (This is not to say that such organizations deal exclusively with persons identified as deviant.) Examples of specialized public agencies (governmental) include police vice and bunco squads, and a special staff within a department of public welfare that investigates cases of welfare fraud, child abuse, and similar matters.

The creation of these groups, one step toward institutionalizing deviance, rests on a prior condition: an agreed upon definition of the nature of the problem and the clientele to be dealt with. Logically, this definition precedes assigning such responsibilities since, in the absence of a definition, no purposive course of action is likely. For example, assigning responsibility for a given problem to police, medical, social welfare, or some other specialized agency requires a prior definition of that problem. Likewise, whether a particular deviant is remanded to a mental hospital, a jail, a prison, a geriatric or nursing home, or elsewhere depends on how he or she is officially defined. (As we will see, the assignment of such definitions is quite problematic and may not be taken for granted.) In another case, the admissions staff of a hospital must be provided a definition (that is, an initial diagnosis) of incoming patients in order to know the area or department of the hospital to which the patient should be sent. Cardiac, orthopedic, obstetric, and similar departmental specializations are near universal. Beyond this, patients may be classified as critical or seriously ill. In any case, as noted in Chapter 1, how we respond to things is shaped by our definition of them.

Institutionalization of deviance also calls for establishing rules and procedures for handling people assigned to various categories of deviance. These rules and procedures tend to become *organized, systematized,* and *stabilized.* Thus, specific roles and statuses (such as a new job classification) may have to be created for the purpose of administering cases. If existing roles and statuses are regarded as sufficient for the task, the responsibility may be assigned to them. Thus, particular people do specific things; in accordance with the principles of division of labor, specific tasks are spread over several functionaries. Stabilization means that by assigning the responsibility of control to an agency, the roles, procedures, and meanings evolved come to have an existence independent of the role players. They become the property of organizations.

Overall, as they appear in specific organizations, these elements of institutionalization reflect bureaucratized methods of handling deviants. Within an agency one finds things characteristic of all bureaucratic organizations: specialized information, specific rules, specialization of tasks, a hierarchy of authority, and impersonal interpersonal relations. Ostensibly, these things are intended to promote achievement of an agency's goals—usually correction, amelioration, containment, and the like. These elements and the meanings that serve as their foundation become part of the social reality of deviance, albeit the reality of specialized groups. These are the realities found in police departments, social work agencies, mental hospitals and clinics, probation departments, prisons, and other organizations that deal with deviant populations. We may refer to this reality—this general body of information and its associated techniques—as the *theory of office*.[3]

Theory of Office. The concept *theory of office* indicates that the institutionalization of deviance involves more than a simplistic notion of bureaucratized routines. Agencies charged with controlling deviants face a problem in social management—what will they do with those persons who come to their attention? The theory of office has evolved to provide an answer to this general question. "Office," as used here, refers to a service, to things done to or for others. In that sense, then, a theory of office is a statement of how an agency will admit and process its clients. Such "theories" also formalize the defining, the classifying, and the labeling (that is, the *registry*) of the client population. Overall, then, theories of office provide a sense of order and meaningfulness to the task at hand. In providing this sense of order, however, a theory of office is evolved and defended, not for rendering treatment or other service, but for solving the difficulties invariably faced by bureaucratic organizations, for promoting a smooth and efficient operation, and for protecting the organization from criticism (Rubington and Weinberg, 1973:118; Newman, 1975; Shover, 1984:71). Let's briefly explore how such matters are handled.

[3]Considering the institutionalization of routines and the theory of office is not intended to suggest that these regulatory elements, rules, and so on, become a "straitjacket," denying practitioners the opportunity to display individuality or inhibiting the creation and application of situationally specific meanings. Thus, for example, while every mental health clinic, prison, and so on has a theory of office, which of its specific features will be applied to any specific case is problematic.

It is characteristic of bureaucracies to handle tasks in routine ways—ideally, with minimal variation between cases of a given kind. Thus, individual cases are to be managed according to the rules, for which bureaucracies are justly famous, and with minimal regard for the idiosyncrasies of the individual case or for personal preferences. Consistent with this ideal, agency functionaries are discouraged from acting on the basis of their private (hence, potentially different and conflicting) definitions of clients and their needs. Private definitions must not be allowed to interfere with the official tasks of the agency. In their place "recipes for action" are provided that serve to routinize tasks. For this purpose agencies develop *typifications* or "standardized categories" in which to place clients and/or cases (Hawkins and Tiedeman, 1975:82) and in terms of which the clients and/or cases may be handled in routine (that is, standardized) ways. Thereby, at least in theory, problems of organizational management are minimized if not precluded.

To prevent the intrusion of private meanings and encourage use of methods consistent with organizational interests, workers are socialized, tutored, and otherwise trained in terms of organizationally preferred routines. For example, beginning professional correctional workers are acknowledged to have no special skills or knowledge about working with offenders. They begin to acquire this knowledge by attending and observing older employees when they interact with inmates. In this way the novice is expected to learn how to deal with offenders and their problems in ways satisfactory to the organization. The novice is coached on how reports are written (what the preferred organizational style is) and how to gather the desired information in the least costly way. Much of this information is provided by allowing novices to review old files "to see how it is done." In these and other ways, recruits are introduced to the *recipe knowledge* that is unique to the agency (Shover, 1984:68–69). Routinization of tasks is thereby enhanced.

Examples of how other control agents dealing with deviants routinize their tasks by use of typifications are abundant. John Van Maanen (1978) notes that police officers use a variety of typifications in their work. These are part of the commonsense wisdom they share about the sorts of people they must deal with in their work. Most noticeable are such types as "the asshole" (also identified as creep, bigmouth, clown, scumbag, shithead, and fool, among others), the suspicious person, and the "know nothing." Although errors occur, in the course of police–citizen encounters officers identify or try to identify citizens in terms of these types. If the identity assigned is that of "the asshole," the citizen in question is likely to be dealt with harshly. The suspicious person is generally treated very professionally, swiftly, and in a "no nonsense" fashion. In either case, the work of the officer is facilitated by such typing. To the extent officers regard such encounters as ordinary, they are inclined to normalize or routinize the way in which they deal with persons perceived as representatives of such categories. "If an encounter [with a citizen] can be normalized, the officer can be relatively confident of the general nature of the interaction and ultimate resolution of the problem" (Lundman, 1980:20).

Like police officers, *public defenders* (tax-supported defense attorneys for indigent defendants) employ standard categories into which "typical" cases may be placed for routine handling. For example, in order to speed up and reduce the cost of processing criminal cases, public defenders and prosecuting attorneys frequently work out an agreement as to how a given case shall be defined (legally classified). To facilitate this process, a number of categories called *normal crimes* have been established in which to place cases. Normal crimes are "those occurrences whose typical features, e.g., the ways they usually occur and the characteristics of the people who commit them . . . are known and attended to by the [public defender]" (Sudnow, 1965:179). Normal crimes frequently dealt with include petty theft, drunkenness, rape, and drug use. A "typical" petty theft is defined as "about 50-50 Negro-white, unplanned . . ., generally committed on lower-class persons and don't get much money, don't often employ weapons, don't make living from thievery,

usually younger defendants with long juvenile assaultive records, etc." (Sudnow, 1965:179). A case that substantially satisfies these criteria will likely be categorized as "normal" and dealt with routinely, thereby facilitating the operation of the agency. Similar routinization of cases may be found in probation departments, in medical practice, welfare agencies, and other organizations.

The immediate importance of these typifications and categories lies in their contribution to the smooth operation of the agency and in the easing of problems likely to be encountered by workers. It is only in terms of a set of typifications or designations that agencies are able to deal with their clients within the limits of budget, staff, and other finite resources. As a case in point, prison inmates may have their level of custody changed (from maximum to medium, for example), not to facilitate "rehabilitation" or because of any character change, but to facilitate the harvesting of crops on the prison farm. Legally and ordinarily, maximum security inmates are not allowed outside the walls of maximum security prisons. However, when an insufficient number of inmates is available for harvest (work requiring inmates to go outside prison walls), a change in classification may conveniently be arranged in order to provide this vitally needed work force (Sykes 1958:25–31; Shover, 1984:71). Thus, official classifications are often designed primarily to serve organizational goals.

Conversely, when the definition of the client lacks clarity, or does not satisfy the existing organizational apparatus, or when the organization cannot ignore the client's uniqueness, the client may well be expelled. For example, in Hackensack, New Jersey, a man in the midst of a sex-change operation who had pleaded guilty to burglary was granted a 90-day suspended sentence—suspended only "because the judge didn't know where the sentence should be served" (*Arizona Republic*, 1977a). A similar case arose in Illinois where Donald Lang, despite being accused of two murders, may never go to trial. Mr. Lang cannot hear, speak, read, or write and is therefore unable to participate in his own defense. For that reason the court has declared him incompetent to stand trial. Until the definitional dilemma is resolved, the accused languishes in the Cook County jail (*Newsweek* 1977:89–90; *Arizona Republic,* 1980d). Lang's case was the subject of a TV movie entitled "Dummy." Finally, in Delhi, New York, a resident jailed for traffic offenses while undergoing a transsexual change and who was a "woman" from the waist up but a "man" from the waist down, had to be searched (appropriately, of course) by female and male deputies, and housed in the jail of the adjacent county where there was an unoccupied floor (*Playboy,* 1980).

Finally, assigning clients to official categories also serves to legitimize the processing of specific cases. That is, backed by the authority of those who categorize or typify, these designations render the treatment or other disposition of specific cases right and proper. For example, a judgment of "incompetency" by a duly convened board of psychiatrists paves the way for the hospitalization or outpatient treatment of a patient. Likewise, official designation of a person as "criminal" legitimizes imprisonment and makes the inmate's presence in prison proper and defensible (Shover, 1984:71). A diagnosis legitimizes medical treatment. (Conversely, a successful malpractice suit against a physician necessitates *delegitimizing* the diagnosis; thereby the treatment may be said to have been in error and the physician liable.) It is only in terms of these designations and their meanings that bureaucratic social control agencies can manage the client population. This defining process, along with other aspects of the theory of office, serves to "shape" persons to the needs of the bureaucratic machinery.

The Case of Total Institutions

The nature of this "shaping" process is familiar to any person who has been inducted into any bureaucratic agency dealing with sizable populations (the military, a university, a prison, and the like). To be sure, the extent to which these efforts are engaged in and the consequences for a person's conception of self vary significantly from organization to organization. But the process is most apparent and most significant in *total institutions,* organizations that demand total subordination of the client population and that severely restrict association between client and "free" population groups (Goffman, 1961:4–5). Examples of total institutions include, among others, precisely those agencies established to deal with various categories of deviant: juvenile detention centers, mental hospitals, prisons, and similar places. This type of organization deserves brief examination.

Admission to these agencies often includes a variety of rituals that serve to eliminate or reduce the individual client's uniqueness or individuality—that is, to reduce the uniqueness of self that may threaten the smooth operation of the agency. Consistent with assuming a master status, the agency tends to erode elements of a person's nondeviant identity and prior conception of self by a "series of abasements, degradations, humiliations, and profanations" (Goffman, 1961:14). For example, as a person enters prison he or she is fingerprinted, photographed (both of which have likely been done numerous times before), subjected to a mortifying rectal (and, if a woman, vaginal) examination, stripped of a name in preference for a number, possibly subjected to a haircut of a standard sort, disinfected, and otherwise "cleansed." These and other admissions procedures are called "*trimming,*" "*programming,*" or "*being squared away*": procedures whereby the new arrival is "shaped and coded into an object that can be fed into the administrative machinery of the establishment, to be worked on smoothly by routine operations" (Goffman, 1961:16).

Shaping is not restricted to the admissions period. Mortifying experiences may be imposed at various points during a person's period of incarceration or hospitalization in order to bring obstreperous, boisterous, or otherwise unruly clients (those who threaten organizational procedures) back into line. For example, in *One Flew Over the Cuckoo's Nest,* Nurse Ratched (Big Nurse) ordered a "cautionary cleansing" of the hair and rectum of patients who had participated in a fishing trip contrary to her wishes (Kesey, 1962:227ff).

Clearly, defiance of authority by clients is intolerable in total institutions. The consequence may be *contaminative exposure,* the defiling of one's person or of things intimately associated with one's self (Goffman, 1961:25).

Other expressions of "shaping" deviant populations to facilitate organizational needs exist in abundance. Upon entering prison, the military, or hospitals, a person is frequently stripped of personal belongings and issued regulation garb and equipment. Access to personal belongings, ranging from clothing to cigarettes, is often restricted in conformity to organizational rules and their rationale. The effect of those restrictions is *personal defacement;* that is, a person is "stripped of his usual appearance and of the equipment and services by which he maintains it" (Goffman, 1961:20). Things that are extensions of self and symbolic of identity are denied.

Mutilation of the body may also be part of the "shaping" process. Included is the use of chemotherapy, electroshock therapy, and surgical techniques such as lobotomy (Kesey, 1962:269; Jackson, 1973:42ff; Chambliss, 1971). Even lacking direct imposition of these forms of mutilation, the simple threat of them may be sufficient to inhibit select behavior patterns, and to intimidate and control the client population. Intimidation and control may also be sought by means of *verbal humiliation.* Being required to address institutional personnel as "mam" or "sir" or by another term of deference (while similar regard is systematically withheld from the client population) is a common example. In some prisons administrative personnel pride themselves on their ability to know and refer to every inmate by number rather than name. To have one's name stripped away is to suffer the removal of a symbol of one's identity and individuality. It is an assault on self.

Though the precise elements of the shaping process vary with the agency and the situation, a not-too-unusual example is provided by Brendan Behan, famous Irish playwright and journalist. In 1936, at age 13, Behan joined the Irish Republican Army and, at age 16, was confined for three years in an English Borstal or reform school. The following, from his writing, informs us of the sort of shaping he experienced when he entered the Borstal.

We were brought to an annexe of the prison; a single-storied building. Inside, a warder, wearing a white coat, stood by a desk, calling out names. As each name was called, the policeman took our possessions from his satchel, the warder listed them, and we signed the list, in our turn. When this was finished, the policeman went off, the warder and he smiling cordial farewells to each other.

"Now," said the warder, "if you've anything in your pockets, turn 'em out."

I turned out my pockets. Except the one I had the cigarettes in, the Capstans I got off the sergeant.

"Will you turn 'em over, Mr. 'Olmes?" said the warder to another.

Mr. Holmes turned us over. He found a bit of shoelace on Charlie.

"Want to practise sailors' knots or something?" Charlie said nothing.

"Why did you not hand it over?"

"I didn't know."

"You didn't know—what?"

"I didn't know it was any harm."

Mr. Holmes roared, "You didn't know it was any harm—what?"

"Oh, I didn't know, sir. Sir, I didn't know, sir, sorry, sir."

The other warder came down, and looked at Charlie. "Remember when you speak to Mr. 'Olmes in future, you'll 'ave respect and haddress 'im properly."

"Or," said Mr. Holmes, "any other hofficer of the service, as Mr. Whitbread will tell you."

Mr. Holmes searched Donohoe, and found a piece of paper in his pocket. The begrudger looked at him.

"You won't want that, you know," said Mr. Holmes. "We give you toilet paper 'ere."

"I know all about what you give 'ere," said Donohoe.

Mr. Holmes passed on to me. Oh dear dilapidated Jesus, why did I keep those bastarding Capstans?

He passed his hands over me and came to them in some excitement. "What 'ave we got 'ere, eh? What? What 'ave we 'ere?—Mr. Whitbread, sir."

Mr. Whitbread came down and stood with Mr. Holmes in front of me. Mr. Holmes held up the cigarettes, and Mr. Whitbread looked at them.

" 'Oo 'ad this little lot, then, Mr. 'Olmes?" asked Mr. Whitbread, who had just seen them taken from my pocket.

"This one 'ere, sir." He spoke into my face. "Tell

101

Mr. Whitbread your name, you."

"Behan, sir."

I put my last name first. In moments of stammering it's easier to pronounce.

"Tell Mr. Whitbread your Christian name," said Mr. Holmes.

"Maybe you don't 'ave any Christian names in Ireland," said Mr. Whitbread.

"Br-Br-Br-Brendan Behan, sir."

"Yes, Behan," said Mr. Whitbread, quietly, looking at his list, "I've got you 'ere all right, I.R.A. man, ain't you? Don't like us much over 'ere, do you, Behan? Pity, you know, seeing as you're going to spend a long, long time with us. About twenty years. That's what the last lot got at Manchester, wasn't it? And you was going to blow us all up, Behan? Weren't you, Behan?" He shouted into my face. "Weren't you?"

"Answer Mr. Whitbread, Behan," said Mr. Holmes reproachfully.

"Not much of the old rebel in you now, Behan, is there? Thought you blokes would 'ave brought over your ox-guns with you," said Mr. Whitbread. "Do you know what an ox-gun is, Behan? It's what they 'ave in Ireland for shooting bull-shit out of."

He looked at the others. Mr. Holmes laughed, and the ginger boy, and Charlie's face was serious and troubled till he looked away from me and laughed with the rest.

"And 'old up your 'ead, when I speak to you."

" 'Old up your 'ead, when Mr. Whitbread speaks to you," said Mr. Holmes.

I looked round at Charlie. His eyes met mine and he quickly lowered them to the ground.

"What are you looking round at, Behan? Look at me."

I looked at Mr. Whitbread, "I am looking at you," I said.

"You are looking at Mr. Whitbread—what?" said Mr. Holmes.

"I am looking at Mr. Whitbread."

Mr. Holmes looked gravely at Mr. Whitbread, drew back his open hand, and struck me on the face, held me with his other hand and struck me again.

My head spun and burned and pained and I wondered would it happen again. I forgot and felt another smack, and forgot, and another, and moved, and was held by a steadying, almost kindly hand, and another, and my sight was a vision of red and white and pity-coloured flashes.

"You are looking at Mr. Whitbread—what, Behan?"

I gulped and got together my voice and tried again till I got it out. "I, sir, please, sir, I am look-ing at you, I mean, I am looking at Mr. Whitbread, sir."

"Well, Behan," said Mr. Whitbread, "now you've learnt that lesson, remember this: We've only three sorts of tobacco 'ere. Three Nuns—none today, none tomorrow, and none the day after."

The others laughed, Mr. Holmes, the ginger boy, and Charlie looking away from me. All except Donohoe, still begrudgingly eyeing the wall.

"Understand that, Behan?"

My face burned and I searched my aching head for my voice.

"Answer Mr. Whitbread, Behan."

"Yes—sir. Yes. Mr. Whitbread."

"Don't you forget it."

"No, Mr. Whitbread, no, sir" (Behan, 1958:35–38).

As this example reveals, there are numerous ways for a person to suffer a mortification or deadening of self as he or she is introduced to total institutions and the master status of deviant. Behaviors and symbols (including names) expressive of a person's prior "innocence" and identity are suppressed if not obliterated and, in their place the person acquires elements of a deviant identity. People are identified as moral "outsiders," and are dealt with as such. This entails more than assuming an alternative status, however. Being identified as "lower" in the moral order of things serves also to justify "treatment" by practitioners in total institutions. We will return to this point shortly in the section "Consequences of Stereotyping." For now it is enough to recognize that being assigned to the status of deviant is often a matter of grave importance.

For all of that, some erosion of the actor's former self and identity may already have commenced prior to contact with a deviance-processing agency. Thus, upon discovery of a person's involvement in deviance, others may begin to perceive him or her in terms of *stereotypes*, group-shared ideas about the nature of people assigned to specific categories. Let's examine stereotypy as it applies to how people acquire a deviant identity.

Stereotypy

For most people, interaction is based to a significant degree on unproven, taken-for-granted assumptions about the others with whom they deal. Storekeepers, bus drivers, office workers, teachers, students, and so on, are ordinarily defined in terms at least minimally consistent with the situation in which we and they interact. For example, whether shopkeepers are kind to animals, like kids, or enjoy a particular style of music ordinarily are not among the criteria used to evaluate such persons because they are not seen as relevant to the role of shopkeeper. There is, after all, a norm of social interaction that, in the absence of contrary information, encourages people to take one another at face value or, alternatively, at least to make judgments of others on the basis of relevant criteria. Thus, lacking contrary information, we are likely to deal with others who are strangers as at least tolerable persons and to approach them as representatives of a relevant typification. Smooth interaction is thereby promoted.

To be sure, characterizations of others are not built in total disregard of external matters. As we noted earlier, such things as speech, general demeanor, style of dress, and the like are often used as *symbols*—that is, stimuli that have learned meanings and values attached to them (Rose, 1965:44f) and that have no objective or essential meaning. For example, a smile is generally invested with positive meaning and the person who flashes a smile is likely to be defined differently from one who either frowns or refrains from smiling. Much of our social interaction rests on definitions of these symbols rather than on some basic or substantial feature of other people.

In addition to speech, dress, and other symbols, how we relate to other people is influenced by the meanings assigned to the statuses they occupy rather than to them as individuals. For example, if one has learned to be distrustful of police as *a category,* it is unlikely that the distrust will be dispelled by a particular smiling officer. This will be particularly true if one regards "cop" as a master status with "untrustworthiness" as an auxiliary trait. The distrust directed against *police in general* is best understood as reflecting a stereotype.

Though people are often reluctant to admit they engage in stereotyping, research evidence reveals it is an extremely widespread practice,

so widespread as to suggest it may well be indispensable for people trying to establish a sense of order in an impersonal, heterogeneous society (Vander Zanden, 1983:19–21). The utility of using stereotypes to characterize people extends to deviants as well as other categories of persons. Thus, just as people have stereotyped ideas about members of various occupational, racial, religious, and ethnic groups, so, too, do they have stereotyped conceptions of various types of deviants. For example, while researching stereotypes of deviants, an investigator asked college students to characterize homosexuals, marijuana smokers, and adulterers, among others. In response, "over two-thirds of the students wrote a highly stereotyped portrait of every deviant type, and the responses . . . were remarkably similar in content—almost as if they were all echoing the same package of images" (Simmons, 1969:27; see also Vander Zanden, 1983:19–23).

Simmons's findings are perhaps predictable because of the homogenizing effect of mass media and the extremely widespread popularity of certain language forms in America. Indeed, being socialized to stereotypic constructions of deviants is by no means uncommon in our society. These constructions are quite prevalent in everyday speech and the mass media. Thomas Scheff (1966:64ff) notes that "children learn a considerable amount of [stereotyped] imagery concerning deviance very early, and . . . much of the imagery come[s] from their peers rather than adults." Some sense of the prevalence of stereotypes of, for example, the mentally ill may be noted in words like *crazy, nuts, cracked, looney, flipped, bughouse,* and others that have, over time, been used to refer to such persons. The content of language is reinforced by media imagery where, in television, for example, the "mentally ill" person

often enters the scene staring glassy-eyed, with his mouth widely agape, mumbling incoherent phrases or laughing uncontrollably. Even in what would be considered the milder disorders, neurotic phobias and obsessions, the afflicted person is presented as having bizarre facial expression and actions. (Nunnally, 1961:74)

These images have become part of the "conventional wisdom" possessed by many Americans pertaining to what the mentally ill look like, how they behave, and, hence, how "normal" people ought to behave toward them.

The social reality of crime and criminals is also reflected in the stereotyped content of our language and the media (Klapp, 1962; Quinney, 1973, 1975; Winick, 1978). Especially notable is the way crime has been portrayed in television programs. Thus, Smythe (1954) reported that most entertainment programs were dramas and that the largest subclass of dramatic programs focused on crime and included extensive character stereotyping. Heroes were characteristically younger and more physically attractive than villains, who were portrayed as being in a state of sexual and physical decline. White Americans comprised 83 percent of the heroes but only 69 percent of the villains. Europeans provided 24 percent of the villains though they were only 14 percent of the character population. Finally, 66 percent of the villain population was made up of Italians. In another study from the 1950s reported by Dominick (1978:115), it was noted that nonwhites seldom engage in police work. More recent analysis of TV program content reveals that "law enforcers . . . were predominantly white males in the prime of life. Eighty-nine percent were male and nearly as many (85 percent) were white" (Lichter and Lichter, 1983:36). These examples indicate that the media deal extensively in stereotyping and are an important source of information concerning what "kinds of people" are appropriate to fill specific kinds of statuses and play specific roles. But these images are not without consequences. Let's give some attention to that matter.

Consequences of Stereotyping. Stereotyping has numerous consequences. First, as part of social reality, the content of stereotypes is often regarded as a valid description of the groups to which it refers. For example, we noted earlier that many physicians have been known to carry on a demanding daily professional routine despite their addiction to drugs. Yet people persist in believing that "junkies are non-productive." Professionally competent addict physicians come to be regarded as "exceptions that prove the rule," that is, that validate the stereotype. On the other hand, the stereotype of physicians (gentle, understanding, wise, ever alert and ready to do his or her duty for humanity) precludes their being perceived as drug addicts. On the basis of *moral congruence,* the statuses of physician and drug addict tend to be mutually exclusive. By assuming the stereotype is largely valid, people think they "know" what a drug addict, a homosexual, a prostitute, and so on is like and feel they are able to recognize one when and if they see one.

Second, stereotypes lead people to anticipate objectionable behavior by deviants. That is, stereotypes have implicit expectations. For example, in the 1978 campaign to repeal civil rights ordinances for homosexuals, antihomosexual forces supported their allegations not on evidence of what homosexuals *had done* but on what it was feared and expected they *would do.* As a case in point, it was anticipated by homophobic spokespersons that gay teachers *would* seek to seduce, molest, or otherwise lead students into a homosexual life style (*Arizona Gay News,* 1978:4). Such anticipatory fears were prominent in Anita Bryant's homophobic campaign at that same time (*Playboy,* 1978:78). To the extent that stereotypes include character traits, people may readily make such predictions. To all intents and purposes, then, the actor "becomes" the thing to which the stereotype refers and is expected to behave accordingly.

Third, largely (if not solely) on the basis of their content, stereotypes bring about the rejection of deviant actors. They are barriers between the deviant and others. If stereotypes are accepted as a valid picture of the deviant's undesirable nature or traits, people are "put off" and may shun the rule breaker. Because the stereotype is often objectified, people are led to assume the deviant "really is that way." Thus, it is not uncommon to find people believing that homosexuals *really are* "limp-wristed faggots" and *can never be* athletic (Garner and Smith, 1977), that blind people *really are* helpless, dependent, and melancholy (Scott, 1969:21), that fat people *really are* jolly, and so on. Because these auxiliary traits are often negatively valued, they serve to justify or excuse others' behaving toward the subject in extraordinary ways. Thus, if people are stereotyped as barbarians, others are entitled to treat them in barbaric ways (Gerbner, 1978:14).

Just as stereotypes serve as the basis for interpersonal rejection, so do they shape and justify the policies that agencies adopt to deal with deviant clientele. A case in point is the way stereotyped perceptions of blind people influence the work of some agencies providing services to the blind. Scott has pointed out that some agencies working with the blind prefer not to deal with all unsighted people, but only with those who conform to the agency's conception of a rehabilitatable blind person, that is, the employable blind and the young—categories felt to have the greatest chance for rehabilitation. Among the reasons why agencies prefer to concentrate on the young and the employable while ignoring other segments of the blind population is that the former conform to a stereotype that can be used effectively in agency fund-raising campaigns wherein themes of "youth, work, and hope" are relied on to elicit support (Scott, 1969:100). Scott also notes that agency personnel have often mistaken *their concept* of the problems of the blind for *the problems themselves*. Blind persons whose behavior fails to conform to these conceptions are regarded as "marginal" to the "real work" of such agencies, that is, educational and vocational training; persons who do not conform to the stereotype are often defined as insoluble cases and their files marked closed. Like the burglar undergoing a sex-change operation, mentioned earlier, they tend to be expelled as clients because the agency is predisposed to handle only cases that conform to its definition of the rehabilitatable blind. Only to the extent that clientele conform to this stereotype can they be fit into the organizational machinery.

As another example, Don Jackson tells us that being identified as a homosexual and being committed to Atascadero State Hospital in California under that state's Mentally Disordered Sex Offender law was grounds for being stripped of all legal rights, perhaps detained for life, and being used as a "guinea pig" in medical/surgical experiments (including experimental use of the drugs prolixin and anectine, electroconvulsive shock, and behavioral conditioning by aversive stimuli to extinguish penile responses (erections) among the patients). A doctor at Atascadero is quoted as saying "These men have no rights: If we can learn something by using them, then that is small compensation for the trouble they have caused society" (Jackson, 1973:43; see also Chambliss, 1971). Rather clearly, among professionals, definitions—including stereotypes—serve to justify treatment.

A fourth consequence of stereotyping is that it serves as the basis for selecting persons to be officially designated as deviant. That is, people are selected to be tagged as deviant not simply because of their involvement in discreditable behavior or, as in the case of the ascribed deviant, because they represent some feared and stigmatized condition. They are singled out because of what stereotypes lead others to think of them. We have already noted at length that differential police reaction to similar behavior among Japanese, black, and white youth was based in part on the stereotyped conceptions police had of these youth. Similarly, it is not uncommon to find schoolteachers stereotyping and judging a younger brother or sister on the basis of the behavior of an older "unruly" child they had in their classroom. These everyday examples reveal the ways stereotypes influence people's perceptions of and, in turn, their actions toward others with whom they deal.

A fifth and final consequence of stereotypes is that they lead to *omittive* acts—that is, to the systematic avoidance of certain acts, words, or conversational topics when in the presence of select categories of stereotyped persons. This tendency reverses what we noted earlier. That is, while stereotypes *prescribe* some responses, they *proscribe* or prohibit others. Examples of how stereotypes lead to omittive or proscriptive acts are numerous. Able-bodied persons tend to avoid or be embarrassed by discussions of sexual behavior, dating, and marriage and childbearing with persons suffering extensive paralysis due to spinal cord injury or with persons who are highly disfigured. Such avoidance is consistent with the stereotype that disabled and disfigured people are asexual. Similarly, it is rare for sighted persons to discuss art such as painting and sculpture with the blind. Likewise, hearing persons tend to avoid conversations with people who have speech and/or hearing defects, a condition interpreted by deaf persons as a sign of others' rejection of them (Higgins, 1980:140). Finally, we have such instances as the store clerk who shuns the shopper with neurofibromatosis (Elephant Man's disease), especially if that person wishes to try on clothing (in some instances such avoidance reflects an aversion born of fear; see Montagu, 1979:26); or the therapist who systematically counsels clients—for example, the disabled—against pursuing select occupations thought by the counselor to be "inappropriate" (Scott, 1969:85). The extreme form of omittive behavior is to ignore and totally avoid acknowledging the presence of the deviant, thereby precluding all interaction.

Though it is possible to overemphasize the importance of the influence of stereotypes on human behavior, it is nonetheless true that in interaction in general, and in particular with people regarded as deviant (occupying a master status), these conceptions play a critical role. For example, most of us have rather limited contact with persons *known to be* deviant. What we tend to know of such people is therefore derived from accounts carried in the mass media or religious writings, from what friends and neighbors say about them, and from public pronouncements by "the professionals" (police, psychiatrists, and so on). Lacking direct contact and independent verifiable information, we find ourselves in an ambiguous position. How shall we relate to these people? How does one interact with the mentally ill? An alcoholic? Someone who has attempted suicide? A criminal of some sort? A homosexual? A quadraplegic? In many cases the ambiguity is reduced (not eliminated) by resorting to stereotypes and responding not to the person but to the definition provided by the stereotype. In short, stereotypes help people to make sense of behavior and people they regard as strange, bizarre, or frightening.

Retrospective Interpretation

Despite their consequences, stereotypes are insufficient for providing justification for official agencies to assign people to the status of deviant. The identification of people as deviant and the legitimation of agency activity calls for greater precision and more extensive documentation and evidence about the deviant actor than stereotypes can provide. In particular, while stereotypes refer to *categories of people,* the task of control agencies requires information about *specific persons,* information that will provide some sense of consistency between a particular actor's behavior and character, on the one hand, and the treatment to be accorded him or her, on the other. As Matza (1969:151) notes, the person who has been *devious* (behavior) must be cast as *deviant* (character). That is, to facilitate the work of the agency, the deviant actor must be made into a case of the thing he or she is alleged to be; to achieve this, behavior (devious) must be linked with character (deviant). To make this link calls for a characterological "transformation" of the actor, a condition effected by the process of *retrospective interpretation* (Lofland, 1969; Schur, 1971). Let's consider this process in some detail.

This transformation is accomplished by means of "reconstructing" or transforming people's character; individuals come to be seen "in a totally new light" (Schur, 1971:52). Consistent with the notion of the master status, people come to be regarded as "nothing but a deviator" (Schur, 1979:231). The importance of this transformation and the mechanisms employed can be seen by the fact that people do not become outsiders simply because they broke some rule or other. Rather, their becoming outsiders follows from the fact that while almost everyone breaks rules, often of a serious nature, people persist in thinking only of the *publicly identified rule breaker* as qualitatively (that is, morally) different from others. This presumed qualitative difference is established by means of retrospective interpretation. Thus, observers look (Latin: *specere*) backward (Latin: *retro*) and carefully examine a person's biography, *selectively* seeking information that is consistent with or "fits" what is now known about the actor's behavior. Accordingly, known rule breakers can be cut off from the respectable portion of society. It is in this "cutting off" and the presumption of difference that we find the essential meaning of the deviant as "outsider," as a "special kind of person." Let's look at some specific examples of this process.

Included among deviants who are regarded as "special kinds of persons" and often treated as "outsiders" are the mentally ill. Charlotte Green Schwartz (1956) has noted that even family members avoid and tend to become alienated from their loved ones who are so diagnosed. As an explanation for this, Schwartz suggests it is because in the perception of others, the mental patient is not just a "different person" but *"he is no longer a person to them.* They sense that something fundamental about the person has been changed. The mental patient is not a person *with* an illness like a man with a broken leg. He is a schizophrenic; in the vernacular, 'he is a mental case' " (Schwartz, 1956:22). The mental patient, then, in contrast to "normals," is a nonperson or in some other way is perceived to be *essentially* different. It is in this sense that the mental patient and other categories of deviant are seen as "special kinds of persons."

For another example, newspapers and other media regularly recast or transform people in this way and define them as a "special kind of person" when they subject alleged rule breakers to extensive but selective biographical scrutiny and, consequently, to "character reconstruction" (Lofland, 1969:149ff). An illustration of this scrutiny involves Jean Harris, convicted murderer of Herman Tarnower, the Scarsdale Diet cardiologist. When the death of Dr. Tarnower at the hand of Jean Harris became known, TV personality and newspaper columnist Andy Rooney (who apparently knew Harris personally) commented as follows:

Most of us were surprised. . . . We were stunned. While it is easy in retrospect to interpret things she did in ways that suggest evil, she did not seem evil. . . . Now, of course, you search your memory for clues that might have made you aware that she may have been a woman capable of buying a gun in Virginia and driving with it in a car to shoot a man in his house 400 miles away. . . . Was the impression I had of Jean Harris as an attractive, intelligent woman wrong, or were those characteristics only a small part of what she was? What other quirks of personality manifested themselves in what actions over the years? (*Arizona Republic,* 1980e)

A second case of character reconstruction is that of John W. Hinckley, Jr., who, in 1981, shot President Reagan. Not long after that event, Hinckley's life was selectively scrutinized by representatives of the press, who summed up their sense of the relevant parts of Hinckley's life in rather negative terms as follows: He didn't play football, excel in school, or have girlfriends; he worked in fits and starts; his life was marked by alienation, a gun fetish, and failure; he failed to graduate from college; he failed to measure up to his brother and sister; he failed to connect with his father; he failed in his efforts to win the heart of a teen-age movie star; he was never a part of this world; he passed from freshman to senior year without leaving a trace; he had a sporadic college career, dropping out at least three times; he lived in one nondescript or seedy apartment after another; he was a wanderer; and he spent time in squalid motels rather than his parents' luxurious home. On the basis of their retrospective excursion reporters concluded that "the person firing [at President Reagan] is just a bit of tan coat, a swatch of sandy hair and a half-seen face in a crowd" (*Arizona Republic,* 1981c). It surely is debatable whether, by any reasonable standard, Hinckley's life and his person could validly be summarized in such terms. Yet it is by means of the selective nature of retrospective interpretation that such abbreviated biographies can be constructed. Only those features of a person's life are noted that reveal a pattern consistent with the known deviation and that allow the actor to be defined as a "special kind of person."

In some instances, the effort to reconstruct character involves trying to discover some previously unrecognized character defect that may help account for the present rule breaking. It is assumed that independent evidence of the defect can be discovered in the person's biography. Accordingly, the deviant's biographical history is minutely examined in order to uncover events symbolic of a character consistent with the current deviant episode. Biographical information that is inconsistent with the known deviance may well be discounted or, if it cannot be ignored, may prompt a shift in the way the behavior is explained. For example, if information cannot be discovered that may plausibly be used as an indicator of a defective character (which would explain the deviant conduct), attention may shift to the psycho-physiological realm and the offender may be examined for possible brain damage. In the celebrated case of Patricia Hearst, background information revealed no clues to a fundamental character defect. Biography provided no plausible explanation for why the heiress to the Hearst newspaper fortune would be an apparently willing participant in the robbery of a Los Angeles sporting goods store and the Hibernia Bank in San Francisco during the time she was alleged to have been a kidnap victim of the Symbionese Liberation Army. In defense of Ms. Hearst, Attorney F. Lee Bailey used the notions of duress and brainwashing. By claiming his client was threatened with being "messed up" unless she participated in the bank robbery, Mr. Bailey was using the concept of duress to make sense of otherwise "unexplainable" behavior. He also employed the metaphor of brainwashing when he delved into "coercive persuasion" (Moritz, 1976:3; see also Szasz, 1976a and 1976b).

Taken together, these efforts constitute the process of retrospective interpretation; new facts are sought and/or old facts are reinterpreted in an effort to establish consistency between the actor's behavior and character (Lofland, 1969:150ff). Finding (or creating) such consistency serves to explain the discreditable conduct and further legitimizes the label. Evil conduct becomes understandable when engaged in by a "special kind of person"—one who, after all, is an "outsider."

Imputational Specialists and Case Records. Contributing to the transformation of a person's identity through retrospective interpretation is the information made available by a host of functionaries called *imputational specialists* (Lof-

land, 1969:136ff). As defined by Lofland, imputational specialists are those persons who, in carrying out their ordinary occupational or professional duties, ascribe characteristics to persons with whom they have contact, characteristics others in the future may use to alter the actor's identity. Examples include the school teacher who records "suspicions" about a child's learning ability, a social worker who makes his or her moral evaluation of a client a part of the latter's file, a probation officer who identifies an offender as "habitually troublesome," or a prison psychologist who converts the "negative" results of a paper and pencil test into definitive statements regarding an inmate's personality. Such entries, of course, refer only to very specific aspects of a person's being, and reflect the perceptions of a growing number of persons in our society (imputational specialists) trained to "find" the very conditions referred to. After all, who is better equipped to "discover" learning disabilities, mental pathology, and crime than teachers, psychologists, and police officers, respectively?[4]

To be sure, not all (indeed, very few) who contribute to these records do so for the purpose of validating a deviant label. Nor am I suggesting that the behavior of these or the other functionaries we will refer to is inspired by malevolence. However, when the need for such validation arises, these files are consulted in a highly selective manner by agency personnel and others so as to discover information that will legitimate the label. Information that is flattering or contrary to what is alleged of the actor is often left open to doubt, or ig-

[4]The growing number of imputational specialists reflects the increasing adoption of bureaucracy as a pattern of social organization during the past two generations. Supplementing the work of these people is the advent of electronic data processing, especially the storage of highly personal information (often of a damaging sort) that is readily collatable into central files. "With some 3.9 billion records on persons stored in thousands of federal data systems, there is mounting concern that computers could be manipulated . . . to control, intimidate or harass citizenry" (*U.S. News and World Report,* 1978; Whiting, 1977). This situation is perceived by some as a potential "information tyranny." Other observers, of course, define the situation quite differently (White, 1982).

nored. On the other hand, data supportive of the label are likely to be accepted unequivocally (Goffman, 1961:155ff). Correct answers to questions asked of prospective mental patients may well be ignored, while incorrect answers are dutifully recorded and taken as evidence of mental illness (Scheff, 1964). Moreover, given the authority ordinarily vested in the agencies engaged in retrospective interpretation, little of one's biography is beyond scrutiny. From the vast array of materials available are selected the misadventures, examples of poor judgment, regrettable incidents, cases of impetuousness, records of intemperance, and other things (which all people have accumulated in quantity) that may have "symptomatic significance." The events recorded in the case history are, then, just the sort that one would consider "scandalous, defamatory, and discrediting" (Goffman, 1961: 155–159). In *One Flew Over the Cuckoo's Nest,* Big Nurse always carried a small pad of paper in her uniform pocket on which to record select events in her patients' daily life. This information was dutifully filed in each patient's record and referred to during "group meeting" for the purpose of degrading or otherwise controlling people's behavior (Kesey, 1962:221ff, 252). Goffman suggests that, far from being an exercise in professional neutrality, the collection, accumulation, and collation of such data is a matter of partisanship, serving the interests of organizations that process deviants. The case of John W. Hinckley, Jr., referred to above, reveals reliance on this sort of information by those trying to construct a biography appropriate to a person who would try to assassinate the president.

Beyond simply being entries in people's files, these materials may be used to develop and support the unanimous belief that the actor is characterologically deviant—that is, is the type of person he or she is alleged to be. The importance of unanimity rests on the fact that its absence promotes conflict. In the absence of substantial agreement regarding the character of the actor, the legitimacy of regarding and responding to the person as a deviant is jeopardized, and the propriety of the actions of the labeling agency may be called

into question. Further, without unanimity, the alleged deviant may well claim to have been falsely and unjustly accused and successfully avoid being labeled. Consensus among the labelers, however, neutralizes the accused's effort at resistance. By effecting consensus, then, the recasting effort achieves greater legitimacy and is more likely to succeed; that is, the actor will officially be certified as an "outsider" (Emerson, 1969:317; Lemert, 1962:112).

Finally, consistent with bureaucratic methods and the "total" character of many deviance control agencies, the content of the case record—the file—often takes on far more importance than the physical person's words or actions. Institutional procedures are oriented in terms of case content, but rarely are they based on the uniquenesses of the deviant population per se. Further, the use of such records may serve to totally depersonalize the individuals to whom they refer. This establishes the distinction between the body and the file. Letkemann notes that

"the file . . . is personified. The comments of others are perceived of as a more accurate reflection of the person than the person himself. In fact, the body is perceived of as a false image. "It" may "give you a line," "give you a snow job." In contrast, the file is trustworthy. It contains absolute legal identity, the fingerprints. In addition, it provides us with the body's character—an account of its values and thoughts by way of psychological tests, charts, and reports. The body's ability is also indicated by aptitude and IQ tests. The body's photograph, evidence toward which one is inclined to react in a more personal manner, is tucked away in an envelope at the back of the file. (1973:18)

Given the process of retrospective interpretation, the establishment of files, and the extraordinary durability of the information contained in case reports—all of which lend considerable emphasis to the "abnormal" and to what is "wrong" with the actor—it may be difficult if not impossible for a person to return to a state of "health" or other socially acceptable status after he or she has experienced a transformation of character and been labeled (Newberger and Bourne, 1978:601; see also Whiting, 1977:766–767).

The Status Degradation Ceremony

In the preceding sections we have talked of a variety of elements related to how individuals get set apart and assigned the status of deviant. We discussed, as relatively discrete elements, the role of total institutions in shaping clients, the ways in which people are subject to being "typed," the ways people are characterized through stereotyping, and the ways in which their character may be "transformed" by means of retrospective interpretation and the examination of select biographical information supportive of a deviant label. It is now necessary to put these discrete elements together in order to perceive their cumulative effect in changing a person's public identity to that of deviant.

The combined influence of these elements is never more apparent than when they are manifest in the *status degradation ceremony*. Like ceremonies in general, these events consist of rituals intended to bring about and give public acknowledgment of a significant change in a person's social position. Similar to ceremonies such as christenings, circumcisions, puberty rites, confirmations, and marriages, degradation ceremonies signal a change in a person's public status. By these rituals "the public identity of the actor is transformed into something looked on as lower in the local scheme of social types" (Garfinkel, 1956:420). Further, at least theoretically, the change in identity effected by these rituals is total. That is, the new status reflects not only what a person has done but refers also to his or her motivational pattern and other aspects of character. Thus, the new identity rests on what a person has done as well as on why he or she is supposed to have done it.

Occurring in the form of court trials, juvenile court hearings, incompetency hearings, psychiatric screening boards, and similar events, degradation ceremonies are expressive of moral indignation. As such, they are not simply amoral transformations of the actor's public identity. They are denunciatory; the actor is stigmatized. In the process of denunciation the actor's former identity (that of a moral being) is virtually destroyed and a totally new identity established. Thus,

The work of denunciation effects the recasting of the objective character of the perceived other: The other person becomes in the eyes of his condemners literally a different and *new* person. It is not that the attributes are added to the old "nucleus." He is not changed, he is reconstituted. The former identity, at best, receives the accent of mere appearance . . . the former identity stands as accidental; the new identity is the "basic reality." What he is now is what, "after all," he was all along. (Garfinkel, 1956:421–422)

For the most part, degradation ceremonies focus on the past and rely on retrospective interpretation; they concern what the actor *has done* and what he or she is assumed to *always have been*. However, degradation ceremonies may also include concern over the future behavior of actors; they may be anticipatory and concern the actor's prospective behavior. The transformation of the actor into a person who is deviant results in the prediction that the actor will continue to behave in ways consistent with what is now perceived to be his or her "essential" deviant self.[5]

On occasion, the anticipatory element of degradation ceremonies becomes quite explicit. This may be seen in a case involving the firing of a self-professed socialist from the faculty of a state university by that school's Board of Regents. The Regents' action was taken contrary to the recommendations of both the university president and two successive faculty committees convened to hear evidence concerning the charges. In disregarding these recommendations and announcing its decision, the Board of Regents stated: "In addition, the Board specifically finds that Dr. Starsky . . . would not consider himself *bound in the future* to obey or enforce the rules and regulations of the University and this Board" (Hoult, 1972:237; italics added). In short, despite the fact that two tribunals found the evidence to be lacking, the Board acted in an an-

[5]The anticipatory element of degradation ceremonies parallels the anticipatory aspect of stereotypes and typification. The similarity is not accidental. In each instance, the actor's character is assumed to be consistent with the "kind of person" who could behave as he or she is alleged to have acted. In the case of stereotypy and typification, the characterological properties are assigned informally; in the instance of the degradation ceremony, these traits are attributed in an "official" and formal manner.

ticipatory manner and concluded that the interests of the university precluded allowing Starsky to continue to teach. Underlying this decision was the image of Starsky as a socialist. We might guess that the moral and characterological meaning of that label for the Regents prevented them from taking any other position. To them, apparently, the label symbolized Starsky's "essential" character.

The Court Trial. One example of a degradation ceremony is the court trial. As ordinarily understood and portrayed in the media, the court trial is a process in which issues of fact are dealt with in order to determine guilt and innocence. This is questionable. Viewed as a process in which reality is constructed, criminal trials involve the determination of whether or not the defendant is the type of person capable of doing the particular crime charged. "In other words, is the defendant a social instance of a thief, murderer, rapist, etc.? Can he be made to represent the crime with which he is charged?" (Hadden, 1973:270; see also Bennett and Feldman, 1981). Two versions of the defendant's character vie with each other: that of the prosecution and that of the defense. To be sure, elements of fact, and different definitions and interpretations of fact, are struggled over. In the final analysis, however, it is the jury's task to render judgment as to which story and which interpretation of fact is the most valid. Not the least of the elements struggled over is the defendant's character. In making its decision, the jury gives formal legitimacy to one version of reality. Let's consider the elements of the trial as a process of creating reality.

Regarding the character of the defendant, prosecutors seek to create an image of that person as one who is different from "normal" people, different, for example, from the sort of person who sits on a jury. To counter this effort, the defense attorney may use any of several approaches. He or she may try to create the belief that (1) the act in question was not deviant, (2) that the defendant was not in control of himself or herself (for example, because of insanity or the effect of brainwashing) when the forbidden act was committed, (3) that the

defendant did not know the act was prohibited and had no intention of defying the law or producing harmful consequences when he or she did the prohibited thing (ignorance), or (4) that the defendant is a victim of a vendetta by the state and is, in fact, a harmless person (Hadden, 1973:272). Regardless of the image sought, the defense goal is to frustrate the prosecutor's effort to create a discreditable image of the defendant.

As an example of story telling, the effort to create reality by both prosecutors and defense attorneys reveals basic strategies. From the prosecutor's perspective, all cases must provide an interpretation of the alleged criminal behavior that jurors may regard as internally consistent. That is, each of the elements of the story—scene, purpose, act, agency, and actor—must be defined and clearly related to the crime. For example, it must be shown that the defendant (actor), on a particular date and time and in a specified place (scene), with full awareness and intention (purpose), by use of some specified means such as threats, force, misrepresentation of self, and so on (agency), did do something proscribed by law such as enter a locked residence or place of business, take another's property, cause someone's death, and so on (act). The tactical maneuvers used by prosecutors to achieve the internal consistency of these elements varies by case. What is important, however, is that all elements be coherent with one another (Bennett and Feldman, 1981:94–96).

The defense, however, has a variety of strategies at its command (Bennett and Feldman, 1981:98ff). One, called the *challenge* strategy, is intended to refute the prosecution's claim that evidence supports the elements of the story. A second strategy is that of *redefinition;* this involves trying to demonstrate that one or more of the story elements provided by the prosecution is ambiguous and, hence, may be defined in alternative ways. For example, if the defense attorney for a person charged with attempted burglary of a store can show that the accused was inadvertently locked in the premises after it closed because he or she (1) was suddenly taken ill and (2) sought relief in a restroom and there fell asleep, it is possible to redefine the element of purpose or intent. A third strategy is *reconstruction*, a tactic calling for altering the whole context in which the action took place. The classic example of this is to have the jury perceive as self-defense what the prosecution calls murder. This can be achieved by "showing that the defendant could have been at the scene without intending to kill the victim, that the defendant had no prior reason to kill the victim, and that the means of causing death reflected a spontaneous response [not premeditated] to serious provocation" (Bennett and Feldman, 1981:104–105). In the final analysis, whatever tactics and strategy are used, all involve retrospective interpretation.

Examples of the use of retrospective interpretation in court trials are abundant in fiction as well as fact. A classic fictional portrayal of the process is found in Camus' *The Stranger* (1954). Shortly after his mother's death, the hero, Monsieur Meursault, chances to meet a petty pimp. In the company of their respective girlfriends, Meursault and the pimp take a weekend outing to the seashore. There they accidentally encounter some enemies of the pimp, an event that ends with Meursault shooting and killing one of them. During the long pretrial and trial, the judge and prosecutor focus their entire attention on Meursault's character while all but totally ignoring the facts of the alleged crime. Interrogation of the defendant and testimony by witnesses establish that M. Meursault does not believe in God, a condition resulting in his being dubbed "Mr. Antichrist"; that Meursault was not distressed by having to send his mother to an institution for the aged; that he displayed "great callousness" by failing to cry or otherwise show appropriate grief at the sad occasion of his mother's funeral; and that he did not linger over her fresh grave as a dutiful son is expected to do. Likewise, Meursault is shown to have visited a swimming pool, initiated a sexual liaison with a woman, and attended a comic motion picture on the day after his mother was buried. Such elements are of "symptomatic significance" for those conducting status degradation ceremonies.

Though having no bearing on the unlawful death, these revelations regarding M. Meursault's behavior, in themselves innocent and subject to reasonable interpretation, are taken to be a reflection of his "defective character" and justification for his condemnation. During the concluding moments of the trial, the Prosecutor speaks to the jury:

Not only did the man before you . . . indulge in the most shameful orgies on the day following his mother's death. He killed a man coldbloodedly, in pursuance of some sordid vendetta in the underworld of prostitutes and pimps. That, gentlemen of the jury, is the *type of man the prisoner is.* (Camus, 1954:121; emphasis added)

To this M. Meursault's attorney replies, "Is my client on trial for having buried his mother, or for killing a man?" (Camus, 1954:121). The prosecutor, stung by the defense attorney's naivete in failing to note the connection between these two facts, replies: "I accuse the prisoner of behaving at his mother's funeral in a way that showed *he was already* a *criminal at heart*" (Camus, 1954:122; emphasis added).

Finally, Camus' tale of the fate of M. Meursault is paralleled by events of everyday life. Thus, in his closing statement in the penalty trial of members of the infamous Manson "family," prosecutor Vincent Bugliosi addressed the jury as follows: "These defendants are not human, ladies and gentlemen. Human beings have a heart and a soul. No one with a heart and a soul could have done what these defendants did to these seven victims. These defendants are human monsters, human mutations" (Bugliosi, 1974:447–448). In this way, the prosecutor gave an indication of the "something special," the "outsider," that is created at status degradation ceremonies.

Constructing Moral Character: The Juvenile Court

Adding to our understanding of the specifics of the processes of categorizing, transforming, and assigning moral character to deviant actors is the systematic observations of Robert Emerson (1969), on the workings of the juvenile court. Based on his work, the following discussion reveals how retrospective interpretation is engaged in and how actors' behavior and character are fused to achieve *moral congruence*. Alternatively, we will see how the absence of such congruence is handled.

Degradation ceremonies involve extensive interaction. In the juvenile court this is largely confined to court officials—probation officers, public defenders and other attorneys, social workers—supplemented by parents and select other witnesses who provide information to the juvenile court judge concerning the defendant and the alleged rule violation. The construction of the offender's moral character is greatly influenced by the types of information provided by these witnesses and by the general demeanor of the offender. How and what information is presented to the court will eventually result in the offender being classified as a "normal" or "abnormal" delinquent.

Pitches and Denunciations. Corresponding to the general division of delinquents into normals and abnormals are two ways by which information may be presented to the court: the *pitch* and the *denunciation* (Emerson, 1969:104). The pitch refers to a presentation designed to cast the offender in the most favorable moral light and have the delinquent defined as "typical"— that is, normal. The pitch is used when probation officers or others wish to keep the accused from being sent to a detention center or from being dealt with in some other harsh way. To achieve a lenient disposition or one that will permit some rehabilitative effort calls for emphasizing the youth's socially approved qualities and ignoring, hiding, or normalizing their opposite. The youth must be shown to have redemptive qualities. Pitches, then, are used to normalize the actor and his or her behavior, thereby providing a foundation for the attribution of a socially acceptable moral character.

The second method of presenting information is the *denunciation,* the purpose of which is to "(a) establish that the present act is of a kind typically committed by a delinquent or criminal-like character and (b) construct a delinquent biography that unequivocally indicates someone of such character" (Emerson, 1969:105). Thus, the denunciation is used to stigmatize the delinquent as a prelude to and

legitimation for imposing severe and restrictive penalties. Consequently, emphasis is placed on the offender's lack of redeeming qualities, and on his or her failings and generally socially unacceptable nature. That is, the offender is seen as abnormal.

Though seeking opposite goals, pitches and denunciations rely on similar techniques and focus attention on the delinquent act and the delinquent's biography. It is these two elements (act and biography) that must be linked in some sensible (meaningful) way to the moral character being presented to the court. We will consider both the act and the biography.

Typing Delinquent Acts and Actors. Earlier it was pointed out that deviance-processing agencies bureaucratize their clients and their actions. An expression of that tendency occurs in the juvenile court, where juvenile offenses are categorized in organizationally convenient ways. Thus, any given delinquent act may be categorized as "typical," "criminal," or "disturbed" (Emerson, 1969:109–110). Associated with each category are distinctive motives (intentions) and distinct kinds of persons (actors). Acts and moral character are perceived to be interdependent. For example, to be perceived as "typical" means that an assault (the illegal act) will be defined as a "fight"—an ordinary event. To be classed as a "criminal" event, the assault must be seen as a mugging with robbery as the associated motive. And the offender's presumed character must be suitably altered to conform to the definition of the act and motive pattern. That is, it is presumed that engaging in criminal assault takes a different "kind of person" than is called for in ordinary fighting. Finally, the "disturbed" category requires the assault be perceived as "vicious," lacking sensible motivation and occurring for "no reason." Such acts are seen as particularly dangerous, risking possible loss of life, and the work of a "disturbed" person.

The offense of sexual misconduct by a female may be similarly categorized. If defined as a case of incidental or nonrepetitive sexual contact, the situation may be regarded as "typical." Though officially frowned on, it is not likely to be seen as the behavior of a person who has a morally unique character. Should the record reveal that the youth's sexual episodes are regular and persistent, however, the chance exists that they will be defined as "criminal," that is, prostitution. Character will change accordingly. Finally, if these sexual encounters are reported to involve several males simultaneously and be orgiastic or a "gang bang," the stage is set for assigning the act and actor to the "disturbed" category. Again, then, the act and moral character are intimately associated in the social construction of the delinquent. The link is established in ways that make sense to the court. It is in terms of the meanings of these categories that the court will respond to the case.

But how do court personnel determine the specific category to which a particular act or actor will be assigned? An answer to this question is important when we recognize that not everything about an event or actor is to be found in official records, and that the content of the record is subject to highly variable interpretation. The presence or absence of information (for whatever reason), as well as how information is transmitted (for example, briefly or in full detail), will shape the definition of the act and actor and, in turn, determine how they are categorized (Emerson, 1969:111). The simple size or bulk of a person's file is itself regarded as symbolic of the extent (and seriousness) of his or her deviant career. Literally, the fatter the file the more likely is the actor to be seen as extensively and deeply involved in deviance. Hence, it contributes to the actor being defined as having a more indelibly delinquent moral character. Investigation of seemingly minor issues such as where a runaway spent the night, and linking the answer to the offender's appearance, may also influence the categorization. For example, how likely it is that a physically clean and neatly attired runaway spent the night sleeping in a doorway or a vacant lot? Is the presence of heavy makeup on the "sexually delinquent girl" indicative of a "typical" or a "criminal" (prostitution) case? Does the presence of several highly salable items in the auto trunk of a suspected juvenile shoplifter suggest a "typical" or a "criminal" case?

In short, categorization of an act and actor is highly problematic, and rests on a combination of several indices, which are themselves assigned meanings that allow acts and actors to be classed as "typical," "criminal," or "disturbed."

Evaluating Biography. Let's turn to the second area of concern: the actor's biography. In investigating the biography, court personnel may be oriented to use the the pitch or the denunciation. The pitch will be used to create the image of a youth whose school record, family situation, known delinquent history, and the like, allows for rehabilitation. A denunciation, on the other hand, is likely to be used for the youth whose background is defined as showing signs of progressive moral decline and the need for strict restraint and punishment. In either case, consulting the biography helps court personnel assess the actor's moral character as well as helping them to "place" the youth in terms of the development of a delinquent career (Emerson, 1969:120–121).

Which presentation is used, pitch or denunciation, depends on the court personnel's definition of where the youth stands vis-à-vis a delinquent career. In turn, the perceived stage of a youth's career rests on (1) the court's definition of his or her general pattern of delinquent behavior (is it characteristically "typical," "criminal," or "disturbed"?) and (2) the meaning of an array of environmental conditions (such as family situation) felt to contribute to serious delinquency (Emerson, 1969:121–132). The first of these concerns generally leads to a standard series of inquiries. Is the present offense one of a series of delinquencies? Has the youth had prior contact with the juvenile court? And, most important, has the youth had previous commitment to a training school, on which basis it may be inferred that a pattern of serious delinquency is well established? Should the presentation be of the denunciatory type, attention will focus on these questions and the details recounted.

Events of a more personal nature will also be investigated. What is the youth's "attitude"; that is, does his or her behavior (especially with respect to the police, the court, and the offense) reflect a "hard-core" delinquent or a person who is amenable to treatment? How does the offender get along with the staff and other students at school? What attitudinal pattern is reflected in the actor's academic record? Who are the actor's friends and how involved are they in delinquent acts? Information concerning all these matters is likely to be readily available, either in the offender's file or in that of others. Each piece of information is subject to collation and retrospective interpretation in an effort to "make sense" of the instance of deviance under investigation.

Turning to environmental conditions, investigation of the actor's biography tends to focus on those things presumed to have "causative" importance. Special importance is likely to be given to family background, particularly parental neglect or other conditions leading to reduced guidance and social control. The amount and kind of parental discipline, general conduct of the home, and whether the parents' behavior conforms to the moral expectations of the court, will affect the court's assessment of the child's moral character and prospects for the future. Basically, the questions posed concern the moral stature of the family. Is the family reputable or disreputable (Emerson, 1969:133; Matza, 1969)? If the latter label is felt to apply to the family, its stigmatizing power may well be transferred to the youth.

If these inquiries fail to provide sufficient information for categorizing of the offender, and if the actor's status remains ambiguous, the court may turn to outsiders for assistance (Emerson, 1969:133–136). A person whose reputation is above reproach (such as a clergy) and who is familiar with the offender may be called on to provide clarity. Clarity may also be provided by calling on expert witnesses such as a psychiatrist. Whether these or other resource persons are used depends on the apparent need to render character and behavior consistent. It is necessary to determine whether the case is typical or atypical. If a case is classed as atypical, the ambiguity of the actor's moral character and, consequently, how the case should be handled, becomes more than usually problematic.

The effort to resolve ambiguities inherent in atypical cases reveals the reciprocal nature of the presumed relation between moral character and behavior (Emerson, 1969:135–136). In typical cases, the delinquent act is inconsistent with the actor's "essentially" positive moral character. In such cases the act is "adjusted" (redefined) to fit the character. If moral character is obscure or uncertain, the benefit of the doubt goes to the juvenile. In atypical cases, however, these elements are interactive and consistent; act and biography point to moral character and, in turn, the constructed moral character reflects back on behavior. A consistent relationship between act and biography is thereby established; the goal of retrospective interpretation is achieved.

Total Denunciation—The "Hopeless Case." We conclude with a brief additional comment on denunciations. It has been noted that the denunciation tends to emphasize the socially negative aspects of a person's behavior and character. When carried to the extreme, and to be successful, denunciations preclude defense for the actor's behavior and weaken any support the actor may have for retaining a moral identity. Such cases, referred to as *total denunciations* (Emerson, 1969:137), call for constructing a "hopeless case." That is, the actor must be presented as one who has (1) had several viable opportunities to refrain from rule-violating behavior, but (2) has chosen to ignore or reject them in favor of delinquent conduct. The repetitiveness of the delinquent behavior—its patterned nature—is then used to support the conclusion that the youth is a "hopeless case," beyond reform, suited only for punitive (rather than rehabilitative) disposition. In view of the number of opportunities to "go straight" and the belief that they were rejected volitionally, the fault is seen to rest solely with the offender. In that sense, there is no defense for the actor's behavior.

Total denunciation disallows a defense in an additional way. First, all parties to the degradation ceremony—officials, witnesses, perhaps family—agree that the actor is a hopeless case. Thus, the actor is fully discredited. Second, disallowing a defense means that there is no meaningful alternative disposition than detention. Such a disposition must be established as a logical and reasonable consequence of the youth having failed to take advantage of the rehabilitative opportunities provided earlier in his or her career. This failure is used to mark the actor's essential character as discreditable. Using "unresponsiveness to rehabilitation" as evidence of defective character, detention becomes the only reasonable disposition of the case.

Finally, anyone who would launch a defense of the actor, suggesting that he or she is yet a socially redeemable person, anyone who would question the propriety of total denunciation of a thoroughly immoral character, must be discounted and such a position discredited. Likewise, persons likely to support the youth, such as parents, are often encouraged to join in the denunciation of the actor, at least to the degree of conceding that he or she should be sent away for "his or her own good." In brief, parents and others are encouraged to concur in the denunciation. In this regard, total denunciation involves a systematic connection, a *circuit of agents* (Goffman, 1973:100), between court officials, next-of-kin, police, and defense counsel (usually a public defender) who engage in a process of *stripping,* that is, official removal of the symbols of a socially acceptable being.

In sum, then, degradation ceremonies mark a change in the definition of a person's moral status. However, this moral recasting is not an automatic consequence of the person's behavior. Consistent with our comments throughout, it can be seen that court officials do not respond to any definitive or objective moral meaning associated with the offender's behavior. The behavior's moral meaning is problematic; it rests on matters of context, biography, and the presentation of materials to the court. Uppermost in this process is the establishment of a sense of consistency among the actor's behavior, biography, and presumed character. In turn, consistency serves to legitimate the court's disposition of the case. Overall, the decisions reached are consequences of a socially constructed reality. Moral congruence is a social construction.

Resistance to Labeling

The theoretical model employed in this book conceives of people as interactive agents who seek to shape their destiny by interacting with elements in their effective environment. Consistent with this model is the assumption that people will not submit meekly to status degradation and moral recasting. As with other aspects of the deviance enterprise, the assignment of moral meanings is problematic, sometimes subject to negotiation. That observation applies as well to efforts to induct people into the status of deviant. In this section we examine how people resist labeling and what factors appear to help them in resisting.

Power: Bargaining and Negotiation as Strategies

One major factor influencing the labeling process is the relative power of the labeler and the labelee. As noted in Chapter 4, the distribution of power in society is rarely, if ever, balanced; it is distributed unevenly. But it is rarely so imbalanced that one party has all, while another has none. This is especially so considering the coalitions, exchange of favors, situational advantages, and other factors that may enhance a person's power position. It should be no surprise, then, that power may be employed in strategic ways by both parties (labeler and labelee) engaged in the labeling process.

One expression of the strategic use of influence to affect labeling is *plea bargaining* (Newman, 1966), whereby defendants in criminal cases plead guilty to reduced charges in return for considerations such as reduced punishment. In exchange, prosecutors are relieved of the need to expend scarce resources to conduct a full-scale prosecution of a relatively minor or routine case. Most pertinent in this strategy is the fact that these pleas are arranged, arrived at through bargaining, by means of which prosecution and defense seek satisfactory outcomes. Each (prosecution and defense) has the ability to influence the other and each exercises "skill"—a clear case of intercursive power. The negotiations involve activity that is far from consistent with stereotyped beliefs about the operation of the criminal justice system. Certainly, negotiated pleas run counter to ideas such as "the punishment fits the crime," that "rules of evidence" are scrupulously adhered to, and that in the American justice system guilt and innocence are determined in adversary proceedings according to the rules of due process. In fact, between 90 and 95 percent of all convictions for crimes in this country are achieved without trial and under conditions substantially at odds with stated ideals (Blumberg, 1967:29; Newman, 1966:3).

Plea bargaining is instructive for students of social reality in that it demonstrates the problematic nature of assessing responsibility. The deviant's responsibility is negotiated and calls for the construction of reality, including the actor's intentions and behavior, as well as the criteria of responsibility. Responsibility, then, is not an absolute (Scheff, 1968:3–4). Negotiation of such matters is, of course, well known among students, particularly in American colleges and universities. It is not uncommon for failing students to "plead their case" before instructors; that is, they seek to avoid having a failing or otherwise unacceptable grade entered in their record. Unacceptable grades have implications for students' images, particularly regarding their capacity to learn and/or their ability to responsibly play the role of student. The consequence of that image for one's employability is immediately obvious. In short, students, like people in general, and publicly apprehended deviants in particular, seek to avoid stigma labels by the process of negotiation.

Efforts to negotiate an acceptable self-image may take more subtle forms. One of these is the effort people make to amass "moral credits" that may be used ("drawn on") at a time when their image as a moral person is jeopardized by public knowledge of wrongdoing. Having these credits available helps support a person's claim to an acceptable social position despite having broken rules. We illustrate with a case involving an unmarried, pregnant high school girl. Throughout her life this girl took pride in being a "good Catholic girl" who

never allowed boys to "take advantage" of her. She then fell in love, submitted to her young man's advances, and became pregnant. Neither wished to marry. Without funds, flight was impossible. For the same reason, and reinforced by very strong religious convictions, abortion was out of the question. Finally, living with her parents in a small town made it readily apparent that in due time her pregnancy would become intolerably public.

The way this girl tried to neutralize the anticipated consequences of her pregnancy was to amass moral credits upon which she could draw when and if she was faced with stigmatization and a spoiled identity. She did this by giving up smoking and what small amount of alcohol she consumed, refraining from parties and other forms of revelry (however mild), doing every extra chore she could to help her parents, working very hard in school to raise her grades—in short, living as ascetic and exemplary a life as one of her age and circumstance could. In these ways she sought to create a highly positive moral image of self, one that would survive the consequences of revealing her pregnancy.

Similarly, in 1980, then Texas Rangers pitcher and Canadian resident Ferguson Jenkins was found guilty in a Canadian court of possession of cocaine. Though guilty, Jenkins was given an absolute discharge and freed without penalty. In announcing this ruling the Ontario Provincial Court Judge told Jenkins, "You seem to be a person who has conducted himself in exemplary fashion in the community and in the country, *building up an account.* This is the time to *draw on that account*" (*Arizona Republic,* 1980f; emphasis added). Jenkins had been a recipient of the Cy Young Award (for outstanding Major League Pitching) and the prestigious Order of Canada. Having been honored in these ways surely placed Jenkins in a position of advantage relative to the disposition of his case. Nonetheless, being freed without penalty was only accomplished as a result of negotiation between Jenkins' defense lawyer and the court.

Avoidance of labeling may also be achieved by people's efforts to "subvert the system."

117

An instructive case is that of some persons who, despite frequent and extensive episodes of drunk driving, manage to avoid being identified as alcoholic and/or convicted of driving while intoxicated (DWI). In a study of the subculture of men who regularly patronize (hang out in) a tavern, Kotarba (1984) discovered that these men's awareness of (1) their constant heavy drinking, (2) the importance of driving in the conduct of their daily affairs, and (3) the potentially damaging personal consequences of being identified as an alcoholic or a drunk driver had marked effect on their conversation and behavior. First, by swapping yarns about how they successfully handle problems associated with driving while intoxicated, these men provide one another with *justifications* for such action and try to minimize the negative official meaning of drinking and driving. Of major importance is avoidance of the idea that they are alcoholic, that they may be "slaves to alcohol," or that they cannot "hold their liquor." Second, conversations also provide these men with *recipe knowledge* concerning how to manage problems that can arise when driving while intoxicated. Included is information on how to deal with the potentially damaging consequences for self feelings when faced with a DWI conviction. Finally, because the tavern these men frequent is also a gathering place for many off-duty police officers, the drinking drivers are able to become acquainted and socialize with officers. This is seen by the drinkers as "a good investment in the future, for they will have a handy reserve of names to drop in case they are stopped while driving. . . . 'name dropping' is the most effective means for avoiding arrest for DWI" (Kotarba: 1984:158). In brief, then, the tavern subculture shared by these men includes a substantial body of knowledge enabling them to protect themselves against the potential of being labeled despite their persistence in behavior they know is officially forbidden. The means at their disposal enable them to "subvert the system"; again, labeling is a highly problematic occurrence.

Still another instance of people trying to avoid labeling involves the tendency of some actors to "put on a performance" in the presence of rule enforcers. Putting on a performance (Lorber, 1967:303) is by no means unusual when people wish to influence or control the conduct of others toward themselves (which is almost always). Where is the child who has never attempted to influence his or her parents' behavior? A person may achieve this control "largely by influencing the definition of the situation which the others come to formulate, and he can influence this definition by expressing himself in such a way as to give the kind of impression that will lead them to act voluntarily in accordance with his own plan" (Goffman, 1959:4). For example, a woman known to the author was stopped by a policeman for speeding. Though she is a highly articulate, intelligent person, she immediately went into her "act," speaking and behaving in a helpless, deferential, self-demeaning manner, professing all the time to be ignorant of the rules. She got off with a verbal warning. On leaving the scene she commented "Mark one for me!"

Another example of this was noted by Richard Nagasawa during his investigation of delinquency in Seattle, Washington (Chambliss and Nagasawa, 1969). In coversation with the Japanese-American boys he studied, it became clear to Nagasawa that they attempted to influence police definitions of their behavior. For example, playing on the already existing favorable bias police had of them, these boys would explain their presence on the streets at unusual hours as a consequence of work or other socially acceptable conditions. During predaylight hours the excuse frequently used was "preparing for newspaper delivery." They often explained late night hours by claiming they were "detained at a late Boy Scout or other socially acceptable club meeting" (personal communication).

Another factor influencing labeling is the offender's demeanor in the presence of police (Piliavin and Briar, 1964). Youthful offenders who display respect for the police and fear of sanctions, and who are penitent (all of which may be feigned) are most prone to be given a formal or informal reprimand and released. However, youth who are "fractious, obdurate, and nonchalant" are more likely to be viewed as "tough-guys" or "punks" and arrested (Piliavin and Briar, 1964:210–211). In addition, evidence suggests that labels may be withheld or less firmly applied if offenders are contrite and willingly acknowledge having violated an important rule. By taking a repentant position the violator (1) acknowledges the legitimacy of the rule and, thereby, (2) establishes a moral consensus (albeit counterfeit) between him- or herself and the control agent (Gusfield, 1967:179). In this way violators are able to influence the behavior of labelers.

Resistance to labeling was also noted by Emerson in his work on the juvenile court, where youths display a number of protective or defensive strategies. One such strategy is *innocence,* whereby the youth professes technical or factual innocence of the charge. This is particularly effective when evidence is conflicting and the case is inconclusive (Emerson, 1969:144–149). A second strategy is to use justifications, either principled or situational. *Principled justifications* require "placing" the youth in a situation involving a conflict of principles (not unlike an "appeal to higher loyalties") the resolution of which allegedly resulted in the violation. *Situational justifications* are used when a youth cites the contingencies of his or her actual situation. Thus, the act is acknowledged to be wrong, but the circumstances are said to have been such as to permit an exception. Third, resistance to labeling frequently involves *excuses,* stories designed to reduce the wrongfulness of the act. Well-handled, "reasonable excuses allow the court to form and maintain an acceptable evaluation of moral character and in this way further favorable dispositions" (Emerson, 1969:153). Elements used in excuses include duress, accident, ignorance, or that one was innocently led into an act that was planned and initiated by others.

A final tactic used by accused persons seeking to obstruct labeling is *counterdenunciation,* that is, attacking the actions and motives and/or character of one's accusers (Emerson, 1969:156ff)—essentially, "condemning one's condemners." As employed by youth facing delinquency charges, this may take the form of trying to diminish one's guilt by attacking and lowering the moral character and reputation of an accuser, however irrelevant that may be. Thus, a youth accused of auto theft attempted to minimize his guilt by identifying the victim as homosexual. Attacks on the moral character of one's accuser is also a highly popular form of defense against the charge of rape. "The standard defense strategy for punching holes in a rape case was (and is) an attempt to destroy the credibility of the complaining witness by smearing her as mentally unbalanced, or as sexually frustrated, or as an oversexed, promiscuous whore" (Brownmiller, 1975:238). Another type of tactic is to counter a denunciation by alleging the complainant's motive is to intimidate the accused, or that the accusation is illegitimate—that is, that the accusation stems from jealousy rather than the person's actual involvement in rule-breaking behavior. As used in political trials (Parker and Lauderdale, 1980:54ff), counterdenunciation may take the form of appealing to higher loyalties or, as noted earlier, may involve an attempt at justification. For example, a man on trial for violation of the Universal Military Training and Service Act (refusal of military induction) likened the prosecution to the defendants at the famous Nuremberg trials of war criminals following World War II. (In the latter instance, the accused defended themselves on the basis of their having been obligated to "follow orders" regardless of the moral implications of doing so.) In the UMTSA trial the prosecutor was cast in the role of blindly serving the government despite its involvement in grossly immoral actions. The defendant, on the other hand, portrayed his refusal of induction as a matter of principle (a matter of "higher loyalties"), reflecting his orientation toward peace and humanity rather than toward the state's policy of war and destruction (Bannan and Bannan, 1974:25). In this and other ways the defendant sought to undermine the legitimacy of the prosecution and point up the impropriety of the charges against him.

In these and many other ways individuals seek to limit the capacity of officials to attach labels. This effort is consistent with the model of human nature used in this volume. As interactive agents, people seek to direct and control the actions of others toward themselves. However, as we will see in Chapter 7, efforts to resist and neutralize the effects of labeling go well beyond our immediate concerns.

Social Distance

An additional factor influencing the probability of labeling is *social distance* (the degree of intimacy and sympathetic understanding between people). As the intimacy and sympathetic understanding between labeler and labelee increase, the probability of being labeled decreases. The operation of this rule of typing was noted in research on unwed fathers, men who had impregnated women to whom they were not married. In most of the relationships studied, the couples had been introduced by friends or family members, had attended school together, regarded themselves as regular dating partners, and in a great majority of cases professed to have strong emotional attachment for one another. These characteristics suggested that the couples shared a common group identity (had minimal social distance) and that typing and labeling would be unlikely. This expectation was fulfilled (Pfuhl, 1978). Similarly, Emerson reports that when complaints against a youth are brought by a person of his or her own age, or by a family member (wherein social distance is minimal) counterdenunciation is likely to succeed and the charges be dismissed. But when the complainant and the accused are socially distant, counterdenunciation is more difficult; that is, charges are less likely to be dismissed (Emerson, 1969:160–161). As Rubington and Weinberg note (1973:9), the tendency is to grant rule breaking in-group members the benefit of the doubt and withhold the attribution of deviant.

As a final example of the role of social distance we refer to the identification of accused persons as child abusers. Newberger and Bourne suggest that physicians are least likely to identify an individual as an abuser if that person and the physician share similar social characteristics, especially similar socioeconomic status. However, if the suspected abuser is perceived to be "socially marginal"—that is, to show signs of poverty, be unemployed,

have a large family, be alcoholic, have a low level of education, and so on, the probability of being confirmed as a child abuser increases substantially (Newberger and Bourne, 1978:601).

Ambiguity of Moral Meaning

Another influence on the labeling process is the clarity/ambiguity of moral meaning. That is, before actors are labeled, their behavior most often is defined as an "uncommon event"—one that might have been otherwise and that has violated a clear and important social rule. In the case of unwed fatherhood, referred to above, the important social rule is "don't impregnate unmarried women." Given this rule, the men responsible for these pregnancies were prime candidates for labeling. Nonetheless, sanctions were almost never imposed. Reconciliation of this apparent inconsistency between rule violation and the absence of labeling leads us to consider the ambiguity in terms of the distinction between the *morality of intention* and the *morality of consequence*.

"Morality of intention" refers to the tradition in which the criteria of blamefulness include the actor's purpose, negligence, recklessness, and knowledge (Packer, 1968:105). On the basis of intention these men are culpable. Each was aware of his purpose (intention) and the possible consequences of his behavior (knowledge), and each behaved negligently or recklessly by ignoring (failing to take adequate precautions against) the risk of pregnancy. In that sense the moral meanings seem clear and the men are sanctionable.

Nonetheless, they avoided being labeled, suggesting that in place of the morality of intention a different morality was employed—the morality of consequence. According to this morality, culpability or blamefulness rests not on the sexual misbehavior, but on how the man behaves following the pregnancy, especially whether he assumes the role of "protector" of the woman. That is, for these men to be labeled seems unrelated to their sexual conduct or its consequence, the pregnancies. If applied at all, the label is attached *ex post facto,* that is, after the man's intentions toward the woman become evident. In other words, whether or not the man "stood by" the woman was more important than his initial sexual misconduct.

The men in this study and those in a position to label them used a "morality of consequence." Very often men referred to a need to "clean things up," that is, to take steps to reduce or eliminate any problems associated with the pregnancy. Such steps included marrying the woman, helping her to meet medical and living costs, arranging and/or paying all or part of the cost of abortion, and otherwise "standing by" her. A morality of consequence was also apparent in the sex codes these men embraced, codes that included the importance of preventing any negative consequences such as pregnancy, venereal disease, and reputational damage as a consequence of sexual behavior. Last, many of the parents of these men and women expressed a morality of consequence by insisting that the man "set things right" or "do the proper thing" with regard to the woman. Fulfillment of these expectations apparently took precedence over their having violated the morality of intention.

While the implications of this study may not be generalized to the labeling process as a whole, there does appear to be a priority or "ranking" of moralities in terms of which the labeling process is sometimes ordered. That is, we have not one rule but two; it seems clear that being sanctioned for violating one rule is dependent on whether one is perceived to be in violation of the other (Pfuhl, 1978:127–128). In short, in some instances, whether or not labeling occurs depends on which moral rule is invoked and under what circumstances it shall be invoked. These things are matters of interpretation. Again, then, labeling is a highly problematic event and a matter of social construction.[6]

[6]According to Jeanette Covington's recent research (1984), one possible defense against labeling is the moral ambiguity of one's offense. Most ambiguous are so-called victimless crimes. Given the ambiguity of the morality of such offenses (their morality is less absolute), an actor's self-justifying accounts may be more effective in resisting the efforts of labelers. Thus, the ability of unwed fathers to resist or avoid labeling may reflect a lack of moral absoluteness concerning that matter.

Odds and Ends

Valuable information concerning the problematics of labeling has also come from investigations in the general field of mental health. Studies have shown that several *factors independent of an actor's behavior or mental state* influence the outcome of investigations to determine a person's legal competency (the legal counterpart of mental illness). These investigations are ordinarily initiated by a complaint filed on the basis of someone's evaluation of the actor's behavior. The outcome of these official investigations (sometimes formal hearings are convened)—that is, whether the actor is declared to be legally incompetent—seems to vary with the age of the alleged incompetent, the composition of the investigating committee, and the type of petition filed in the case.

The younger the client the less likely he or she is to be declared incompetent. Perhaps this pattern stems from the positive valuation assigned youth and, conversely, the increased tendency of older people to become economically dependent and/or to be seen as nonproductive members of society. Second, if investigative bodies consist of psychiatrists, the probability increases that a decision of incompetence will result, likely as an expression of the psychiatric construction of reality. Being trained to identify mental illness, psychiatrists do precisely that! Third, as social distance between the petitioner and the alleged incompetent decreases (that is, as petitioner and actor become more intimately associated), so does the likelihood that a judgment of incompetence will result. A petition filed by members of a family against one of its members has less chance of being supported than it would otherwise. Reluctance to assign a label of mental illness in such cases is likely to reflect community definitions of family interrelations. In any case, it is quite clear that labeling is influenced by factors other than the mental state of the person under examination (Haney and Michielutte, 1968:241).

Additional research on the subject of labeling the mentally ill—this time on lunacy hearings—reveals

that those persons who were able to approach the judge [in a lunacy hearing] in a controlled manner, use proper eye contact, sentence structure, posture, etc., and who presented their stories without excessive emotional response or blandness and with proper demeanor, were able to obtain the decision they wanted, whether it was release or commitment—despite any "psychiatric symptomatology." (Miller and Schwartz, 1966:34)

Research also shows that the outcome of admissions hearings at some state hospitals for the mentally ill is conclusively influenced by whether or not the alleged incompetent is represented at the hearing by a private attorney. Thus, in 81 admission cases studied, it was found that "61 (91%) of those without legal counsel ($N = 66$) were admitted, but only 4 (26%) of those with legal counsel ($N = 15$) were admitted" (Wegner and Fletcher, 1969:69). It was also found that this relationship between legal representation and admissions decisions persisted when the patient's behavior was held constant. That is, even when the patient met psychiatric criteria for admission, his or her chances of being admitted were significantly lower with legal representation than without (Wegner and Fletcher, 1969:70–71).

As these data reveal, then, the attribution of a deviant label is far from an automatic or inevitable consequence of rule-breaking behavior. Due to the influence of several factors, many of which are quite tangential to the principal issue of the actor's behavior, labels may be changed (as in the case of plea bargaining) or entirely withheld (as at many competency hearings).

However, labeling and the general demeanor of the deviant are not totally independent of one another. Evidence reveals that in some cases the deviant contributes to his or her own discovery and official stigmatization. One such example was revealed in research comparing homosexuals discharged from military service with honorable discharges and those receiving less than honorable discharges (LHD). It was found that the probability of receiving an LHD is greater for those homosexuals in the military who are highly active sexually than for those who have infrequent sexual contact. The probability of receiving an LHD is also greater for those who select their homosexual partners from among military person-

nel. In short, it is not just practicing homosexuality that influences being labeled and sanctioned. Official labeling is also influenced by the perceived character of the actor's behavior, a matter over which actors are able to exert some influence (Williams and Weinberg, 1970).

In brief, then, the dynamics of status degradation and labeling are influenced by many factors, suggesting that the outcome of these proceedings is far from certain and, like other aspects of the deviance process, may not be taken for granted.

Summary

This chapter has focused on "creating deviants," that is, on the informal and formal procedures by which people come to regard themselves and come to be regarded by others as deviant—on how people's selves are recast to conform with what is known of their deviant behavior. This has entailed a consideration of deviance as a status—achieved and ascribed, primary and secondary—and consideration of the seeming capacity of a person's deviant status—a master status—to obscure the balance of his or her self.

Extended consideration was also given to the institutionalization of deviance—to how responsibility for responding to deviant persons is assigned to bureaucratic organizations, how these organizations operate, and what their consequences are for the client population. Of major importance are (1) the principal rationale for the conduct of these agencies—the theory of office—and (2) how, in total institutions, these agencies socialize the client to a role consistent with that of a person who is seen as essentially deviant. Not the least important element in this process is the influence of stereotypes. Relying on the work of imputational specialists, and by a process of retrospective interpretation, a biography of the deviant is constructed that validates the label assigned to him or her. In this way an actor's character and behavior may be shown to be consistent. A further consequence is that the conduct of the agency vis-à-vis the client is legitimized. The culmination of much of the labeling process is noted in the degradation ceremony—such as court trials and similar procedures.

Overall, being cast as deviant is a consequence of a process that may have only a marginal relationship to a person's prior behavior and the meaning assigned to it. An example of how behavior, actor, and actor's biography are linked together, demonstrative of the problematic outcome of the labeling process, was provided by an extended consideration of the degradation ceremony of the juvenile court.

Part of what renders the outcome of these proceedings problematic—uncertain—is that the decisions reached are negotiable (hence, unpredictable), subject to the influence of several situational factors, and altogether resistable. Consideration was given to several factors influencing the labeling process.

For all of that, some people do get labeled. Their principal identity does come (at least officially and publicly) to be that of deviant. What are the effects of a "spoiled identity"? We turn now to a consideration of the consequences of labeling and stigma.

6 Consequences of Stigma

Introduction

We have noted that most people who break rules are never publicly identified as rule breakers. That is, most are never formally assigned the status and identity of deviant. Further, many of those who are formally processed and labeled deviant are able to challenge labelers and avoid the potentially serious consequences of labeling. In short, whether an attempt is made to label a rule breaker, and whether such an attempt is successful, is far from certain. However, it is equally apparent that many people do get labeled, often indelibly, with the result that their public identity is "spoiled" and they are burdened with the consequences of stigma. This chapter deals with identity spoilage and stigma, that is, with the personal and social consequences of being labeled. We are concerned with what happens to people when they "become the thing they are named" (Manning, 1975:2). In addressing these matters we consider the third phase of the deviance process identified by Kitsuse: how people are accorded the treatment defined as appropriate for deviants.

To adequately represent this aspect of the deviance process and to avoid misunderstanding, we begin by examining the concepts of stigma and spoiled identity. To better understand the consequences of stigmatization, we follow this discussion with a brief treatment of the theoretical aspect of the labeling perspective. We then consider the practical consequences of labeling in both social psychological (personal) and social terms. Finally, we deal with and attempt to make sense of conflicting research evidence bearing on disputed aspects of the labeling process. Throughout our analysis we will adhere to the relevant elements of the Paradigm of Definition presented in Chapter 1.

Stigma and Spoiled Identities

The term *stigma* (plural: *stigmata*) refers to a mark or brand (such as that imposed on slaves) indicating the bearer's low *social position* and others' perception of the bearer as an "outsider." Such stigmata have long been used to call public attention to people's low *moral position* as, for example, in the case of criminals. This sense of stigma is demonstrated in Nathaniel Hawthorne's famous novel *The Scarlet Letter,* wherein the heroine, Hester Prynne, is required to wear the letter "A" (for adulteress). In this case the stigma represents not only someone's violation of moral rules, but the despicability and shame of the guilty person.

The case of Hester Prynne also reveals that stigmata reflect on the bearer's identity. Earlier we noted that the labeling process includes an effort to establish consistency between behavior and character; that is, to establish that one who is known to have done deviance must be made deviant. In keeping with this, a person who bears a discrediting stigma is taken to be an instance of the thing described by that sign. Thus, the scarlet "A" on Hester Prynne's garment symbolized her moral defect. The bearer's public identity is that of a person who is spoiled, morally corrupted, or otherwise tainted (Goffman, 1963:19).

To be sure, not all stigmata are alike. Goffman suggests three types (1963:4–5). First, there are *abominations of the body,* that is, conditions such as physical deformities resulting from birth, illness, or accident that are regarded as repugnant or odious and that may be used to place the individual in a discredited category. These are most often associated with cases of ascriptive deviance. A classic example of someone with such a stigma is Quasimodo, in Victor Hugo's *Hunchback of Notre Dame.*

Second are *blemishes of character,* qualities inferentially based on the person having engaged in things like crime, homosexuality, or political radicalism; having attempted suicide; having been diagnosed as mentally ill; and the like. Again, character and behavior are rendered consistent. As an example, political radicals are often taken to be (characterologically) dangerous, impulsive, and aggressive, while adulterers are often assumed to be (characterologically) immoral, promiscuous, and insecure (Simmons, 1969:29). Finally, there are *tribal stigma.* In Goffman's terms, these are the "stigma of race, nation, and religion, . . . stigma that can be transmitted through lineages and [that] equally contaminate all members of a family" (Goffman, 1963:4). Examples include skin color and names that have specific religious and/or national connotations. In most cases, these stigmata, like abominations of the body, are matters of ascription rather than achievement.

Regardless of type, all stigmata share one sociological feature: They symbolize that one occupies a *master status.* As Goffman notes: "an individual who might have been received easily in ordinary social intercourse possesses a trait that can obtrude itself upon attention and turn those of us whom he meets away from him, breaking the claim that his other attributes have on us" (Goffman, 1963:5). In theory, then, stigmata denote a person's morally *spoiled identity*—social undesirability—and take precedence over other qualities to which the person may lay claim. On the basis of the attributed "spoilage," the person is rejected.

With these few definitions and examples in mind, let us now place the issue of stigmatization and its consequences into a larger theoretical framework. By examining stigmatization from the symbolic interactionist perspective, we may better appreciate its social and social psychological consequences.

Consequences of Labeling: Theory

Theoretical Foundations
The origins of the labeling perspective are found in the work of Charles Horton Cooley

and George Herbert Mead. These scholars employed a *symbolic interactionist* perspective, a form of social psychology stressing the idea that human behavior and personality rest on people's facility for developing and using language (symbols) to transmit meaning. In this perspective human interaction rests largely on these meanings; hence social interaction becomes symbolic interaction. Most important is the symbolic interactionist contention that a person's self-image or self-concept emerges in interaction with others.

An example of this contention is Cooley's idea that people's self-feeling consists of three elements: (1) how they imagine they appear to another person, (2) their imagination of how the other judges their appearance, and (3) a resulting self-feeling (Cooley, 1902:184). As a result of this interactive process, people evaluate their behavior, attitudes, and general appearance on the basis of how they think others evaluate these same things. Cooley noted that "we always imagine, and in imagining share, the judgments of the other [person's] mind" (Cooley, 1902:184–185). From such imaginings we derive self-feelings such as shame, pride, mortification, and embarrassment, among others.

The position taken by George Herbert Mead is compatible with that of Cooley. According to Mead, people are able to see themselves as objects as a result of *role taking,* that is, putting themselves in another's position and identifying with that person (Meltzer, 1967:9). Taking the role of the other depends on the ability to use symbols to communicate or transmit meanings. By learning the symbols commonly employed in the groups with which one associates—family, neighborhood, friendship cliques, and so on—a person learns others' meanings and definitions of things and tends to internalize them. People are then able to put themselves in others' roles—take the role of the other—and have others' perspectives become their own. "The standpoint of others provides a platform for getting outside oneself and viewing oneself as others do. The development of the self is concurrent with the development of the ability to take roles" (Meltzer, 1967:10). This, as well as the development of a self-conception, is the consequence of the socialization process. It is through this general process that identity is acquired. As Peter Berger notes, "identity is socially bestowed, socially sustained and socially transformed" (Berger, 1963:98). It is the theory underlying this transformation of a person's self in relation to stigmatizing labels that concerns us. To better appreciate how these matters pertain to labeling deviants, let's expand briefly on these theoretical issues.

As we noted in Chapter 5, the concepts of primary and secondary deviant contrast with one another. Major differences between them are (1) their concern for the degree to which the lives of primary and secondary deviants are organized around the facts of their deviance and (2) the difference in the way they view themselves, that is, their self-concept. As indicated, the primary deviant's transgressions are unknown to public agencies and do not become the subject of a public forum (a degration ceremony). They have not been publicly labeled. In the absence of labeling, it is assumed, the primary deviants' rule breaking remains incidental and subordinate to the actors' law-abiding behavior. In their own eyes as well as others', the actors continue to be regarded as "essentially innocent." To appreciate how actors may be transformed from "essentially innocent" to "basically evil" persons by reason of labeling calls for brief examination of the distinction between the concepts of *essential* or *substantial self* and the concept of *situational self*.

In writing about the self, Mead distinguished between the "I" and the "Me" as phases of people's personality. "Phases" means that the distinction between the "I" and the "Me" is analytical only, and that in Mead's view these elements are integrated to form the personality (Natanson, 1973:17). Viewed analytically, the "I" refers to that aspect of self that is "independent of any particular situations, what the individual considers himself to be at all times" (Douglas, 1967:280–281). As such, the "I" corresponds roughly to what other scholars have referred to as the *essential* or *substantial self*. Thus, the terms *essential* and *essence* have been used to refer to those aspects

of self that transcend particular situations and that reflect what one is "really" thought to be, that is, "in essence," "in the first place," "all along," "in the final analysis," "originally" (Garfinkel, 1956). Similarly, the term *substantial self* has been used to refer to the "complex of meanings—or characteristics—which are imputed to a person as a whole (as a substance), not as a player of special roles in special scenes and times" (Douglas, 1967:282).

The "Me", on the other hand, refers to the "*social self,* the object that arises in interaction" (Charon, 1979:82). That is, the "Me" corresponds to people's *situated selves*—to the way people refer to themselves when self is considered in terms of specific roles and statuses. Viewed this way, people have many situated selves; theoretically, they have one for every situation or activity they are involved in.

Consistent with the idea that the "I" and the "Me" are integrated, Douglas (1967:282) suggests that assigning a substantial self ("I") to an actor is a consequence of having previously assigned a series of situated selves ("Me") to the person. Ultimately, one comes to acquire a substantial self due to having been repeatedly identified in particular ways ("good Joe," "sweet gal," "jerk," "scum bag," and so on). Once established, the substantial self ("I") begins to take command, as it were, and subtly influences the subsequent situated selves assigned to the actor. To recapitulate, the assignment of successive situated selves over a prolonged period leads to the development of a substantial self, a notion of what the person "really is." In turn, the nature of the substantial self places limits on what sorts of situated selves might thereafter appropriately be assigned to the actor. A degree of consonance between these selves will be established.

How the substantial and situated selves relate to the process of labeling deviants may now be made clear. As indicated above, a person's self (or selves) is reflected in the name(s) used to refer to the actor; such names as "jerk," "creep," "bright," and so on are both the terms by which people are known and the linguistic categories to which they are assigned. In short, the names people use to refer to themselves, and by which others know them, serve to "locate" or place people in the social order and to rank them relative to others. That is, some names are more prestigious and more highly valued than others. It is the names by which we and others know us that constitutes our *identity*.

A person's identity, however, derives from several sources. One of these is the labels imposed on people guilty of some transgression.[1] As Rosenberg indicates, these transgressions are usually referred to by the use of verbs such as drinking, stealing, indulging, selling, and so on (1979:10). So, one is drinking alcohol, stealing money, indulging in drugs, or selling sexual favors. Once it is certified that the actor has engaged in the transgression, he or she is "located" in a category reserved for persons of his or her sort. Thus, the drinker is "located" or categorized as alcoholic, one who steals is categorized as a thief, one who uses drugs becomes an addict, and one who sells sexual favors becomes a prostitute. In each instance a noun takes the place of the verb; *when nouns replace verbs and are used as devices to characterize people, labeling has occurred.*

The implications of being known by these nouns are several and have a direct bearing on the consequences of stigma (Rosenberg, 1979:12ff). First, just as we noted earlier in the case of stereotyping, people are responded to in terms of these names and the categories to which they are assigned. Likewise, occupants of each category are subject to a set of expectations. Thus, regardless of whether they satisfy the expectation, people known as criminals, drug addicts, or mental patients are expected to display certain behaviors and traits

commonly felt to be characteristic of persons of that type. Second, these names serve as the basis for ranking and evaluating people. If, in the current scheme of things, the names by which people are known have strong negative meaning (as in the case of stigmatizing names), they are likely to be appropriately devalued. In short, the names by which people are known are directly linked with their perceived social worth. Finally, consistent with the symbolic interactionist perspective, these names or labels impact directly on how people judge themselves, that is, on how people feel about themselves. Thus, at least theoretically, people who are known by negatively valued names are likely to experience correspondingly negative feelings of self.

In summary, these theoretical considerations suggest that (1) how people are defined, evaluated, and responded to by others is reflected in the names others use to identify them, and (2) how people are defined, evaluated and responded to by others have important consequences for their self-feelings. Theory predicts, then, that labeling is likely to have both social psychological and social consequences. Before examining that prediction, however, there is one additional preliminary issue to consider: deviance amplification.

Amplification and Stabilization of Deviance

As we've seen, the labeling process is intended to identify a person as deviant. If the process is successful, the labelee comes to occupy the status of deviant and is expected to play the role, that is, display the appropriate behavior. As with any status, deviance is linked to a set of meanings (in this case, moral meanings symbolized by the stigma) that are appended to the occupants of the status. Occupying a status and playing the role likely results in the incumbent being socialized to the role, which process includes learning the self-feelings appropriate to that role.

These considerations have led to a major proposition of the labeling perspective that may be called the *amplification hypothesis*. Briefly, this hypothesis states that *"rule breakers become entrenched in deviant roles because they are*

---

[1]Rosenberg (1979:10–12) suggests five other categories of identity: (1) *social statuses* based on people's age, sex, occupation, and so on; (2) *membership groups,* including those based on ethnicity or cultural background, religion, sociopolitical affiliation, friendship groups, interest groups, and other categories such as race; (3) *derived statuses,* those positions one occupies on the basis of prior statuses, such as war veteran, ex-con, divorcee, and so on; (4) *social types,* referring to the names given people as they are located in standard categories based on their interests, attitudes, behavior, and so on, including such typifications as egghead, jock, jerk; and (5) *personal identity,* usually referred to by a person's unique name or, in some cases, a social security number or fingerprint.

labeled 'deviant' by others and are consequently excluded from resuming normal roles in the community" (Mankoff, 1971:201; emphasis in original). This proposition arose very early in the development of the labeling perspective. Tannenbaum (1938) maintained that to "dramatize" the evil of the wrongful act serves only to perpetuate the conflict between the rule breaker and society, a conflict likely to have negative consequences for the actor's self-image. Tannenbaum writes:

From the community's point of view, the individual who used to do bad and mischievous things has now become a bad and unredeemable human being. From the individual's point of view there has taken place a similar change. He has gone slowly from a sense of grievance and injustice, of being unduly mistreated and punished, to a recognition that the definition of him as a human being is different from that of other boys in his neighborhood, his school, street, community. This recognition on his part becomes a process of self-identification and integration with the group which shares his activities. (1938:17)

It was Tannenbaum's view that the community reaction, more than a person's behavior or character, was the critical factor in stabilizing people in the position of deviant.

Echoing this viewpoint, Kai Erikson maintains that community response to deviants, particularly deviants experiencing degradation ceremonies, leaves the actor in a position from which there may be little or no escape. Underlying community rejection is the negative moral meaning attributed to the deviant and symbolized by the stigma. In turn, "the community's reluctance to accept the deviant back helps reduce whatever chance he might otherwise have for a successful readjustment" (Erikson, 1964:17). Community rejection, then, is alleged to be a fundamental element in people becoming secondary deviants.

Another contributor to the labeling perspective, Howard Becker, takes a similar position. Becker maintains that "one of the most crucial steps in the process of building a stable pattern of deviant behavior [becoming a secondary deviant] is likely to be the experience of being caught and publicly labeled as a deviant" (1973:31). It is claimed that, rule-violating behavior aside, whether or not one's deviant ori-

entation becomes crystallized is at least partly dependent on others' reactions to the alleged deviant. Again, Tannenbaum:

The first dramatization of the "evil" which separates the child out of his group for specialized treatment plays a greater role in making the criminal than perhaps any other experience. . . . The process of making the criminal . . . is a process of tagging defining, identifying, segregating, describing, emphasizing, making conscious and self-conscious; it becomes a way of stimulating, suggesting, emphasizing and evoking the very traits that are complained of. . . . The person becomes the thing he is described as being. (1938:19–20)

A fourth theorist, Edwin Lemert, has also suggested that an individual's conception of self as a deviant and his or her involvement in the deviant role rest on "a progressive reciprocal relationship between the deviation of the individual and the societal reaction" (1951:76). The stages of this progressive reciprocal relationship are as follows:

1. primary deviation, i.e., one breaks rules;
2. social penalties are imposed; these are
3. followed by more deviation;
4. penalties becoming stronger and are accompanied by rejection of the deviant actor; this is followed by
5. further deviation in association with resentment and hostility directed at those imposing the penalties;
6. deviance is then defined as intolerable resulting in stigmatizing the errant actor;
7. in response to the stigma and penalties actor's deviant conduct is strengthened; this leads to
8. the actor's acceptance of the conception of self as deviant and orients his or her life around the status of deviant. (Lemert, 1951:77)

Leslie Wilkins has also commented on this aspect of labeling. According to Wilkins, the action of social control agents (police, and so on) against the rule breaker, rather than suppressing the offensive behavior, may only isolate and alienate the person. By their action, control agents exclude the violator and, however unintentionally, promote a negative self-conception in the person. Rather than encourage conformity, these consequences of labeling only push the deviant further from "normal" society. Social rejects may then "tend to develop their own values which may run counter to the values of the parent system, the system which defined them as 'outliers' " (Wilkins, 1965:92). Further, as officials receive added information concerning the behavior of deviant groups, reactions intended to curb that behavior persist, perhaps even increasing in intensity. Wilkins contends this action-reaction-action cycle is repetitive in nature and may "continue round and round again in an amplifying circuit" (1965:92).

Applying the amplification model specifically to drug users, Jock Young suggests that the interaction process between deviants and control agents (police) influences both groups. For example,

(i) the police act against the drug-users in terms of their stereotypes;
(ii) the drug-user group finds itself in a new situation, which it must interpret and adapt to in a changed manner;
(iii) the police react in a slightly different fashion to the changed group;
(iv) the drug users interpret and adapt to this new situation;
(v) the police react to these new changes; and so on. (1971:33)

The deviance amplification cycle may be stated in slightly different terms. First, as we noted earlier, to be publicly identified as deviant is to be cloaked with the mantle of a master status. In addition to having the capacity to obscure other (perhaps morally acceptable) statuses and alter the actor's identity (Payne, 1973:36), there is an implicit set of expectations linked to the master status. Not the least of the alleged effects of this status and the associated expectations are the fear and suspicion they arouse in the audience—conditions that may subtly "call for" the detested behavior. The detested behavior is "called for" in the sense that it is the behavior the audience anticipates and acknowledges or responds to. The master status reduces the probability that the actor will be credited with other behaviors, especially law-abiding behaviors. After all, rule violators are expected to violate rules!

Should the actor conform to these expectations, his or her behavior serves only to confirm the original label. The label becomes a self-fulfilling prophecy. Conversely, failure of the deviant actor to conform to the expectations of the deviant status may not be acknowledged (Tannenbaum, 1938:477). On the basis of these circumstances, it is theorized that the moral meaning of a person's deviance may create a barrier that prevents the actor from occupying normal statuses or engaging in normal social intercourse. The actor is regarded as a moral pariah and is so treated.

Second, because others may respond to the actor in terms of the master status, and because self-feelings are derived from others' reactions, the actor may come to regard himself or herself in terms consistent with the moral judgments expressed by others and symbolized by the stigmatizing label. These self-attitudes, as well as the limitations placed on a person's role-playing opportunities, become central facts of his or her life.

Taken together, these conditions lead to the proposition that as a result of responses to the actor's behavior or condition by official control agencies and others in the community, labeling may occur, which, in turn, may result in the actor becoming entrenched or "engulfed" in the role of deviant (Lemert, 1967a: chapter 3; Schur, 1971:67ff; Schur, 1973:115ff; Becker, 1973:31, 179). The actor thus enters the stage of secondary deviance.

In the secondary stage the actor's deviant status is theorized to have social and social psychological consequences. It is also alleged (Tannenbaum, 1938) that being publicly declared deviant serves to perpetuate one's deviant conduct. In short, community rejection and social control create and maintain *deviant careers* (Rose, 1968:43). As an extension of this contention it has been proposed that by following a public policy of judicious nonintervention (Lemert 1967b:96–97) or radical nonintervention (Schur, 1973:153ff) many of the long-term negative consequences of labeling may be avoided.

A Cautionary Note

Having introduced several theoretical elements of the labeling perspective and some of their implications for deviant actors, let us briefly identify what these elements of the perspective *do not* mean.

First, these remarks do not mean that labeling and amplification are simple, mechanistic or nonproblematic results of authorities imposing their definitions on defenseless rule violators. The action of one group (deviant or control agent) does not compel the action of the other in some deterministic or behavioristic sense (Douglas, 1971a:144ff; Kotarba, 1984:159). Quite the reverse is the case. As our model of human nature indicates, people are interactive agents who *adapt* to and even transcend elements in their environment. Young notes that the deviant group is not to be thought of as "a pinball inevitably propelled in a deviant direction, or . . . the police [as] . . . the cushions of the machine that will inevitably reflex into a reaction triggered by the changing course of the deviant group" (1971:34). Nonetheless, negative responses by the community and its representatives are major environmental conditions with which labeled persons and groups must deal.

Second, to say that labeling by members of the community or their representatives is the foundation for secondary deviance is emphatically *not to locate the origins of rule-violating behavior in people's response to that behavior.* The point is missed if the theoretical proposition outlined here is taken to mean, for example, that mental hospitals drive people insane, that police and prisons force innocent people to engage in crime, or that narcotics treatment facilities make addicts of people. Indeed, labeling theory has little or nothing to say about the first causes, that is, the etiology, of rule-violating conduct. Rather, the contention is that prior to being labeled, when a person is a primary deviant, his or her violations are incidental to a host of nondeviant roles. The person is yet officially "innocent." Labeling, however, may significantly alter that condition (Lemert, 1967a:17).

Thus, these comments are *not to suggest that the responsibility for the rule violator's action is shifted from the actor to the social audience* (Nettler, 1974:209) or that "the moral burden of control is shifted from the victim (the labelee) to the victimizer (the control agents)" (Davis, 1975:172; Piven, 1981:491). On the other hand, we do suggest that being labeled may

effectively reduce the degree of self-control or self-ordination the actor is able to exercise. Labeling, we contend, "places the actor in circumstances which make it hard for him to continue the normal routines of everyday life and thus provoke him to 'abnormal' actions" (Becker, 1973:179). In this sense, then, *though it is not a first cause of rule-breaking behavior,* labeling is believed to intensify, enlarge, and perhaps prolong a person's involvement in a deviant role.

Third, and last, these remarks should not be interpreted to mean that labeling automatically prevents actors from participating in all forms of normal social interaction (Davis, 1975:174). Whether or not, and the degree to which, labeling becomes an impediment to such things is problematic, depending on a variety of conditions which we will consider later in this chapter.

With these points in mind, let us now turn to an examination of the data in an effort to determine how validly theory describes the everyday experiences of deviant actors.

Consequences of Labeling: Practicalities

That naming things may have profound consequences for the thing named is a truism needing no defense. Its consequences are never greater than when the naming involves assigning morally loaded labels. Even children have a sense of this when they utter the rhyme "Sticks and stones may break my bones, but words will never hurt me." What children know from experience is that labels can raise serious doubts and questions about the fundamental worth of the person toward whom they are directed. How smart can one be who is tagged "stupid," how brave one who is labeled a "yellow belly," how strong one who is dubbed "puny," how attractive one who is referred to as "cow" or "fatty," how feminine one who is labeled "tomboy," or how manly one who is called "sissy"? In a literal sense, each label casts a bit of doubt, perhaps a small moral shadow, on the person's sense of self and feeling of self-worth.

What children experience, however, is not

totally analogous to the experiences of deviants who have been formally labeled in some way or other. However hurtful at the time, these childhood episodes seem characteristically to be short-lived. This seems also to be the case for persons whose behavior or condition is regarded as only nominally or *marginally deviant,* that is, "behavior existing on the border of conventional and deviant worlds" (Briedis, 1975:481). These experiences are marked departures, though, from the prolonged and agonizing experience of those persons who endure the consequences of stigma for years. As an example, consider the following:

I was 4 years old when I started school. My mother had told them I was 5; I was somewhat precocious, and she may just have wanted to get me out of the house. But butch haircut or not, some boys in the third grade took one look at me and said, "Hey, look at the sissy," and they started laughing. It seems to me now that I heard that word at least once five days a week for the next 13 years, until I skipped town and went to the university. Sissy and all the other words—pansy, fairy, nance, fruit, fruitcake, and less printable epithets. I did not encounter the word faggot until I got to Manhattan. I'll tell you this, though. It's not true, that saying about sticks and stones; it's words that break your bones. (Miller, 1971:48)

In short, it should be acknowledged at the outset that the social psychological and social consequences of stigma and labeling are potentially extremely damaging. We may appreciate this by examining the experience of persons who have been effectively labeled and stigmatized, and whose public identity is therefore changed. We will first examine the consequences of labeling for self-attitudes and follow with a consideration of its social effects.

Social Psychological Effects of Labeling

By means of symbolic interaction people acquire a mental life, are able to experience self, become the subject of their own thoughts, and may come to define themselves as others do. These contentions lead to the idea that a change in self-regarding attitudes may well occur after a person is publicly labeled deviant (Matza, 1969:143ff; Lemert, 1967a:17). We will

consider the practical meaning of this change for secondary and for primary deviants.

The Secondary Deviant. The secondary deviant tends to be perceived and related to by others in terms of his or her spoiled identity. How that experience may contribute to negative self-attitudes is seen in the case of skid row winos. For these men, three distinguishable identities are relevant to our discussion. The first is the *popular identity.* Commonly labeled "bums," sometimes "derelicts" or "transients," these men are popularly seen as "people who fail abysmally, are dependent on society, lack self-control, drink too much, are unpredictable, and often end up in jail for their criminal behavior" (Spradley, 1970:66). Examination of these labels reveals their dual use; that is, they serve as a means to (1) impute characterological traits to these people while (2) the ascribed traits are taken as evidence of the actor's lack of social worth. Together these names become the stuff of a spoiled identity. For example, "derelict" refers to one who lacks respectability because of *being* neglectful, undependable, and unfaithful. "Transient," in the pejorative sense, refers to one who *is* unsettled, migratory, impermanent, and unstable; on those grounds the person cannot be relied on. These personal qualities reinforce the popular belief that the way of life of the skid row wino is "irrational, immoral, and irresponsible" (Spradley, 1970:66).

A second identity these men share is their *medical identity,* the basis of which is the idea that their objective condition (poverty, nomadism, and so on) stems from a disease, specifically, alcoholism. Unlike some illnesses that beset people, alcoholism is often perceived to directly influence a person's *being.* For example, although there are all kinds of human diseases and illnesses, it is relatively rare for those conditions to become the basis of a personal noun. We never refer to the victim of a stroke or a heart attack as other than a victim; there are no personal nouns by which these people are known. These conditions are not perceived to change the victim's essential self; they do not form the basis for moral judgment. In the case of alcoholism, however, one *becomes* an alcoholic. Similarly, one who suffers paralysis of the lower limbs *is* a paraplegic, one who cannot see *is* blind, and one deprived of hearing *is* deaf. In each instance, at least in American culture, the malady is fused with one's essential character (Romano, 1982:66–67). It matters little that the criteria for some of these conditions, such as alcoholism, lack specificity. Simply, in the nature of stereotypy, a person who is perceived to suffer the condition is burdened with the popularly associated traits (Spradley, 1970:66). These traits, however, are pregnant with moral meaning, as the highly stigmatizing aspects of blindness and alcoholism make evident; such people are marked as morally inferior (Scott, 1970:258). The nouns by which these people are known are not merely descriptive; they are every bit as evaluational as the adjectives they replace (Rosenberg, 1979:30).

Finally, the skid row resident is concerned with his *legal identity*. Blending with elements of his popular identity, traits associated with the legal identity are morally loaded. Police view these men as vagrants and criminals guilty of at least the moral offense of public drunkenness (Spradley, 1970:67). On the basis of his research, Egon Bittner concludes that "in the view of the experienced patrolman, life on skid row is *fundamentally* different from life in other parts of society . . . skid row is perceived as the natural habitat of people who lack the capacities and commitments to live 'normal' lives on a sustained basis" (1967:705; emphasis added). Clearly, the quality of life is seen as a consequence of the character of the people living there.

Attitudes held by police are shared by laypeople and the press. Howard Bahr reports the negative reaction of a rural person on first encountering skid-row people in Chicago:

We went through "skid row" and saw a "gutter" man which was to be picked up by the paddy wagon when the police see him. There are supposed to be a lot of those men on the street who have passed out from drunkenness. I'm glad we only saw one. I wouldn't dare walk down that street because I was scared just looking at the people. (1973:59)

And in the daily press one reads as follows:

Dirty, disheveled, sometimes dangerous and often traveling in packs, an unprecedented number of panhandlers and bums drift daily around New York City.

A team of . . . reporters has ranged through New York day and night . . . seeking out the beggars and homeless drifters with neither the will nor the energy to work.

They found that many of the young alcoholic drifters are potentially violent and will threaten passersby who turn down their touch. (Furey, 1961:59–61)

As we noted in Chapter 5, the stereotypic beliefs about representatives of deviant categories—for example, that skid row alcoholics are disinclined to be "normal"; that the blind are helpless, melancholy, frustrated, and live in a "mental void" (Scott, 1969:4); and that stutterers are constitutionally different from nonstutterers (Lemert, 1951:151)—come to be reified, that is, take on "objective" character. This knowledge then constitutes the reality that guides the thoughts and actions of "normals" vis-à-vis the deviant. This reality provides the framework for evaluating and judging the deviant and his or her behavior. It is these beliefs, for example, that lead some sighted persons to shun the blind (Scott, 1969:24), that may interfere with the establishment of intimate (perhaps sexual) relations between normals and the physically handicapped (Kriegel, 1974:233ff), that encourage some police and others to view the skid row resident with fear and apprehension (Bahr, 1973:231), and that leads people to insist that homeless persons "be kept out, locked up, segregated in some place with 'others of their kind' " (Bahr, 1973:64).

Alteration of Self-Feelings. Consistent with symbolic interaction theory, research yields substantial support for the idea that self-feelings among some deviants often correspond to the public (medical, personal, or legal) conceptions of them. James Spradley asked men arrested for public drunkenness "What do you feel is the worst thing about appearing in court on a drunk charge?" Fifty-three percent replied it was "the public humiliation" (Spradley, 1970:190–191). Specific elements leading to humiliation included their physical appearance upon entering court and the difficulty of maintaining an acceptable social image. Said one man, "Your appearance, it is *degrading* to lay in the drunk tank over the weekend and appear in court—no shave, no comb to even comb your hair, clothes all wrinkled" (Spradley, 1970:191; emphasis added). Another man commented, "A person is usually sick and dirty from laying on the concrete floor and to have to appear in front of a lot of people in that condition is very *humiliating*" (Spradley, 1970:191; emphasis added). Others mentioned their fear of confronting and possibly being recognized by court spectators. One man summarized the feelings of many with one word: "Degradation."

Degrading experiences for these men are not limited to their appearance in court. From their first encounter with police on the street, the skid row habitué is likely to be spoken to in highly insulting ways; these people are *defamed*. Some of these insults consist of the terms used by police (among others) to refer to these men: tramp, wino, bum, drunk, dehorn, skid row bastard. Men also report having to endure threats to their person when they have to deal with police. Such threats as "Shut up or we will beat the shit out of you" are designed to inform the person that he is the power subject and that the police are the power holders. Together with the use of defamatory names, these experiences leave these men with the idea that theirs is an inferior identity (Spradley, 1970:141).

Also affecting self-conception is the fact that these men are frequently robbed of their possessions by police (reported by 23 percent of Spradley's respondents). This experience effectively informs these men that their claim to respectability and consideration is diminished. In an impersonal society where a person's identity is crucially linked to material possessions, especially money, the loss of such symbols and *the apparent lack of means to effect their return,* may well have a critical influence on one's feelings of self (Spradley, 1970:145). Added to this is the ever-present threat of physical assault by police and/or jailers if the man takes other than a passive stance regarding his treatment. Thirty-five percent of Spradley's subjects reported that police "rough you up," "hit you," "take shoes to you," "club you," "shake the hell out of you," "work you over," "slam your face on something," "split your head open," "bounce you off his knee," or "drag you someplace" (Spradley, 1970:148–149). These men are left with a marked sense of their vulnerability. As Spradley suggests, the entire experience suffocates any self-assertiveness they may harbor. They are effectively stripped of the opportunity to display any autonomy or self-determination (Sykes, 1958:73–76; Spradley, 1970:161).

These and many other experiences, hidden from public view and often denied by officials, comprise the reality and ritualized experience of such men at the hands of the law. These experiences, especially being jailed, are critical in their life.

[In jail] they find the remaining shreds of respectable identity stripped away as they become participants in an elaborate ritual—that of making the bucket. Identity change takes place for these men as they are labeled "bums," cut off from former roles and identities, treated as objects to be manipulated, and coerced into being acutely aware of the new definitions of social interaction, space, time, and identity which are part of the jail. (Spradley, 1970:223–224)

Persisting over an extended time span, such experiences lead to the actor being engulfed in the deviant role.

Role Engulfment. As used by Edwin Schur (1971:69ff), *role engulfment* refers to the long-term social psychological impact of labeling on the deviant. It is a consequence of others relating to the deviant largely in terms of a spoiled identity and is a subaspect of secondary deviance. To the degree that social interaction is restricted by reason of a person's deviant identity, that is, as people respond to the actor more in terms of the master status of deviant and less often in terms of socially acceptable identities, the master status becomes more salient for the actor. Becoming engulfed in one's deviant status, then, is a *cumulative process,* the outcome of which is that people may define themselves in the same negative way that others do. A person's "I," or essential/substantial self, becomes that of deviant.

Engulfment is well demonstrated by the way some people are socialized to the role of the blind and adopt the "true believer" mode of adjustment. In this case the blind

adopt as a part of their self-concept the qualities of character, the feelings, and the behavior patterns that others [those who can see] insist they must have. Docility, helplessness, melancholia, dependency, pathos, gratitude, a concern for the spiritual and the aesthetic, all become a genuine part of the blind man's personal identity. (Scott, 1969:22)

The expectations that the sighted have of the blind are communicated to the blind in subtle and not-so-subtle ways. Agencies established to "rehabilitate" the blind sometimes expect these people to be more "normal" than sighted people, requiring the blind to meet expectations that sighted people are not expected to meet. For example, in the case of a blind college student, one agency required that he "pass" a Minnesota Multiphasic Personality Inventory test (which, incidentally, has never been standardized for the blind) as a condition of continuing his tuition grant. What sighted student must "pass" (even submit to) such a test in order to obtain scholarship aid, and what, we wonder, constitutes "passing" in this case? Since it is theoretically (and practically) impossible to be more normal than normal, the agency is encouraging its charges to become and remain dependent. The opportunities for self-sufficiency provided by higher education, opportunities consistent with the idea of rehabilitation, are apparently contrary to some of the stereotyped expectations of the blind.

In another sense, however, blind people may be expected to *avoid* displaying attributes of normality. Thus, one student, blind from birth, was unable to write normal script and was restricted to braille. To place a signature on any document, then, called for him to mark an X on paper. Finding this degrading and onerous, the student sought to get a signature stamp, a simple device allowing for elimina-

tion of the X and a measure of dignity. The proposal was rejected by the rehabilitation agency working with this person. Instead, officials insisted the student learn to write in cursive, a truly formidable task for one who has never seen what handwriting looks like. In short, the signature stamp may provide the student more freedom than the agency felt he should have and rejected his use of it.

Also contributing to the blind person's dependency on others and his or her engulfment is the tendency for some agencies to reject the use of dog guides by the blind and to encourage the use of a cane. Canes, according to many blind people, are more restrictive than dogs: They are difficult to handle, can be accidentally run between the legs of passersby, get caught in revolving doors, become jammed in cracks in sidewalks or sewer grates and are thus easily bent or broken, and are difficult to handle in automobiles and public conveyances unless they are collapsible. Most important, the cane cannot be trained and has no memory. In short, canes are quite limited in their ability to enhance the blind person's mobility, independence, and sense of freedom.

An alternative to the cane is the dog guide. More than promoting mobility, such dogs help their masters feel a freedom unavailable with canes. As one blind college student related, "They're more than guide dogs. It's like a companion—like the child you never had" (*Arizona Republic,* 1981d). Additionally, the dog guide may serve as a "bridge" between its blind master or mistress and others. This is particularly the case in that dogs may serve as a substitute for eye contact, conceded to be a vital aspect of initiating and maintaining social interaction. Despite the apparent social and other advantages of a dog, many rehabilitation agencies persist in rejecting their use and opt for reliance on a cane (Scott, 1965:136).

Engulfment is also apparent in the characteristically discouraging approach agencies sometimes take regarding the employability of the blind person (Scott, 1965:136ff). Agencies often tell their clients that they will be faced with problems when they seek a job, that there are few jobs for the blind, that employers are reluctant to hire the blind, and so forth. What clients are not told is that there are many blind attorneys, physicists, mathematicians, auto mechanics, farmers, and others. That is, the blind are able to occupy a far greater range of occupational roles than stereotypic notions suggest. To restrict the blind person's awareness of such possibilities is to encourage the "true believer" mode of adjustment and promote role engulfment. Again, self-feelings reflect others' definitions.

Engulfment also occurs among others who display abominations of the body and are stigmatized on that basis. One such case is that of Mary Benchley, who was born with a markedly deformed lip, a wide, flat, and generally malformed nose, and poorly aligned teeth. Though operated on for a harelip when she was one year old, Mary Benchley's disfigurement persisted. In school Mary's classmates made fun of her, called her names such as "split lip" and "crooked talking," and she was often laughed at by others when called on to recite. As she grew up she was systematically excluded from adolescent groups and was forced to engage in solitary forms of recreation. In seeking employment Mary also found her disfigurement was a handicap. Even minor jobs were denied her, she felt, because the potential employer desired "someone prettier." In seeking surgical correction of her condition at thirty-four, Mary Benchley stated

that her whole life had been greatly influenced by her appearance and by her speech defect. While she found it exceedingly embarrassing and difficult to make people fully understand her when she talked (she carried a slip of paper with her name written on it), she felt that her appearance had been the greater handicap in obtaining jobs and making friends. She stated that not only had people ridiculed her and stared at her, but she had been the victim of pity, questions, jokes, and nicknames. All her life she felt rejected by others because of her deformity, and *this caused her to feel depressed, inferior, and anxious.* (Macgregor et al., 1953:34–35; emphasis added)

Engulfment is not restricted to ascriptive deviants. Similar experiences and resultant self-feelings are reported by some law violators. In one case, a young man named Ken was

charged with passing a $20 check without sufficient funds, a result of his failure to keep accurate records of his bank transactions. His sentence was one year on probation. Ken's initial reaction was that the episode was no more than a "minor inconvenience." His friends reacted either with "disbelief or levity." Of his intimate associates, only his family displayed anger or displeasure over Ken having broken the law. To Ken, the most distressing reaction came from the community at large—a small rural town populated largely by a single ethnic group. Describing them as "harsh," Ken felt the townsfolk branded him a criminal and reacted to him in accordance with that definition. He describes the reaction as follows:

(They reacted like) "you're going to have to watch him now," "he's a known criminal now," "he's an outcast," or "you'll have to watch him he could be dangerous," you know. Completely (banned)!

At first, I just looked at it like, they had to be putting me on. I mean their reaction was so (unbelievably) violent. . . . Uh, my God! what is this? You know, (I just couldn't believe it was happening).

Then—I thought maybe (the) next thing they would tell me is I'm a hardened felon, you know, I go out and knock people in the head for money—I couldn't believe it—but *that's the type of community we had. "If you was good—you was good. If you was bad—you was horrid!"* Uh, it's just one of those type deals. (Frazier, 1976:135; emphasis in original)

To add to these difficulties, the parents of Ken's girlfriend refused to admit him to their house, would not permit the girl to come to the door, and told Ken never to come to their house again (Frazier, 1976:136).

On the basis of repeated experiences of this sort, Ken reports that his attitude toward self began to change.

when I got this from people it started making me very bitter . . . you know, like, "what the hell— *if I'm going to be named a criminal I might as well be one I guess."* I never went out and done anything, I mean . . . but that was my outlook. And getting more and more so. I mean, "if they're going to condemn me for that, what was their reaction gonna be if I actually did do something serious." Uh, actually I got a little more defensive from then on. . . . (Frazier, 1976:136; emphasis in original)

Clearly, we note in Ken's case the tendency of the master status to take precedence, influencing the way others related to Ken. Apparently, to the townsfolk, the only salient identity Ken had was his spoiled identity.

The Primary Deviant and Symbolic Labeling. In contrast with the secondary deviant, theory suggests that the primary deviant does not experience "symbolic reorganization at the level of self-regarding attitudes and social roles" (Lemert, 1967a:17), that primary deviants do not come to know themselves and are not known by others as deviants "in the first place." Because their rule breaking remains "private," the term *deviant* is not applied to them as it is to secondary deviants. Their rule breaking is alleged to have less impact because a deviant image is not being reflected back to them from others. Therefore, the public image of primary deviants remains moral. If a person's rule breaking has any impact on self-evaluation, the impact is assumed to be transitory and restricted to the person's situated self. Theoretically, then, it is assumed that primary deviants maintain a moral conception of their substantial self. However logical, and though it may apply to the bulk of rule breakers, this theoretical position does not apply to all. Appreciation of cases that depart from theory calls for an examination of symbolic labeling.

Symbolic labeling refers to the application of stigma without benefit of public ceremony; it is a matter of self-labeling and points up the fundamental distinction between the formal, *official process of labeling,* and the subjective process of *labeling one's self* as a consequence of an awareness of the public meaning of one's actions (Warren and Johnson, 1972; Rotenberg, 1974).

Examination of this concept is necessary to appreciate the social psychological consequences of rule breaking for some unlabeled persons. However important for those experiencing them, degradation ceremonies are experienced by very few rule breakers. Formal labeling is atypical. Goode notes that "most of the people who would be considered 'deviants' were their behavior to become known to the general public do not conform to this [public labeling pattern]" (1975:580). For example, the bulk of the male homosexuals studied by Gagnon and Simon (1968:353) were subjected to no formal stigmatizing process. The atypicality of formal labeling has also been noted by Warren and Johnson (1972), who, like Gagnon and Simon, contend that most homosexuals never have their personal sexual activities become a public issue. Despite that, many members of the gay community define "themselves as essentially *being homosexual* (i.e., in terms of their substantial self), and tend to organize their lives around the fact of possessing this *symbolic* (as opposed to publicly applied) *stigma*" (Warren and Johnson, 1972:77; italics in original). What seems true of homosexuals seems equally plausible for a wide array of other categories of deviants. Many other persons

appear to be largely symbolically labeled as deviants in American society; thus, their "escalation" to the status of secondary deviance (with its implications of a [deviant] "substantial-self") results *not* from (official) *acts of labeling,* typically at least, but through more informal and amorphous processes of *being-labeled,* or having an identity infused with the cognizance of its public opprobrium. (Warren and Johnson, 1972:77)

Symbolic labeling is wholly consistent with symbolic interactionist theory. As we have noted, people have a mental life. They are able to engage in self-scrutiny, interact with themselves (behave reflexively), evaluate their acts and condition in terms of public rules and meanings and, consequently, develop self-regarding attitudes. Symbolic labeling rests on precisely these elements. Given (1) knowledge of social rules and their moral meanings, (2) acknowledgment to self that one is engaged in disapproved behavior, and (3) a sense of the low esteem in which "such persons" are held, the rule violator may then proceed to label himself or herself in ways consistent with public meanings. The outcome may well include a revision of his or her substantial self.

To appreciate this process it is necessary to recall that symbolic labeling occurs in a context replete with expressions of the public meanings of deviant acts and actors. For example, even in the absence of formal conversation on the topic, sexually active teenagers may be well aware of their parents' negative judgment of premarital sexual conduct. Isolated derogatory comments about venereal disease, premarital pregnancy, or remarks about "parents not being able to trust young people" are often sufficient for the teenagers to infer these meanings (Briedis, 1975:482–483). On a more public level, jokes about fat people, minority people, the mentally retarded (moron jokes), the physically handicapped, "queers," drunks, persons with speech impediments, and so on, provide the sort of knowledge that leads to humiliation and denigration of self, not unlike the consequences of formal degradation ceremonies. One author describes the demeaning consequences of exposure to this knowledge:

Sometimes I find myself drawn as if into a net by the abuses and sneers of the hostile world. I hear the vile joke or the calumnious remark, and must sit in silence, or even force a smile as it were in approval. A passenger enters an elevator and remarks, "When I come out of a barber shop, I have a feeling I smell like a fag. I better watch out or some goddamn queer'll pick me up on the way home." The operator laughs, and I find myself forcing a smile, joining in the humiliating remark that is, unknowingly, directed against myself. (Cory, 1951:10)

In similar fashion, obese people experience the humiliation of knowing the public conception of fatness and fat people. As Millman notes, some overweight women are caught up in several conflicting emotions and definitions of their condition. On the one hand, many wish never to have the topic of their weight discussed because of its humiliating potential. On the other hand, if they lose weight they want to be complimented, but yet dislike the implication of the compliment, that is, that they have been grossly overweight (Millman, 1980:80–81). It seems clear that many obese people define their condition and themselves in the same negative way that so many others do and that obesity is a central fact of their life.

Everyday language also reveals the low esteem in which some people are held. This is exemplified in the case of people who are short. Our vocabulary is filled with taken-for-granted expressions that demean shortness: "putting people down," "belittling people," "being shortsighted," "getting the 'short end' of the stick," and "being shortchanged" are but a few examples (Feldman, 1975). And, of course, who can forget popular songs about short people?

Similar expressions and consequent experiences are shared by many other categories of primary deviants. They serve to socialize the deviant, provide evidence of the disdain in which he or she is held, and inform the rule breaker of the presumed difference between so-called normals and the substantial self of "people like them." On the basis of this socialization, the primary deviant may well experience social psychological difficulties.

Guilt, Shame, Transparency, and Bedevilment. Among the difficulties faced by the primary deviant are guilt and shame. Manifest by feelings of self-disgust and other negative attitudes, and often accompanied by a verbal expression of a desire to withdraw from public view ("I could have crawled in a hole and pulled it in after me!"), guilt and shame derive "from a horror of being disapproved of by others, particularly by meaningful or significant others, and from the fact that the values of these others have often been accepted by the rule breaker" (Sagarin, 1975:315). Guilt and shame may be expected, then, among those persons who anticipate that others will judge their behavior negatively. The self-abnegation that is so much a part of guilt feelings is a derivative of symbolic interaction; people judge themselves as they *expect* others will judge them.

Knowing their behavior is banned and punishable means, too, that rule violators must face the prospect of losing social acceptability among some persons if information about their behavior becomes widely known. As a result, they face the task of managing their secret. They are concerned with *transparency*— that is, with whether or not they will be able to keep their secret and from whom it ought to be kept (Matza, 1969:150). For example, a liberated young woman who had sexual affairs with several men reported having guilt feeling based on her awareness of her parents' attitude toward premarital sex. She commented as follows:

Dr. D: Earlier you said you feel guilty.
JM: Because of my parents. My parents don't know about my personal life. I imagine they have had their suspicions at times, but my mother is adamant about sexual experience before marriage. It would destroy her if she knew about me, I think. (Denes, 1977:35)

Similarly, research on unwed fathers revealed that men experience considerable *bedevilment* (Matza, 1969:146ff) as a consequence of their involvement in these extramarital pregnancies. That is, they anticipate losing social acceptability among some persons if information about their behavior becomes public. Thus, many unwed fathers were concerned that public knowledge of their involvement would bring down the law on them, that their families would reject them, that it would be grounds for expulsion from school or other groups, and that friends and neighbors would reject them. As a result, they, too, had to confront the problem of transparency and the task of managing their secret (Pfuhl, 1978; Briedis, 1975:484–485).

The horrors of discovery may be noted in other contexts, as well. For example men who frequent *tearooms* (a public place, often a restroom, where impersonal homosexual encounters occur) take great precautions to reduce the potential threat of discovery, to protect their anonymity and avoid unwarranted intrusion (Humphreys, 1970:26, 131; Corzine and Kirby, 1977). These precautions, consisting primarily of information control, serve to "exclude the potentially threatening and uninitiated intruder, . . . [and] protect participants from biographical disclosure; and locales are chosen for an ease of access that keeps wives, employers, and other from discovering the deviant activity" (Humphreys, 1970:131). The lack of such controls increases the threat that one will be discovered and exposed; the consequence is "a double nightmare of flight from fear and pursuit of satisfaction" (Humphreys, 1970:133).

Worry over discovery is also characteristic of many persons who drink a great deal but wish not to acknowledge that they are alcoholics. Sometimes the drinker seeks to avoid disclosure by attempting to be humorous about his or her behavior. At other times the drinker engages in outright deceit and lying (Hough, 1974:17).

It is important to note that a person's degree of concern over these matters does not necessarily reflect or vary with the frequency of his or her involvement in rule violations. This is evident in Rossman's investigations of *pederasts,* males over 18 years of age who engage in sexual acts with adolescent boys. Many of the men studied by Rossman had engaged in a sexual act with a boy only once or twice in their entire life and, at the time of the research, had not had sexual contact with boys for several years. Nonetheless, these men lived in constant fear that their past would be revealed. Caution, fear, and secrecy—from officials, psychiatrists, and one another—characterized these men's lives. Any publicity, research, or public attention was greatly feared, so much so that some pederasts threatened Rossman's life if he persisted in investigating this topic (Rossman, 1973:30).

Finally, evidence of the occurrence and potency of self-labeling can be found among some victims of rule breakers who, by a curious bit of legerdemain, are regarded equally as culpable of wrongdoing as their offenders. A case in point is the victim of incest. Observers suggest that some incest victims suffer a derogation of self-image, not merely because they were victimized in this way, but because of the guilt they bear for having participated in the proscribed act. Complementing the sense of guilt is the matter of transparency. As one incest victim related,

The hardest problem I had was that in the period after I left home I was convinced that anybody who saw me could tell that I was bad and that no man would ever want me because I was so bad. That was one of the hardest things to get over. At times the old conviction that I'm a bad woman comes up. To this day, the issue of whether I'm a good or bad woman is alive for me. (Justice and Justice, 1979:182)

The foregoing examples point out the very real difficulty of distinguishing between so-called secondary and primary deviants on the basis of their respective social psychological experiences. The major social psychological distinction between these categories of deviants (that secondary deviation entails substantially altered psychic structure and self-regarding attitudes, while primary deviation has only limited implications for these matters) involves differences of degree rather than kind. The issue of how central or prominent in a person's life rule breaking is—the matter of saliency—seems not to fully differentiate the primary from the secondary deviant. The centrality of primary deviants' rule breaking is seen in the quantities of time and energy they sometimes devote to avoiding identification, and the guilt they suffer in private. Likewise, we must note the sometimes all-consuming fear of transparency and the anticipation of others' negative responses when their involvement in deviation is revealed. Indeed, for primary deviants equipped with an active imagination, these burdens may be at least as great as those borne by publicly identified rule breakers who experience social reaction and are able to deal with matters accordingly. In short, primary as well as secondary deviants seem to organize life around the facts of their deviance (Lemert, 1967a:40–41). As regards the social psychological consequences of being labeled and stigmatized, then, it may well be that many of the theoretically suggested differences between primary and secondary deviants are based on less than a full appreciation of the practical aspects of everyday life.

Social Consequences of Labeling

It has been noted that the labeling process may result in the erection of barriers that restrict/limit deviants' participation in the normal social life of the community. To the degree that the stigmatized condition dominates the consciousness of others, it imposes limitations on their interaction with deviants. For example, Davis (1961:123–125) notes several ways that the meanings of physical handicaps intrude on and influence interaction between disabled and able-bodied persons. First, physical disabilities may become the "focal point of interaction," influencing conversation, introducing an element of strain into the relationship, and making the interaction a time of general discomfort. Second, is the "inundating potential" of the handicap; that is, the disability (deafness, blindness, and so on) may overwhelm the interaction. For example, rather than good humor, spontaneity, gaiety, and laughter, there may be silence, pity, fear, and avoidance as the stigmatized condition dominates. Third, stigmatized conditions often constitute a "contradiction of attributes." Thus, consistent with stereotypic ideas and the concept of moral congruence, persons exhibiting stigmata tend not to be perceived as occupants of "normal" roles and statuses and are denied the attributes of those occupants. If the stigmatized person displays the attributes of "normals" relative to occupation, interests, and so on, a sense of discordance may result. Finally, Davis notes that stigmatized conditions frequently introduce an element of ambiguity into a relationship because many people do not know what to predict about the behavior, interests, and capabilities of the disabled. The taken-for-granted expectations the able-bodied have of one another are unsuitable, it is felt. Again, then, a sense of ambiguity and strain may be experienced. We will refer back to these influences shortly.

A further set of barriers arises because as a person assumes the master status of a deviant with appropriate character traits, his or her identity becomes that of an "outsider" who cannot be trusted (Becker, 1973:1). Despite the irrelevance of a person's deviance to any particular social role, the deviant may be denied access to legitimate (nondeviant) positions. For example, though a person's sexual preference may have nothing to do with his or her ability to play a given occupational role, certain jobs may be closed to persons known or suspected to be homosexual. This situation has been reported on by David Kopay, a collegiate and professional football player who publicly acknowledged his homosexuality. In Kopay's experience, despite his qualifications to fill the role of football coach, public rejection of homosexuals prevented his being employed in that capacity (Kopay and Young, 1977:61–63, 182). Similarly, the International Association of Chiefs of Police have adopted a resolution opposing the hiring of homosexuals for police work, arguing that the role of police officer is totally inconsistent with a person who is an "open, obvious, ostentatious" homosexual (*Arizona Republic,* 1977b). In 1975 the U.S. Air Force took a similar position in the case of Tech. Sergeant Leonard Matlovich following a public acknowledgment of his homosexual preference. In seeking to oust Matlovich from the Air Force the argument was made that "the presence of homosexuals in the service . . . could impair recruitment; other young men might feel anxious about living in close quarters with them . . . homosexuals cannot command respect as officers and non-coms and are prey to blackmailers" (*Time,* 1975a). Five years after he was discharged for admitting his homosexuality, Matlovich was ordered reinstated by a federal court judge (*Arizona Republic,* 1980g). Two months later the government agreed to pay Matlovich $160,000 to settle the court battle with him rather than allow the decorated Vietnam veteran to remain in the armed forces (*Arizona Republic,* 1980h). The case of Sergeant Matlovich resembles that of homosexual WACS (*Time,* 1975b), as well as that of homosexuals in the armed forces during World War II. During that time, homosexuals were regularly discharged from the armed forces; called "blue angels" because their discharges were printed on blue paper, gays were and continue to be regarded as a threat to the armed forces (Berube, 1983).

These cases reflect people's tendency to perceive deviants as a threat to the smooth integration of statuses and roles characteristic of "normal" social existence. For example, it is taken for granted that occupants of legitimate statuses and roles are at least minimally suited to those positions. That assumption leads people to attribute at least a minimal degree of harmony to existing social arrangements and relationships. However, when these statuses and roles are occupied by known deviants, such assumptions are difficult at best, perhaps impossible, and a sense of unease is likely to follow. Simply stated, people who are deviant

are assumed to possess traits rendering them incapable of satisfying normal role expectations. Hence, many people reject the idea that prostitutes can make good wives or good mothers, that a drug addict can play legitimate roles satisfactorily, or that convicted felons can be permitted to occupy positions of trust. Similarly, many people are loath to allow homosexuals to play the role of teacher, fearing their children will be corrupted (*Playboy,* 1978:78). People are taken to be the same as the thing symbolized by the label; they have a moral defect. The alleged moral defect "fixes" them in the position of "outsider" and helps shape others' responses. As our examples show, a basic response is to avoid contact in order to prevent contamination.

Protection of Territories. To contaminate something is to pollute it, corrupt it, or otherwise render it impure. To a great extent, the restrictive social conditions faced by many rule breakers reflect the efforts of people to work against what is often perceived to be the contamination of territories by deviants (Lyman and Scott, 1967). As used here, territories are multiple: public, home, interactional, and body. *Public territories* are those areas to which one has freedom of access by reason of citizenship. Nations, schools, cities, and similar public areas are examples. Closely related and not always distinguishable from public territories are *home territories,* places where people "have a relative freedom of behavior and a sense of intimacy and control over the area" (Lyman and Scott, 1967:238). Clubhouses, country clubs, gay bars, and hobo jungles are cases in point. Third are *interactional territories,* any place where people may engage in social interaction. That is, every interaction occurs in some physical place (someone's apartment, a street corner, a tavern) that, for the duration of the interaction, is enclosed by an "invisible boundary." These interactional territories may be identified by people's resistance to their being penetrated by persons other than the interactants. Finally, there is *body territory,* "the space encompassed by the human body and the anatomical space of the body" (Lyman and Scott, 1967:241). That body territories exist may be noted in the way people selectively grant and withhold the right of others to view and touch their body. This territory has been described as the most sacred of all, as evidenced by the numerous restrictions societies establish concerning the time, place, and relationship between persons who may legitimately view and/or touch the naked body of another, engage in sexual intercourse, and so on. In marriage, of course, body territory ordinarily approximates home territory by granting rights to spouses that traditionally have tended to be withheld from others (Lyman and Scott, 1967:241).

Each of these territories may be (and is) encroached upon and misused by those who *violate* them (by making unwarranted use of a territory), *invade* them (cross their boundaries without entitlement), or *contaminate* them (pollute, corrupt or otherwise render them impure by use or definition). In the first instance, children may play hide-and-seek in a cemetery, while a man may make use of a public restroom designated for women only. In the second case, "adult" theaters and bookstores or taverns may be established in close proximity to schools or churches, or in residential areas from which they had previously been absent. By reason of this type of invasion, the third form of encroachment, contamination, may occur. That is, in the perspective of some persons and groups, a territory may be rendered impure by such usage.

Viewed in terms of these forms of territories and the ways they may be misused, many of the restrictions imposed on deviants become understandable. Given a sense of the deviant as a *pariah,* someone afflicted with a grave moral defect, the "normal" person or group may well feel that the deviant's presence constitutes an encroachment of one sort or another. The rapist is one who *violates* the victim's bodily territory. If the victim is a married woman the rapist is also violating the spouse's home territory. The attempt to convert public restrooms into meeting places (tearooms) by homosexuals and the wildcatting of beaches by nude bathers are seen as *invasions* of public territory. Should such efforts succeed, the en-

croachment may be regarded as an instance of contamination.

If the presence of the deviant is regarded as an intolerable encroachment, any of several reactions may occur. One possible reaction is *turf defense,* a popular expression of which is the delinquent gang that seeks to physically resist the invasion of its territory by a rival gang. More consistent with the standard conception of deviance, however, is the case in Chicago wherein residents of the Edgewater district banded together (with support from the Chicago Police Department's Gang Crime Unit) to resist thefts, muggings, harassment, and other crimes being committed against the residents by a local gang (Law Enforcement Assistance Administration, 1977:3, 7). Perhaps the classic example of turf defense is citizen opposition to the location of prisons, jails, halfway houses, and similar facilities in or in proximity to residential areas (*Arizona Republic,* 1980i).

A second reaction in defense of territory is *insulation,* that is, "placement of some sort of barrier between the occupants of a territory and potential invaders" (Lyman and Scott, 1967:246). There are several common examples of this. The use of their native language by foreign students on university campuses or by residents of an ethnic enclave (such as a Chinatown) keeps "outsiders" at bay. More common is the careful use of facial expressions to communicate to others that an interactional home territory ought not be invaded.

Finally, there is the tactic of *linguistic collusion,* used to protect interactional and home territories. Most often this defense consists of an elaborate linguistic form that outsiders may not readily understand and that automatically identifies them as ineligible for participation. The special argot developed by some occupational groups (musicians), ethnic groups (blacks), and other groups (Val Gals who employed Valspeak) (*Time,* 1982b) are cases in point.

As applied to many of the restrictions imposed on deviants, these reactions reflect a tendency toward defense or protection of one or another territory. For example, in gay bars (often regarded as home territories) efforts are often made to regulate, if not suppress, open displays of homosexual affection in order to protect the license of the establishment (Cavan, 1966:71–72). To protect interactional territory, the peers of youngsters who are obese or who have a physical handicap often quite bluntly exclude them from participating in regular activities.

Other Restrictions and Consequences. The social limitations imposed on stigmatized people go beyond territorial protection. For example, those with felony convictions may experience restrictions on employment. Evidence of this is contained in Schwartz and Skolnick's (1964) study of the effects of a criminal court conviction on employability. These authors conclude that a convicted felon is substantially more likely to encounter employment difficulties than a person having no convictions; indeed, the person *without* a record is nine times more likely to receive a positive response from a potential employer than an equally qualified person *with* a criminal record. What is even more revealing about these data, however, is that those who were accused but later acquitted (officially declared innocent) were also very likely to experience employment problems. This, it should be noted, is likely to occur despite the idea that a person who is acquitted of a crime is innocent (legally) and, according to our system of justice, should not be subject to sanction (Schwartz and Skolnick, 1964:108–109).

The general impressions derived from Schwartz and Skolnick's research are reinforced by the findings of other studies. An experimental study of Canadian employers' responses to job applicants reveals that a record of conviction for violation of marijuana laws has serious implications for employability (Erickson and Goodstadt, 1979). Erickson and Goodstadt report that the perceived level of seriousness of an applicant's offense is less important to prospective employers than the simple fact that they were convicted. That is, "the status of criminal took precedence over that of drug user in determining the employ-

er's response" (Erickson and Goodstadt, 1979:214) to a person's application for employment.

Severe limitations on employment are also reported among the disabled (Safilios-Rothschild, 1970:262ff). To be sure, employment opportunities available to the disabled vary with the subject's age, sex, race, educational level, work history, degree and type of disability, and so on. Nonetheless, overall, only a fraction of the employable disabled are employed. Those that are employed tend, on the average, to have less severe afflictions and be better educated. The disabled who are employed tend to receive fewer promotions and are often restricted to less prestigious jobs than the ones they held before they became disabled. Added to this is the tendency for some employers to subject disabled employees to constant observation and evaluation—more than they impose on able-bodied workers. These experiences sometimes have a profound influence on the self-feelings of the disabled. To be limited to work roles beneath one's level of ability and training is humiliating, evidence of one's devalued position. Acceptance by others, then, is partial. For some it is likely that a forthright rejection would be preferable to halfhearted or counterfeit acceptance. Taken together, then, these studies indicate that labels may serve as barriers to full social participation.

Exclusion is also well demonstrated in the case of the mentally ill. In studying hospitalized mental patients, Schwartz (1956) discovered that such patients receive few visits from relatives or friends. Visits that did occur were anxiety-provoking, and visitors (with the exception of the patient's mother) tended not to return. Half the patients studied had no visits from persons other than family and, of those having visits, 41 percent were single or occasional visits. In seeking to account for this pattern of avoidance and isolation of patients, Schwartz's informants indicated that mental patients are nonpersons. "They are afraid of what a 'nonperson' might do because he no longer is guided by the controls 'people' have" (Schwartz, 1956:22). Such comments are clearly consistent with theory: Alleged characteristics of deviants are perceived as inimical to "normal" social interaction.

Further support for theory is found in the research by Phillips (1963) and by Loman and Larkin (1976). Phillips investigated factors related to the rejection of the mentally ill, focusing specifically on the "extent to which people's attitudes toward an individual exhibiting disturbed behavior are related to their knowledge of the particular help-source that the individual is using or has used" (1963:963). In this study, "help-source" refers to clergy, psychiatrists, marriage counselors, mental health clinics or hospitals, and the like, where people may go to seek help when they feel they have an emotional or mental health problem. It was hypothesized that "individuals exhibiting identical behavior will be increasingly rejected as they are described as not seeking help, as utilizing a clergyman, a physician, a psychiatrist or a mental hospital" (1963:965). Interviews concerning five case abstractions representing a variety of mental health conditions were conducted with a sample of 300 married white females. Data supported Phillips's hypothesis that the likelihood of being rejected increases progressively when "an individual exhibiting a given type of behavior . . . is described as seeking no help, as seeing a clergyman, as seeing a physician, as seeing a psychiatrist, or as having been in a mental hospital" (1963:968). Thus, *regardless of behavioral differences,* persons described as needing assistance with emotional problems tend to be rejected. Apparently, the more clearly the help-source identifies (that is, labels) the help-seeker as a person with mental health problems, the greater the tendency toward rejection.

A study of the rejection of the mentally ill by Loman and Larkin (1976) reached similar conclusions. In this study, an effort was made to determine the relative influence of three independent variables (the actor's behavior, the actor's account of that behavior, and labels) on two dependent variables: (1) audience rejection and (2) assessment of the social competence of persons declared to be mentally ill. The "audience" in this study consisted of students enrolled in a general sociology course who were exposed to two different videotaped counseling sessions reflecting "fairly reasonable and common explanations of [a student's] poor academic progress" (Loman and Larkin, 1976:557). In one version of the counseling session the lack of academic progress was accounted for by the impersonality of the school atmosphere and the attitudes of the teachers. In the second version the "distressed student" accounted for academic difficulties in ways that could readily be interpreted as paranoid. Data revealed that the actor's behavior and the account of that behavior (two of the independent variables) had little relationship to audience rejection of assessment of competence (dependent variables). However, the "label" was significantly associated with both dependent variables. That is, rejection and a low assessment of the subject's social competence were associated with labeling. Loman and Larkin contend that this association reflects people's agreement with the stereotypic characterizations implied by the label (1976:560). Again, then, it appears that the meaning conveyed by labels, *irrespective of manifest behavior,* is significantly associated with how people respond to deviant actors.

The socially restrictive consequences of stigma may also be found among ascriptive deviants. Employers often establish physical criteria for employees (such as height and weight restrictions) regardless of whether the criteria are pertinent to job performance (Barker, 1948:31). Failure to satisfy these criteria may result in unemployability, however "fit" a person may be in other respects. Such things as obesity, deafness, or the loss of a limb or paralysis, may result in intense social ostracism if only because these conditions are felt to interfere with many aspects of life, public and private. Regarding obesity, for example, evidence suggests that being excessively overweight has an influence on college acceptance, particularly among females (Cahnman, 1968:290). According to the New England School Study,

Twice as many obese persons were found in the high school female population than in the female college population (23.3 percent vs. 11.2 percent), with a less large but still considerable difference for boys (18.0 percent vs. 13.7 percent). Correspondingly, two-thirds more of the non-obese girls went on to college than the obese (51.9 percent vs. 31.6 percent) and only three fifths as many non-obese females as obese began to work directly after high school without further training of any kind (17.4 percent vs. 28.9 percent); the difference between non-obese and obese males was insignificant. There was no significant difference for females or males regarding motivation to attend high-ranking colleges, academic performance, and social class (SES of origin), whether they were obese or not. (Cahnman, 1968:290)

Research among the blind also reveals that ascriptive deviants experience social deprivation in their relationships with sighted people. Reflecting *omittive behavior,* subjects in one study of the blind (all of whom were residents of the Federal Republic of Germany) reported feeling "ignored" and "overlooked" by sighted people when they entered restaurants, shops, and so on. Overall, in their relations with sighted people, 88 percent of these blind persons reported that they suffered from the prejudices of the sighted. Others commented that they were made to feel like "outsiders" and that they felt "forced into the status of a deviant person" (Meyer, 1981:360).

The consequences of stigma, then, extend into the most private spheres of life. For homosexuals, being identified as gay is often taken by others as an invitation to violence. The result is the widespread practice of gay bashing, a practice that often enough ends in the death of the victim (Sagarin and Macnamara, 1975). Additionally, homophobia traditionally has interfered with the proper delivery of health care to the homosexual minority, a situation that has intensified with the discovery of AIDS. And after it was revealed that she had had a lesbian relationship with her secretary, tennis star Billie Jean King is estimated to have lost at least $500,000 in fees for endorsements (*Arizona Republic,* 1981e). Further, the first baby born in Litchfield, Illinois, in 1980 was denied the traditional gifts given to such infants; the baby girl's parents were not married at the time of her delivery (*Arizona Republic,* 1980j). Traditionally, the "fat boy" is excluded from a game of ball and the "fat girl"

is ignored as a dating partner. For those with defective hearing, limited ability to communicate affects relations with family and friends. The hard-of-hearing man

has trouble understanding what his wife is saying, especially if he is reading the paper, and his wife is talking while she is making noise in the kitchen. This kind of situation frequently leads at first to a mild dispute and later to serious family tension. The wife accuses the husband of inattention, which he denies, while he complains in rebuttal that she mumbles. Actually, he eventually does become inattentive when he realizes how frustrating and fatiguing it is to strain to hear. When the same individual tries to attend meetings, to visit with friends, or go to church services and finds he cannot hear what is going on or is laughed at for giving an answer that is unrelated to the subject under discussion, he soon, but reluctantly, realizes that something is wrong with him. He stops going to places where he feels pilloried by his handicap. He stops going to the movies, the theater or concerts, for the voices and the music are not only far away but frequently distorted. Little by little his whole family life may be undermined, and a cloud overhangs his future and that of his dependents. (Sataloff, Sataloff, and Vassallo, 1980:358)

Not the least of the difficulties faced by people with a hearing impairment stem from the fact that their condition runs counter to taken-for-granted assumptions. One such assumption is that people ordinarily can hear, speak, and see. Higgins (1980:150) reports the fatal shooting of a deaf mute by a robber; apparently, the deaf mute was shot as a consequence of his inability to hear and respond to the robber's demands.

Persons with a physical disability may experience isolation and other social consequences. Fink, Skipper, and Hallenbeck (1968) report that as the mobility of physically disabled wives decreases, so, too, does the husband's satisfaction with the companionate aspect of the marital relation. Husbands of severely disabled wives often attempt to spend more time at home with their wives, but often find this less than satisfactory, especially because this frequently calls for a suspension of activities in which both persons once engaged and from which they derived considerable pleasure. Included here are mundane but important things like visiting friends, attending movies, and going on automobile trips. As one husband commented

Well, it hurts if you can't get out with the family and do things that other families do. Such as, for instance, through the paper you see a show you'd like to see. Other families say, "Well, let's go." They put on a clean shirt and they do, and that's had its effect on me. . . . You can't just pick up and do something on the spur of the moment. It just can't be done. To go somewhere it takes planning, to be sure there's electrical outlets where you're going for the respirator. If we go to the show, I always go there first, talk to the manager, find out where we are going to be, see there's AC current there for her equipment. So it's not an easy thing just to go visiting. (Fink, Skipper, and Hallenbeck, 1968:68)

These restrictions bring us to a consideration of "courtesy stigma."

Courtesy Stigma. Several of the examples cited in the preceding section reveal that the consequences of stigma are not restricted to those to whom it is directly applied. The term *courtesy stigma* points to the fact that a stigma often "spreads from the stigmatized individual to his close connections" (Goffman, 1963:30). Examples include the spouse and offspring of the mental patient (Yarrow, et al., 1955; Freeman and Simmons, 1961), the families of mentally retarded children (Birenbaum, 1970), families of convicted felons, parents of gays (Miller, 1971), and many others who may share some of the discredit assigned to the stigmatized individual. An intimate affiliation with a stigmatized person may become a social psychological as well as a social liability.

Social psychologically, courtesy stigma frequently results in painful self-examination, self-condemnation and guilt, conditions often found among parents of homosexuals and disabled children. Many of these parents believe they have "failed" their children and thus experience guilt and shame (Simpson, 1977:15; Hobson, 1976; Henderson and Bryan, 1984:167–168). Such feelings are sometimes built on the idea that the homosexuality or disability results from parental failings that make them culpable (Bieber, et al., 1962:chapters III

and IV; Henderson and Bryan, 1984:165). Expressive of this guilt and self-blame is the following letter, written by a parent to a homosexual author:

I blame myself for the fact that my son is homosexual. I know that it is a nearly incurable disease. I confessed my son's predicament—he is 16—to our family doctor, and he said that in rare cases the disease can be cured, but he said that the cure is a long and costly one and would be far beyond our means. . . . He said that while the boy may not be an actual menace to society, there is always the possibility of arrest and disgrace. . . . Do you think we should send him away someplace? Are there hospitals where for a minimal charge he might . . . ? I would hope that he would be well treated. . . . We have never discussed the fact that he is queer. His father refuses to allow the subject to be mentioned in our home. (Miller, 1971:73)

In social terms parents of gays and the disabled also reveal the effects of courtesy stigma. Thus, it is not uncommon to hear parents of gays tell of the difficulty they experienced in acknowledging to family and friends that they have a homosexual child. Parents worry how their own "coming out" will influence their social life, their business affairs—whether or not they will be condemned as defective parents, and so on (*New York Times,* 1983b). Parents of the disabled sometimes report similar problems, as well as family discord and marital strain (Henderson and Bryan, 1984:162, 172–174).

In other instances courtesy stigma takes a more vicious form. Thus, in Indianapolis, Indiana, the one-time foster mother of a man executed for murder was sent a wooden chair wrapped in wire as a "commemoration" of the execution of her foster son. She is also the object of crank phone calls, is referred to as the "Electric Lady", and, in general, is the target of anger directed against the deceased foster son (*Arizona Republic,* 1982c).

Also reflecting self-blame and torment is the fear of stigma that often accompanies having one's spouse declared mentally ill and hospitalized. As one wife said, "I live in a horror—a perfect horror—that some people will make a crack about it to Jim (the child) and suppose after George (the husband) gets out that everything is going well and somebody throws it up in his face. That would ruin everything. I live in terror of that" (Schwartz, 1956:20). Associated with these concerns was the fear that people will be disrespectful, suspicious, or fearful of the husband upon his release from the mental hospital. "The wives feared that their husbands would suffer from social discrimination—their husbands would not be able to get jobs; they would be avoided by old friends; their children would be excluded from play groups; and, in general, their family would be looked down upon" (Schwartz, 1956:21).

These fears are not limited to the subjective level; they often become the basis of action intended to prevent their realization. For example, wives of men who are mentally ill often avoid telling others of the husband's condition or reveal no more than is absolutely necessary. However, this tactic may give rise to new difficulties.

Many wives had to invent devious excuses [for their husband's absence] backed up with still more excuses and explanations. They had to be careful about who knew and who did not. Some tended to cut off old associations by avoiding them or moving away, leaving no forwarding address. With neighbors and friends they acted strained and remote. There was always the fearful possibility that the "truth" might be discovered. Life for such a wife became complicated and uneasy. Her fears led her to limit her relationships with others precisely when she needed them more than ever. Her own behavior cut her off from many little services friends might perform for her. It also reduced the possibility that she could talk about her problems and difficulties to a sympathetic listener. . . . This behavior—which, by the way, is often undertaken at the husband's request—is an attempt to "protect" him from unfriendly attitudes, but it does so at the expense of *isolating both the wife and the husband.* (Schwartz, 1956:21; emphasis in original)

Similar tendencies are found among parents of children declared mentally retarded. For such people, interfamily visiting is often curtailed, fewer invitations are extended, vacations may be highly limited, and entire families may change their place of residence (Schonell and Watts, 1956:217).

Not all persons and groups closely associated with the stigmatized seek to minimize public awareness of that affiliation and/or of the stigma. Thus, the parents of John Hinckley, Jr., after a period of profound guilt, confusion, and self-blame, entered the field of mental health and now make public appearances and give speeches supporting the mental health movement. They also founded the American Mental Health Fund to promote public awareness of mental health needs (*People Weekly,* 1984a). Others affected by courtesy stigma affiliate with persons similar to themselves in order to overcome their difficulties. Two examples are the Children of Gays/Lesbians and the Federation of Parents and Friends of Lesbians and Gays. The first organization encourages children to come to terms with their parents' homosexuality, to overcome fear of ostracism, to feel free to bring friends into the home, and to view homosexuality as a viable lifestyle. The second organization offers emotional support for parents and children of gays, and seeks to keep family bonds intact. Thus, despite courtesy stigma, there are people who manifest a willingness to accept those who are stigmatized and who strive to achieve a degree of normalcy in social relationships (Birenbaum, 1970).

Deviance Amplification

Our earlier theoretical discussion noted that negative community responses to the deviant, especially (but not only) responses of social control agencies, are alleged to promote the amplification and perpetuation of deviance. It was Tannenbaum's (1938) contention that *dramatization of evil* led to the actor having a negative definition of self and to the perpetuation of rule violations. Sharing in this view are Erikson (1964), Wilkins (1965), Lemert (1967a) and Becker (1973). Each contends that community rejection of the actor may encourage *career* deviance, that is, movement of an individual from the status of primary deviant, through a sequence of movements and positions, to that of secondary deviant wherein identity and behavior are principally deviant (Becker, 1973:24–39). In short, labeling stabilizes deviance; "deviation begets deviation"

(Lemert, 1967a:25). However logical this proposition may appear, some evidence supports it and some does not. We will examine both types and then try to resolve the contradictions.

Examining the Evidence: Pro

A considerable number of studies supporting the amplification hypothesis focus on delinquency. Davis (1973) concluded that a positive relation exists between a person's involvement with a juvenile justice system and his or her subsequent involvement in delinquency even though the person had little or no commitment to delinquency. Evidence supporting amplification has also been reported by Klein (1974). Comparing police departments with high and low rates of juvenile *diversion* (channeling youth away from the criminal justice system), Klein shows that recidivism rates among youth are higher among departments having lower diversion rates (where offenders are treated formally and channeled into the justice system) than among departments that have high diversion rates (1974:297).

Additional support comes from Gold and Williams' (1969) semiexperimental study of 35 pairs of matched apprehended and unapprehended juvenile offenders. "In 20 of the 35 comparisons, the apprehended member of the pair subsequently committed more offenses than his unapprehended control. In 10 of the 35, the unapprehended control committed more offenses. Five pairs committed an equal number" (Gold and Williams, 1969:8). In an earlier study conducted in one city, Gold (1970) reached similar conclusions. Again using matched pairs of apprehended and unapprehended delinquents, Gold found that "in 11 of the 20 pairs, the apprehended youngsters went on to commit more offenses than the unapprehended youngsters, in four they committed less, and five the same number" (1970:107). Gold concludes that not only does apprehension fail to deter, it appears to be a stimulant to further violations.

More recent research (Farrington, 1977) using a population of 383 British youth as sub- jects revealed similar results. Farrington compared the self-reported delinquency scores of 285 unlabeled youth with those of 98 publicly labeled youth. "In agreement with the deviance amplification hypothesis, the 98 publicly labeled youths had very significantly higher self-reported delinquency scores at age 18 than the . . . 285 non-labeled youth" (1977:114). Subsequent examination of this data, to test the plausibility of alternative explanations of his findings, led Farrington to persist in his support of the amplification hypothesis as it applies to delinquents.

But does the amplification hypothesis apply to categories of deviants other than delinquents? In one instance, as we noted earlier, agencies established to rehabilitate the blind frequently encourage (if not require) their clients to "play the kind of deviant role traditionally reserved for the blind" (Scott, 1965:138). To the extent the client meets agency expectations, stereotypic beliefs are actualized; the client becomes the "true believer" and is entrenched in his or her deviance in terms of both identity and behavior.

A similar condition is noted by Fred Davis's (1961) study of polio victims, mentioned earlier. In a number of ways the polio victim's disability becomes the issue of principal concern in his or her relations with able-bodied persons. Thus, the disability may become the "focal point of interaction," a condition others respond to first and foremost in both speech and action; it may "inundate" or overwhelm all other attributes the disabled person may have (reminiscent of the notion of "master status"), with the result that interaction is shaped by these perceptions (definitions); and third, attributes that are contradictory or irrelevant to the disability tend to be subordinated, while those consistent with it tend to be emphasized. This is characterized by the experience of a particularly pretty woman polio victim who often hears new acquaintances say "How strange that someone so pretty should be in a wheel chair" (Davis, 1961:124). Finally, the disability becomes a source of interactional ambiguity for both the able-bodied and the disabled person. For example, to what activities is it appropriate to invite the disabled? And under what circumstances should the disabled person accept or decline the invitation? Regardless of the answer, each question may be seen to focus on the disability. To the extent the disability becomes the central issue *around which other aspects of life are organized,* we may say the disabled person is entrenched in the position of a career deviant.

Additional support for the amplification hypothesis stems from research on mental illness. In his analysis of mental illness as a social status, Thomas Scheff (1966:84ff) proposes that amplification of one's role as a person who is mentally ill is encouraged by two processes leading the patient to accept that role. The first process involves rewarding the patient for playing the deviant role, that is, concurring in the diagnosis and behaving accordingly. This process is promoted partly by the doctor's "apostolic function" (Balint, 1957) and partly by the unequal distribution of power between patient and physician. *Apostolic mission* or *function* means that doctors usually have well-developed and firmly held ideas about how people with particular illnesses should act. In the process of making a diagnosis, the physician subtly (or otherwise) encourages the patient to accept the diagnosis he or she thinks is appropriate; acceptance of the diagnosis is greatly enhanced by the physician's power over the patient. This is a consequence of the physician being "well trained, secure, and self confident in his role in the transaction, whereas the client is untutored, anxious, and uncertain about his role. Stated simply, the subject, because of these conditions, is likely to be susceptible to the influence of the [physician]" (Scheff, 1968:6). The physician's efforts are reinforced by the action of other staff and hospital patients. For example, Caudill et al. (1952) have pointed out that conversation between patients on psychiatric wards often revolves about how valuable it is for patients to accept that they are in a mental hospital and that if a patient wants to "get well" and be released he or she had best work with (accept the definitions provided by) the physician. How patients encourage one another to accept

a deviant identity is noted in the following exchange between patients (Scheff, 1966:86):

New Patient: "I don't belong here. I don't like all these crazy people. When can I talk to the doctor? I've been here four days and I haven't seen the doctor. I'm not crazy."

Another Patient: "She says she's not crazy." (Laughter from patients.)

Another Patient: "Honey, what I'd like to know is, if you're not crazy, how did you get your ass in this hospital?"

New Patient: "It's complicated, but I can explain. My husband and I. . . ."

First Patient: "That's what they all say." (General laughter.)

The second process leading to amplification is that of deviants sometimes being punished if they seek to abandon the deviant role and return to a normal role (Scheff, 1966:87; Lemert, 1951:433–441). As an example, we have already observed the employment and other restrictions imposed on ex-convicts and the disabled, and the general exclusion of the mentally ill. Such discrimination, extending into social and marital areas as well as the occupational, serves to block deviants' efforts to reassume a normal role. Thus, not only are people rewarded for accepting the deviant role, but they are often punished if they make an effort to abandon that role.

A similar argument in support of the amplification hypothesis is based on Jacqueline P. Wiseman's study of the experiences of skid row men (1970). Those men who seek employment (try to abandon the deviant role) as part of their rehabilitation often report having a particularly difficult time.

In part, this is because . . . his union membership has lapsed during drinking bouts, or he cannot get a job in his trade as an electrician, metal worker, or one of the other crafts because so much of this work is tied in with contracts demanding security clearance for all workers.

To be unbondable means that the Skid Row man cannot work on many jobs connected with the handling of money or expensive equipment. His status as an alcoholic (or ex-alcoholic) means he cannot work around heavy machinery because of high-risk insurance provisions. Add to this his age, his loss of current experience in his field, and the suspiciously long gaps in his job record (which are hard to explain in any case), and the picture of a virtually unemployable man emerges. (Wiseman, 1970:229)

In summary, evidence and commentary based on examination of juvenile delinquents, the blind, polio victims, the mentally ill, exconvicts, the disabled, and the alcoholic support the view that labeling, by a complex interactive process, may encourage the entrenchment of people in the role of secondary deviant and stabilize them in that position. But, one may ask, is there no contrary evidence? Indeed, there is.

Examining the Evidence: Con

One argument in opposition to the amplification hypothesis is that labeling has no permanent consequence on the deviant. For example, as a result of his study of physician drug addicts, Charles Winick (1964) notes that few doctors are prosecuted for this form of rule breaking and, in contrast to the "street" addict, most physicians treated for addiction at the U.S. Public Health Service Hospital remained off drugs, were not stigmatized, and maintained a successful professional life.

A study of physicians charged with medical malpractice reveals similar conditions. Schwartz and Skolnick (1964) report that of 58 physicians interviewed about the occupational consequences of malpractice lawsuits, "fifty-two reported no negative effects of the suit on their practice, and five of the remaining six, all specialists, reported that their practice *improved* after the suit" (Schwartz and Skolnick, 1964:11, emphasis in original).

These studies suggest that the very protective stance taken by members of the medical profession toward its members may serve to guard physicians, even those formally declared to have engaged in malpractice, from the burden of stigma. These physicians contrast sharply with those who lack a significant power base (Hessler, 1974:151; Schwartz and Skolnick, 1964:115). Another factor likely to be protecting the physician from long-term negative effects of stigma is high occupational status. Given the popular definition of that status, including physicians' alleged devotion to service and competence, and the associated

tendency of laypeople to defer to doctors just because they are doctors, it is unlikely that these members of the upper world would be subject to prolonged disprivilege. Similarly, we cannot help recalling the relative lack of deviance amplification in the case of former Vice President Spiro T. Agnew as a result of his having engaged in political corruption and tax evasion (*Newsweek,* 1973) or in the cases of Charles Colson, John Dean, and other highly placed persons involved in the Watergate affair.

A second argument contradicting the amplification hypothesis is that in some cases, rather than perpetuating deviance, labeling actually reduces it. This argument is consistent with the more traditional view that punishment deters (Sutherland and Cressey, 1978:339–340). In her study of shoplifters, Mary Owen Cameron (1964:151) reports "very little or no recidivism" among adult pilferers apprehended by store detectives but not turned over to police or formally charged. Cameron suggests the adult pilferer does not think of himself of herself as a thief prior to apprehension (which, she says, is an illusion); arrest and interrogation break down such illusions. Coupled with fear, shame, remorse, and a lack of support from friends and family, the destruction of these illusions as "front work" forces pilferers to regard themselves as others do, that is, as rule breakers. Cameron suggests that for some people the horror of that perception is enough to deter further violations (1964:161–166).

A second example of how labeling may deter further rule breaking is the case of members of Alcoholics Anonymous. In his study of the therapeutic dynamics of AA, Milton Maxwell (1967) identifies two factors associated with symbolic or formal labeling that combine to help the alcoholic achieve sobriety. First, the drinker must accept the fact that he or she has a drinking problem that cannot be controlled alone and that anything less than total abstention is impossible. This amounts to acknowledging and accepting the label and identity of the alcoholic. Second are the associated feelings of disillusionment and despair, followed by the discovery of hope. As many alcoholics say, they feel "licked," "down and out," "beaten," that they have their "backs to the wall," or are at "the end of their rope." Such despair, however, is frequently combined with (dissipated by?) hope in the form of a recovered alcoholic, someone who has shared their despair and escaped it. Maxwell comments,

A meaningful [to the actor] coming together of disillusionment and hope seems to be a very individual matter. It may occur early as in the case of what A.A.'s call "high bottoms." It may not occur until after many years of suffering ("low bottoms"), and it may not occur at all, but there is nothing fateful about it. . . . Whether disillusionment and hope intersect early or late, it appears that both are prerequisites for readiness to seek or accept help. (1964:214)

Resolving the Pros and Cons

It is readily apparent that the arguments and evidence bearing on the amplification hypothesis are contradictory. But all is not hopeless confusion. We may resolve many of these contradictions and make sense of the competing claims by noting that while labeling may be and often is associated with people becoming more firmly entrenched in the deviant role, such entrenchment and amplification (becoming a "career deviant") is not inevitable; many other factors intervene between *being* labeled (formally or informally), on the one hand, and *career deviance,* on the other. Let's examine some of these intervening factors.

Ascriptive vs. Achieved Rule Breaking. Appreciation of the consequences of labeling for career deviance calls for distinguishing between ascriptive and achieved deviance. In the case of the highly visible ascribed deviant, such as the obese, the dwarfed, the blind, or the ugly, social reaction may be all that is required for one to become entrenched in the deviant role. Such persons "are not handicapped because their physical and/or visible traits prevent them from playing any particular roles but rather because of the invidious labeling process and the absence of factors which might tend to mitigate its effects" (Mankoff, 1971:207). Given the involuntary character of the deviance of these people, the status assigned them depends on audience reaction rather than on their acts or intentions. Therefore, in the case of the ascribed deviant, labeling may be considered sufficient to stabilize people in a deviant career.

In the case of achieved deviants, however, the relationship between labeling and amplification or career deviance is less clear. On the basis of evidence derived from examination of embezzlement, marijuana use, and homosexuality, Mankoff notes that people frequently become involved in deviant careers *in the absence of public labeling* and stigma. Thus, he contends, social reaction is not a *necessary condition* of (one that always precedes) career deviance. Stated differently, one may become a habitual rule breaker without formal labeling, and one may become largely (if not entirely) law-abiding despite having been labeled. Neither is social reaction a *sufficient condition* (one that is always followed by its effect) of prolonged participation in deviance among achieved deviants. Many achieved deviants who are labeled are able to adapt to this condition in ways unavailable to the ascribed deviant (Mankoff, 1971:209–211). In short, career deviance is less likely to be associated with labeling in the case of the achieved than in that of the ascribed deviant.

Formal vs. Informal Labeling. Examination of the preceding studies suggests that amplification of deviance most frequently (*not* inevitably) occurs when deviant actors experience registry and processing by public social control agencies (especially by those that are governmental, such as police and courts). Conversely, amplification is least likely to occur when actors are dealt with informally or by representatives of private organizations (such as store detectives in the case of shoplifting). Despite exceptions, the studies examined in the preceding discussion suggest that persons caught up in the bureaucracy of official deviance-processing agencies are more, rather than less, likely to be indelibly influenced by that experience. The reasons for this are numerous and interrelated. First, being specialists in imputation, such agencies tend to be more "expert" in their trade and, as creators of official files, have a more extensive and lasting impact on the identity of their clients. More, given their governmental status, the stamp of disapproval applied by such agencies tends to carry more authority, an authority toward which people are inclined to be most deferent. Most important, however, is that by their character and mandate, formal social control agencies are more likely to perpetuate than to discontinue stigmatizing labels. For example, unlike Weight Watchers, whose ostensible purpose is to eliminate obesity and extinguish the label, police, courts, and prisons perpetuate the reality of the actor's presumed defective character. Not the least important basis of the label's indelibility is that it legitimates the activity of the agency. Thus, as a matter of organizational interest it is predictable that formal/public social control agencies will have a more amplifying effect than others. Again, however, such agencies do not operate in a vacuum. Consequently, their effect is moderated by the actor's ability and opportunity to negotiate with and influence agency actions. With that in mind, let's consider power and socioeconomic status as elements that may help us make sense of seemingly contradictory evidence.

Power and Socioeconomic Status. The opportunity of the labeled deviant to avoid becoming involved in career deviance may be greatly enhanced by *power,* that is, the control he or she may exert over others' behavior by whatever means available, including the use of economic wealth. For example, if the long-term consequences of labeling involve discrimination or occupational restrictions, these may be compensated for or substantially lessened depending on the power base of the offender. Of course, in some cases the actual exercise of power is unnecessary; *merely having access to power* may be sufficient to forestall the negative potential of labeling. As a case in point, let's examine the outcome for both corporations and individuals of what has been termed the "Incredible Electrical Conspiracy," "the biggest criminal case in the history of the Sherman [Antitrust] Act" (Smith, 1970:132).

This case involved charges of price fixing, rigging of bids, and the dividing of markets on the manufacture and sale of electrical equipment with an annual value of $1.75 billion. The conspiracy extended over a period of eight years and included the largest manufacturers and distributors of electrical equipment in the United States (General Electric, Westinghouse, Allis-Chalmers, McGraw-Edison, Carrier, and 24 other companies of varying size). For their part in this conspiracy, the offending corporations were fined a total of $1,787,000, with the largest fines being levied against G.E. ($437,500) and Westinghouse ($372,500). To corporate giants, such fines are piddling, "no more unsettling than a $3 parking fine would be to a man with an income of $175,000 a year" (Geis, 1977:120). More substantial were the damage claims against these corporations by municipalities and other purchasers of their equipment. Despite the size of these settlement payments (alleged to total about $160 million in 1964) a company like General Electric could charge the bulk of these off against taxes (Geis, 1977:120).

Except for fines of a relatively inconsequential sort, these corporations suffered no appreciable (if any) damage to their public image (identity). A survey of national newspaper coverage in the days immediately after the defendants admitted their guilt revealed the case received very little media coverage. Only 16 percent of newspapers surveyed (of a sample of 15 percent of all newspapers sold in the United States) gave front-page coverage to the story. Those that did give it front-page coverage gave it no more than one column. Fifty-four percent gave one column or less on an inside page, and 30 percent never mentioned the story ("Notes and Comment," 1961). A second survey (of 30 newspapers accounting for 20 percent of all newspapers sold in the United States), taken after the sentences were handed down, revealed that

forty-five percent of the newspapers in the survey kept the story of the sentencing off the front page. Fewer than a handful of the surveyed papers mentioned the names of any of the sentenced corporations other than General Electric and Westinghouse, and most of the newspapers devoted substantially all their headline space and coverage to the executives who received prison sentences. None of the newspapers emphasized that the *corporations* were actually guilty of committing *crimes*. ("Notes and Comment," 1961:289; footnote 35; emphasis in original)

In this case moral stigma appears to have been withheld from the guilty corporations. Words like *crime, guilt,* and *corporation* were never linked together. Thus, the image of the corporation was protected, no blacklisting of the offending companies occurred, and business as usual was the order of the day.

But what of the executives? Prior to their indictment these men had played roles leading to the idea they were "pillars of the community," including church deacons or vestrymen, president of the chamber of commerce, hospital board member, Community Chest fund raiser, bank director, Little League organizer, and the like. They had *moral credit.* As we might expect, several of these men were dismayed over the prospect of being relegated to the status of "jailbirds" (Smith, 1970). As things turned out, they had little to worry about. Of 45 corporation executives who were involved, 7 received jail sentences of 30 days and 24 were given suspended jail sentences. The maximum fine imposed on these men was $12,500 and in one case that entailed two conspiracies (Smith, 1970:530). The seven who went to jail were later described by officials as model prisoners, got a five-day reduction in sentence for good behavior, and were released. One "executive resigned from his original job, indignant that his salary had not been paid while he was in jail, and shortly thereafter he was appointed president of another corporation at an estimated annual salary of $65,000" (Bloch and Geis, 1970:311). About a month after paying his penalty, a second executive assumed the presidency of another company at an annual salary of $74,000 (Geis, 1977:129).

The outcome of this case is consistent with Sutherland's (1945) classic analysis of the differential implementation of law in white-collar crime cases. It was Sutherland's contention that a combination of fear of and admiration for businesspeople prompted courts to be more lenient when judging their violations than when judging those of other offenders. This leniency and the image that "the man of business is a man of virtue" is also facilitated by the cultural homogeneity between the media and industry as interest groups (Sutherland, 1945:72). Given the combination of these factors, the modest penalties in the electrical conspiracy case and the absence of protracted stigma are not surprising. These results are consistent with the cases of addict physicians and physicians charged with malpractice, cited earlier.

It would be naive, of course, to suggest that the seemingly protected position afforded some offenders is purely and simply a matter of power, that some professionals and business-people have sufficient clout to withstand the effort of the state to regulate their conduct. Interacting with and supplementing the privileged position of some people is the ambivalence and conflict that exists concerning the appropriateness of applying criminal sanctions in cases of violations of occupational regulations. Simply stated, there is a distinction between the legal code, on the one hand, and people's moral codes, on the other. In a heterogeneous society these several codes are unlikely ever to be entirely consistent with one another. As such, there will always be instances in which public support for legal regulation will be questioned and in which applied criminal sanctions will seem modest relative to those applied in other sorts of cases, such as in instances of crime against persons (see Ball and Friedman, 1965). In short, what may appear to be a consequence of a power game is more validly described as a result of the interaction of power and several other factors, not the least of which are the conflicting elements of social reality in a heterogeneous society.

A final example of how power and wealth interact with other factors to protect some people against stigmatization and career deviance is found in the case of college students. In reporting the results of research into systematic crime and deviance among students at an elite college (deviance that included property destruction, drug dealing, grand theft, auto theft, and gang rape), Stuart Hills notes that students display a sense of "invincibility" based on their belief that their social class position and the influence of their parents renders them immune from arrest and, if arrested, immune from prosecution. As one student reported:

There is no way in hell that the (town) police force would ever nail a (Preppy) for dealing. There's too much influence at (Preppy University) and they know it. Sweet _____ (the Director of Student Services) and _____ (a college vice-president) both have a good conception of what is going on. Yet, I've never heard of anyone getting busted. It would ruin the lily-white reputation parents have of (Preppy U.). (Hills, 1982:266)

It seems clear that students' protected position stems in part from the fact that, as noted earlier, organizations operate to maximize rewards and minimize strains. For school administrators and the police to press charges and pursue these matters would be too much trouble. Thus, we may confidently propose that the career consequences of labeling will vary inversely with the power and socioeconomic status of the labelee. Status and power sometimes "insulate" rule breakers against the long-term effects of labeling and deviance amplification.

Motives. Whether or not labeling promotes career deviance also hinges on the motives for the behavior. The motives that underlie the actor's decision to engage in rule breaking do not necessarily cease after the initial violations occur. On the basis of persistent motives, the actor may pursue a deviant career despite the absence of formal labeling and regardless of an opportunity to refrain from rule breaking and to reassume a nondeviant status. Thus, the Cantonsville Nine, on trial for (admittedly) having destroyed government property (military draft files) as an expression of their opposition to U.S. involvement in Vietnam, were described by their attorney William Kunstler as being "proud" of what they had done; Kunstler also noted that the defendants perceived their actions as "one of the shining moments in their personal lives" (Bannan and Bannan, 1974:129). Quite clearly, the motives of these defendants, founded on religiously based convictions, are unlikely to be altered one way or another, by public condemnation. Conse-

quently, it is quite plausible to contend that some people will persist in a pattern of rule breaking because they are committed to that behavior, because they like what they are doing, or for other reasons (Mankoff, 1971:211–212).

Other Factors. On the basis of their own and others' research, Thorsell and Klemke (1972:397–402) suggest that a variety of other conditions may influence deviance amplification. First, they propose that when labels are assigned confidentially (as by private organizations rather than public agencies) to people who have limited commitment to deviant behavior (many shoplifters, for example), the probability of deviance amplification is reduced.

Second, they suggest that when the labelee identifies with the labeler, and shares the labeler's general moral sense, labeling is most likely to retard further deviance. This proposition is consistent with the work of Maxwell on alcoholics, cited earlier, and with that of Carol A.B. Warren (1974b). Contrary to the amplification hypothesis, Warren reports, first, that negative labeling by former members of the stigmatized category (such as ex-cons, ex-drug users, and ex-alcoholics) promotes identification between labeler and labelee and stimulates a change in the deviant's lifestyle and behavior. Second, Warren reports that labeling occurring within the confines of a voluntary membership group (such as a weight loss group) is more likely to promote a positive change in the labelee's behavior and identity than when labeling occurs in total institutions such as jails or prisons (Warren, 1974b:307–308).

Unlike labeling as a result of degradation ceremonies, that which occurs in voluntary groups, often of a therapeutic sort, has the goal of promoting a "positive" change, one the actor desires. Such labels are defined as part of therapy and are applied by those with whom the actor identifies. Moreover, labels applied in these settings are transitory; they are applied to promote abandonment of (rather than engulfment in) a morally questionable condition. Often, too, labels so applied are stripped of negative meaning. Thus, in AA, alcoholism is medicalized; it is a disease to be treated rather than a moral defect leading to the actor's condemnation.

Third, Thorsell and Klemke suggest that the nature of community response to the labeled deviant is critical as an insulator against a person's becoming entrenched in the deviant status. Especially important are positive, supportive relations with significant others such as family and friends. Such relations serve to maintain social integration between the labelee and the larger community; the disintegrative potential of labeling is thereby frustrated.

Finally, these writers propose that when labels can be relatively easily removed, as in the case of "closing" records of juvenile delinquents or "sealing" other public documents, the actor has less chance of becoming involved in career deviance. Simply stated, the record and the label are no longer visible and, hence, do not work to shape relationships between offenders and others. Offenders are given a "second chance."

Summary

The aim of this chapter has been to examine the social-psychological and social consequences of stigma and identity spoilage. Employing an interactionist approach, theory suggests that the attribution of stigmatizing labels to actors, and behaving toward actors in terms of the moral meaning of those labels, may result in a substantial transformation in the actors' public identity and self-concept. By and large, the evidence we have examined, taken from a wide variety of ethnographic and other research, supports the contention that many people who are publicly labeled do, indeed, suffer social psychological consequences, specifically a decline in self-feelings. For the most part, we may say that such feelings reflect (1) the social relations between deviant actors and their condemners, (2) the actors' internalization of the moral meaning linked to their deviant status, and (3) the fact that deviant actors are often responded to by others rather exclusively in terms of their deviant (that is, spoiled) identity.

These consequences are not limited to those who are publicly labeled. Through the process of symbolic labeling, undetected rule breakers—primary deviants—may label themselves and experience the burden of guilt and shame and the fear of public disclosure. These social psychological consequences, identified as role engulfment, are most properly seen as the outcome of a cumulative process. In addition to the social psychological consequences, stigmatization may also have social consequences of varying intensity and duration, extending not merely to deviant actors, but, by way of courtesy stigma, to those with whom they are intimately associated.

Most important, we have attempted to show that these consequences stem not from any indelible characterological or other defect possessed by the actor, but from the audience's definition of the deviant as unacceptable, morally defective, and, hence, difficult to relate to in normal ways. These definitions are sustained by negative stereotypy. Consistent with these meanings, we have seen that normals often erect barriers to avoid contact with and contamination by those whom they regard as defective. These barriers obstruct normal social interaction and, in turn, may encourage some stigmatized persons and groups to become more deeply involved in the deviant role, that is, to have their deviance amplified.

Evidence bearing on the validity of the deviance amplification hypothesis is conflicting. Much of this conflict reflects the state of the sociological art, methodological matters, and other issues beyond the scope of this volume (Meade, 1974). Nonetheless, by refining our perspective, it is possible to make sense of the broad and conflicting claims. Consistent with this, we examined several factors that research and experience indicate have an influence on the amplification process.

First, we distinguished between ascribed and achieved deviance, suggesting that the influence of labeling on a person's behavior and identity is likely to be less damaging in the case of the achieved than the ascribed deviant. This, we contended, is a consequence of the greater role of voluntarism in the case of achieved than ascribed deviance.

Second, we focused on the labelee's ability to wield power and his or her location in the social structure. Simply, representatives of some groups are better able to insulate themselves from the effects of labeling.

Third, we noted that the motives underlying a person's involvement in rule-violating behavior may well encourage career deviance independent of labeling. Motives may render labeling quite incidental to some cases of career deviance.

Finally, a host of other influential elements have been discussed, including (1) the circumstances under which labeling occurs, (2) the labelee's commitment to rule-breaking behavior, (3) the identification between labeler and labelee, (4) the nature of others' responses to the labelee, especially within primary groups, and (5) whether or not the label may be easily expunged or its visibility reduced.

Taken together, these considerations suggest that it is inappropriate to make unqualified claims that *in and of itself* labeling has either positive or negative effects on target populations. In the final analysis, the effect of labeling and stigma is mediated by a variety of interrelated elements. Not the least of these is the actor's ability to manage stigma. It is to that issue that we now turn.

7 Managing Stigma

Introduction

An earlier chapter stressed a model of human nature that emphasized people's active role in shaping their destiny. According to this model, people interact with, adapt to, and sometimes overcome elements in their world. Rarely are they so passive as to allow themselves to be buffeted about, willy-nilly, by whatever forces come their way. As an example, we noted people's efforts to negotiate with labelers in an attempt to resist or modify the tags placed on them. A second example of people's effort to shape their destiny involves *stigma management,* that is, any of a variety of methods employed, individually or collectively, either to control information about their spoiled identity or otherwise alter the meanings attributed to them in order to reduce the social significance of their deviance. In this chapter we examine the many ways in which deviant persons and groups seek to manage their stigma. In examining this issue we deal with the fourth and final element of the deviance process.

In considering people's efforts to manage stigma, we do not suggest or imply that such efforts are universal or that attempts are necessarily successful to any specific degree. For one thing, the idea of stigma is simply inapplicable to some people. That is, it is entirely possible "for an individual to fail to live up to what we effectively demand of him, and yet be relatively untouched by his failure; insulated by his alienation, protected by identity beliefs of his own, he feels that he is a full-fledged human being, and that we are the ones who are not quite human" (Goffman, 1963:6). Second, some deviants concur with public attributions and accept their stigma and shame, as we may note among minority group members who express self-hatred (Vander Zanden 1983:326–328). In neither of these instances do people confront and deal with the stigma directly. In the first case the stigma is ignored, while in the second case people capitulate and accept its meaning as valid.

Contrary to these instances is the tendency of many stigmatized people to deal more directly with their stigma. Some acknowledge the stigma and seek to correct or otherwise overcome it. For example, people who are paralyzed struggle to walk, run, or engage in other physical activity characteristic of "normals," while *transsexuals,* people who, through surgery and socialization seek a gender and/or sex identity other than that to which they were born, undergo psychotherapy, hormone injections, and radical surgery to alter their sex organs (Humphreys, 1972:137; Kando, 1973). Still others may use their stigmatized condition to achieve secondary gains—for example, to explain or justify other shortcomings or deficiencies. The stigma becomes an excuse for ill-success to which it has no relevance (Goffman, 1963:10).

The aspects of stigma management with which we will deal differ from these in that we are concerned with those modes of adjustment pertinent to situations in which "normals" and the stigmatized are in contact. Management of one's stigma, therefore, becomes a *social* matter; that is, an effort must be made to control or otherwise influence the information others may acquire or have about one's condition. For some, this control takes the form of trying to avoid the disclosure of damaging information; for others, it involves trying to make already disclosed information less obtrusive and stigmatizing. For still others, it entails trying to bring about a change in the meaning customarily assigned to the stigma. However, regardless of the form it takes, successful stigma management calls for an effort to influence the construction of reality. The stigma must be dealt with if the actor wishes to minimize his or her differentness. These comments require some qualification.

Analysis of stigma may profit by noting the variation in the public nature of stigma. In some cases people possess stigmata that are not readily or immediately noticed by or known to others. Examples include sterility in a male, a person's ethnic origin, or the fact that a person is a former mental patient or prison inmate. In general, this group also includes those who have been symbolically labeled and have managed to keep their deviance secret. Such cases of stigma fall into the category of the *discreditable,* that is, people who would likely be discredited were their deviance to become public. In contrast are persons whose stigma is either self-evident (blindness, obesity, a physical handicap, skin color) or is or may be assumed to be known by others. These cases represent the *discredited.* Our consideration of stigma management will follow this distinction as it pertains to individualized efforts to manage stigma.

Individualized Stigma Management

The Discreditable

Secrecy and Information Control. Erving Goffman suggests that people who are discreditable often confront the problem of whether "to display or not to display; to tell or not to tell; to let on or not to let on; to lie or not to lie; and in each case, to whom, how, when and where" (Goffman, 1963:42). People who carry an undisclosed stigma have to reckon with the possibility that people accept them unwittingly—that is, without knowing—and that if their stigma became known to others their acceptance (which is based on ignorance and unintentional) would be replaced by rejection. In an effort to avoid rejection, those who possess an undisclosed stigma have a pervasive need for secrecy.

This concern for secrecy has been noted by Humphreys (1970), Corzine and Kirby (1977), and Delph (1978) in their studies of impersonal sexual encounters among men. Concern for secrecy during these sexual encounters in public restrooms ("tearooms") and other public settings such as roadside rest areas, is marked by the emergence of the role of *watchqueen,* that is, a watchman or lookout who remains alert to the possible intrusion by police or other strangers who may pose a threat to those engaged in sex (Humphreys, 1970:26–27). Even where no such role exists, concern for secrecy remains paramount. Because these encounters often involve persons who are married, or engaged in professions, or who otherwise maintain an acceptable public identity, participants rarely exchange personal information. Telephone numbers, addresses, and surnames are seldom given out. Other information is purposely left vague or ambiguous in order to prevent participants from being identified and having their involvement disclosed (Corzine and Kirby, 1977:173). In other cases, those who are discreditable attempt to *pass,* that is, by controlling information about themselves, they seek to occupy a status by fraudulent means. In either case, secrecy is of utmost importance. So, too, is secrecy important to persons who seek sex partners by advertising in sex tabloids. Such ads invariably omit names and addresses and invite interested respondents to make anonymous contact through a post office box. In the case of swingers with children, considerable effort is put forth to "keep their children from listening in on phone conversations on the extension phones, intercepting mail and finding photographs of other couples either in the nude or engaging in sexual activity" (Bartell, 1971:30). In other instances swingers design their homes so as to ensure privacy and prevent surprise visits from curious children. Thus, houses are built with wings separated by pairs of locking doors, are soundproofed, and are connected only by intercom for emergency purposes (Bartell, 1971:31).

Finally, concern over information control is not a transitory condition, but one that extends over long periods of time, a fact that, for many people, serves only to compound life's difficulties. This is demonstrated in the following letter written to the author of a biographical piece on being homosexual:

I have been working on this letter and trying to send it for more than three months now. . . . I have been married for over 20 years, have a daughter who is 20 and in college, and another who is 18 and will start college in the fall. We have a beautiful home and, I feel, a good life together. My wife is my best friend, but she has a very Victorian view of sex; it is performed more as a duty than anything else. . . . For me the thrills, excitements and beauties of sex have always come from men. I don't like the lying, the hiding, the excuses that go on because of my situation. I would like to open the door and have gay friends to my house and have the knowledge accepted. Has this ever been done successfully? If so, how? How can you change a person's mind when "homosexual" is a very dirty word, although they have lived over 20 years with one, lovingly? Any ideas, please? (Miller, 1971:69)

If nothing more, these examples attest to the fact that deviants feel compelled to give careful attention to the management or control of information about themselves that would reveal their discreditable condition.

Information control involves a variety of general techniques. First, it may entail avoiding contact with *stigma symbols,* signs that would call attention to or reveal a person's debased or deviant condition (Goffman, 1963:43). For example, it has been suggested that, historically, for a black person to "pass" and establish a totally white identity called for "sociological death and rebirth." That is, passing required a black person to sacrifice his or her educational credentials if they were acquired at a black school, to abandon all contact with family and friends so as to avoid the risk of being identified, and to suffer the loss of work and other references that might reveal one's racial identity (Drake and Cayton, 1962:163). Among transsexuals, passing may require name changes and a move to a new community, as well as new friends, jobs, and so on (Kando, 1973:98; Bogdan, 1974), in addition to having their birth certificates altered so that the sexual identification thereon is consistent with their newly acquired sexual iden-

tity (*Arizona Republic,* 1981f). For unwed fathers, avoidance of contact with stigma symbols sometimes involves abandoning the pregnant woman or encouraging her to take residence in some distant place. By avoiding all contact with the pregnant woman (who symbolizes his failing), the man seeks to control information concerning his moral rule violation (Pfuhl, 1978).

A second general technique of information control involves the use of *disidentifiers,* that is, symbols used to prevent a person from being conceived of as deviant (Goffman, 1963:44). Again referring to premarital pregnancies, a number of couples marry prior to the birth of the baby. Regardless of other reasons for marrying, one acknowledged result is the legitimation of an otherwise illicit union and ensuing birth. In that way the principals are provided with a positive image, one that would at least protect them against the full impact of having their deviance revealed (Christensen, 1953; Pfuhl, 1978).

A pervasive concern over disclosure, which leads to the use of disidentifiers, is also found among Mexican male homosexuals. Much of this concern stems from the tight grasp the Mexican family maintains over unmarried male members. Given this grasp, these men greatly fear being seen in the company of effeminate males or being seen entering or leaving places where known homosexuals gather—either of which is likely to be taken as evidence of one's own homosexuality. To avoid disclosure of homosexuality, these men frequently maintain social contacts with women, periodically engage in heterosexual intercourse with prostitutes, and publicly whistle or make suggestive remarks at passing women (Carrier, 1976).

The use of disidentifiers and the maintenance of secrecy may become thoroughly woven into the fabric of a person's life. This is revealed by research among lesbians. For example, maintaining secrecy may necessitate adjustment of speech patterns. One lesbian respondent reported that as a result of having cultivated a self-protective sensitivity, she became so accustomed to anticipating her utterances that she lost a great deal of spontaneity in her speech and at times found herself being quite inarticulate (Ponse, 1976:318). In other instances, lesbians cultivate speech patterns and discuss topics intended to misinform their audience about their sexual preference. For example, in order to establish and maintain a heterosexual image, some lesbian women will speak publicly about their boyfriends or unrequited love affairs. Others may establish a standing relationship with a man so as to have a male companion on select occasions (Ponse, 1976:318). Another disidentifying device used by some lesbians is to habitually dress in ways suggestive of their being "superfeminine" or straight (Ponse, 1976:319). In all these ways people seek to avoid projecting cues that would reveal their homosexual orientation.

In some cases the need to use disidentifiers is so widespread as to make it profitable for others to provide such services. Thus, at a major western state university an enterprising female student provided an "Alibi Service" to other female students. Limiting herself to ten customers at one time, this student provided a bogus mailing address and phone number for young women living with boyfriends despite their parents' objections. The service included collecting and delivering mail to subscribers, as well as answering the phone and giving callers the appropriate message or alibi for each person. For this service the fee was $20 per month (*State Press,* 1980).

Managing undisclosed stigma may call for a third general tactic: leading a *double life.* Leading a double life requires a person to impose severe restrictions on his or her choice of associates and friends. For example, other than highly impersonal and instrumental contacts, some homosexuals refuse to have any association with heterosexuals. Having a drink after work with a heterosexual co-worker or dropping by a heterosexual neighbor's residence to talk, are things to be scrupulously avoided lest one's identity be revealed. When intermingling between homosexuals and heterosexuals does occur, there remains the question of whether or not to tell or to lie, and to whom. Leading a double life is often an attempt to resolve the tensions and anxieties that arise from this intermingling. Thus, many people who are gay

strictly separate their homosexual and heterosexual friends. The success of this tactic is debatable, as one lesbian informant notes:

Oh boy, I've lived a double life like you wouldn't believe all my life and sometimes the pressure was so enormous I thought I was going to explode. We'd sit around and have coffee, the girls in the office, and they'd say . . . this woman looks like a man . . . Omygod that's a queer and I'd sit there and listen to this kind of stuff and . . . until I'd just get violent sometimes. And there's been a few times when it's been all I could do just to keep from jumping up and saying, "Look you guys have lunch with me, we've socialized together for fifteen years. I'm queer!" I've wanted to do it so bad that you know, I uh, almost explode! Because you know . . . Why? I mean, what would I have accomplished anyway—I would have lost more than I had gained. (Ponse, 1976:327–328)

The foregoing suggests that the preservation of secrecy calls for the development of "a more heightened awareness and a sharper perspective on ordinary affairs and everyday encounters than those for whom concealment is not an issue" (Lyman and Scott, 1970:78). Conditions of ordinary social interaction that "normals" take for granted often must be given considerable attention by those seeking to conceal their stigma. As we have noted, spouses of mental patients go to great lengths to conceal the family stigma. Stutterers frequently develop tricks to disguise their speech problem, such as anticipating the inclination to use "difficult" words and then selecting a less troublesome substitute. The colostomy (surgical formation of an artificial anus) patient finds it necessary to select a theater seat so located as to provide quick and easy access to a lavatory. And the covert homosexual must watch every word and gesture for fear of revealing his or her true self. In each case, the paramount concern is never to relinquish control over information about self.

The development of this sensitivity is not without unintended consequences. For example, at the same time and precisely because it helps them to maintain a heterosexual identity, the reliance on a male companion may frustrate some lesbians' desire to become more involved in the gay community. The price of a heterosexual image, then, is at least partial isolation from intimate association with one's reference group. As Ponse remarks, "the veils of anonymity are often as effective with one's own as with those from whom one wishes to hide" (1976:319).

Another price the discreditable must sometimes pay is the strain and tension that secrecy imposes on what would otherwise be quite ordinary and relaxed situations. Thus, referring to the four years he served prior to "coming out" (publicly revealing his homosexuality), a gay police officer indicated "it was very stressful to keep it hidden. What I'm going through now [being dismissed from the police force and seeking reinstatement]—with all the publicity—is stressful, but not nearly so stressful as keeping it hidden for so long" (*Arizona Republic,* 1980k). For persons maintaining control of information, taken-for-granted activity such as casual conversation with co-workers or others about friendships, about how one spent a weekend, or about the types of leisure activity they engage in may be the basis for heightened tension lest they slip and reveal their deviation. They cannot afford to be free and open; they must always be circumspect. To have the desired effect, secrecy may require a person to lead a double life, replete with alienation, dissonance, and uninterrupted vigilance for fear that damaging information will fall into the wrong hands.

The Role of Others. The management of discreditability is aimed at influencing others' perceptions and, hence, affecting self–other relations. The outcome of these efforts, however, may not rest solely with the deviant actor. In many cases successful management is achieved only with the assistance of others. Quite often this takes the form of a mutual pretense between the deviant and others, or a false or *counterfeit secrecy* (Ponse, 1976:323). In such instances, despite mutual awareness, both the deviant and others tacitly agree to preserve the fiction that there is nothing different or unusual about the deviant or his or her actions. For example, Ponse cites a case of counterfeit secrecy between a lesbian and her mother. In this instance, despite incontrovertible evidence to the contrary, a facade of heterosexuality (normality) was maintained, with both parties refusing to discuss the situation. Conversation between mother and daughter excluded such topics as boyfriends, marriage, childbearing, and other things that would call for acknowledgment of the unrecognizable (Ponse, 1976:325–326). This same strategy has been noted among some Mexican male homosexuals, many of whom continue to live in the parental home long after the age when young men are expected to have established their own residence. Between such men and their families—and even when their homosexuality is known to several members of the family—there may exist a "conspiracy of silence" or "counterfeit secrecy."

The homosexually involved individuals thus continue to act in such a way that they do not expose themselves to unknowing relatives, neighbors, or friends. They may continue to maintain the fiction, for example, that some day they will marry and have children; and social occasions at the house may be organized as though their interests were heterosexual. (Carrier, 1976:367)

Similarly, a 33-year-old woman who is obese suggests that "other people put fat people in the closet. They don't talk about it and don't acknowledge it. No one will use the word *fat* in front of you. They use circumlocution, like *zoftig* or *heavy,* or say that you have a pretty face" (Millman, 1980:14–15). As in the case of leading a "double life," counterfeit secrecy demands a price. The obscuring and denial of one's identity in this way serves not only to reinforce both the idea of one's unacceptability and some degree of self-alienation, but also to erect barriers between self and others from whom one might conceivably obtain emotional support. Topics of conversation and areas of interaction become highly attenuated and social relationships become strained. The tension the person seeks to avoid may be intensified by the very means employed to reduce it.

The Discredited

In contrast to the problem of the discreditable, which is to control information, the discredited face the problem of seeking to reduce the relevance of the stigmatized condition by attempting to maintain a positive, if not normal, self-image and public identity. A variety of tactics may be used to achieve this goal.

Destigmatization: Purification and Transcendence. *Destigmatization* refers to the processes whereby one may negate or expunge a deviant identity and replace it with one that is essentially nondeviant or normal. Carol A.B. Warren (1980) proposes two methods whereby individuals may achieve this change in identity: purification and transcendence. Drawing on Warren's work, let's briefly examine these two methods.

Purification refers to the process whereby a person's old and defective self is replaced by a new moral self, either by sacred or secular means. In the sacred method, the person is transformed from "sinner to saint"; by this means, expressed in religious terms, he or she experiences "rebirth" and is "born again." In being reborn, the effect of the prior degradation ceremony is reversed. In that ceremony, an essentially moral identity and self are obliterated and replaced by those that are immoral. In sacred (as well as secular) purification the "lower order" self is exchanged for one of a "higher order." This rebirth is achieved by means of the actor extinguishing the condemned behavior and/or engaging in behavior that may be seen as having a spiritual base, such as charitable works involving self-sacrifice. As an example, we may cite Malcolm X, former leading figure in the Black Muslims, who rose from hoodlum, thief, dope peddler, and pimp to become one of the most dynamic leaders of the Black Revolution in the United States. In Warren's terms Malcolm X "became an abstinent, educated Black Muslim from being a wild-living, uneducated atheist, [while] Charles Colson of Watergate fame, . . . passes from being a 'crooked, power-hungry politician' to a 'humble and repentant Christian'" (1980:63).

Much the same process is found in the secular form of purification, wherein a defective moral identity is replaced by means of moral action. In this form, the purifying moral action is likely to be prolonged, extending over years, and of a relatively dramatic sort. Again, Warren provides the example of John Profumo, former British War Minister who became involved in a sex scandal with a call girl and fell from grace. His purification was accomplished by years of voluntary work with the poor and alcoholics of London (1980:64).

In contrast with purification, destigmatization by *transcendence* is more applicable to the case of the ascribed deviant who is unable to assert control over his or her stigma (as the achieved deviant may extinguish his or her offending behavior). Thus, while in purification the old, defective self is "erased," in transcendence the old self—or at least symbols of it—persist. The achievement of destigmatization, then, requires the deviant to "rise above," that is, transcend, his or her condition by means of some persistent type of action that is unexpected among people with their type deviation. In short, transcendence calls for a person to display a "better" self rather than to eliminate the former self (Warren, 1980:64–65).

Several examples of destigmatization by transcendence come to mind: John Merrick, the Elephant Man (Montagu, 1979; Warren, 1980:65); author, lecturer, and humanitarian Helen Keller (deaf and blind); President Franklin D. Roosevelt (polio victim); English poetess Elizabeth Barrett Browning (an invalid due to spinal injury); Russian author Feodor Dostoevsky (epileptic); and contemporary comedian Jerry Jewell (cerebral palsy) (Gleidman and Roth, 1980:41; Graves, 1980). For these and many other ascribed deviants (the spinal cord injured person who skis, the postpolio gymnast, the lame swimmer, and so on), the only way they may experience destigmatization is to achieve extraordinary success or become expert in areas of endeavor ordinarily closed to persons such as themselves (Goffman, 1963:10). For persons who are discredited, these destigmatization processes roughly parallel the effort made by some discreditable persons to build up moral credits against the time their deviation may become known.

Deviance Disavowal. Still another tactic used by the discredited is *deviance disavowal,* that is, repudiation of or denial that their behavior or

162

condition is abnormal (Davis, 1961). This tactic may be used by both achieved and ascribed deviants. Seen as an effort to *normalize,* deviance disavowal seeks to render normal and morally acceptable that which has heretofore been regarded as abnormal and immoral (Davis, 1961:126). As such, the process of disavowal, if successfully carried out, normalizes relations between the deviant and others.

As a technique of managing stigma, deviance disavowal has been observed among those convicted of sexual offenses against children (McCaghy, 1968). Convicted child molesters frequently allude to the influence of alcohol as an explanation and a way of normalizing the situation. As examples, men state:

"If you been drinking a lot your passions get aroused." "I was intoxicated and couldn't account for myself." "I was drunk. I didn't realize their age and I was half blind. I've always been a drinker." "Drinking is the reason. I could always get women. I can't figure it out. A man's mind doesn't function right when he's got liquor on it." (McCaghy, 1968:48)

Essentially, these men contend that the offense would never have occurred had it not been for their intoxicated condition and that it is more or less "normal" for alcohol to have this effect on people. They allege alcohol caused them to do what their "true character" would not otherwise permit. Their problem is perceived to be simple: They sometimes drink to excess and then do "stupid things." However, the "stupid thing" is not symbolic of the molester's substantial self. By this means, men attempt to explain their behavior, absolve themselves of responsibility for their wrongdoing, and avail themselves of the image of a normal, socially acceptable, moral person. They make a bid to be seen as persons who have many of the same positive social attributes possessed by others. Thus, they make the effort to "normalize" their identity while acknowledging their rule breaking.

The Disavowal Process. The disavowal process consists of three stages. The first is marked by *fictional acceptance of the deviant as normal and equal to others.* Interaction between the deviant and others is characterized by politeness, curiosity, and privacy. Ordinarily, we may expect others to exhibit some curiosity about aspects of the deviant that symbolizes his or her differentness, be it obesity, a physical handicap, a record of wrongful behavior, and the like. Despite this curiosity, the norms supporting the value of privacy require that people "refrain from remarking or otherwise reacting too obviously to those aspects of [deviant] persons which in the privacy of our thought betoken important differences between ourselves" (Davis, 1961:126). Despite curiosity, then, people generally tend to honor the norms of privacy and conduct themselves according to the standards of politeness. Feigning avoidance of the thing that is very much on people's mind amounts to *civil inattention.*

That such fictions are practiced is noticeable by the horror that sometimes arises when they are stripped away, especially by innocent children. As an example, we may note the instance in which a very overweight babysitter was greeted by her three-year-old charge with the loud exclamation "You're fat!" Davis tells of another occurrence provided him by a young woman informant with a physical handicap.

I was visiting my girlfriend's house and I was sitting in the lobby waiting for her when this woman comes out of her apartment and starts asking me questions. She just walked right up. I didn't know her from Adam, I never saw her before in my life. "Gee, what do you have? How long have you been that way? Oh gee, that's terrible." And so I answered her questions, but I got very annoyed and wanted to say, "Lady, mind your own business." (Davis 1961:127)

Feigning normalcy and equality permits existence of the fiction of "no difference" between the deviant and others. Most important, this permits prolongation of the interaction to the point that people may be able to relate to the deviant in terms other than those linked to his or her deviance. At this point, the second stage of deviance disavowal commences: *the facilitating of normal role taking by the deviant.* This stage is reached when people are able to interact with the deviant in terms of his or her nondeviant statuses. Interaction is no longer restricted by the characterological imputations linked to the master status. Terms such as *blind, crippled,* and so on, can be used without embarrassment when talking with a blind or disabled person. Often this stage is actively promoted by the effort of the deviant to project images, attitudes, and concepts of self other than those of a deviant.

Development of this stage of disavowal calls for reciprocity between the deviant and the normal. That is, as the deviant disavows his or her "abnormality" and makes a bid for redefinition of self, the nondeviant must respond in a manner consistent with the cues proffered by the deviant. The nondeviant's support of the effort at disavowal confirms the deviant's bid for self-redefinition; equally important, it helps promote "normalization" of the very same traits that may originally have been the basis of the actor's rejection. When interaction between the deviant and others reaches a level such that the deviant condition is no longer regarded as a handicap, it may be said that one has "broken through" the interactional limitations imposed by the master status (Davis, 1961:128). Interaction becomes spontaneous rather than forced, natural rather than artificial.

Breaking through leads to the third and last stage of the process—*institutionalizing* (that is, sustaining) *normalized relationships.* Institutionalization does not mean that the special condition of the deviant (for example, that he or she cannot see, or is confined to a wheelchair, or has a prison record) is ignored. Rather, it means that these conditions are ultimately acknowledged and worked into the ordinary relationship that prevails between deviant and others. Davis suggests this normalization is reached in either of two ways.

First, there is "overnormalization," in which a person "normalizes his perceptions to such an extent as to suppress his effective awareness of many of the areas in which the handicapped person's behavior unavoidably departs from the normal standard" (Davis, 1961:130). This pattern exists when a person, unthinkingly, schedules events, appointments, activities, and so on, that turn out to be inconvenient, embarrassing, or uncomfortable for the deviant.

For example, the person makes reservations for dinner at a usually crowded restaurant without telling the management that one of the diners will be confined to a wheelchair. In short, the deviant is being encouraged to "give up" his or her abnormality.

The second method is the reverse of the first. That is, here the nondeviant joins the deviant in defying the stereotypic definitions that prevail in the larger community (Gowman, 1956:71). In doing this, the nondeviant seeks to affirm his or her belief in the deviant's capabilities. As expressions of this repudiation we may note the case of the able-bodied person mildly and jokingly chiding a paraplegic friend for being "so damned helpless," or the hearing person who asks a hearing-impaired friend why she failed to respond to a question by inquiring when she last "cleaned out her ears." For persons who embrace stereotypic conceptions of the physically handicapped, such remarks are horrifying in that they violate the standards of "good taste" and civil inattention. However, for those involved in normalized relations, the perception of such remarks as horrifying is taken as evidence of the definer's lack of enlightenment. Essentially, such remarks announce that the disability is defined as a "small part" of the individual (Levitin, 1975:552).

A word of caution is in order. These comments concerning disavowal and normalization are not made to suggest that these processes are panaceas for the ills of the stigmatized person, or that all instances of apparent acceptance constitute genuine cases of normalization. As Marcia Millman (1980:78) notes regarding the case of some overweight women, acceptance of the deviant in certain roles (such as confidante and friend) by others does not necessarily extend to their being accepted in other roles (such as competitor in the dating game). Indeed, in some instances, a person's obesity is the basis for the friendship. That is, to the insecure female seeking to be active in the dating game, the fat girl who is felt to be unable to compete favorably in that game is a "safe" friend. In short, what appears to be normalization may be counterfeit. Further, disavowal may constitute a catch-22. That is, if deviants assume others accept them as normal and behave accordingly, they risk rejection. "On the other hand, if they never take the risk of presenting themselves as normal, they relinquish any chance of ratification [of normalcy], of participating in the world and its pleasures" (Millman, 1980:78). Stigmatization does seem to pose rather difficult problems.

Deviance Avowal. In contrast to disavowal, some people attempt to manage their stigma and avoid or limit devaluation by acknowledging their condition or wrongful action while simultaneously working to effect a positive social identity and achieve positive social statuses (Levitin, 1975:550–551). By openly declaring that they are handicapped or otherwise stigmatized, people may be said to engage in *deviance avowal* (Turner, 1972). For example, people who are temporarily handicapped sometimes use the technique of avowal by proclaiming that "this deviance will *not always* be me" (Levitin, 1975:551). In taking this path, the deviant individual is not simply resisting the label *permanently disabled,* but is seeking to discourage the idea that *any* such label is appropriate. That is, he or she resists the application of any label that symbolizes the removal of the attribution of normality.

Avowing his or her deviance while making a bid for normality may demand considerable time, effort, and imagination on the part of the stigmatized person. For example, avowal may call for an effort to relate the details of the particular condition to any person who will listen. In telling the story, emphasis will be placed on the prognosis of early recovery (even when this is not medically justifiable), thereby emphasizing the temporary nature of the condition. The basic message is that "this handicap will *not always* be who I am" (Levitin, 1975:554). Examples of this effort include the temporarily disabled person who announced the temporary need of a wheelchair and its anticipated "disappearance" by painting "Houdini" on the chair (Levitin, 1975:552). Another device used by temporarily disabled persons is to inquire of others about their own past illnesses or disabilities, thereby reminding them that they, too, may once have been afflicted.

The goal is to limit others' opportunities to "draw lines" between him- or herself and the stigmatized person.

The permanently handicapped who seek to convey the basic message that their "handicap is *not all* of who I am" (Levitin, 1975:554) engage in this same effort. For its members, the National Association to Aid Fat Americans encourages the view that people are other things in addition to being fat and that fatness should not be allowed to dominate a person's life. (Millman, 1980:17). To emphasize the latter point, messages of avowal often carry information about the untainted aspects of self.

For both the temporarily and the permanently disabled, broadcasting details and providing cues that will permit others to relate to them in terms of a nondeviant role facilitates their own normal role taking (as in the second stage of the disavowal process). If this effort is successful and the preferred definition accepted by "normals," the final stage of normalizing relations between deviants and others is reached.

Moreover, avowal seeks to separate the *deviant condition* from the *deviant role.* Thus, alcoholics who have "taken the cure" and have their drinking under control may acknowledge they are alcoholics, but stress that they no longer are drunks. In making the separation between condition and role, it becomes possible for the deviant and/or others to overlook, forget, or redefine the prior "failing." Indeed, as we noted earlier, a person's prior, now controlled, deviance becomes the basis of a *derived status,* a position based on the person's prior status.

Stigma Management and Socialization. Use of the techniques of disavowal and avowal to successfully manage encounters with nondeviants does not come easily or automatically. The techniques must be learned as part of the ongoing biography of the deviant. The deviant must be socialized to his or her role. Promoting that socialization are other deviants with whom one may interact directly and indirectly (as through the media) and from whom cues may be acquired on how to minimize role problems. Of greatest importance, however, are service and social organizations serving the various segments of the larger stigmatized population. The importance of these organizations—about which, more later—rests on the fact that stigmatized persons most often must go outside standard groupings, such as family, "to find socialization experiences toward establishing a more complete identity" (Barthell, 1983:148). Thus, overwhelmingly, parents and siblings of stigmatized persons are themselves part of the larger community and are therefore unable to serve as complete role models for the stigmatized person. Over 90 percent of deaf people have hearing parents; paraplegics and quadriplegics come from able-bodied families; most gays have straight parents; and so on. The absence of immediately available role models, then, increases the dependence of the stigmatized on organizations established to serve their unique needs.

Examples of the socialization provided by such organizations may be found in the many journals, magazines, and other printed material they produce and distribute to their clientele. One such journal is *Paraplegia News,* which contains articles written by "insiders" to help handicapped persons adjust to their condition, find fulfillment, and handle distressing encounters with nonhandicapped persons. Such an article is Sue Odgers's (1978) "Sex on Wheels," which outlines for the disabled female what "kinds of men" she may encounter and how they may be dealt with. In much the same way that the able-bodied characterize the disabled, Odgers typifies the sorts of sometimes well-meaning, but hopelessly ill-informed, able-bodied men she has encountered. Examples are Mr. Curious, Mr. I Understand and Can Help, Mr. I Have the Remedy, and so on. Additionally, the author indicates how these occasionally clumsy persons and awkward encounters can be dealt with with dignity, and she presents her own romantic fantasy. Perhaps the latter is most important in that (1) it serves to normalize sexuality among the disabled (and thereby counters the tendency of stereotypes to desexualize such persons), while at the same time (2) helping disabled women deal effectively with the world on their own rather than others' terms.

For the obese, the National Association to Aid Fat Americans provides a newsletter containing valuable information on the pros and cons of medical treatments for obesity, buying clothes, finding understanding physicians, employment opportunities, and so on. This is the sort of recipe knowledge nondeviants take for granted but that is not part of the ordinary socialization processes in our society.

Humor also is used to sensitize and help people manage their stigma. Many of the journals addressed to the physically handicapped carry cartoons designed to promote disavowal or avowal, normalize stigmatized conditions, diminish their limitations, and assist the actor to anticipate and respond to recurring events. Hopefully, then, problems may be reduced and stigma managed more gracefully.

The audience toward whom these are aimed also includes the "normal" population. Successful stigma management may require a change in the normals' perception of and behavior toward the deviant. Ideally, then, the stereotyped conceptions of deviants and their presumed characterological defects must be addressed and altered, thereby promoting greater empathy for the deviant. Exemplifying this effort is the Lily Tomlin characterization of Crystal, the Terrible Tumbleweed (*Paraplegia News,* 1978:24–25). In this characterization, admittedly a burlesque, Crystal is a young quadriplegic woman confined to a CB-equipped "blow-job" wheelchair dubbed the Iron Duchess. Conforming to anything but the stereotype of a quadriplegic, Crystal is traveling coast to coast in her chair; thus far she has traveled 1,900 miles in one year and seven months. When she arrives in California, says Crystal, she will go hang gliding at Big Sur, perhaps the first (and maybe the last) quadriplegic to do so. Liberally sprinkled with gallows humor (in the middle of one hang gliding experience Crystal got her catheter caught in a crosswire and crashed), Tomlin's characterization is designed to bring to the attention of the public things the rules of good taste and civil inattention require be avoided. By the use of satire, Tomlin questions the appropriateness of such restrictions and stereotypes. In their place (hopefully) is empathy and a greater sensitivity to the needs and capabilities of the disabled.

The success of this effort is admittedly problematic and unknown. Tomlin's mail includes letters from normals indicating that such frankness is more than some people can manage. Others perceive the characterization to be in bad taste. But among disabled persons, Crystal is well accepted as a means of telling their story "with warmth, honesty, total humanity and humor." (*Paraplegia News*, 1978:24).

Accounts: Excuses and Justifications. In addition to the foregoing techniques of stigma management, people whose deviance (notably, deviance by achievement) is known frequently seek to manage their moral burden by using any of a variety of *accounts*—statements designed "to explain unanticipated or untoward behavior" (Scott and Lyman, 1968:46). Two kinds of accounts are *excuses* and *justifications*.

Excuses consist of a variety of fairly standard, socially approved phrases or ideas used by people to bring about a softening of the moral breach they are involved in and to relieve themselves of responsibility for the deviant condition (Scott and Lyman, 1968:47). One type of excuse is the *appeal to accidents*. This is employed when people claim their conduct and its consequences are the result of things (for example, an environmental irregularity such as a hazard or a momentary bodily weakness) over which they have no control. A second type of excuse consists of *appeals to defeasibility*. As an example, a person may seek to absolve himself or herself of responsibility by claiming to have acted on the basis of "misinformation arising from intentional or innocent misrepresentation of the facts by others" (Scott and Lyman, 1968:48). Had valid information been available, they contend, they would have acted differently; its absence serves as a mitigating force. A third category of excuse includes those that rest on *biological drives*. For example, popular phrases such as "boys will be boys" and "that's what you'd expect from a woman" refer to the idea that some behaviors really are sex-linked traits. As a result, behavior is fatalistically attributed to conditions over which people are believed to have no influence. Again, then, people are granted some measure of relief from responsibility. A fourth and final type of excuse is *scapegoating*, excusing their behavior on the basis of traits (negative) possessed by others. For example, a Mexican girl excuses her behavior by claiming that "I was always getting into fights because some girls are vipers; they get jealous, tell lies about each other, and start trouble" (Lewis, 1961:143). Given the unacceptable traits of others, the actor's behavior becomes understandable and the actor is less blameworthy.

A second category of accounts is *justifications*, ideas that "neutralize an act or its consequences when either is called into question" (Scott and Lyman, 1968:51). The unique feature of justifications is that they call for an acknowledgment of the wrongfulness of the *type* or *category* of act in question while seeking to have the *specific instance* in question defined as an exception. For example, taking the life of another person is generally wrong. Yet, as we have noted, it is justified under conditions of war and self-defense, among others.

When the act and its consequences are called into question, when the seeming contradiction between the general rule and the specific case is raised, people may resort to any of a variety of justifying ideas to account for their behavior while keeping the general rule intact. Called "techniques of neutralization," many of these devices were considered in Chapter 2.

To these techniques of neutralization must be added two other forms of justification: the *sad tale* and *self-fulfillment*. "The sad tale is a selected (often distorted) arrangement of facts that highlight an extremely dismal past, and thus 'explain' the individual's present state" (Scott and Lyman 1968:52; see also Goffman, 1961:150–151). As an example, Harold Greenwald (1958:32–36) relates the "sad tale" of a call girl whose biography included the experience of the depression of the 1930s, a period of residence in an orphan asylum, being sent to a series of foster homes (in one of which the foster father allegedly forced her to perform fellatio on him and in another of which she was regularly punished for things she had not

167

done), loneliness, and so on, finally culminating in her engaging in sex in return for material reward. This array of conditions is regarded as an explanation and justification for the woman's prostitution.

In employing *self-fulfillment* a person justifies his or her rule violation on the ground that it is an aid to a higher and more complete realization of praiseworthy goals. For example, the ingestion of some drugs (such as peyote, marijuana, LSD) has been justified by some people on the ground that these chemicals "expand consciousness" and enhance one's sensibility to people and things in the environment. Syllogistically, sensibility is good (self-fulfilling), the chemicals enhance one's sensibility, therefore the ingestion of these chemicals is justifiable.

Covering. A final technique used by individuals to manage a discredited condition is *covering,* referring to an array of tactics whereby one seeks to present his or her stigma in the least offensive way—that is, to minimize the stigma so as to ease any associated tension (Goffman, 1963:102–104). One method of covering seeks to divert attention from one form of stigma to a second, hopefully lesser, stigma. As an example, Goffman cites the blind person who wears dark glasses symbolizing his or her blindness, in an effort to cover defacement or disfigurement that may exist in the region of the eyes (Goffman, 1963:102–103). A second form of covering is that in which the discredited person avoids displaying "failures" that would call attention to his or her stigma and that might interfere with social interaction. As an example, Goffman refers to the near-blind person who refrains from reading in public since to do so would require bringing the page to within a few inches of his or her face. Such a display would call attention to the handicap and perhaps contribute to problems of acceptance by others (Goffman, 1963:103). Very similar is the case of extremely obese people, especially women, who have stylish clothes made to order and always have their hair stylishly cut in order to effect the most favorable public image (Millman, 1980:9).

Collective Stigma Management

The several stigma management techniques thus far considered are essentially individual modes of adaptation; their successful use seldom calls for the assistance of more than a few others. We turn now to a different mode of adaptation, one calling for group or collective effort.

In an office building corridor hangs a poster displaying the silhouette of a person in a wheelchair. The caption reads: "You gave us your dimes. Now we want our rights." In San Francisco and other cities many prostitutes have organized and hustle for their rights as well as dollars. They belong to COYOTE, "a loose woman's organization" (the acronym stands for "Call Off Your Old Tired Ethics"), aiming to "reform the way American society hassles, punishes and stigmatizes its prostitutes" (*The Missoulian,* 1973). At a major western state university, Free Spirit, the gay student organization annually sponsors a "gay awareness" week designed to change what gay people regard as misconceptions concerning homosexuality, and to educate the public and promote understanding of gay life by straights. And, again in San Francisco, Bob Goldman's National Stuttering Project is attempting to "off the pig"—that is, have the cartoon character Porky Pig declared a menace—and promote the self-enhancement of the nation's 2.6 million stutterers (*Time,* 1977).

These examples represent the work of an apparently growing and increasingly varied number of *voluntary associations* (groups seeking to promote the common interest of the membership, affiliation being noncoercive) established by those who have been stigmatized. Included are associations of those who are deviant by ascription as well as by achievement. They are the people—dwarfs, alcoholics, gamblers, the overweight, drug addicts, the physically disabled, homosexuals, the aged, and mental patients, among others—who have, largely since the late 1960s and 1970s, sought to establish an organizational apparatus to help themselves solve some of the dilemmas of deviance. In the following section our concern will be focused on these associations, their origin, the forms they take, and the role they play in the larger deviance process. We will focus on the efforts of deviant groups to engage in moral entrepreneurial activity.

Before turning to specifics, it is important to recognize that the moral entrepreneurial efforts of deviant groups is an acknowledgment that the capacity to effect change in social reality and influence the rule-making apparatus of society is not restricted to groups identified as "the establishment," "the powerful," and so on. Indeed, as noted earlier, stereotypically, superior economic groups in society wield great power, but so, too, do other groups. Further, deviant segments of society do not necessarily occupy positions of impoverishment. Thus, as just one example, within the homophile community of San Francisco there exists tremendous wealth as well as persons occupying influential positions in almost every conceivable occupation and profession. In short, a valid analysis and understanding of the deviance process must avoid that one-sidedness "which grants the capacity to create and communicate meanings only to the powerful who name and shape deviance, when they name and enforce rules" (Piven, 1981:493). Quite fundamentally, what follows is in harmony with the power model introduced earlier.

Origins of Voluntary Associations

Some sociologists believe that the presence of voluntary associations among deviants represents a relatively new phenomenon in history; at least, they give the impression that the prevalence of such groups has increased markedly in the past few decades (Sagarin, 1969; Becker, 1970). While perhaps true in general, the validity of this notion varies with the specific group under consideration, the virulence of social opposition directed toward it, its size and power relative to nondeviant groups, and several other factors. Adding to the confusion in this general realm is the fact that, until recently, the history of the activity of some groups, especially their involvement in resistance, has not been investigated (Katz, 1976:335). The

idea that the recent appearance of voluntary associations among deviants represents a new phenomenon (rather than being simply a matter of increased visibility and an expansion of a long-standing tendency) also fails to reckon with the fact that "the tree presupposes a root." In fact, secret societies, with which some present-day voluntary associations have continuity, were quite common among preliterate peoples and have a history dating from the most ancient times (Heckethorn, 1965).

Secret Societies. What is meant by the term *secret societies?* These may be defined as associations that place a premium on concealment and that engage in ritual designed to maintain secrecy. In sharp contrast with groups that admit almost anyone to membership and hide nothing from outsiders, secret societies are "organized around the principles of exclusiveness and secrecy" (MacKenzie, 1967:14). Recruitment is selective and activities are protected from public scrutiny. "Secrecy is the condition of the group's existence, and is maintained as far as possible over the whole range of its activities" (MacKenzie, 1967:14). Beyond this uniformity of organizational style, secret societies have historically exhibited considerable variation in focal concerns: religious, political, scientific, military, as well as criminal and antisocial. Among the better-known groups of the latter sort were Chinese secret societies, many of which "enrolled criminals, miscreants, delinquents, and outcasts as members and mercenary thugs" (Lyman, 1974:23). Chinese secret societies also provided an organizational base from which persons could launch both individual and collective protests against oppression. "By joining a secret society, an individual acquired a sworn fraternity of comrades, a protective group, and the force to counter the strength of the traditional societies" (Lyman, 1974:41). A purely native American secret society is the Invisible Empire Knights of the Ku Klux Klan.

Secret societies are often formed by persons engaged in behavior defined as deviant by the dominant standards of society. As such, secret societies may be said to emerge out of and provide an index of social conflict in a society. This is particularly the case of those whose activities are perceived to be heretical, revolutionary, or in some other sense threatening to vested interests in the society. The secrecy of such groups is understandable as a means of obscuring their deviation from public view (MacKenzie, 1967:300). However, secrecy also colors the relationship between those who share the secret vis-à-vis those who do not. For those involved, sharing fosters a sense of mutual confidence and trust; without these conditions, the protective advantage of secrecy is lost. In the absence of secrecy, the discreditable person may become discredited (Simmel, 1950:346).

Another feature of secret societies is their aristocratizing effect on the membership. That is, "by joining one another, those who want to distinguish themselves give rise to the development of an aristocracy, i.e., a sense of themselves as a superior and privileged class, which strengthens and . . . enlarges their position and self consciousness" (Simmel, 1950:346–365). By separating and forming a group, people may acquire a heightened and positive sense of their specialness; belonging to such groups becomes honorific. (This element is readily recognized among members of social and academic groups on American college and university campuses.) As a counter to degradation, this aristocratizing effect encourages members to regard themselves as "chosen people" (Warren, 1980:67). Because aristocratization leads to a redefinition of the stigmatized traits or behavior, such symbols may become honorific and, as among homosexuals, for example, the basis for calling for widespread deviance disavowal (Lauritsen and Thorstad, 1974:7; Howard, 1970:11). The importance of this for those who have been publicly discredited or who experience symbolic labeling seems obvious.

Finally, belonging to secret societies provides members with a sense of freedom unavailable in other settings. Within the confines of the secret organization opportunities exist to behave in ways that public social regimentation and the threat of punishment seek to prevent. Indeed, Simmel proposes that the "widespread diffusion of secret societies is usually proof of public un-freedom, or a tendency toward . . . political oppression" (Simmel 1950:361). Belonging to a secret society provides a person with the opportunity (freedom) to express his or her uniqueness, albeit deviant, while minimizing the costs and danger of being open. Secret societies provide opportunities for association with sympathetic others and for self-expression without fear of censure. Within the limits of its safety, the secret society permits one to abandon the *fronts* (the managed images of self) so necessary for those engaged in deviance (Goffman, 1959:22ff).

The Deviant Community. An important aspect of secret societies is that they overlap and have continuity with the creation of communities of deviants. Community here refers not to a physical thing (that is, not a geographical area having a political identity and name), but rather, as a psychic and social thing (a state of mind and a set of relationships). It is psychological in that it is the "sense of oneness, of brotherhood and sisterhood" (Warren, 1974a:13) shared by people who are set apart by the stigmatization of their ethnicity, sexual inclinations, disability, or other behavior. It is a social thing in that it consists of people whose lifestyle reflects their oneness with others.

To say communities are psychic and social things does not mean they cannot be found in physical places. Among professional thieves of the 1920s and 1930s, these "places" included the speakeasies, restaurants, saloons, cigar stores, and other places where professional gangsters congregated (Sutherland, 1937:158–159). For the homeless men and women, vagabonds of the road of that same era, social centers existed in the form of "jungles" or "places where the hobos congregated to pass their leisure time outside the urban centers" (Anderson, 1923:16). In such places, matters of interest to hobos were discussed, songs sung, stories told, meager foodstuffs shared, and solidarity established among people who had turned their backs on the world and who were at ease with one another (Reitman, 1975). Among homosexuals such places are the baths, bars, gymnasia, motels, clubs, resorts, and other locations catering to that population. Among striptease dancers it is the gay bars and hotels where these women may gather under at least minimally hospitable circumstances (McCaghy and Skipper, 1969). Involvement in such communities of outcasts provides many outsiders with a new identity—a rebirth, as it were—that permits them to shed some or all of the symbolic stigma they may have acquired (Hills, 1980:179–181).

Communities such as these do not arise in a simple, deterministic, or mechanistic fashion. Nor are they automatic consequences of societal condemnation of the people who populate them. Rather, these communities develop out of the choices people make to affiliate with persons like themselves. In some cases (as, for example, among segregated ethnic or racial minorities, or military personnel being treated in specialized centers for spinal cord injuries), a person may have few viable options from which to choose. For most of those who are discredited and discreditable, however, affiliation allows them to express what is best not revealed in the presence of nondeviants. For homosexuals, involvement in the "gay world" permits them to experience the pleasures of their sexuality, to hold hands with a lover, to engage in honest communication, to feel they are indistinguishable from and accepted by others. To be involved in such communities is to be exposed to their subcultures. The change in self-image and the exhilaration that may result from this is expressed by one young homosexual as follows:

I knew that there were homosexuals, queers and what not; I had read some books, and I was resigned to the fact that I was a foul, dirty person, but I wasn't actually calling myself a homosexual yet. . . . And the time I really caught myself coming out is the time I walked into this bar and saw a whole crowd of groovy, groovy guys. And I said to myself, there was the realization, that not all gay men are dirty old men or idiots, silly queens, but there are some just normal looking and acting people. . . . I saw gay society and I said, "Wow, I'm home." (Dank, 1971:187)

For striptease dancers, community means an opportunity to interact with similarly situated others without being perceived and treated as sex objects (McCaghy and Skipper, 1969). For dwarfs it means an opportunity to escape the prying stares of normals and to experience a semblance of ordinary social life (Sagarin, 1969:203).

In seeking after such experiences, the comfort of sympathetic others, deviants are no different from nondeviants. What does appear to be unique is that heretofore secret societies (by definition) and deviant communities have spawned few *public* associations. However, as noted, the past few decades have seen a remarkable upsurge in their number. Let's consider the bases for that change.

Increasing Voluntary Associations

How may we account for the recent increase in the number and visibility of voluntary associations among deviants? The answer is neither altogether clear nor very precise. Very likely, the increasing number and variety of such associations, and especially their more public nature (as compared with secret societies), is linked to a variety of social changes, that have occurred over the past century or so. Of major importance is urbanism and all it represents (Sagarin, 1969:29). As urbanism has increased, so, too, has the opportunity to effect anonymity. People have been permitted to remain faceless and nameless in increasingly larger cities. Anonymity has also provided a greater opportunity than ever before for society's outsiders to meet with like-minded others and indulge their appetites despite the opposition of public morality.

If anonymity has not been immediately available, increasing geographic mobility has made possible the short- (or long-) term change in geographic location. By means of quick trips to nearby urban places, people "could organize and join an association, go to its meetings, and then return . . . home . . . with few people knowing. . . . Thus the anonymous society—as opposed to the secret one—was born" (Sagarin, 1969:29).

Another possible contributor to the growth of voluntary associations among deviants has been the increasing tendency, during the 1920s and 1930s, of Americans to look upon many deviations as the reflection of an underlying emotional disorder, one calling for sympathy rather than punitive condemnation. Apparently helped along by the increasing popularity of the ideas of Sigmund Freud and psychoanalysis, the shame and stigma associated with some deviations began to decline (Sagarin, 1969:30). Thus, "the rise of dime-store psychoanalysis—the easy explanation of deviant or odd behavior as the product of childhood traumas that might have happened to anyone . . . helped the public to absolve [some] deviants of responsibility for what they do" (Becker, 1970:343). Taken together, these views may be said to have encouraged a change in the definition of some forms of deviance by promoting an image of the rule breaker as something other than a "sinner whose consignment to hell is a foregone conclusion" (Becker, 1970:343). This changing reality of deviance paved the way for increased organizational (especially political) activity among segments of the deviant population.

Closely linked to this changing definition of deviance is the increasing public tolerance for some behaviors previously regarded only as revolting. Rather than condemning, people have, over the course of several decades, become more inclined to attribute deviance to extenuating circumstances, to accept the idea that deviants can be reformed, and to be less inclined to take harsh punitive action against them (Becker, 1970:343). More recently, these tendencies have been paralleled by court decisions intended to restrict the use of extralegal methods by law enforcement agencies controlling deviants. For example, public officials have been prohibited by courts from interfering with the right of protest organizations to demonstrate peacefully, such actions being protected by the 1st and 14th Amendments to the Constitution, which guarantee the right to assemble peacefully and seek redress of grievances (Boggan et al., 1975:14).

The reluctance in some areas to deny constitutional protection to deviant minorities has also contributed to the recent increase in voluntary associations among outsiders. In some cases, this reluctance has apparently been based on the fear that to deny such rights to one group might bode ill for other groups in the future. One example of this reluctance is the defeat at the polls in California of the so-called Briggs Amendment, which would have required the dismissal and prevented the hiring of known homosexuals as teachers in that state's public schools (Gregory-Lewis, 1978:7ff). A second example involves the Seattle, Washington, initiative to repeal that city's gay rights law. The Seattle City Council unanimously condemned the initiative as "misguided, confused, dangerous, deceitful, frightening and un-American" (Anderson, 1978). That sentiment was echoed by the Community Relations Committee of the Jewish Federation of Seattle. In a resolution, that Committee condemned the repeal of civil rights for gays, claiming it "is a denial of human and civil rights which, if allowed to pass, could become part of an epidemic, which will spread to other individuals who are minorities by virtue of their race, religion, sex, political beliefs or natural origin" (Anderson, 1978). The initiative was defeated at the polls by an approximate 3:2 margin (Mayerson, 1978). What is most important is that victories of this sort stimulate and encourage similar efforts among other groups who perceive themselves as oppressed.

Finally, and perhaps most important, is the influence of the social protests of the 1950s, 1960s, and 1970s. Of special significance is the development of the counterculture during that time and the agonizing political upheavals concerning black liberation and America's role in Vietnam (Altman, 1971). Prior to that time, control of the *public morality* of this nation was, by and large, in the hands of white, Anglo-Saxon, Protestants (Schrag, 1970). At least on the public level, no viable challenge to that control had existed prior to the development of black protest in the 1960s and, simultaneous with that, the challenge of youth. Each in their own way, blacks and youth demanded the right to their own culture and insisted on its legitimacy. Each collectivity called for a new social reality and new identities. In doing so, each provided a model to be followed by the other groups who felt oppressed.

Promoted by these several conditions, recent

years have seen a rapid increase in the number and variety of voluntary associations among deviants of almost every sort. Within this vast array of collectivities, however, there exist rather marked differences. Let's consider these differences.

Types of Associations

Not all organizations of deviants are alike. Indeed, such organizations may be classified on two different dimensions: (1) the *dominant method* by which they seek to achieve their objective and (2) the *orientation* of the association with respect to the major or legitimate values of society. Let's explore these two dimensions.

Dominant Method: Expressive and Instrumental Groups. Regarding the dimension of dominant method, two major types of association are distinguishable, the expressive and the instrumental. *Expressive groups* are those that "exist primarily to furnish activities for members" (Gordon and Babchuk, 1959:25). Serving members' needs is an end in itself. Thus, a principal concern of many groups is to provide social and recreational opportunities for the membership. Often there is an interest in providing information (legal, medical, dietary, and the like) or services (legal, transportation, education) for the followers. For the most part, expressive groups do not concern themselves (that is, confront and seek to deal) with issues of the larger society. Rather, these groups tend to be apolitical, choosing to foster various methods of *evading stigma*—that is, helping the individual correct his or her "fault" or "defect," aiding people to adopt a socially acceptable lifestyle, or providing the support and succor of other stigmatized persons (Humphreys, 1972:141). Essentially, the posture of expressive groups promotes adaptation to (rather than removal or alteration of) stigma.

The second type of organization included under this dimension is the *instrumental.* These are groups that "serve as social influence organizations designed to maintain or create some normative conditions or change" (Gordon and Babchuk, 1959:25). They are designed primarily to resist or promote change. This is not to suggest that these organizations are unconcerned with the welfare of members; indeed, just the opposite is the case. Rather, these associations are "designed to benefit members by organizing them to change, in some small way, what to them [is] a significant aspect of the social system" (Sagarin, 1969:84). Unlike expressive groups, instrumental types seek to *counter or remove the stigma* linked to their differentness (Humphreys, 1972:141). As we will see, it is these associations that are involved in the politicization of deviance (Horowitz and Leibowitz, 1968).

Value Orientation: Conformative and Alienative Groups. The second dimension by which we may differentiate voluntary associations concerns the group's orientation toward legitimate social values. Again, two major orientations are discernible. First is the *conformative* type, referring to the tendency of some groups to be in accord with major social values (Lyman, 1970:37). That is, despite their sometime interest in social change, these groups do not address themselves to basic social values and institutional arrangements. Rather, attention is focused on a realignment of social priorities, the altering of specific social policies, or changes in select laws. In other cases conformative groups may work to alter the moral meaning of their particular brand of deviance. However, in seeking these changes, conformative groups pose no necessary challenge to the existing political, religious, economic, or other institutions of society.

The second type of group noted under this dimension is the *alienative,* referring to groups hostile to the major legitimate values and institutions of society (Lyman, 1970:37). Though less prevalent, this type of group tends toward a radical or revolutionary posture. *As perceived by their membership,* the problems such groups face are endemic to the society, a consequence of the way the society is structured and operated. As such, the alienative group is hostile to and "attacks"—for the most part, verbally—dominant social values and institutions.

A Typology of Associations. By combining the dimensions of organizational method and value orientation, we may establish a fourfold classification or typology of voluntary associations (Table 7-1). Representing *ideal types*— that is, a hypothetical conception of groups against which actual groups may be compared—this framework reflects a somewhat imperfect placement as to the location of actual groups. It is imperfect, first, because the groups identified do not reflect in practice the unqualified commitment to or display of the ideal traits linked to each type. Second, in the course of time the complexion of groups may change in important ways. As a case in point, we need only contrast the Ku Klux Klan of the 1880s with the rechartered Ku Klux Klan of today. Despite these limitations, this typology establishes a working classification of voluntary associations. Let's examine the major types.

The first type of association is the *expressive-conformative* type. One popular group of this sort is Weight Watchers, a commercial organization composed of overweight persons. The official purpose of the association is to provide dietetic advice and information to members and, in weekly meetings, provide support and encouragement for those who are dieting. Another organization of this type is Recovery, a self-help group established to provide social and rehabilitative assistance to former psychi-

atric patients. Nationwide, this organization has a reported 7000 members and approximately 1000 local chapters. Finally, there is Little People of America. This organization limits membership to persons who are 4'11" in height or less and to either proportionate or disproportionate dwarfs. LPA provides an information exchange for members, assists dwarf couples wanting to adopt children of that type, assists "normal" parents who have dwarf children, and in other ways seeks to help members solve problems unique to little people.

Equally prevalent are groups of the *instrumental-conformative* type. Examples of these include several of the organizations mentioned in the preceding discussion. COYOTE, for example, has as its principal goal the decriminalization of prostitution. The goals and activities of COYOTE are disseminated through an official newspaper called *Coyote Howls*. Another organization of this type is the League of Lefthanders. Founded in 1975, the League seeks equality for lefthanded people in a society favoring righthandedness. Among its activities is an effort to make lefthanded items more available at prices comparable to righthanded items, and to eliminate or reduce job discrimination based on handedness. Lastly, we may include the National Gay Task Force, an asso-

TABLE 7-1
A Typology of Voluntary Deviant Associations*

DOMINANT METHOD	ATTITUDE TOWARD DOMINANT SOCIAL VALUES	
	CONFORMATIVE	ALIENATIVE
EXPRESSIVE	Weight Watchers Recovery Little People of America	Old Order Amish Black Muslims
INSTRUMENTAL	COYOTE League of Lefthanders National Gay Task Force	Redstockings The Feminists

*Adapted from: Stanford Lyman, *The Asian in the West* (Reno/Las Vegas, Nevada: Western Studies Center, Desert Research Center, 1970): p. 37. Used by permission of Stanford Lyman.

ciation dedicated to the elimination of discrimination based on a person's sexual preference. The Task Force coordinates the efforts of local gay organizations, seeks to effect change in the media use of stereotypes when dealing with homosexual topics, and lobbies legislative bodies on behalf of gay rights. Each in its way, these organizations seek social change, but are not generally perceived to pose a threat to the basic institutional character of society.

Third, there are organizations we may refer to as *expressive-alienative*. Characteristic of this type is the Old Order Amish, a religious group once confined to Lancaster County, Pennsylvania, but now found in 20 states as well as Central and South America and Canada. A splinter group of the Mennonite Church, the Old Order Amish are believers in a literal translation of the Bible and regard themselves as a "chosen people," "a royal priesthood." As such, they have rejected almost all aspects of modern industrial civilization. This includes their homes and clothing which are stark (but highly functional) by modern standards, the rejection of bodily adornments of all kinds, the rejection of automotive vehicles and bicycles, the tendency to shun elections except to vote against school board candidates who are unsympathetic to their views, and the rejection of insurance and federal social security, preferring to rely on mutual aid for individual assistance (Kephart, 1982:51–55). In these ways members of the Old Order Amish reflect their expressive tendencies as well as their steadfast rejection of (alienation from) modern American life and values.

A second group fitting the expressive-alienative category is the Black Muslims, an ascetic religious group originating in the 1930s. Their expressive tendencies are revealed in their emphasis on group solidarity, mutual aid, self-discipline, and general conformity of the membership to a stringent code of personal and social morality (Lincoln, 1961:80). The Black Muslims demonstrate their alienative tendencies by their repudiation of established religious bodies in this country and their effort to become aligned with Islam (Lincoln, 1961:218), as well as their call for black separation, that is, a repudiation of racial, economic, and political integration with white society (Lincoln, 1961:87–93).

The final type of association is the *instrumental-alienative*. Representative of this category are a vareity of women's liberation groups reflecting varying degrees of political activism and radicalism. Generically, these organizations are referred to as the Women's Liberation Movement. Many of the specific organizations affiliated with this movement are unstructured and unconnected, and reflect widely differing ideologies. Specific groups recently representative of the alienative wing of the movement are Redstockings and The Feminists. According to the Redstockings Manifesto, the enemy is men; women are oppressed and exploited by men who, as a class, use the dominant institutions as tools of oppression. Men are perceived as controlling the cultural, political, and economic institutions, as well as having the force to retain their position as oppressors. All men are rewarded by the existing system. That system must go (Morgan, 1970:533ff). The Feminists, a splinter group from the New York National Organization for Women (NOW), call for the elimination of marriage and family as we know them because these perpetuate traditional male–female role playing. Likewise, "political institutions such as religion [must be eliminated] because they are based on philosophies of hierarchical order and reinforce male oppression of females" (Papachristou, 1976:235). Such views led The Feminists, at the height of their activity, to be regarded as "one of the more prolific sources of radical feminist ideas" (Freeman, 1975:82).

Thus, in brief, we see that voluntary associations cover a wide range of interests and activities, and pursue a variety of goals. The relevance of these associations, however, is best seen when they are viewed in terms of the dynamics of the larger deviance process. Let's turn now to that matter.

The Deviant as Moral Enterpreneur

Having considered the historical and contemporary basis for voluntary associations of deviants, as well as their variety, let us now turn to a consideration of the role played by those organizations in the broad context of the deviance process. Viewed as expressions of a *general social movement*—that is, an uncoordinated and general shift in the values of people (Blumer, 1955:200)—the social changes we have noted (particularly the youth movement and black liberation in the 1950s and 1960s) signaled the emergence of new orientations and sensitivities among large segments of our population. Many people were exhibiting a new sense of self, a general dissatisfaction with their position in society, and a desire for an extension of rights and privileges heretofore unrealized. To be sure, the directions toward which people were striving, the new images of self and the values being sought, and so on, may have been vague during the early period of this movement. Yet out of such periods of indefiniteness come specific social movements (such as women's liberation, gay liberation, fat liberation) and the myriad voluntary associations that identify themselves with and that together comprise the more general humanitarian movement (Mauss, 1975:45). Let's give thought to these associations viewed as moral entrepreneurial groups, small parts of a larger social movement especially prominent in our society since the 1950s.

Forming Entrepreneurial Groups
How each association or group emerges varies as a consequence of the uniqueness of the organization's purpose, the time and place of its creation, and the persons forming it. Despite this uniqueness, however, it seems clear that most associations grow out of the friendship and other communications networks that constitute a part of the communities and subculture of deviance (Freeman, 1973). Initially, these associations are small, loose-knit, relatively unstructured entities. Indeed, as elements of either the general humanitarian movement or a specific social movement, in their early period, these entities lack definite character and are scarcely noted. It is only later, following a period of group proliferation and internal solidification, that they become recognized as part of a movement. Between the time of their initial formation and this rec-

ognition, statements of group purpose become clarified. Uncoordinated shifts in people's values begin to take direction. Almost before people are aware of what is occurring, "microscopic indicators [of unrest] coagulate into recognizable groups" (Humphreys, 1972:56). Let's consider some specifics bearing on how this may occur.

A Sense of Dissatisfaction. Earlier it was proposed that the work of the moral entrepreneur begins with a sense of dissatisfaction with some facet of the status quo. That observation is as applicable to the rule-creating work of deviant groups as to any other. In the case of deviants the dissatisfaction arises out of their individual and collective experience (biography), particularly the experience of social oppression and the burdens linked with stigma. Given their shame and publicly discredited condition, many are "driven out" of legitimate society and often enough have little chance of returning. Others are subjected to a variety of forms of social oppression, be it legal-physical, occupational-financial, or ego-destructive (Humphreys, 1972:chapter 2). For some people it is discrimination, for others it is prejudice, and for some it is the ignominy of being approached with the tolerance granted an "inferior" by a "superior." For those who remain in the "closet" (the discreditable) there is the ever-present need to engage in "front work," to maintain a facade of normality, to be on their guard, to never let on or reveal that aspect of self. In short, each type of deviant, by definition, comprises a class of social rejects, such rejection being a manifestation of the dominant reality.

These experiences may be softened and their consequences modified slightly by a person's involvement in the deviant community. It is in the context of that community that we must view this experience. We may include, as elements of these communities, beliefs and interests. *Beliefs* refer to the convictions and the sense of reality shared by those who have experienced stigmatization and who participate in and share the deviant subculture. Beliefs come to be shared as a result of people congregating and interacting with one another. As in the case of rule creators in general, interpersonal relations among the stigmatized lead to an awareness of and a heightened sensitivity to the experience of oppression and the need for change. Through association the deviant becomes aware that he or she is not alone, that other like-minded and sympathetic persons exist. Other outsiders, particularly in the aggregate, come to be perceived as a source of refuge in a malevolent environment.

However, the easing of problems provided by participation in the deviant community is not to be confused with their final solution. The deviant community does not comprise the totality of experience. To some extent, deviants of whatever sort must continue to be involved in the life of the larger society. As such, they continue to be the experiencing persons, that is, those who suffer the impact of the dominant reality and for whom that reality is a problem (Toch, 1965:7). It is from the ranks of those who perceive conditions as problems that members of expressive and instrumental groups are drawn. As an element of their biography, people experience the hardships of stigmatization and are thereby drawn together to establish organizations to alleviate those hardships.

The Quest for Change. Beyond experiencing problems and defining them as intolerable, people must regard change and the resolution of problems as an attainable goal. Change must be conceivable. To embrace the idea that change is possible and become involved in creating associations working to promote it rests, finally, on the individual's conscious desire to engage in that enterprise (Toch, 1965:12). Together with like-minded others, such persons may be said to be in search of meaning and change.

Persons in search of meaning may be regarded as sensitive and alert to ideas and proposals that have relevance to their problem, especially those ideas that appear to promise change. Such persons may be said to be *susceptible* (Toch, 1965:12–13). That is, susceptible persons are suggestible and likely to engage in selective perception. Being oriented toward change, they are more than ordinarily prone to

perceive others' proposals as promising vehicles of change. Susceptibility, of course, is a matter of degree, just as its manifestation may take an active or passive form.

Affiliation with such organizations is often decided on the basis of the appeals proffered by members. Like other moral entrepreneurs, spokespersons for voluntary associations seek to spread their message, to render it appealing to those who are susceptible. Indeed, the appeals made by such persons are explicitly addressed to those who are susceptible. In turn, given this tendency, appeals are likely to be found meaningful by audience members. It is when susceptible people encounter beliefs they define as appealing that they may decide to affiliate. As examples of appeals made to elements of susceptibility, we may point to the Little People of America. Appeals made to dwarfs and midgets to join this organization speak to increasing their medical knowledge about their physical condition,[1] to helping people with occupational problems and other inconveniences, and, most important, to providing members with an opportunity to expand their social life by meeting other little people (Weinberg, 1968:67; Truzzi, 1968). The appeal of "trim down" or weight-watching organizations often speaks to people's wish to be relieved of the "disease" or "sin" of being overweight (Allon, 1973). As with other organizations, these examples demonstrate that appeals are couched in terms consistent with the problems, interests, and goals of potential members. Often the appeals offer satisfaction of a variety of needs.

An equally important element of appeals is

[1]The accumulation and dissemination of medical information concerning dwarfism reflects an abiding concern among dwarfs and midgets for the physical basis of their condition and its correction and prevention. As an example, biologists engaged in research in the field of recombinant DNA anticipate that isolation of the gene governing human growth will ultimately provide a cure for dwarfism. (See Howard and Rifkin, 1977:31.) More recently, researchers have developed a man-made hormone that duplicates one secreted naturally by the pituitary gland and that promotes growth. For extraordinarily tiny children (for example, a four-year-old child with the height of a 20-month-old) such developments give some promise of normal height. (*Arizona Republic,* 1981g)

the *ideology* put forth by various movements. As used here, ideology refers to the beliefs a group of people hold in common and what they expect to achieve as a collectivity (Toch, 1965:21). Ideological statements help define the organization in terms of specific beliefs and goals. For example, the National Organization for the Reform of Marijuana Laws (NORML) identifies its goals as seeking an end to all criminal penalties for possession and use of marijuana. The National Association to Aid Fat Americans seeks to change the social reality of obesity; it is dedicated to the proposition that "fat can be beautiful." The American Sunbathing Association, a nudist organization, identifies its goal as the cultivation of healthy minds and healthy bodies. Sometimes, of course, the meaning of ideological statements is not so apparent as these examples suggest. In some instances the meanings are more obscure. An example is found in the case of the KKK, the purpose of which is phrased in the following vague, sweeping terms: the "protection and maintenance of distinctive institutions, rights, privileges, principles and ideals of pure Americanism and to the defense and preservation of the Constitution as originally written and intended" (*Encyclopedia of Associations,* 1978:887).

In addition to the foregoing, some of the "ideological" material generated and disseminated by these organizations consists of *bureaucratic propaganda,* that is, material "produced by an organization for evaluation and other practical purposes that is targeted for individuals, committees, or publics who are unaware of its promotive character" (Altheide and Johnson, 1980:5). Consequently, the apparent meanings of these statements of goals and other justificatory material ought not be taken at face value. Viewed as "official" information, these things are intended to facilitate the need of the respective organizations *as such.* Nonetheless, and despite their sometime obscure character, these materials strike a sympathetic chord among the oppressed who seek change. As a result, these materials are the link between organization goals and members' interests; they are the things susceptible people want to hear.

In summary, the formation of entrepreneurial groups of deviants may be said to arise out of the same general conditions and processes that give rise to any other moral entrepreneurial groups. These include a dissatisfaction with the status quo, a shared perception that existing conditions are intolerable and that change is desirable and conceivable (Humphreys, 1972:48).

Tactics of Change

Just as the bases for deviants forming voluntary associations and entering into moral entrepreneurial activity parallels those found among nondeviants, so, too, do these groups engage in similar tactics. This may be seen in their respective effort to transform troubles into issues, to seek legitimacy and cognitive change, their resort to the media to promote visibility, an effort to change reality, and, finally, their interest in altering public policy. In this section we give brief consideration to each of these matters. In this examination, however, our concern will necessarily be confined to instrumental groups—those concerned with altering some aspect of the normative condition of society.

Troubles and Issues. In pursuing social change, instrumental groups composed of deviants use tactics similar to those used by other moral crusaders. For example, one tactical similarity is the effort to demonstrate that, despite popular beliefs to the contrary, the existing public policy regarding a specific type of deviance is contrary to the public interest, broadly conceived. Efforts will be made, for instance, to demonstrate that the existing policy toward the deviant minority (discrimination, oppression, and so on) could readily be visited on other groups now considered to be legitimate. Or it may be suggested that the cost to society of maintaining and perpetuating a condition of deviance (as with criminalizing and imposing harsh penalties for marijuana use and possession, and other victimless crimes) is excessive and counterproductive. Thus, prior to its becoming a relatively popular perspective, the National Organization for the Reform of Marijuana Laws (NORML) was making the point that zealous enforcement of marijuana laws diverts significant numbers of law enforcement personnel and other resources from policing more important and socially damaging matters, such as violent crime (NORML, n.d.:1). In this way the problem faced by the deviant minority is enlarged to encompass others; the cost of the "cure" to society at large is construed so as to suggest it is more of a burden than the "disease." As with other moral entrepreneurial tactics, then, "troubles" are converted into "public issues."

Gaining Legitimacy. A second tactical similarity between deviant and nondeviant moral entrepreneurs is the promotion of legitimacy by gaining the support of prestigious and respected others. This means that a major concern among the groups under consideration is to bring about a redefinition of the stigmatized condition. A portion of this redefinition effort involves changing the moral meaning of the offending condition, that is, the promotion of legitimacy (as opposed to simply seeking decriminalization). In the pursuit of legitimacy, deviant groups engage in diverse tactics. One of these is to seek a sympathetic response from already established and respected professions in their respective area of expertise. To the extent a sympathetic response is obtained, the stigmatized group can expect at least tacit support and some enhancement of legitimacy.

One example of this has been the tacit support lent to the gay liberation movement by psychologists questioning the designation of homosexuality as "abnormal behavior," and by the American Library Association's opposition to classifying books on homosexuality under the heading of "Sex Perversion," on the grounds that such a designation was "inaccurate, bad librarianship, and oppressive to homosexuals" (Spector, 1977:52; Spector and Kitsuse, 1977:13–14). To the extent that the implied reclassifications occur, the tendency exists for a stigmatizing designation to be extinguished and be replaced by one of a morally neutral sort. It should be clear that as these names (that is, classifications) change, we may

expect some change, too, in the moral identity of these groups.

On a lesser scale, instrumental groups may seek legitimacy by attempting to call attention to the similarities between themselves and socially respected persons and collectivities. As a case in point, one issue of *Coyote Howls,* the official newspaper of COYOTE, pointed out the mutuality of goals between Margo St. James (founder and leader of COYOTE) and Father dePaul Genska, a Franciscan monk who administers a group serving the needs of street women in New York City. The apparent message here is that if COYOTE and a segment of the Roman Catholic church share goals, then COYOTE cannot be all bad (*Coyote Howls,* 1978:9). To further promote the organization's legitimacy, the same issue of *Coyote Howls* printed portions of a letter written by Mrs. Dorothy Wachter (mother of Margo St. James) to then First Lady Rosalynn Carter on the occasion of Mother's Day. First, the letter drew a parallel between their respective children; second, it pointed out how blessed mothers are who have children such as theirs; and, third, it made reference to the "dedicated" and "crusading" work engaged in by Margo St. James (*Coyote Howls,* 1978:4). One may easily regard this effort as an attempt to elicit some legitimating support from the First Lady.

As a final instance of seeking legitimacy through testimonials, NORML lists as members of its Advisory Board several prominent physicians, attorneys, educators, and religious personalities.

Use of the Media. A third tactical similarity between deviant and nondeviant moral crusaders is their resort to the media to achieve visibility, attract adherents, and solidify the ranks of followers—efforts that are seemingly indispensable. We have already noted the wide variety of devices—many of which involved the media in one form or another—used in the campaign in China to "liberate" the bound foot of Chinese women. A similar historical example of resort to the media is found in the case of the Scientific Humanitarian Committee, a German organization formed in 1897 and regarded as the first gay liberation group. In 1903 that group published a pamphlet entitled *What People Should Know About the Third Sex* in order to provide a "generally understandable and convincing piece of propaganda that will make it possible to reach the broadest layers of the public with a refutation of the false conceptions that still often hold sway about the nature of Uranianism [homosexuality]" (Lauritsen and Thorstad, 1974:14). The pamphlet went through nineteen editions within four years.

In a similar way, many contemporary groups create and maintain their own official publications, such as we noted in the case of COYOTE. Other examples include the monthly newsletter of the Little People of America and the Gray Panthers' (a group serving the interests of the aged) quarterly newsletter and book. Indeed, such publications are so common as to suggest they are an indispensable feature of such organizations. Circulated among members, these publications heighten people's awareness of events of interest to them, promote interaction, and encourage members to engage in letter writing and other activity intended to bring about desired change. Of course, such materials are also circulated to government administrators and others close to the seats of power whose support is necessary for the success of the movement. Supplementing these efforts are the established (profit-making) newspapers and magazines serving a select segment of the deviant population. Examples include *The Advocate* (a newspaper) and *Alternate* (a magazine) serving gays, and *Paraplegia News, Mainstream,* and *Accent on Living,* all of which serve the disabled.

Concern over access to the media extends well beyond the establishment of "in-house" or official organs among such groups. Related to the issue of gaining legitimation is the problem of gaining visibility among the general public. For this purpose, access to more orthodox media becomes important. So, too, is the issue of how representatives of disprivileged groups and issues or incidents of importance to them are portrayed in the media. For that reason many disprivileged groups have worked to get representatives hired by the media. In the case of blacks, women, and others, this has proved beneficial in terms of the amount and "slant" of the coverage media provide these collectivities.

A group for whom this benefit has not yet been realized is homosexuals. In the view of many people, the treatment of the issue of homosexuality in the orthodox press is "timorous, shallow, and hypocritical" (Pierson, 1982:28). To the extent that information about homosexuals and homosexuality is available in the orthodox media, it tends to reflect a heterosexual slant. This is because homosexuals working in the media remain "closeted" and therefore have little or no influence on shaping news coverage. "So far as is known, the [San Francisco] Chronicle is the only mainstream daily to have actively sought out a gay reporter" (Pierson, 1982:33).

Not the least of the resulting problems is that the legitimacy of interests of the gay community, as well as the identity of that community, are jeopardized by the perpetuation of negative sterotypy and bias. One example that outraged homosexuals and others was the CBS-TV broadcast "Gay Power, Gay Politics" on April 26, 1980. That broadcast, the content and nature of which is too extensive to be dealt with here, led to a complaint being filed against CBS-TV with the National News Council. The complaint charged that the broadcast misrepresented the gay community in San Francisco by means of "the systematic use of hearsay, oversights, exaggerations, distortion, inflammatory buzzwords, leading questions and misleading and deceitful editing" (*Columbia Journalism Review,* 1981:76). Of the 11 members of the National News Council hearing and voting on the complaint, 9 concurred, 1 dissented, and 1 dissented in part. In short, overall, the Council found the complaint justifiable.

Orthodox media coverage of gay issues generated similar concern in Toronto, Canada. There, it has been alleged, the leading daily papers, the *Toronto Star* and *Toronto Sun,* gave extensive coverage to the charge of obscenity brought against the gay newspaper, *The Body Politic.* However, the *Star* gave only limited coverage and the *Sun* gave no coverage to the acquittal of *The Body Politic* following a trial. Such bias in the media, it is felt, jeopardizes the effort of the gay community to achieve legitimacy (Zwicker, 1982).

Lastly, a problem for deviant spokespersons is having their activity and perspective defined as newsworthy by newsworkers and, hence, deserving of recognition. In playing the role of "newsmaker" and seeking access to media channels, spokespersons for deviant interests often find it necessary to establish at least a "counterfeit" legitimacy in order to overcome obstacles to news coverage and have their perspective broadcast. One method used to effect such an image of legitimacy is to establish an organization (often more apparent than real), specifically for the purpose of presenting self to media newsworkers (Altheide, 1974). A second method of securing media coverage is to *stage* events that have a high probability of being defined by newsworkers as worthy of coverage. Thus, deviant associations may purposely generate events likely to receive media coverage. For example, groups opposed to nuclear electrical generating plants have staged acts of civil disobedience in order to promote confrontation with police, have themselves arrested, and force a court trial. The ultimate goal of this tactic is to gain media attention and use the trial as a means to bring their message to the attention of a larger audience (Shuey, 1978:3, 25).

Reconstructing Reality. A fourth parallel between the tactics of deviant and other moral crusaders is their construction of realities. As we saw earlier, a major task of the moral entrepreneur is to create "new moralities" and to alter the meaning of conditions, behavior, and so on. In the case of the deviant moral entrepreneur, this effort most often takes the form of reconstructing dominant reality, that is, countering popular beliefs concerning the causes and consequences of the stigmatized condition/behavior, and contesting existing stereotypes and elements of myth regarding the group in question.

A prime example of a group seeking to alter dominant beliefs and taken-for-granted under-

standings is the efforts of a California organization called Fat Underground to counter popular beliefs concerning the advantages and consequences of dieting. Fat Underground maintains that dieting is not an aid to better health, serves no lasting purpose, and may actually "wreck" people's health by contributing to increased stress and high blood pressure. Further, they state that in the United States "reducing is a $10 billion industry annually. Someone is making a lot of money off the public's fear of fat. Your (temporary) loss is their gain and they want to keep it that way" (*Before You Go On a Diet,* n.d.).

Similarly, gay liberationists have long worked to promote a change in the popular beliefs concerning the causes and character of homosexuality. Beginning in the 1860s in semiformal fashion in Europe, and continuing with the work of the Scientific Humanitarian Committee between 1896 and 1935, representatives of the homophile community have long challenged public beliefs about homosexuals and homosexuality as well as public policies stemming from those beliefs (Lauritsen and Thorstad, 1974). A recent example of the desired change in social reality promoted by such efforts is the diagnostic reclassification of homosexuality by the American Psychiatric Association (APA). For nearly 100 years the APA had classified homosexuality as a sexual deviation and a manifestation of a mental disorder. Then, to a great extent due to the agitation by representatives of the homophile community (including protests and demonstrations at psychiatric conferences and several APA conventions), in 1973 the APA reclassified homosexuality and identified it as a "sexual orientation disturbance." In announcing this reclassification the APA stated that

The category of homosexuality is now replaced by "sexual orientation disturbance" which is described as follows: This category is for individuals whose sexual interests are directed primarily toward people of the same sex who are either disturbed by, in conflict with, or wish to change their sexual orientation. This diagnostic category is distinguished from homosexuality, which by itself does not necessarily constitute a psychiatric disorder. Homosexuality per se is one form of sexual behavior, and like other forms of sexual behavior which are themselves not psychiatric disorders, is not listed in this nomenclature of mental disorders. (American Psychiatric Association, 1973)

A forced referendum on this change revealed that 42 percent of the voting psychiatrists opposed the new classification (Spector and Kitsuse, 1977:20). Clearly, not all practicing psychiatrists accept this change. What is most relevant for gay liberationists, however, is that in the politics of deviance, a significant symbolic victory was achieved. By a vote of 58 to 42 percent, a new and official definition of homosexuality had been created. Officially, homosexuality was no longer a disease or mental disorder, but a "way of life" equal to heterosexuality. In creating this new reality, the legitimacy of homosexuality had been significantly advanced.

Another example of the reconstruction of reality is found in the case of alcoholism. Though references to alcoholism as a disease appeared as early as the eighteenth century (Catanzaro, 1968:5), a systematic movement to institutionalize that view was not evident prior to the 1930s, when a physician, W.D. Silkwood, with the support of Alcoholics Anonymous, proposed that alcoholism is an allergy. Somewhat later, E.M. Jellinek consolidated the view of alcoholism as a disease with the publication of his book *The Disease Concept of Alcoholism* (1960). Though not accepted by everyone, and despite the difficulty of isolating uniform, consistent, and progressive symptoms, the idea of alcoholism as disease has paved the way for a general redefinition: Alcoholism is now popularly regarded as "problem drinking" (McCaghy, 1976:271–272). This redefinition is more than mere semantics. By this change people who are perceived to be alcoholic are relieved of the moral burden once carried by those labeled as drunks. With alcoholism being considered an illness, the social response to the inebriate leads to treatment and rehabilitation rather than punishment; excess consumption of alcohol is converted from a legal to a medical problem.

A final example of an effort to alter existing moral meanings by deviant crusaders is the case of legalized abortion. Over the past 15 years, largely through the efforts of the National Association for the Repeal of Abortion Laws, representatives of the women's liberation movement, and other crusaders, the meaning of abortion has been altered for a substantial segment of the population. With abortion long described as a barbarous ritual, cloaked in secrecy and available only at exorbitant rates paid to quacks and criminals operating in dingy "kitchen table" surroundings, restrictive abortion laws were generally seen as necessary to protect women from the unscrupulous and to safeguard the family. Accordingly, legal restrictions were staunchly supported by and were incorporated into the basic tenets of fundamentalist faiths and the Roman Catholic Church. In sharp contrast, groups favoring repeal of restrictive abortion laws saw these regulations as totally evil, inhumane, and unjust. They perceived abortion as a medical issue to be decided privately between women and their physicians. To have the choice of abortion, "was simply the right of personal decision, the right of a woman to control the creative powers of her body, to bring into the world only a child she truly wanted and loved" (Lader, 1973:xiii).

Though it may not be attributed solely to the efforts of pro-repeal forces, it is yet noteworthy that in recent years there has been a substantial change in public attitudes toward abortion. Thus, based on independent nationwide samples of college and noncollege youth, a report by Daniel Yankelovich shows that between 1969 and 1973, during which years the abortion revolution was in full flower, the proportion of noncollege youth regarding abortion as morally wrong declined from 63 percent to 48 percent. The general moral code of college youth is reported to be even less strict in that only 32 percent of the people interviewed in 1973 regarded having an abortion as morally wrong (Yankelovich, 1974:87, 91, 93). In 1981 Yankelovich reported that 60 percent of the respondents polled in the United States favored the legal right of women to decide to have or not have an abortion up to the third month of pregnancy (Yankelovich, 1981:60).

Altering Public Policy. As indicated in Chapter 4, the creation of "new moralities" is intended to have either instrumental or symbolic consequences. To be sure, no direct link may be established between changes in moral meanings and individual actions. Nonetheless, we may observe alterations in public policy that are consistent with the moral meanings sought after by crusading deviant minorities. With that as a "measure of success," let's inquire briefly into what may be the outcome of the moral entrepreneurship of deviant groups. At the outset, it is well to recognize that, in an area so fraught with currents and crosscurrents of moral meaning, where each success is almost immediately tempered by a setback, few if any sweeping generalizations may be proffered. More prudent, it appears, is to note that winning "battles" must not be equated with winning "wars." It is perhaps also true that the experience (whether of success or failure) of one segment of the deviant population has no necessary relationship to the experiences of other segments. Here, then, we will focus on specifics, withholding more general impressions for later.

One area that has undergone substantial change is alcoholism. As we noted, the view that alcoholism is a disease, though not without its critics, has become well established. Consistent with this change in definition has been the establishment over the nation of alcohol detoxification centers and diversionary treatment programs (Siegel, 1973). As alternatives to incarceration, this change in public policy is a marked departure from tradition, according to which behaviors associated with drinking (such as public drunkenness) were defined as crime, the responsibility of the police and court system. Problem drinkers, ranging from the intoxicated driver to the inebriated felon, tend now to be defined as needing treatment and rehabilitation rather than punishment. At present, some limited departure from this trend has developed in the form of a legal "crackdown" on drunk drivers. Spurred by the emotional influence of "horror stories" and official statistics on the consequences of drunk driving, a Presidential Commission on Drunk Driving has been established and many states

have enacted laws mandating severe penalties for drunk driving. Not the least important contributor to this reversal is the organization known as Mothers Against Drunk Drivers (MADD) (*Time,* 1982a; *Newsweek,* 1982a; *U.S. News and World Report,* 1983).

Despite this reversal *in policy* it is unlikely that the larger consequences of the medicalization of alcohol dependency will be changed. In short, the institutional nature of the treatment perspective seems secure. Not the least of the reasons for its security is that decriminalization has reduced the burdens borne by police and courts. Thus, the city of Boston reported 12,627 arrests for public drunkenness in 1973. In 1974, one year after decriminalization, there were 8755 reported cases of protective custody for public intoxication, a reduction of 39 percent (Rubington, 1975:413). In the span of six years, 1969 through 1974, police–inebriate contacts were reduced by more than 10,000. As a result of less frequent contact between police and inebriates may also come changes in the definitions these groups have of each other and in inebriates' definitions of self (Rubington, 1975).

A second area subject to redefinition and altered public policy in recent years is marijuana use. Groups working to decriminalize marijuana possession (such as NORML) were instrumental in disseminating information indicating the nonrational nature of antimarijuana legislation and law enforcement. Aided by representatives of the medical profession, it became fashionable to regard pot smoking as a relatively harmless source of pleasure. Any problems associated with its use were seen as infrequent and superficial (Goode, 1972:183). Operating as lobbies and pressure groups, organizations worked to bring about a reduction in criminal penalties for marijuana possession. These groups appear to have succeeded in several jurisdictions. In 1973 Oregon reduced the penalty for marijuana violations to a fine. Between 1975 and 1977 Alaska, California, Colorado, Maine, and New York followed suit. Reform proposals have been considered in other states, especially due to the growing recognition of the medicinal value of marijuana for victims of glaucoma and for cancer patients undergoing chemotherapy. Thus, in 1978 New Mexico legalized the therapeutic use of marijuana. Finally, in the absence of formal revision of law, informal nonenforcement of possession laws seems to have been widely adopted as policy.

Despite these changes, there is at present a concerted effort over the nation to counteract the relaxed view of and approach to marijuana use. First, the earlier view of the limited and superficial consequences of marijuana use are being contested by claims concerning the drug's effect on higher mental and psychological functioning, as well as its alleged negative physiological effects including "impaired lung function, decreased sperm counts and sperm motility, interference with ovulation and prenatal development, diminished immune response and possibly lung cancer" (*Newsweek*, 1982b:40). Second, while enforcement of possession laws have been relaxed, many jurisdictions have increased their enforcement efforts aimed at producers and distributors. This change seems to parallel an increase in the domestic production of marijuana to the point that it is now regarded as the nation's third most valuable cash crop—valued at more than $10 billion annually (*Newsweek*, 1982b:37). Simultaneous with this more zealous law enforcement effort, however, is the contrary view that growing marijuana should be legalized; the rationale for this is that legalization would make it possible to regulate and tax that very valuable crop (*Newsweek*, 1982b:42–43). It is clear that this ebb and flow of public policy and sentiment reflects interpersonal conflict and the existence of competing realities concerning marijuana use, as well as the changing distribution of power in society. Certainly the conflict over the morality of pot is far from resolved.

Also subject to widespread public and official attention over the past several years is homosexuality. Consider the following evidence. In 1971 a gay candidate was elected president of the student body of the University of Minnesota; East Lansing, Michigan, and San Francisco became the first cities to enact civil rights protections for gay people; and in Hawaii so-

domy statutes were repealed. In 1973 the American Psychiatric Association reclassified homosexuality. In 1974, then U.S. Representative Bella Abzug (N.Y.) introduced a bill in Congress to ban discrimination against gay people, and Elain Noble, an avowed lesbian, was elected to the Massachusetts House of Representatives. In 1975 Pennsylvania Governor Milton Shapp ordered an end to discrimination in hiring gays for state jobs; in California a bill was signed into law decriminalizing consensual sex between adults; the U.S. Civil Service Commission announced an end to its policy prohibiting employment of homosexuals; six additional states repealed sodomy statutes and ten more cities passed gay rights ordinances. In 1977, Dade County (Miami), Florida, passed and then repealed an ordinance banning discrimination against gay people in housing and employment. In that same year several other cities repealed similar ordinances, largely because of the mobilization of opposing sentiment by Anita Bryant and sympathetic others. In 1978, however, such repeal efforts were resoundingly defeated in California and Seattle, Washington. In 1977 Harvey B. Milk became the nation's first openly gay city official when he was elected to the San Francisco Board of Supervisors. In 1983 Gerry E. Studds (D-Mass.) became the first sitting member of Congress to declare he is a homosexual, although there is an alleged 30 or more other gay members of Congress who remain "in the closet" but who may be expected to lend support to legislation consistent with or reflecting the interests of the homosexual population (*Arizona Republic*, 1983c). In 1984 the California legislature passed a bill that would outlaw job discrimination against homosexuals in that state (*Arizona Republic*, 1984a), and the U.S. Supreme Court announced (for the first time in almost 20 years) that it will hear a gay rights case stemming from a lower court ruling that "bars Oklahoma public schools from firing teachers, substitute teachers, or teacher's aides for advocating [for example, while testifying before a legislative committee or speaking on a public panel] gay or lesbian conduct" (*The Advocate*, 1984a). Finally, in 1984 California

Governor George Deukmejian signed into law a bill (Assembly Bill 848) "which will enable gay and lesbian victims of anti-gay violence to sue their attackers" (*The Advocate,* 1984b).

To be sure, not all these developments went unchallenged. Nor may this be taken as a time of "clear victories" for the homophile movement. Thus, for example, Supervisor Harvey Milk was the victim of an assassin (Shilts, 1982), and the 1984 anti-discrimination bill in California was vetoed by Gov. Deukmejian. Nonetheless, the decade of the 1970s and the early 1980s have likely witnessed more concern over public policy regarding gay rights than any other period. The ultimate goal of such activism is that homosexuals not be differentiated as a group (Weinberg and Williams, 1974:287).

The activism and sometime militance of minority activists is not confined to groups concerned only with voluntaristic deviance. Equally active are the disabled who have been identified as a "new minority," an "awakening minority" whose members are "finally making themselves heard by lobbying for bills that will aid their cause, by attending city council meetings, and by addressing service clubs" (Watson, 1978:20). Following the model established by other instrumental groups, the disabled have learned that "action brings reaction."

Although not yet a full-fledged civil rights movement such as other disprivileged groups, there have been great changes in public policy concerning the disabled in recent years. Of major importance was the passage by Congress of the Rehabilitation Act of 1973. Among its several sections, this law (1) requires affirmative action hiring of disabled workers, (2) ensures physical accessibility of the handicapped to public and private buildings, (3) requires affirmative action among contractors doing more than $2500 worth of business annually with the federal government, and (4) bans job discrimination against disabled persons in agencies (public or private) receiving federal funds (Gleidman and Roth, 1980:267). In the absence of quality education for the disabled, however, the intent of the Rehabilitation Act would likely never be realized.

For that reason, with the assistance of organizations such as the National Education Association, Congress passed in 1975 the Education for All Handicapped Children Act (Public Law 94–142). This Act stipulates a "free appropriate public education in an environment that would be the least restrictive for the handicapped child's normal development. The handicapped student would no longer be an exile" (*NEA Today,* 1983:2). This Act is not without its critics, however, since it allegedly fails to address the basic prevailing conception of disability and the disabled, namely, the view that disability is a "disease" and the disabled are socially inferior (Gleidman and Roth, 1980:chapter 9). However valid a criticism, it remains true that the All Handicapped Children Act reflects a significant change in public policy concerning disabled children as a segment of the population. With emphasis on the principle of providing a special educational opportunity *appropriate to the individual's needs,* the law is designed to eliminate hasty and detrimental labeling of the disabled (such as the identification of a dyslexic child as "lazy" or "retarded") and to promote the mainstreaming or integration of the disabled into the life of the community (Hoye, 1983).

Seen as facilitators of mainstreaming, these recent changes in public policy, however much they may be subject to debate and continuing clarification, represent a dramatic change from the circumstances of a mere generation ago, when the prevailing policy was to institutionalize and isolate disabled persons. Perhaps the most dramatic and highly personalized expression of a changing image of disabled persons is the selection in 1984 of George L. Murray, a wheelchair marathoner, from among 50 amateur athletes in the United States as a Wheaties world champion. As such, Mr. Murray's photo will appear on Wheaties cereal boxes (*Mainstream,* 1984).

Taken together, these examples of public policy change, many of which rest on the efforts of disvalued people to challenge their deviant status, reflect the increasingly politicized nature of deviance in our society. We will conclude with a consideration of that issue.

The Politicization of Deviance

No complete consideration of the endlessly complex political nature of deviance is possible in these few paragraphs; the topic is the stuff of volumes (Gamson, 1968 and 1975; Piven and Cloward, 1977; Lauderdale, 1980; Schur, 1980). Rather, our purpose in this section is merely to give focus to this general matter, with which we dealt in specific terms in Chapter 4 and subsequently.

The alterations in social reality and public policy that we have considered have implications of the utmost significance for the analysis and understanding of the phenomenon of deviance. First and most obviously, these materials make it clear that deviance cannot be adequately apprehended as a "morality play" in which forces supporting the eternal verities and virtues embraced by the "right-minded" are pitted against the forces of evil manifest in one or another aberration. On the contrary, the politicization of deviance strongly suggests that the deviance process is a dialectic, a kind of power game in which conflicting interests vie with one another for the official stamp of legitimacy. In no case is one interest the *inherent* moral superior of its opposite. It is a power struggle in which the "prize" is the incorporation (symbolically or instrumentally) of one morality into public policy and the simultaneous deviantizing (Schur, 1979:39) of its opposite.

Second, to suggest that deviance is best seen as a power struggle rather than a morality play means, too, that issues of deviance are unlikely to be validly described as absolute and unarguable. On the contrary, they are matters that are everlastingly negotiable to one degree or another. To the distress of many, traditionally dominant moral meanings, especially concerning sexual matters, are increasingly likely to be defined as problematic and subject to compromise. Persons and groups ranked high by traditional public standards are no longer automatically assumed to possess moral superiority—especially by those who traditionally have been politically marginal. Even former President Jimmy Carter admitted to looking on women "with lust" and to having "committed adultery" in his heart (*Playboy,* 1976:87). Perhaps more than ever, legitimacy is perceived as challengeable, as well as a quality available to those with the clout to achieve it. Clearly, the politicization of deviance means the existing structure of public rules and their enforcement has taken on new meaning (Horowitz and Leibowitz, 1968:296). The prevailing views seem neatly summarized by the lapel button reading "Question Authority!"

Third, the foregoing materials surely suggest that nothing is deviant or nondeviant but that defining makes it so. In the context of "deviance as politics," this notion cautions against adopting the simplistic idea that deviance reflects moral essences that, in turn, are reflected in public policy. Rather, to view deviance as politics raises the question of what processes are involved in the elevation of one definition of morality to a position of legitimacy and the simultaneous derogation of an alternative morality. Based on our analysis, we contend that these processes are fundamentally political, reflect the moral heterogeneity of our society, are influenced by the distribution of power, and are essentially the same whether engaged in by moral crusaders or by those seeking freedom from stigma (Schur, 1980:190).

The developments and activities recounted here also indicate that deviant groups, in increasing number and diversity, have abandoned the traditionally subordinate political role assigned them by representatives of legitimate society. To be sure, historically, power subjects have protested the treatment accorded them by power holders (Gamson, 1975). Rarely, however, did power subjects seek to alter their position vis-à-vis the power holders (Becker, 1970:241), seek to have their position legitimized by the public at large, or openly campaign for votes either for a candidate of their choice or to bring about approval or rejection of an initiative on the ballot. The increasing tendency of contemporary groups to resort to these and similar tactics signals the fact that "deviants have become more self-conscious, more organized, more willing to fight with conventional society than ever before. They are more open in their deviance, prouder of what they are and less likely to be treated as others want to treat them without having some voice in the matter" (Becker, 1970:344). More than ever, seen in political terms, the deviance process reflects elements of an intercursive power model.

Increasingly abandoned, too, is the idea that the stigmatized and the oppressed shall be satisfied with being "ministered to" in therapeutic terms. Indeed, the activities we have recounted indicate progressive rejection of the traditional idea that "being different" is in some way pathological, a condition necessarily calling for "correction" by psychiatry, surgery, social work, counseling, or some combination of these. This amounts to an utter rejection of the "correctional" orientation that has so long dominated in the field of deviance. Such rejection and repudiation is the other side of the coin of self-acceptance among those heretofore rejected by legitimate society. Evidence of such a posture is found in the repudiation by the disabled of the social pathology model of handicap (Gleidman and Roth, 1980: chapter 3), by the principled attack on the tendency of well-meaning, able-bodied persons (such as celebrity Jerry Lewis) to infantilize and promote pity for victims of muscular dystrophy by categorically referring to such persons as his "kids" without regard for their age. In this capacity, Lewis and others have been identified as people who have "mouths like sewers" (*Achievement*, 1981).

Finally, recent developments indicate that "the line between the social deviant and the political marginal is fading. It is rapidly becoming an obsolete distinction" (Horowitz and Leibowitz, 1968:285). Indeed, to cite just two examples: Given the political activism of representatives of the gay liberation movement (Shilts, 1982) and the recognition among the disabled of the link between personal worth, dignity, and self-respect, on the one hand, and political power and activism, on the other (Funk, 1981:1), one is tempted to say the disfranchisement of such people *as voting blocs* already is obsolete. If so, and though we must allow for the possibility of change, its obsolescence may spell the end of an elitist conception of the political process wherein only majorities

ruled (with the possible exception of a few powerful minorities). Politically active deviant associations are a marked departure from tradition and testify to the flourishing of "minoritarian" politics (Horowitz and Leibowitz, 1968:288).

These changes are wholly consistent with the model of human nature and society used throughout this volume. Politicization of deviance is reflective of persons who deal actively with their environment, who *interact with* rather than simply *respond* to external pressures. The collective effort of these groups to confront, manage, and overcome their stigma is reflective, too, of deviance as a conflict process between sometime subordinates and sometime superordinates. Consistent with our earlier analysis of power and lawmaking, the work of these voluntary associations reveals that law is indeed an instrument for the realization of the values and interests of groups having power.

Summary

In this chapter we have examined the diverse means by which people seek to deal with stigma. To facilitate analysis of stigma management by individuals, a distinction was made between the *discreditable* and the *discredited*. Among the discreditable, stigma management appears to involve a rather universal set of properties, including the manipulation of *stigma symbols,* a reliance on *disidentifiers,* and the sometime need to lead a "double life." Such techniques are acknowledged to have varying degrees of success, depending on the circumstances under which they are used and the person's facility in employing them. Even with the active complicity of others, as in the case of counterfeit secrecy, however, the use of these devices may sometimes exact a substantial price, particularly the substitution of one set of tensions for another.

Turning to the discredited, those whose stigma is publicly known, we noted the use of deviance *disavowal,* a process having three analytically discernible stages, each of which is intended to facilitate normalization of relations between deviants and others. We noted disavowal is a process wherein the deviant makes a claim to normality and the nondeviant honors that claim; the key to successful disavowal is reciprocity. A second technique of management among the discredited is deviance *avowal,* whereby a person acknowledges the deviance but simultaneously indicates that it is only one part of his- or herself. Essentially, avowal is an effort to avoid being engulfed by the *master status.*

Stigma management may also be promoted by socialization to the deviant role. A major element in that socialization is to recognize and overcome the stereotyped typifications of the deviant role. Other "tools" used to manage one's moral burden include *excuses,* which seek to reduce the moral breach in which the person has been engaged, or *justifications,* which are intended to deny the negative moral implications associated with the person's actions. Justifications may take the form of any of several *techniques of neutralization, sad tales,* or *self-fulfillment.* The use of these techniques is a commonplace occurrence wherein people employ a variety of verbal devices (we are tempted to say "tricks") in order to absolve themselves of moral responsibility and promote a redefinition of their actions. In a microscopic sense, people are engaged in an effort to create a reality leading to modification of others' definition of them and, in turn, a modification of their status as discredited persons.

Turning from individual to collective methods of stigma management, extensive consideration was given to various forms of *voluntary associations.* To better understand these associations, their origins were examined; we noted their continuity with *secret societies,* and we linked their recent increase in number and visibility with a variety of changes in American society over the course of the past century. Of most immediate importance in explaining their present status are the political upheavals experienced by the United States during the 1960s and 1970s, and the broader humanitarian social movement that began during that period, as well as the more specific movements that continue at present.

Viewing these associations as moral entrepreneurial groups, we also examined their activities and the existential conditions to which they are related: the experience and definition of conditions as intolerable and the resulting desire to pursue change. In examining the tactics used by instrumental groups, several similarities were noted between them and other moral crusaders. That such similarity exists reflects the widespread institutionalization of the means to alter public policy and create "new moralities" by collective effort. Most important, we suggested, these activities reflect a fundamental change in the nature of deviance in this society—a shift requiring that deviance be viewed as a political rather than a moral and therapeutic issue.

Epilogue

For those who have followed our analysis to this point, let us now summarize, draw a few conclusions, and do a bit of projecting.

Early in this book I said I had no "final truths" to impart. Given our perspective, it should be evident that "final truths" concerning moral matters are anything but final. Seen as social constructions, "final truths" reflect only the value orientation of their author. What I have tried to provide is a mode of analysis that will enable people to understand deviance and its opposite, respectability, as socially constructed categories, parts of a humanly created social order.

Our analysis of the dialectic of deviance as a social construction began with the effort of moral entrepreneurs to create new moralities and assign negative moral meaning to conditions that distress them, progressed through the stages by which these meanings become institutionalized and part of public law, and concluded with the effort of "outsiders" to alter official reality and normalize their condition. Hopefully, this effort has resulted in establishing a firm distinction between rule breaking and deviance, between the *actions* and *conditions* of people, on the one hand, and the *social reaction* to them, on the other. Equally important is the hope that this exercise has clearly explained the process by which these distinctions are established, maintained, and changed, revealing that deviance and respectability are social creations resulting from the attribution of moral meanings to people and things. By noting the ongoing nature of this process we may conclude that deviance (and its counterpart, respectability) is unending, that it is part and parcel of the uninterrupted effort of people to create and maintain order in a heterogeneous and conflictful environment. It is part of the process whereby people create order by assigning meanings to things that have no essential meaning, the process by which people create order in an absurd world (Lyman and Scott, 1970). However, to say that social order, including deviance, is a social construction and dependent on defining is *not to say* it is *merely* a matter of semantics, that is, a matter of words. To be sure, deviance entails the attribution of meaning (as the word *semantics* suggests), but it entails far, far more. It is by naming things that people make sense of the sociocultural world and organize their responses to it. To suggest the social construction of deviance reduces to *mere* semantics (as if that were nothing) is to ignore people's ability to objectify their creations, mock those whose lives are burdened by the consequences of these objectified meanings, and, in general, trivialize the entire process.

In concluding our study we might ask where this analysis leads us. For example, are we to conclude from this study that the elimination of deviance is to be found in ceasing to make rules? That is, if deviance results from rule making, is it reasonable to suggest we end rule making? Theoretically and logically that may be so. But practically it is a pointless suggestion; a lack of rules will not alter people's interests, allay their fears, or reduce the bodily and/or psychological harm from which they seek protection. Or, again, does the foregoing analysis lead to the idea that deviance can be eliminated by adopting an ethic of "anything goes"? That is, does the answer to the "deviance problem" lie in withholding moral meanings from the activity and conditions of others? Reasoning of the "anything goes" type leads to the idea that "across-the-board normalization" is the ultimate answer. Were that suggestion to be put forth as a basis for social policy, we suspect that it would be labeled "suicidal." Viewed practically, the notion of "anything goes" is foolish in that it ignores the idea that reality is multiple, that interests, values, and related goals—however narrow and petty or lacking in rationality they may appear—are often assigned cosmic importance and defended to the death. In short, "anything goes" fails to reckon with fundamental aspects of the definitional model and is not based on a valid, defensible image of everyday life. Indeed, the very idea that deviance can be ended, that it can be overcome, that we can win the "war against crime," and so on flies in the face of all that has been included in the preceding chapters. Deviance is no more likely to disappear than is respectability; the one necessitates the other.

However, to say that deviance is a persistent feature of collective life does not mean deviance will remain static, that it will not change. Thus, while the deviance process will persist, the substantive aspects of deviance will change. For example, we can look forward with confidence to continued change in those conditions and activities defined as objectionable. One example is pornography. What most people might agree is pornographic or erotic art and literature has existed since time immemorial. Nonetheless, the current struggle over pornography in this country is as fresh and as impassioned as ever. Extending well beyond matters of morality, the current struggle has been joined by representatives of diverse interests including religion; government; feminist groups; and organizations of professionals such as educators, librarians, and child psychologists—as well as the publishing, motion picture, and television (especially cable service) industries, each of which has a strong financial interest in the issue. The outcome of this struggle cannot be foretold. What does seem certain, however, is that out of the interaction of these many interest groups altered definitions of pornography, erotica, and obscene and salacious art and literature will emerge. And who knows, perhaps one day it will be officially decided that films of humans killing one another are more obscene than films of humans making love to one another; it may come to pass that scenes of tenderness, such as a man kissing a woman's breast, will be rated R (perhaps even G), while scenes of a man committing sexual assault will be rated X.

As another example of the changing substance of deviance, consider the recent changes in lifestyle in our society. A few decades ago any departure from the traditional pattern of monogamous marriage was seen as a sign of immorality and decadence and a threat to the social order. More recently, such diverse patterns as group marriage, bisexual and homosexual liaisons between consenting adults, communal living, one-parent families, and open cohabitation have become more prevalent and accepted in at least some segments of society. By means of normalization, patterns of living once defined as deviant and prohibited are now classified as "alternative lifestyles." Thus, a Phoenix, Arizona, court in 1980 granted custody of her two daughters to a white lesbian ex-convict with a black lover, despite the objections of the woman's relatives (*Arizona Republic,* 1980l). In 1981 a woman in California gave birth to a child that will be reared by her transsexual brother-turned-sister, who is married and confined to a wheelchair (*Arizona Republic,* 1981h). And in a Brooklyn, N.Y., Family Court a 22-year-old man won the right to adopt his 26-year-old homosexual lover (*Arizona Republic,* 1981i).

Change in moral/legal meanings can also be seen in the case of marital rape. Since time out of mind husbands have been exempt from prosecution for rape of their spouses though they may have used (sometimes extreme) physical means to force their wives to perform sexual acts. However, in 1977 the spousal immunity clause was deleted from Oregon's rape statute. Thereafter, at least technically, husbands in that state could be charged and brought to trial for raping their wives. In 1978 John Rideout was so charged, although he was later acquitted of the charge of first-degree rape (Russell, 1982:17ff). By 1980 two more states—Nebraska and New Jersey—had eliminated the spousal exemption. In 1981 it was reported that the rape laws in California, Connecticut, Florida, Iowa, Massachusetts, Minnesota, and New Hampshire were similarly changed. However, simultaneously, 12 other states "extended the privilege of husbands to rape their wives to men who are cohabiting with women with whom they are not legally married" (Russell, 1982:21–22). Such contradictions reflect the dialectics of the deviance process and the fact that elements of social reality are multiple and often in disagreement.

But changes in deviance involve more than the foregoing. At a more fundamental level, changes in public policy in recent decades in our society and in other western nations indicate that we are at a time of increasing selectivity in the implementation of public law. Thus, it seems that banning and the criminalization of behavior increasingly occur only when (1) the act is defined as offensive or morally blameworthy either by a substantial majority of the population or an exceedingly powerful minority, and (2) where a victim may be said to clearly have suffered some overt and demonstrable harm (Sklar, 1979). Progressively, behavior that lacks one or the other of these elements is subject to less vigorous official condemnation and its practitioners to less strenuous control. Examples that come to mind include abortion, use of mood-altering substances (especially marijuana and cocaine), prostitution, homosexuality among consenting adults, and gambling (Geis, 1972), among others.

Placing this development in an historical framework and employing an intercursive power model suggests that we may have reached the point when declaring conditions immoral, deviant, or criminal has become progressively more difficult. This increased difficulty seems, first, to be a consequence of the increased politicization of deviance. That is, given previously oppressed groups' recently achieved sense of power and willingness to employ countervailing tactics to secure and/or protect their interests, as well as their awareness that labeling is negotiable if not altogether resistable, we may have passed the point when rule makers could easily and willingly criminalize or otherwise publicly condemn people and behavioral forms. Second, some observers suggest this trend is promoted by an awareness that "the criminal law is too expensive and cumbersome a process, its police resources and court time in too high demand and too short supply, its effects on people's lives . . . too drastic, the methods its enforcement officers

must use to uncover the so-called 'victimless crime' (entrapment, informers) too degrading to allow its use against conduct that produces no provable harm, creates no victim" (Sklar, 1979:71).

Evidence of this is seen in the case of abortion. Regardless of one's definition of abortion, the conflict that has ensued these many years reveals that it is no longer reasonable to expect the entire nation to "jump to the moral rope" of heretofore dominant and powerful interest groups, not even the Roman Catholic Church or fundamentalist Protestant bodies. Neither, it seems, are people intimidated by the support of the antiabortion forces by President Reagan or the terrorist attacks on family planning and abortion counseling clinics. Similarly, where once the support of the gay community was a political "kiss of death," aspiring candidates for public office now vie with one another for its vote (*Arizona Republic*, 1983g). This is to be expected as the moral pluralism of our society becomes increasingly manifest in the political arena.

Further, we can expect the process of banning to require progressively more demonstrable evidence of the harm or damage alleged to result from the conditions and behavior to be declared deviant. As a result, and because so much of what people fear are "things of the mind," we may look for a narrowing of the parameters of official deviance. Existing rules will continue to fall into disuse ("administrative decriminalization"), some will be formally repealed or otherwise modified, and new rules will be rather more difficult to enact.

These comments on the perceived direction of change certainly do not mean we can anticipate an "end to deviance." The changes noted will be met with marked resistance, as many of them now are; "backlash" will persist. I am not suggesting we are moving toward a time of greater compassion or tolerance for human differences, or that we are less interested in controlling deviants than previously (Pfuhl, 1985). By all means, we will continue to witness people's efforts to differentiate between themselves and others and to denigrate those others. We will continue to witness such cases as: the refusal of a U.S. Marine detachment conducting a Toys for Tots campaign to enter a gay bar to retrieve donated toys (*Arizona Republic,* 1983e); a Baptist school cancelling its scheduled basketball games with another private school after years of competition because the school's officials learned their opponents are Roman Catholic (*Arizona Republic,* 1983f); an Illinois high school student being kicked out of the National Honor Society by high school officials when they learned she was pregnant (*Arizona Republic,* 1984d). In short, what some may define as pettiness, prejudice, and distrust will persist. So will the tendency to brutalize "outsiders."

The one thing these anticipated changes *do not* herald is that our society, from a moral perspective, is "going to hell in a handbasket," or that we are headed for a state of utter moral degradation. *Moral degradation* is a term people who are distressed and troubled apply to situations that disturb them greatly, over which they have little or no control, and to which they have not yet reconciled themselves. Viewed dispassionately, all we may note with assurance is that public moral codes are changing and that the boundaries between public and private morality are in flux. Over time we have become more aware of the diverse and socially harmless ways in which people organize their private lives, more aware of the breadth of private morality. As this awareness has increased, so, too, has our sense of the irrelevance and futility of perpetuating a public morality to which we pay only lip service. As a consequence, many seek a revision of public rules to bring them more in line with the moral diversity of everyday life.

The type and direction of the change that concerns me is exemplified by the contrast afforded by the cases of Ralph Ginzburg in the 1960s and of Vanessa Williams in 1984. In the former case, Publisher Ginzburg was fined $28,000 and sentenced to five years in federal prison for sending his magazine, called *Eros,* and two other obscene publications through the U.S. mails. Though there was an outcry in support of Ginzburg based on First Amendment rights and against the severity of his punishment, the U.S. Supreme Court (in a 5 to 4 decision) upheld the conviction, with Justice William J. Brennan announcing that Ginzburg was guilty of "the sordid business of pandering" (*Time,* 1966:56). In sharp contrast is the case of Vanessa Williams, the first black Miss America. In 1984, Bob Guccione, publisher of *Penthouse* magazine, released photographs of Miss Williams in the nude posing with a female partner in scenes of apparent lesbian sexual behavior. In response to the publication of the photographs, officials of the Miss America Pageant reportedly found that they "sullied" the image of Miss America; they were "appalled" and found the photos repugnant. Miss Williams was stripped of her status as Miss America. For his part, publisher Guccione, who rationalized his actions by claiming the photos were desirable in the eyes of his readers (recall Ginzburg's "pandering"), was publicly criticized for displaying poor taste and timing in releasing the photographs when he did, and for possibly behaving unethically in releasing pictures without Williams's written authorization to do so (*People Weekly,* 1984b). Beyond these relatively mild consequences and a momentary public interest in the matter (based, one suspects, on the novelty of the pictures rather than on their supposed "threat" to society), nothing more was heard of the incident. Clearly, the Ginzburg and Williams cases represent very different periods in the social history of our society, particularly in terms of the public moralities in vogue at these respective times.

Changes of this sort are to be expected as practitioners of varied forms of behavior and moralities seek legitimacy and an opportunity for free expression of what has heretofore been condemned and/or cloaked in secrecy. Again, because moral meanings are human constructions rather than natural law expressions, it may be a bit unrealistic to expect such constructions to stand unchanged and absolute for all time. Rather than being absolute, morality is situationally based. As such, all we may reasonably expect, and what we continually experience, is a periodic change of face.

Glossary

abominations of the body
conditions of one's person resulting from birth, illness, or accident that are commonly regarded as repugnant and perceived as stigma.

achieved status
a social position occupied by reason of the official or public definition of a person's behavior; contrasts with *ascribed status*.

advocacy journalism
the tendency of some journalists to play the role of special pleader without, simultaneously, playing the counter role of critical questioner.

affinity
a general condition leaving one more or less attracted to engaging in a specific pattern of behavior.

alienative group
one that is hostile to or rejects major legitimate values and institutions of the society.

appeal to higher loyalties
a technique of neutralization wherein one justifies his or her rule breaking as a result of being faced with equally binding but mutually exclusive obligations; whichever obligation is satisfied automatically results in violation of the other.

ascribed status
a social position occupied on the basis of the official or public definition of a quality a person is assumed to possess; contrasts with *achieved status*.

autoerotic fatalities
deaths resulting from the use of injurious agents or procedures (for example, asphyxia) to heighten sexual arousal during masturbation.

auxiliary status traits
a set of subsidiary or secondary conditions usually associated with persons occupying a master status.

avowal
a technique of stigma management whereby an actor acknowledges his or her abnormal condition while simultaneously seeking a positive social identity and social status.

awareness
a necessary condition of rule making in which would-be rule makers perceive objective elements as a threat.

banning
assigning or infusing an activity or condition with negative moral meaning; to proscribe the activity as bad, evil, immoral, wrong.

bedevilment
a concern of some rule breakers that if information about their deviation becomes public they will suffer a loss of social acceptability.

blemishes of character
personal qualities attributed to persons known or thought to have engaged in immoral conduct that are themselves stigmatizing.

bureaucratic propaganda
following Altheide and Johnson, "any report [including statistical as well as verbal materials] produced by an organization for evaluation and other practical purposes that is targeted for individuals, committees, or publics who are unaware of its promotive character and the editing processes that shaped the report."

bureaucratization
the process of developing formal organizations and roles, a division of labor, and systematic procedures to deal with specific phenomena. *See institutionalization.*

canons of the scientific method
a series of postulates forming the foundation of the scientific method.

career deviance
a sequence of changing movements, stages, and positions through which one passes, possibly resulting in being identified publicly as deviant, excluded from nondeviant activities, and defining self as deviant.

circuit of agents
a network of role players who concur in the official denunciation and stripping of an actor of his or her social acceptability.

coalition
formal or informal, covert or overt cooperative relations between groups, usually for the pursuit of limited goals.

commitment
a felt obligation to persist in a line of action because of the anticipated negative consequences of discontinuing that line of action.

condemnation of condemners
a technique of neutralization in which one focuses attention on his or her condemners and their alleged immorality; intended to render the accused relatively less reprehensible in appearance.

conflict perspective
the idea that society is the arena of disagreement and conflict between various segments of society regarding values, interests, and morality. See *consensus perspective*.

conformative group
one that tends to embrace dominant social values.

consensus perspective
the idea that the members of society are in essential agreement as to the core values and moral meanings extant in the society; has several implications in sharp contrast with those of the conflict perspective.

contaminative exposure
defiling or dishonoring of one's person or the things associated with one's self.

contracultural
referring to values regarded as inconsistent and in conflict with the values held to prevail in the larger society.

counterfeit secrecy
a mutual pretense between a deviant and others wherein, despite their shared knowledge of the actor's deviation, neither makes reference to it in speech or action.

courtesy stigma
the stigma experienced by those (parents, friends, and so on) intimately associated with persons directly stigmatized.

covering
(cover) the use of a variety of devices or tactics designed to help one present his or her stigma in the least offensive way or to minimize its impact.

crimes without victims
the unlawful but willing exchange of goods and services.

declaratory argument
in law, the belief that the absence of a law against a thing is equal to official endorsement of that thing.

defounding
the classification of events as misdemeanors that satisfy the legal criteria of felonies.

denial of injury
a technique of neutralization in which the wrongfulness of one's actions is reduced by redefining the wrongful action; theft becomes "borrowing," assault becomes a "fist fight," vandalism becomes a "prank," and so on.

denial of responsibility
a technique of neutralization in which deviant actors attribute their behavior to the pressure of external forces over which they have no control.

denial of the victim
a technique of neutralization in which the victim is "transformed" into a deserving target of the offender's wrath; the victim becomes an "evildoer," while the rule breaker becomes a "moral avenger."

denunciation
at a status degradation ceremony, a method presenting information so as to stigmatize the actor and promote the imposition of severe and restrictive penalties; contrast with *pitch*.

destigmatization
the process engaged in for the purpose of eliminating one's deviant identity and replacing it with one that is perceived to be nondeviant or normal.

determinism
(deterministic) any philosophy stressing the causal influence of conditions and events felt to be necessary to the occurrence of subsequent conditions or events.

disavowal
the tendency of some deviant actors to repudiate or deny that their condition or behavior is abnormal; the effort to normalize that which heretofore has been defined as abnormal.

discreditable
referring to that segment of the deviant population whose deviation is not publicly known, who have been symbolically labeled, and who manage to keep their deviance secret.

discredited
referring to those persons whose stigma is self-evident or may be assumed to be known by others.

disidentifier
any symbol used to prevent one being identified as deviant.

diversion
a technique used in some places to divert youthful offenders from the criminal justice system; involves "treating" rule breakers informally rather than processing them through the institutionalized justice system.

effective environment
the highly individualized objects people experience and the meaning people give to these objects.

empiricism
a series of operations or methods used in doing science; emphasizes the importance of sensory experience as the basis of knowledge. See *positivism*.

epistemology
the study (or theory) of the nature and basis of knowledge, its validity and its limits.

essential self
See *substantial self*.

etiology
the study of the cause or origins of a thing; in deviance, of the actions regarded as immoral.

excuse
one form of an account or explanation for behavior that allows the actor to avoid acceptance of full responsibility for the act.

expressive group
one that exists principally for the purpose of serving the immediate personal and/or social needs of the membership. See *instrumental group*.

externalization
one aspect of the process rendering subjective meanings objective; refers to the overt manifestation of initially subjective meanings, preferences, techniques, and the like.

holy crusade
the efforts of moral entrepreneurs that are defended and supported by scriptural and other worldly references.

ideal type
a hypothetical conception of a phenomenon against which actual expressions of the thing may be compared.

identity
a part of self-concept; the variously derived labels or names by which persons are known and on the basis of which they are classified or categorized.

institutionalization
the processes associated with bureaucratized methods: development of organized and systematized rules and roles and the stabilization of these as the "property" of formal organizations. See *bureaucratization*.

instrumental goals
in law, referring to the use of law to directly influence the actions of others.

instrumental group
one that exists principally for the purpose of serving as a "social influence organization," seeking to resist or promote change; in contrast to expressive groups, instrumental groups tend to be political. See *expressive group*.

integral power
usually applied to a situation wherein the distribution of power is so unbalanced as to appear unilateral. See *intercursive power*.

intercursive power
usually applied to a situation in which power is distributed in a bilateral or multilateral fashion, albeit unequal (asymmetrical) in its distribution. See *integral power*.

interest groups
groups organized on the basis of shared and distinctive interests of the members, generally functioning to perpetuate and serve the interests of the membership.

internalization
the process (in socialization) whereby seemingly objective knowledge is acquired by people, resulting in the fusing of self and others.

justification
an explanation for one's behavior wherein one accepts responsibility for the action but denies any immoral or negative aspect to the action.

justification, principled
a justification that entails a conflict of principles, the resolution of which is alleged to be the basis of one's rule-violating action.

justification, situational
a justification resting on actual or alleged situational conditions that permit the wrongful act to be defined as an exception.

legitimacy
a legal, authorized, and public status.

master status
a status that tends to supersede and obscure other statuses one occupies simultaneously.

moral absolutes
universal moral standards and meanings held to apply at all times and places; moral absolutism; contrasts with *moral relativism*.

moral congruence
the consistency in moral meaning (positive or negative) of statuses and their associated auxiliary traits.

moral entrepreneurs
groups (seldom individual actors) who take the initiative and engage in the "business" of (1) defining existing moral rules, (2) seeking to change existing moral rules, or (3) seeking to create moral rules where none exist.

moral relativism
the belief that moral meanings are situationally rooted, changeable, and dependent upon people's construction of them; contrasts with *moral absolutism*.

morality of consequence
a moral code in which one's blamefulness rests on the results of his or her initially wrongful actions, including whether or not these consequences are dealt with by the actor. See *morality of intention*.

morality of intention
a moral code in which one's blamefulness is based on his or her purpose, knowledge, negligence, and recklessness. See *morality of consequence*.

motives
the complex of meanings individuals regard as sufficient reason for their behavior.

mutilation of the body
any of a variety of techniques resulting in one being maimed or in having his or her physical person altered significantly; chemotherapy, shock therapy, and surgical techniques may be included.

myth(s)
socially constructed tales serving to explain events; in the case of deviance, myths often seek to cast rule breaking in counterinstitutional terms.

neutralize
to treat or accommodate to a negatively defined condition by means of altering its definition and reducing its significance.

nominalism
a philosophical position stressing the idea that there are no universal essences.

normal crimes
following Sudnow, a range of offenses commonly dealt with by public defenders and which, therefore, may be handled in routine ways.

normalize
to perceive the unusual or the atypical as ordinary and normal.

objectivation
an aspect of the process of rendering subjective meanings objective; entails the naming of things, the name (independent of the referent) taking on a reified character. Applies to knowledge in general.

objective
referring to the idea that events and qualities of events and conditions are external to human consciousness, that is, that they exist independent of mind; the reverse of *subjective*.

office, theory of
an aspect of the institutionalization process; a rationale for the methods employed by formal organizations to fulfill their task; renders the task meaningful and provides a sense of order.

omittive behavior
the avoidance of people, acts, words, or conversational topics, and so on, when confronted by or in the presence of select segments of the deviant population.

ontology
the study of being and reality, and the essence and relations of things.

optimize
to treat something in optimistic ways despite a general negative definition of the thing.

pederast
(pederasty, pedophilia) one who has an erotic craving for children, sexual attraction to children, deriving sexual gratification from them.

personal defacement
the marring or spoiling of one's ordinary appearance by removal of the materials and services by which that appearance is maintained.

pessimize
a neologism identifying the tendency to perceive things negatively and, on that basis, regard them as intolerable.

pitch
at a status degradation ceremony, a method of presenting information so as to cast the offender in the most favorable moral light; contrasts with denunciation.

plea bargaining
a process whereby defendants in criminal cases and prosecutors negotiate a plea, usually of guilt; the defendant may receive a reduction in the charge and/or penalty, while the prosecutor is freed of the necessity of expending scarce resources in acquiring a conviction.

positivism
the idea that the proper way to study reality and man is to employ the methods of science. See *empiricism*.

power
following Wrong, "the production of intended effects by some men on other men." In general terms, a variety of means used to control the behavior of others.

pressure groups
interest groups that work to protect their interests by recourse to public law.

primary deviance (deviant)
the initial stage in a deviant career; one whose rule breaking is incidental to his or her involvement in socially acceptable behaviors; akin to secret deviance. See *secondary deviance*.

primary sexual identity
one's fundamental sexual inclination, either heterosexual, homosexual, or bisexual; not to be confused with sex roles, sex norms, or other cultural prescriptions or proscriptions, or one's actual behavior.

pure deviant
similar to secondary deviant; one whose rule breaking is known and responded to by others.

rate
a ratio relating the size of one number to that of another.

recipe knowledge
general normative information concerning what is and is not considered correct and on which people base routine daily activities.

reflexive activity
self-interaction; one becomes the object of his or her own thoughts or action.

reification
the process or result of defining and behaving toward things that are abstract as if they were material and concrete.

retrospective interpretation
a complex cognitive process in which the character of a known deviant actor is rendered consistent with his or her behavior; involves characterological transformation.

role engulfment
long-term social psychological consequences of labeling; a cumulative process wherein one's deviant identity becomes increasingly central in his or her relations with others.

scapegoating
attributing one's problems to the alleged deficiencies or weaknesses of others.

secondary deviance (deviant)
an advanced stage in a deviant career characterized by the centrality or salience of others' reactions to one's rule breaking; one whose life becomes organized about the facts of his or her deviance. See *primary deviant*.

secret deviant
one whose rule breaking is neither publicly recognized nor responded to as such. Similar to *primary deviant*.

secret society
an association organized around the principles of exclusiveness and secrecy of membership; activity of the group may be highly variable (religious, political, and so on) and either deviant or nondeviant.

self-concept
a complex of meanings or definitions people have of themselves, acquired in interaction with others.

self-fulfilling prophecy
an initially false definition of things that is reacted to in such a way as to promote its validation.

sequential models
explanatory systems in which causal factors are seen to develop over time and that are alleged to operate at different times. See *simultaneous models*.

simultaneous models
explanatory systems in which all causal factors are assumed to be operative at the same time. See *sequential models*.

situated moral meanings
the application of general or abstract moral meanings to specific situations and their consequent departure from the abstract meaning.

situated self
self-regarding feelings that arise in interaction and that are associated with specific situations, roles, and statuses; corresponds to Mead's "me"; contrasts with *substantial self*.

situated transactions
a series of interactions between two or more persons, limited to the time and place they are in one another's physical presence.

social causation
the perceived (socially created) relationship between things and events, and in terms of which people respond to these things and events.

social distance
the degree of sympathetic understanding between people or groups of people.

social reality
the meanings (definitions, conceptions, and typifications) people assign to things in their environment and in terms of which they seek to introduce order to their world.

status degradation ceremony
any of a variety of public rituals intended to bring about and give public legitimacy to a reduction in one's public status.

stereotypes
group-shared ideas about the nature of a category of people.

stigma
a sign or symbol indicating the bearer's low social and/or moral position.

stigma management
any of a variety of methods used individually or collectively to promote control of information about one's deviation and spoiled identity; efforts to alter moral meaning attributed to persons having a spoiled identity so as to reduce the significance of their deviance.

stigma symbols
signs that call attention to one's deviation or spoiled identity.

stripping
official removal of the symbols by which one identifies himself or herself as a socially acceptable person.

subjective
referring to those things having their origin in the mind, perception, or consciousness of the actor; contrasts with *objective*.

substantial self
corresponding to Mead's "I," refers to that aspect of self felt to be independent of specific situations and what the person considers themselves to be "in essence"; contrasts with *situational self*.

symbolic goals
in law, the use of law to legitimate the goals and purposes of some groups without directly influencing others' actions.

symbolic interactionism
a form of social psychology stressing the idea that human behavior and personality rest on people's ability to create and use symbols to transmit meaning.

symbolic labeling
self-labeling; the application of stigma without benefit of public ceremony.

symbolic universe
an integrated set of ideas/meanings providing a sense of orderliness and legitimacy to the elements comprising the institutional order.

symbols
stimuli that have learned meanings and values attached to them.

tearoom
a public place, such as a restroom, where impersonal homosexual encounters occur.

techniques of neutralization
any of a variety of methods of "devices" used to reduce (neutralize) the binding force of moral norms on the actor and assist him or her to maintain a socially acceptable image of self despite having violated rules. See *appeal to higher loyalties, condemnation of condemners, denial of injury, denial of the victim.*

territories, home
places where one has freedom of behavior and a sense of intimacy, as well as control over the area.

territories, interactional
places where people engage in social interaction; the space in which a specific interact occurs.

territories, public
places to which one has access by reason of citizenship.

test case
in law, a court case promoted by interest groups in the belief that the decision is likely to influence future cases resting on similar points of law and in which the interest group has an abiding concern.

total institutions
organizations that demand total subordination of the client population and that severely restrict interaction between clients and nonclients.

transfer of authority
the investing of ideas, proposals, and the like with legitimacy on the basis of the prestige of those with whom they are identified, such as heroes, esteemed public figures, and others.

transparency
a concern on the part of rule breakers that others may "see through" them and perceive them as deviant.

transsexual
one who, through surgery and socialization, seeks a change in gender and/or sex identity.

tribal stigma
conditions such as nationality, skin color, and so on that are transmitted through lineages or families and regarded by others as stigmatizing.

turned on
used in two senses: (1) aware of and knowledgeable about a thing as a result of experience; (2) converted to a behavior as a result of experiences defined as pleasurable and satisfying.

typification
the way(s) people classify events, objects, or other people and in terms of which they respond to them.

unfounding
a technical/legal tactic whereby alleged violations of law are declared to have no factual basis, most often because the alleged violation is perceived by authorities to be unprosecutable.

variable
any phenomenon that can change, be measured, or be quantified.

voluntary association
a group seeking to promote the common interest of the membership, affiliation being noncoercive.

willing
a condition in which one is open or free to engage in a given pattern of behavior at a specific time and place.

Bibliography

Achievement, The National Voice of the Disabled
  1981   "An Open Letter to Jerry Lewis." November:2.

Adler, Patricia and Peter Adler
  1978   "Tiny-Dopers: A Case of Deviant Socialization." *Symbolic Interaction* 1(Spring):90–105.

Advocate, The
  1975   "L.A. Police Department's Position on Gay People." February 26:8.
  1984a   "Supreme Court Finally Accepts a Gay Case," October 30:22.
  1984b   "Gay-Bashing Bill Signed in California," October 30:23.

Akers, Ronald L.
  1964   "Socio-Economic Status and Delinquent Behavior: A Retest." *Journal of Research in Crime and Delinquency* 1 (January):38–46.

Alinsky, Saul D.
  1972   *Rules for Radicals, A Practical Primer for Realistic Radicals.* New York: Random House.

Allon, Natalie
  1973   "Group Dieting Rituals." *Society* 10 (January/February):36–42.

Altheide, David Lynn
  1974   "The News Scene." Unpublished Ph.D. dissertation. San Diego: University of California.
  1976   *Creating Reality, How TV News Distorts Events.* Beverly Hills, Calif.: Sage Publications.

Altheide, David L. and John M. Johnson
  1980   *Bureaucratic Propaganda.* Boston: Allyn and Bacon.

Altman, Dennis
  1971   *Homosexual Oppression and Liberation.* New York: Avon Books.

American Druggist
  1968   "The Pharmacist as a Drug Addict." December 2, 1968. Cited in Paul R. Elmore and Larry Cohen, "Addiction Among Pharmacists and Physicians," Pacific Sociological Association, Anaheim, Calif., April 1970.

American Psychiatric Association
  1973   Press release. Pp. 19–20 in M. Spector and J.I. Kitsuse, *Constructing Social Problems*, Menlo Park, Calif.: Cummings Publishing.

Anderson, Nels
  1923   *The Hobo, The Sociology of the Homeless Man.* Chicago: University of Chicago Press.

Anderson, Robert T.
  1968   "From Mafia to Cosa Nostra." Pp. 269–279 in Marcello Truzzi, ed., *Sociology and Everyday Life.* Englewood Cliffs, N.J.: Prentice-Hall.

Anderson, Scott P.
  1978   "Dispatch." *The Advocate.* October 4:8ff.

Anonymous
  1974   "Shooting Up: Autobiography of a Heroin Addict." Pp. 59–68 in Jerry Jacobs, ed., *Deviance: Field Studies and Self Disclosures.* Palo Alto, Calif.: National Press Books.

Aptheker, Herbert
  1943   *American Negro Slave Revolts.* New York: International Publishers.

Arizona Gay News
  1978   "Perspective." November 23:4.

Arizona Republic (Phoenix)
  1975   "Priests Ordered to Refuse Communion to Women in Groups." April 9:A-14.
  1977a   "Jail Avoided by Defendant in Sex Change." March 9:B-11.
  1977b   "Chiefs of Police Oppose Homosexuals as Officers." October 7:A-8.
  1980a   "Berrigans, How Can They Be Faulted For Their Devotion?" (Colman McCarthy), October 15:A-7.
  1980b   "What Is the Point of Leading People into Violating the Law?" (William Raspberry), October 10:A-7.
  1980c   "Series of Sex Killings Worry Californians," September 21:B-15.
  1980d   "Fate of Deaf Accused Killer Remains Tangled in Legal Web," October 10:A-13.
  1980e   "Jean Harris and the Scarsdale Diet Doctor" (Andy Rooney), March 27:A-18.
  1980f   "Jenkins Found Guilty but Freed without Penalty," December 19:D-1.
  1980g   "Gay Airman Is Ordered Reinstated," September 10:A-5.
  1980h   "Homosexual Settles Case with Military," November 25:A-9.
  1980i   "Glendale Residents Oppose Halfway House Despite Switch," February 26:A-5; March 1:B-1.
  1980j   "Town Denies Gifts to Illegitimate Child," January 5:A-10.

1980k   "Fired Gay Police Officer Plans Fight to Regain Job," September 10:B-1.

1980l   "Phoenix Lesbian Wins Custody of Young Daughters From Court," April 14:A-1.

1981a   "Denver Woman Declares War on Pulpit Tyranny," November 28:F-4.

1981b   "Coalition Determined to Clean up 'Sodom and Gomorrah,' " February 11:A-2.

1981c   "John W. Hinckley, Jr., a Wanderer with Nowhere to Go," April 6:A-1 and A-3.

1981d   "Shared Vision: Blind Student and Canine Companion Walk 10 Miles to Demonstrate Superiority of Guide Dogs to Canes," December 12:A-1 and A-13.

1981e   "Endorsements Dry up for Billie Jean King," September 29:C-9.

1981f   "Transsexuals Seek Changes in Birth Records," October 4:AA-7.

1981g   "Tests Start on Man-made Hormone Designed to Spur Children's Growth," December 20:A-8.

1981h   "Transsexual's Wish Comes True: Sister Bears Child for Her," January 18:B-5.

1981i   "Homosexual Given OK to Adopt Lover," February 5:E-9.

1982a   "Conscience Haunts Purse Thief," May 2:B-8.

1982b   "Junkie Doctors 'Adept' at Hiding Habit," February 17:B-10.

1982c   "Cruel Reminders Haunt Foster Mom of Executed Killer," March 14:B-9.

1982d   "Reagan Urged to Decree Anti-pornography Week," October 21:A-16.

1983a   "Addicted Doctors Saved by Self-help," February 14:A-1.

1983b   "Anti-porn Fight Began as Favor to Priest," March 28:A-9.

1983c   "Gay Power, Fledgling Political Movement Strives to Be Lobbying Force in Congress," December 25:C-3.

1983d   "Special-interest Funds Listed for 80 Freshmen in Congress," October 2:A-12.

1983e   "Gay Bar Rotten, to Corps; Toys Rescued," December 23:A-12.

1983f   "Baptistball, Old Rival 'Discovered' to Be Catholic, Is Crossed off Schedule," December 31:A-1.

1983g   "Democratic Hopefuls Vying for Gay Support," December 11:AA-20.

1984a   "Gay Rights Bill Poses Dilemma," March 8:A-6.

1984b   "Center Ranks Suicide as No. 2 Death Cause for Well-to-do Teens," May 15:A-2.

1984c   "Churches Take Stock Against Nuclear Ads," January 5:A-3.

1984d   "Honor Group Expulsion of Pregnant Teen Illegal," September 5:A-6.

Ashman, Charles R.
1973   *The Finest Judges Money Can Buy and Other Forms of Judicial Pollution.* Los Angeles: Nash.

Babbie, Earl
1979   *The Practice of Social Research.* 2d ed. Belmont, Calif.: Wadsworth.

Bahr, Howard M.
1973   *Skid Row: An Introduction to Disaffiliation.* New York: Oxford University Press.

Balint, Michael
1957   *The Doctor, His Patient, and the Illness.* New York: International Universities Press.

Ball, Harry V. and Lawrence M. Friedman
1965   "The Use of Criminal Sanctions in the Enforcement of Economic Legislation: A Sociological View," *Stanford Law Review* 17 (January):197–223.

Bannan, John F. and Rosemary S. Bannan
1974   *Law, Morality and Vietnam.* Bloomington, Ind.: Indiana University Press.

Barber, Bernard
1973   "Resistance by Scientists to Scientific Discovery." Cited in William J. Chambliss, ed., *Sociological Readings in the Conflict Perspective.* Reading, Mass.: Addison-Wesley.

Barker, Roger G.
1948   "The Social Psychology of Physical Disability." *Journal of Social Issues* 4 (Fall):28–38.

Barnes, Harry Elmer and Negley K. Teeters
1951   *New Horizons in Criminology.* 2d ed. Englewood Cliffs, N.J.: Prentice-Hall.

Bartell, Gilbert D.
1971   *Group Sex, A Scientist's Eyewitness Report on the American Way of Swinging.* New York: Peter H. Wyden.

Barthell, Charles N.
1983   "Deaf and Gay: Where Is My Community?" Pp. 147–157 in William P. McCrone, Roger L. Beach and Frank R. Zieziula, eds., *Networking and Deafness.* Silver Spring, Md.: American Deafness and Rehabilitation Association.

Bay, Christian
1967   "Civil Disobedience: Prerequisite for Democracy in a Mass Society." Pp. 163–183 in David Stolz, ed., *Political Theory and Social Change.* New York: Atherton Press.

Becker, Howard S.
1960   "Notes on the Concept of Commitment." *American Journal of Sociology* 66 (July):32–40.

1966   *Social Problems, A Modern Approach.* Ed. New York: Wiley and Sons.

1970   *Sociological Work, Method and Substance.* Chicago: Aldine.

1973   *Outsiders, Studies in the Sociology of Deviance.* Rev. ed. New York: Free Press.

Before You Go On a Diet

n.d.   Fat Underground, P.O. Box 597, Venice, California 90291.

Behan, Brendan
1958   *Borstal Boy,* New York: Avon Books.

Bell, Daniel
1962   *The End of Ideology.* Rev. ed. New York: Free Press.

Bell, Robert R.
1976   *Social Deviance, A Substantive Analysis.* Rev. ed. Homewood, Ill.: Dorsey Press.

Bennett, Lerone, Jr.
1965   *Confrontation: Black and White.* Baltimore: Penguin Books.

Bennett, W. Lance and Martha S. Feldman
1981   *Reconstructing Reality in the Courtroom, Justice and Judgement in American Culture,* New Brunswick, N.J.: Rutgers University Press.

Bensman, Joseph and Robert Lilienfeld
1979   *Between Public and Private, Lost Boundaries of the Self.* New York: Free Press.

Berelson, Bernard and Patricia J. Salter
1946   "Majority and Minority Americans: An Analysis of Magazine Fiction." *Public Opinion Quarterly* 10 (Summer):168–190.

Berger, Peter L.
1963   *Invitation to Sociology, A Humanistic Perspective.* New York: Doubleday Anchor.

Berger, Peter and Thomas Luckmann
1967   *The Social Construction of Reality.* New York: Doubleday.

Berkowitz, Leonard and Nigel Walker
1967   "Laws and Moral Judgements." *Sociometry* 30 (December):410–422.

Berrigan, Philip
1971   *Prison Journals of a Priest Revolutionary.* New York: Ballantine Books.

Berube, Allan
1983   "Coming Out Under Fire." *Mother Jones* 8 (February/March):23–29ff.

Best, Joel and David F. Luckenbill
1980   "The Social Organization of Deviants." *Social Problems* 28 (October):14–31.

Bieber, Irving et al.
1962   *Homosexuality, A Psychoanalytic Study of Male Homosexuals.* New York: Vintage Books.

Birenbaum, Arnold
1970   "On Managing a Courtesy Stigma." *Journal of Health and Social Behavior* 11 (September):196–206.

Bittner, Egon
1967   "The Police on Skid-Row: A Study of Peace Keeping." *American Sociological Review* 32 (October):699–715.

Blaustein, Albert P. and Clarence C. Ferguson
1957   *Desegregation and the Law: The Meaning and Effect of the School Desegregation Cases.* New Brunswick, N.J.: Rutgers University Press.

Bloch, Herbert A. and Gilbert Geis
1970   *Man, Crime, and Society.* 2d ed. New York: Random House.

Blok, Anton
1974   *The Mafia of a Sicilian Village, 1860–1960, A Study of Violent Peasant Entrepreneurs.* London: Basil Blackwell and Mott Limited.

Blumberg, Abraham S.
1967   *Criminal Justice.* Chicago: Quadrangle Books.

Blumer, Herbert
1955   "Collective Behavior." Pp. 165–222 in Alfred McClung Lee, ed., *Principles of Sociology.* New York: Barnes and Noble.

1956   "Sociological Analysis and the Variable." *American Sociological Review* 21 (December):683–690.

Bogdan, Robert
1974   *Being Different: The Autobiography of Jane Fry.* New York: Wiley and Sons.

Boggan, E. Carrington et al.
1975   *The Rights of Gay People, The Basic ACLU Guide to a Gay Person's Rights.* New York: Avon Books.

Bordua, David J.
1962   "Some Comments on Theories of Group Delinquency." *Sociological Inquiry* 33 (Spring):245–260.

Box, Steven
1981   *Deviance, Reality and Society.* 2d ed. New York: Holt, Rinehart and Winston.

Boyle, Bob
1978   "Legalizing Pot Could Net State Big Tax Money." *Florida Times-Union* (Jacksonville), August 13.

Briar, Scott, and Irving Piliavin
1965   "Delinquency, Situational Inducements and Commitment to Conformity." *Social Problems* 13 (Summer):35–45.

Briedis, Catherine
1975   "Marginal Deviants: Teenage Girls Experience Community Response to Premarital Sex and Pregnancy." *Social Problems* 22 (April):480–493.

Brodie, Fawn
  1945   *No Man Knows My History*. New York: Alfred A. Knopf.

Brody, Jane E.
  1984   "Autoerotic Deaths of Youths Causes Widening Concern," *New York Times*, March 27:17 and 20.

Brown, Claude
  1966   *Manchild in the Promised Land*. New York: Signet Books.

Brown, J.W., D. Glaser, E. Waxer and G. Geis
  1974   "Turning Off: Cessation of Marihuana Use After College." *Social Problems* 21(April):527–538.

Brown, Richard H.
  1977   "The Emergence of Existential Thought: Philosophical Perspectives on Positivist and Humanist Forms of Social Theory." Pp. 77–100 in Jack D. Douglas and John M. Johnson, eds. *Existential Sociology*. New York: Cambridge University Press.

Brownmiller, Susan
  1975   *Against Our Will: Men, Women and Rape*. New York: Simon and Schuster.

Bryan, James H.
  1967   "Apprenticeships in Prostitution." Pp. 146–164 in John H. Gagnon and William Simon, eds., *Sexual Deviance*. New York: Harper and Row.

Buckner, H. Taylor
  1978   "Transformation of Reality in the Legal Process." Pp. 311–323 in Thomas Luckmann, ed., *Phenomenology and Sociology, Selected Readings*. New York: Penguin Books.

Bugliosi, Vincent (with Curt Gentry)
  1974   *Helter Skelter, The True Story of the Manson Murders*. New York: W.W. Norton.

Burns, W. Haywood
  1963   *The Voices of Negro Protest in America*. New York: Oxford University Press.

Bustamente, Jorge A.
  1972   "The 'Wetback' as Deviant: An Application of Labeling Theory." *American Journal of Sociology* 77 (January):706–718.

Cahnman, Werner J.
  1968   "The Stigma of Obesity." *The Sociological Quarterly* 9 (Summer):283–299.

Cameron, Mary Owen
  1964   *The Booster and the Snitch, Department Store Shoplifting*. New York: The Free Press.

Camus, Albert
  1954   *The Stranger*. New York: Random House.

Carmichael, Stokely and Charles V. Hamilton
  1967   *Black Power*. New York: Random House.

Carrier, J.M.
  1976   "Family Attitudes and Mexican Male Homosexuality." *Urban Life* 50 (October):359–375.

Catanzaro, Ronald J.
  1967   "Psychiatric Aspects of Alcoholism." Pp. 31–45 in David J. Pittman, ed., *Alcoholism*. New York: Harper and Row.
  1968   *Alcoholism, The Total Treatment Approach*. Springfield, Ill.: Charles C. Thomas.

Caudill, W. et al.
  1952   "Social Structure and Interaction Processes on a Psychiatric Ward." *American Journal of Orthopsychiatry* 22 (April):314–334.

Cavan, Ruth S.
  1928   *Suicide*. Chicago: University of Chicago Press.
  1969   *Juvenile Delinquency: Development, Treatment, and Control*. 2d ed. Philadelphia: J.B. Lippincott.

Cavan, Sherri
  1966   *Liquor License*. Chicago: Aldine.

Chambliss, William J.
  1969   *Crime and the Legal Process*. New York: McGraw-Hill.
  1971   "A Visit to San Miguel." *The Humanist* 31 (July/August):24–25.
  1973a   *Sociological Readings in the Conflict Perspective*. Reading, Mass.: Addison-Wesley.
  1973b   "The Saints and the Roughnecks." *Society* 11 (November/December):24–31.
  1975   *Criminal Law in Action*. Santa Barbara, Calif.: Hamilton.
  1978   *On the Take, From Petty Crooks to Presidents*. Bloomington, Ind.: Indiana University Press.

Chambliss, William and Richard H. Nagasawa
  1969   "On the Validity of Official Statistics: A Comparative Study of White, Black, and Japanese High-School Boys." *Journal of Research in Crime and Delinquency* 6 (January):71–77.

Chambliss, William J. and Robert B. Seidman
  1971   *Law, Order, and Power*. Reading, Mass.: Addison-Wesley.

Charon, Joel M.
  1979   *Symbolic Interactionsim: An Introduction, An Intrepretation, An Integration*. Englewood Cliffs, N.J.: Prentice-Hall.

Chernin, Kim
  1981   *The Obsession, Reflections on the Tyranny of Slenderness*, New York: Harper and Row.

Christensen, Harold T.
  1953   "Studies in Child Spacing: I-Premarital Pregnancy as Measured by the Spacing of the First Birth from Marriage." *American Sociological Review* 18 (February):53–59.

Clark, Brian
  1978   *Whose Life Is It Anyway?* New York: Avon Books.

Clark, John P. and Eugene Wenninger
  1962   "Socio-Economic Class and Area as Correlates of Illegal Behavior Among Juveniles." *American Sociological Review* 27 (December):826–834.

Clausen, John A.
  1976   "Mental Disorders." Pp. 103–139 in Robert K. Merton and Robert Nisbet, eds., *Contemporary Social Problems.* 4th ed. New York: Harcourt Brace Jovanovich.

Cleland, Max
  1982   *Strong at the Broken Places.* New York: Berkley Books.

Coburn, Judith
  1983   "Terror in Saigontown, U.S.A." *Mother Jones* 8 (February/March)14ff.

Cohen, Albert K.
  1955   *Delinquent Boys: The Culture of the Gang.* Glencoe, Ill.: The Free Press.

Columbia Journalism Review
  1981   "National News Council Report." January/February:76–83.

Commission on Obscenity and Pornography
  1970   *Report of the Commission on Obscenity and Pornography.* New York: Bantam Books.

Connell, Noreen and Cassandra Wilson
  1974   *Rape: The First Sourcebook for Women.* New York: New American Library.

Conrad, Peter
  1975   "The Discovery of Hyperkinesis: Notes on the Medicalization of Deviant Behavior." *Social Problems* 23 (October):12–21.

Cooley, Charles Horton
  1902   *Human Nature and the Social Order.* New York: Charles Scribner's Sons.

Cory, Donald Webster
  1951   *The Homosexual in America: A Subjective Approach.* New York: Greenberg.

Corzine, Jay and Richard Kirby
  1977   "Cruising the Truckers: Sexual Encounters in a Highway Rest Area." *Urban Life* 6 (July):171–192.

Covington, Jeanette
  1984   "Insulation from Labeling." *Criminology* 22 (November):619–643.

Coyote Howls
  1978   "Letters to the Madam." n.d. Volume 5 (Ball Edition).

Cressey, Donald R.
  1969   *Theft of the Nation, The Structure and Operations of Organized Crime in America.* New York: Harper and Row.

Dahrendorf, R.
  1959   *Class and Class Conflict in Industrial Society.* Stanford, Calif.: Stanford University Press.
  1964   "Out of Utopia: Toward a Reorientation of Sociological Analysis." Pp. 209–227 in Lewis A. Coser and Bernard Rosenberg, eds., *Sociological Theory: A Book of Readings.* New York: Macmillan.

Dank, Barry M.
  1971   "Coming Out in the Gay World." *Psychiatry* 34 (May):180–197.

Davis, F. James
  1976   "Beliefs, Values, Power, and Public Definitions of Deviance." Pp. 50–59 in F. James Davis and Richard Stivers, eds., *The Collective Definition of Deviance.* New York: The Free Press.

Davis, Fred
  1961   "Deviance Disavowal: The Management of Strained Interaction by the Visibly Handicapped." *Social Problems* 9 (Fall):120–132.

Davis, Nanette J.
  1975   *Sociological Constructions of Deviance, Perspectives and Issues in the Field.* Dubuque, Iowa: W.C. Brown.

Davis, Richard L.
  1973   "The Labeling Perspective and Juvenile Delinquency." Unpublished Ph.D. dissertation. University of New Hampshire.

Dawley, David
  1973   *A Nation of Lords.* New York: Doubleday.

Delph, Edward William
  1978   *The Silent Community, Public Homosexual Encounters.* Beverly Hills, Calif.: Sage Publications.

Denes, Magda
  1977   *In Necessity and Sorrow, Life and Death in an Abortion Hospital.* Baltimore: Penguin Books.

Dentler, Robert A. and Lawrence J. Monroe
  1961   "Early Adolescent Theft." *American Sociological Review* 26 (October):733–743.

Dickson, Donald T.
  1968   "Bureaucracy and Morality: An Organizational Perspective on a Moral Crusade." *Social Problems* 16 (Fall):143–156.

Dictionary of American Biography
  1930   "Anthony Comstock." Volume IV. New York: Charles Scribner's Sons.

Dohrenwend, Bruce P.
  1975   "Sociocultural and Social-Psychological Factors in the Genesis of Mental Disorders." *Journal of Health and Social Behavior* 16 (December):365–392.

Dominick, Joseph R.
1978   "Crime and Law Enforcement in the Mass Media." Pp. 105–128 in Charles Winick, ed., *Deviance and Mass Media.* Beverly Hills: Sage Publications.

Douglas, Jack D.
1967   *The Social Meanings of Suicide.* Princeton, N.J.: Princeton University Press.
1970   *Deviance and Respectability.* Ed. New York: Basic Books.
1971a   *American Social Order, Social Rules in a Pluralistic Society.* New York: Free Press-Macmillan.
1971b   "The Rhetoric of Science and the Origins of Statistical Social Thought: The Case of Durkheim's Suicide." Pp. 44–57 in Edward A. Tiryakian, ed., *The Phenomenon of Sociology.* New York: Appleton-Century-Crofts.
1977   "Shame and Deceit in Creative Deviance." Pp. 59–86 in E. Sagarin, ed., *Deviance and Social Change.* Beverly Hills, Calif.: Sage Publications.

Douglas, Jack D. and Paul K. Rasmussen, with Carol Ann Flanagan
1977   *The Nude Beach.* Beverly Hills: Sage Publications.

Drake, St. Clair and Horace R. Cayton
1962   *Black Metropolis, A Study of Negro Life in a Northern City.* New York: Harper and Row.

Dunford, Franklin W. and Philip R. Kunz
1973   "The Neutralization of Religious Dissonance." *Review of Religious Research* 15 (Fall):2–9.

Durkheim, Emile
1951   *Suicide, A Study of Sociology.* (Translated by John A. Spaulding and George Simpson.) New York: Free Press-Macmillan.

Emerson, Robert M.
1969   *Judging Delinquents, Context and Process in Juvenile Court.* Chicago: Aldine.

Empey, Lamar T.
1982   *American Delinquency, Its Meaning and Construction.* Homewood, Ill.: Dorsey Press.

Encyclopaedia Britannica
1974   "John Brown." *Micropaedia,* Vol. II:308; "Carry Nation." *Micropaedia,* Vol. VII:207. Chicago: Helen Hemingway Benton.

Encyclopedia of Associations
1978   "Invisible Empire Knights of the Ku Klux Klan." Volume 1, National Organizations of the U.S. Section 9, Public Affairs Organizations. Chicago: Gale Research Co.

Ennis, Philip H.
1967   *Criminal Victimization in the United States, A Report of a National Survey.* Washington, D.C.: U.S. Government Printing Office.

Epstein, Edward Jay
1977   "Peddling a Drug Scare." *Columbia Journalism Review* (November/December):51–56.

Erickson, Patricia G. and Michael S. Goodstadt
1979   "Legal Stigma for Marijuana Possession." *Criminology* 17 (August):208–216.

Erikson, Kai T.
1964   "Notes on the Sociology of Deviance." Pp. 9–21 in Howard S. Becker, ed., *The Other Side, Perspectives on Deviance.* New York: Free Press.

Etzioni, Amitai
1964   *Modern Organizations.* Englewood Cliffs, N.J.: Prentice-Hall.

Fairfield, L.
1959   "Notes on Prostitution." *British Journal of Delinquency* 9 (January):164–173.

Faris, R.E.L. and H. Warren Dunham
1939   *Mental Disorders in Urban Areas: An Ecological Study of Schizophrenia and Other Psychoses.* Chicago: University of Chicago Press.

Farrington, David P.
1977   "The Effects of Public Labeling." *British Journal of Criminology* 17 (April):112–125.

Federal Bureau of Investigation
1985   *Uniform Crime Reports.* Washington, D.C.: U.S. Government Printing Office.

Feldman, Egal
1967   "Prostitution, the Alien Woman and the Progressive Imagination, 1910–1915." *American Quarterly* 19 (Summer):192–206.

Feldman, Saul D.
1975   "The Presentation of Shortness in Everyday Life—Height and Heightism in American Sociology: Toward a Sociology of Stature." Paper presented before The American Sociological Association, Denver, Colorado.

Fink, Stephen L., James K. Skipper, Jr. and Phyllis N. Hallenbeck
1968   "Physical Disability and Problems in Marriage." *Journal of Marriage and the Family* 30 (February):64–73.

Fontana, Vincent J.
1973   *Somewhere a Child Is Crying, Maltreatment—Causes and Prevention.* New York: New American Library.

Franklin, John Hope
1956   *From Slavery to Freedom: A History of American Negroes.* 2d Rev. ed. New York: Alfred A. Knopf.

Frazier, Charles E.
1976   *Theoretical Approaches to Deviance: An Evaluation.* Columbus, Ohio: Charles E. Merrill.

Freeman, Howard E. and Ozzie G. Simmons
1961 "Feelings of Stigma Among Relatives of Former Mental Patients." *Social Problems* 8 (Spring):312–321.

Freeman, Jo
1973 "Origins of the Women's Movement." *American Journal of Sociology* 78 (January):792–811.
1975 *The Politics of Women's Liberation.* New York: David McKay.

Frutig, Judith
1975 "Griffin Seeks Probe on Hoffa Mystery." *The Christian Science Monitor,* December 4:50.

Funk, Robert
1981 "A Disenfranchised People: Disabled Citizens and the Right to Vote." *Disability Rights Review* 1 (October):1–2ff.

Furey, Thomas
1961 "Wave of Bums Sweeps Over Parks, Streets." *New York World Telegram.* Cited in Howard M. Bahr, *Skid Row, An Introduction to Disaffiliation.* New York: Oxford University Press.

Gable, Richard W.
1958 "Political Interest Groups as Policy Shapers." *Annals of the American Academy of Political and Social Science* 319 (September):84–93.

Gagnon, John H. and William Simon
1968 "Homosexuality: The Formulation of a Sociological Perspective." Pp. 349–361 in Mark Lefton, James K. Skipper, and Charles H. McCaghy, eds., *Approaches to Deviance: Theories, Concepts, and Research Findings.* New York: Appleton-Century-Crofts.

Galliher, John F. and Allyn Walker
1977 "The Puzzle of the Social Origins of the Marihuana Tax Act of 1937." *Social Problems* 24 (February):367–376.

Gamson, William A.
1968 *Power and Discontent.* Homewood, Ill.: Dorsey Press.
1975 *The Strategy of Social Protest.* Homewood, Ill.: Dorsey Press.

Garfinkel, Harold
1956 "Conditions of Successful Degradation Ceremonies." *American Journal of Sociology* 61 (March):420–424.

Garner, Brian and Richard W. Smith
1977 "Are There Really Any Gay Male Athletes? An Empirical Survey." *Journal of Sex Research* 13 (February):22–34.

Geis, Gilbert
1972 *Not the Law's Business? An Examination of Homosexuality, Abortion, Prostitution, Narcotics and Gambling in the United States.* National Institute of Mental Health. Washington, D.C.: U.S. Government Printing Office.
1977 "The Heavy Electrical Equipment Antitrust Cases of 1961." Pp. 117–132 in Gilbert Geis and Robert F. Meier, eds., *White Collar Crime, Offenses in Business, Politics, and the Professions.* New York: The Free Press.

Geller, Allen and Maxwell Boas
1969 *The Drug Beat.* New York: McGraw-Hill.

Gerbner, George
1978 "Deviance and Power, Symbolic Functions of Drug Abuse." Pp. 13–30 in Charles Winick, ed., *Deviance and Mass Media.* Beverly Hills: Sage Publications.

Gibbs, Jack P. and Walter T. Martin
1964 *Status Integration and Suicide.* Eugene, Ore.: University of Oregon Press.

Glaser, Daniel
1971 *Social Deviance.* Chicago: Markham.

Gleidman, John and William Roth
1980 *The Unexpected Minority, Handicapped Children in America.* New York: Harcourt Brace Jovanovich.

Goffman, Erving
1959 *The Presentation of Self in Everyday Life.* New York: Doubleday Anchor Books.
1961 *Asylums, Essays on the Situation of Mental Patients and Other Inmates.* New York: Doubleday Anchor Books.
1963 *Stigma, Notes on the Management of Spoiled Identity.* Englewood Cliffs, N.J.: Prentice-Hall.
1973 "The Moral Career of the Mental Patient." Pp. 95–105 in Earl Rubington and Martin S. Weinberg, eds., *Deviance, The Interactionist Perspective.* 2d ed. New York: Macmillan.

Gold, Martin
1966 "Undetected Delinquent Behavior." *The Journal of Research in Crime and Delinquency* 3 (January):27–46.
1970 *Delinquent Behavior in an American City.* Belmont, Calif.: Brooks/Cole.

Gold, Martin and Jay R. Williams
1969 "National Study of the Aftermath of Apprehension." *Perspectus, A Journal of Law Reform* 3 (December):3–38.

Goode, Erich
1972 *Drugs in American Society.* New York: Alfred A. Knopf.
1975 "On Behalf of Labeling Theory." *Social Problems* 22 (June): 570–583.
1981 "Drugs and Crime." Pp. 227–272 in Abraham S. Blumberg, ed., *Current Perspectives on Criminal Behavior.* New York: Alfred A. Knopf.

Goode, William J. and Paul K. Hatt
1952   *Methods in Social Research.* New York: McGraw-Hill.

Gordon, C. Wayne and Nicholas Babchuk
1959   "A Typology of Voluntary Associations." *American Sociological Review* 24 (February):22–29.

Gowman, Alan G.
1956   "Blindness and the Role of the Companion." *Social Problems* 4 (July):68–75.

Graves, William
1980   "I Want to Make People Laugh." *Mainstream, Magazine of the Able-Disabled* 5 (June):9 and 15.

Greenwald, Harold
1958   *The Call Girl, A Social and Psychoanalytic Study.* New York: Ballantine Books.

Gregory-Lewis, Sasha
1978   "Politics, Californians Face Proposition 6 and Will It Be Written, Mene, Mene, Tekel Upharsin?" *The Advocate,* November 15:7ff.

Grosswirth, Marvin
1982   "Medical Menace, Doctors Hooked on Drugs." *Ladies Home Journal* 94 (March):141–144.

Gusfield, Joseph R.
1955   "Social Structure and Moral Reform: A Study of the Women's Christian Temperance Union." *American Journal of Sociology* 61 (November):221–232.
1967   "Moral Passage: The Symbolic Process in Public Designations of Deviance." *Social Problems* 15 (Fall):175–188.

Hacker, David W.
1977   "She's Against Gay Rights." *National Observer,* March 12:1, 16.

Hadden, Stuart C.
1973   "Social Dimensions of Jury Decision Making." *International Journal of Criminology and Penology* 1 (August):269–277.

Halverson, Guy
1975   "The Politics of the Gun Trade." *The Christian Science Monitor,* November 14:19.

Haney, C. Allen and Robert Michielutte
1968   "Selective Factors Operating in the Adjudication of Incompetency." *Journal of Health and Social Behavior* 9 (September):233–242.

Haney, Robert W.
1960   *Comstockery in America.* Boston: Beacon Press.

Hardert, Ronald A. et al.
1977   *Sociology and Social Issues.* 2d ed. Hinsdale, Ill.: Dryden Press.

Harris, Richard N.
1973   *The Police Academy: An Inside View.* New York: Wiley and Sons.

Hawkins, Richard and Gary Tiedeman
1975   *The Creation of Deviance, Interpersonal and Organizational Determinants.* Columbus, Ohio: Charles E. Merrill.

Hazelwood, Robert R., Park Elliott Dietz and Ann Wolbert Burgess
1983   *Autoerotic Fatalities.* Lexington, Mass.: D.C. Heath, Lexington Books.

Hazlett, Bill
1976   "30,000 Children Sexually Abused, LAPD Reports." *Los Angeles Times,* November 19:I,3,25.

Heckethorn, Charles William
1965   *The Secret Societies of All Ages and Countries.* New Hyde Park, N.Y.: University Books.

Henderson, George and Willie V. Bryan
1984   *Psychosocial Aspects of Disability.* Springfield, Ill.: Charles C. Thomas.

Henshel, Richard L. and R.A. Silverman, eds.
1975   *Perception in Criminology.* New York: Columbia University Press.

Henslin, James M.
1971   "Criminal Abortion: Making the Decision and Neutralizing the Act." Pp. 113–135 in James M. Henslin, ed., *Studies in the Sociology of Sex.* New York: Appleton-Century-Crofts.

Hertz, Robert
1960   *Death and the Right Hand.* Glencoe, Ill.: Free Press.

Hess, A.G. and D.A. Mariner
1975   "On the Sociology of Crime Cartoons." *International Journal of Criminology and Penology* 3 (August):253–265.

Hessler, Richard M.
1974   "Junkies in White: Drug Addition Among Physicians." Pp. 146–153 in Clifton D. Bryant, ed., *Deviant Behavior, Occupational and Organizational Bases.* Chicago: Rand McNally.

Higgins, Paul C.
1980   *Outsiders in a Hearing World, A Sociology of Deafness.* Beverly Hills: Sage Publications.

Hills, Stuart L.
1971   *Crime, Power, and Morality: The Criminal-Law Process in the United States.* Scranton, Pa.: Chandler.
1980   *Demystifying Social Deviance.* New York: McGraw-Hill.
1982   "Crime and Deviance on a College Campus: The Privilege of Class." *Humanity and Society* 6 (August):257–266.

Hobson, Laura Z.
1976   *Consenting Adult.* New York: Warner Books.

Holzner, Burkart
1972   *Reality Construction in Society.* Rev. ed. Cambridge, Mass.: Schenkman.

Horowitz, Irving Louis and Martin Leibowitz
1968 "Social Deviance and Political Marginality: Toward a Redefinition of the Relation Between Sociology and Politics." *Social Problems* 15 (Winter):280–296.

Horton, Paul B. and Gerald R. Leslie
1965 *The Sociology of Social Problems.* 3d ed. New York: Appleton-Century-Crofts.

Hough, Henry Beetle
1974 "Becoming an Alcoholic." Pp. 15–32 in Charles H. McCaghy, James K. Skipper, Jr., and Mark Lefton, eds., *In Their Own Behalf: Voices from the Margin.* 2d ed. New York: Appleton-Century-Crofts.

Hoult, Thomas Ford
1969 *Dictionary of Modern Sociology.* Totowa, N.J.: Littlefield, Adams and Co.
1972 *March to the Right.* Cambridge, Mass.: Schenkman.

Howard, John
1970 "The Transformation of Stigma: An Analysis of The Gay Liberation Movement." Paper read at meetings of the Pacific Sociological Association, Los Angeles, Calif.

Howard, Ted and Jeremy Rifkin
1977 *Who Should Play God? The Artificial Creation of Life and What It Means for the Future of the Human Race.* New York: Dell.

Hoye, Pamela
1983 "Mainstreaming vs. Special Education, The Law Demands What's Best For The Child." *Mainstream, Magazine of the Able-Disabled* 8 (June):9–15.

Hughes, Everett Cherrington
1945 "Dilemmas and Contradictions of Status." *American Journal of Sociology* 50 (March):353–359.

Hughes, Graham
1964 "The Crime of Incest." *Journal of Criminal Law, Criminology, and Police Science* 55 (Sept.):322–331.

Humphreys, Laud
1970 *Tearoom Trade, Impersonal Sex in Public Places.* Chicago: Aldine.
1972 *Out of the Closets, The Sociology of Homosexual Liberation.* Englewood Cliffs, N.J.: Prentice-Hall.

Inciardi, James A.
1974 "Drugs, Drug Taking and Drug Seeking: Notations on the Dynamics of Myth, Change and Reality." Pp. 203–220 in James A. Inciardi and Carl D. Chambers, eds., *Drugs and the Criminal Justice System.* Beverly Hills: Sage Publications.

1978 *Reflections on Crime, An Introduction to Criminology and Criminal Justice.* New York: Holt, Rinehart and Winston.
1979 "Heroin Use and Street Crime." *Crime and Delinquency* 25 (July):335–346.

Jackson, Don
1973 "Dachau for Queers." Pp. 42–49 in Len Richmond and Gary Noguera, eds., *The Gay Liberation Book.* San Francisco: Ramparts Press.

Jellinek, E.M.
1960 *The Disease Concept of Alcoholism.* New Haven, Conn.: College and University Press.

Johnson, John M. and Diana A. Bohon-Bustamente
1982 "Mass Media Reports and the Emergence of Deviance: Aspects of a Media Politics Model." Paper read at meetings of Society for the Study of Social Problems, San Francisco, Calif.

Johnson, Michael P.
1973 "Commitment: A Conceptual Structure and Empirical Application." *The Sociological Quarterly* 14 (Summer):395–406.

Justice, Blair and Rita Justice
1979 *The Broken Taboo.* New York: Human Sciences Press.

Kando, Thomas
1973 *Sex Change, The Achievement of Gender Identity Among Feminized Transsexuals.* Springfield, Ill.: Charles C. Thomas.

Kaplan, Abraham
1964 *The Conduct of Inquiry.* San Francisco: Chandler.

Kasen, Jill H.
1980 "Whither the Self-made Man? Comic Culture and the Crisis of Legitimation in the United States." *Social Problems* 28 (December):129–148.

Katz, Jonathan
1976 *Gay American History, Lesbians and Gay Men in the U.S.A.* New York: Thomas Y. Crowell.

Kephart, William M.
1982 *Extraordinary Groups, The Sociology of Unconventional Life-Styles.* 2d ed. New York: St. Martin's Press.

Kesey, Ken
1962 *One Flew Over the Cuckoo's Nest.* New York: Signet, New American Library.

Kirkpatrick, Clifford
1955 *The Family, As Process and Institution.* New York: Ronald Press.

Kitsuse, John I.
1962 "Societal Reaction to Deviant Behavior: Problems of Theory and Method." *Social Problems* 9 (Winter):247–256.

Klapp, Orrin E.
1962   *Heroes, Villains, and Fools: The Changing American Character.* Englewood Cliffs, N.J.: Prentice-Hall.

Klein, Malcolm W.
1974   "Labeling, Deterrence, and Recidivism: A Study of Police Dispositions of Juvenile Offenders." *Social Problems* 22 (December):292–303.

Klockars, Carl B.
1974   *The Professional Fence.* New York: The Free Press.

Kopay, David and Perry Deane Young
1977   *The David Kopay Story, An Extraordinary Self-Revelation.* New York: Bantam Books.

Korn, Richard R. and Lloyd W. McCorkle
1959   *Criminology and Penology.* New York: Henry Holt.

Kotarba, Joseph A.
1975   "America Acupuncturists: The New Entrepreneurs of Hope." *Urban Life* 4 (July):149–177.
1984   "One More for the Road: The Subversion of Labeling Within the Tavern Subculture." Pp. 152–160 in Jack D. Douglas, ed., *The Sociology of Deviance.* Boston: Allyn and Bacon.

Kriegel, Leonard
1974   "On Being Crippled." Pp. 233–246 in Charles H. McCaghy, James K. Skipper, Jr., and Mark Lefton, eds., *In Their Own Behalf: Voices from the Margin.* 2d ed. New York: Appleton-Century-Crofts.

Krisberg, Barry
1975   *Crime and Privilege, Toward a New Criminology.* Englewood Cliffs, N.J.: Prentice-Hall.

Kuhn, Manford H.
1967   "The Reference Group Reconsidered." Pp. 171–184 in Jerome G. Manis and Bernard N. Meltzer, eds., *Symbolic Interaction, A Reader in Social Psychology.* Boston: Allyn and Bacon.

Lader, Lawrence
1973   *Abortion II: Making the Revolution.* Boston: Beacon Press.

Latham, Aaron
1976   "The Pike Papers: An Introduction." *The Village Voice* (supplement), February 16:70.

Lauderdale, Pat, ed.
1980   *A Political Analysis of Deviance.* Minneapolis, Minn.: University of Minnesota Press.

Lauritsen, John and David Thorstad
1974   *The Early Homosexual Rights Movement (1864–1935).* New York: Times Change Press.

Law Enforcement Assistance Administration Newsletter
1977   "Mother of 10 Leads Fight Against Gang." December 6:3ff.

LeGrand, Camille E.
1973   "Rape and Rape Laws: Sexism in Society and Law." *California Law Review* 61 (May):919–941.

Lemert, Edwin M.
1951   *Social Pathology, A Systematic Approach to the Theory of Sociopathic Behavior.* New York: McGraw-Hill.
1962   "Paranoia and the Dynamics of Exclusion." Pp. 106–115 in Earl Rubington and Martin S. Weinberg, eds., *Deviance, The Interactionist Perspective.* 2d ed. New York: Macmillan.
1967a   *Human Deviance, Social Problems, and Social Control.* Englewood Cliffs, N.J.: Prentice-Hall.
1967b   "The Juvenile Court—Quest and Realities." Pp. 91–106 in *Task Force Report: Juvenile Delinquency and Youth Crime.* President's Commission on Law Enforcement and Administration of Justice. Washington, D.C.: U.S. Government Printing Office.

Lemkau, Paul V. and Guido M. Crocetti
1967   "Epidemiology." Pp. 225–232 in Alfred M. Freedman and Harold I. Kaplan, eds., *Comprehensive Textbook of Psychiatry.* Baltimore: Williams and Wilkins.

Letkemann, Peter
1973   *Crime as Work.* Englewood Cliffs, N.J.: Prentice-Hall.

Levitin, Teresa E.
1975   "Deviants as Active Participants in the Labeling Process: The Visibly Handicapped." *Social Problems* 22 (April):548–557.

Levy, Howard S.
1966   *Chinese Footbinding, The History of a Curious Erotic Custom.* New York: Walton Rawls.

Lewis, Oscar
1961   *Children of Sanchez.* New York: Random House.

Lichter, Linda S. and S. Robert Lichter
1983   *Prime Time Crime.* Washington, D.C.: The Media Institute.

Lincoln, C. Eric
1961   *The Black Muslims in America.* Boston: Beacon Press.

Lindesmith, Alfred
1940   " 'Dope Fiend' Mythology." *Journal of Criminal Law and Criminology* 31 (May/June):199–208.

Lofland, John
1969   *Deviance and Identity.* Englewood Cliffs, N.J.: Prentice-Hall.

Loman, L. Anthony and William E. Larkin
1976 "Rejection of the Mentally Ill: An Experiment in Labeling." *The Sociological Quarterly* 17 (Autumn):555–560.

Look
1938 "Tell Your Children." November 22:24–25.

Lorber, Judith
1967 "Deviance as Performance: The Case of Illness." *Social Problems* 14 (Winter):302–310.

Lowry, Ritchie P. and Robert P. Rankin
1969 *Sociology, The Science of Society.* New York: Charles Scribner's Sons.

Luckenbill, David F.
1977 "Criminal Homicide as a Situated Transaction." *Social Problems* 25 (December):176–186.

Lundman, Richard J.
1980 *Police and Policing, An Introduction.* New York: Holt, Rinehart and Winston.

Lyman, Stanford M.
1970 *The Asian in the West.* Reno/Las Vegas, Nev.: Western Studies Center, Desert Research Institute.
1974 *Chinese Americans.* New York: Random House.

Lyman, Stanford M. and Marvin B. Scott
1967 "Territoriality; A Neglected Sociological Dimension." Social Problems 15 (Fall):236–249.
1970 *A Sociology of the Absurd.* New York: Appleton-Century-Crofts.

Macgregor, Frances Cooke et al.
1953 *Facial Deformities and Plastic Surgery, A Psychosocial Study.* Springfield, Ill.: Charles C. Thomas.

MacKenzie, Norman
1967 *Secret Societies.* New York: Holt, Rinehart and Winston.

Mainstream, Magazine of the Able-Disabled
1984 "The Wheaties Breakthrough." Vol. 9 (February):4, 8–9.

Mankoff, Milton
1971 "Societal Reaction and Career Deviance: A Critical Analysis." *The Sociological Quarterly* 12 (Spring):204–218.

Manning, Peter K.
1971a "Fixing What You Feared: Notes on the Campus Abortion Search." Pp. 137–166 in James H. Henslin, ed., *Studies in the Sociology of Sex.* New York: Appleton-Century-Crofts.
1971b "The Police: Mandate, Strategies, and Appearance." Pp. 149–193 in Jack D. Douglas, ed., *Crime and Justice in American Society.* Indianapolis: Bobbs-Merrill.

1975 "Deviance and Dogma." *The British Journal of Criminology* 15 (January):1–20.

Maris, Ronald W.
1969 *Social Forces in Urban Suicide.* Homewood, Ill.: Dorsey Press.

Markle, Gerald E. and Ronald J. Troyer
1979 "Smoke Gets In Your Eyes: Cigarette Smoking as Deviant Behavior." *Social Problems* 26 (June):611–625.

Marx, Gary T.
1974a "Ironies of Social Control: Authorities as Possible Contributors to Deviance Through Non-enforcement, Covert Facilitation, and Escalation." Revision of paper read at International Sociological Association meetings, Toronto, Ontario, Canada.
1974b "Thoughts on a Neglected Category of Social Movement Participant: The Agent Provocateur and the Informant." *American Journal of Sociology* 80 (September):402–442.
1980 "The New Police Undercover Work." *Urban Life* 8 (January):399–446.

Marx, Paul
1978 "Legislation Corner." *Mainstream, Magazine of the Able-Disabled* 3 (September):18.

Matza, David
1964 *Delinquency and Drift.* New York: Wiley and Sons.
1969 *Becoming Deviant.* Englewood Cliffs, N.J.: Prentice-Hall.

Mauss, Armand L. and Associates
1975 *Social Problems as Social Movements.* Philadelphia: J.B. Lippincott.

Maxwell, Milton A.
1967 "Alcoholics Anonymous: An Interpretation." Pp. 211–222 in David A. Pittman, ed., *Alcoholism.* New York: Harper and Row.

Mayerson, Robert
1978 "Saving the Queen City's Honor." *Seattle Sun,* November 15:1ff.

McCaghy, Charles H.
1968 "Drinking and Deviance Disavowal: The Case of Child Molesters." *Social Problems* 16 (Summer):43–49.
1976 *Deviant Behavior: Crime, Conflict and Interest Groups.* New York: Macmillan.

McCaghy, Charles H. and James K. Skipper, Jr.
1969 "Lesbian Behavior as an Adaptation to the Occupation of Stripping." *Social Problems* 17 (Fall):262–270.

Meade, Anthony C.
1974 "The Labeling Approach to Delinquency: State

of the Theory as a Function of Method." *Social Forces* 53 (September):83–91.

Meltzer, Bernard N.
1967 "Mead's Social Psychology." Pp. 5–24 in Jerome G. Manis and Bernard N. Meltzer, eds., *Symbolic Interaction, A Reader in Social Psychology*. Boston: Allyn and Bacon.

Merton, Robert K.
1957 *Social Theory and Social Structure*. Rev. ed. Glencoe, Ill.: Free Press.

Merton, Robert K. and Robert Nisbet
1971 *Contemporary Social Problems*. 3d ed. New York: Harcourt Brace Jovanovich.

Meyer, Erich
1981 "The Blind and Social Deprivation." *International Journal of Rehabilitation Research* 4(3):353–364.

Miller, Dorothy and Michael Schwartz
1966 "County Lunacy Commission Hearings: Some Observations of Commitments to a State Mental Hospital." *Social Problems* 14 (Summer):26–35.

Miller, Merle
1971 "What It Means to Be a Homosexual." *New York Times Magazine*, January 17:9ff; October 10:67ff.

Millman, Marcia
1980 *Such A Pretty Face*. New York: W.W. Norton.

Mills, C. Wright
1959 *The Sociological Imagination*. New York: Oxford University Press.

Milner, Christina and Richard Milner
1972 *Black Players, The Secret World of Black Pimps*. Boston: Little, Brown.

The Missoulian
1973 "Hookers' Guild Formed in 'Frisco." June 26:12.

Molotch, Harvey and Marilyn Lester
1974 "News as Purposive Behavior: On the Strategic Use of Routine Events." *American Sociological Review* 39 (February):101–112.

Montagu, Ashley
1968 "Chromosomes and Crime." *Psychology Today* 2 (October):43–49.
1979 *The Elephant Man, A Study in Human Dignity*. New York: E.P. Dutton.

Morgan, Robin, ed.
1970 *Sisterhood Is Powerful, An Anthology of Writings from the Women's Liberation Movement*. New York: Random House.

Moritz, Frederic A.
1976 "Hearst: What Evidence to Bar?" *The Christian Science Monitor*, February 6:3.

Movahedi, Siamak
1975 "Loading the Dice in Favor of Madness." *Journal of Health and Social Behavior* 16 (June):192–197.

Murphy, Fred F., Mary M. Shirley and Helen L. Witmer
1946 "The Incidence of Hidden Delinquency." *American Journal of Orthopsychiatry* 16 (October):686–696.

Natanson, Maurice
1973 *The Social Dynamics of George Herbert Mead*. The Hague: Martinus Nijoff.

National Center for Health Statistics
1982 *Vital Statistics of the U.S., 1978. Vol. II-Mortality*, Part A. D.H.H.S. Publication No. (PHS) 83-1101, Washington, D.C.: U.S. Government Printing Office.

National Commission on the Causes and Prevention of Violence
1970 *Law and Order Reconsidered*. New York: Bantam Books.

National Commission on Marihuana and Drug Abuse
1972 *Marihuana: A Signal of Misunderstanding*. Washington, D.C.: U.S. Government Printing Office.

National Observer
1977 "Views from Readers: On Anita Bryant and 'Gays.'" April 16:12.

National Organization for the Reform of Marijuana Laws
n.d. *Statement in Support of the Need to Reform Marijuana Laws*. Washington, D.C.

NEA Today
1983 "Heart of the Law," March, p. 2.

Nettler, Gwynn
1974 *Explaining Crime*. New York: McGraw-Hill.

Newberger, Eli H. and Richard Bourne
1978 "The Medicalization and Legalization of Child Abuse." *American Journal of Orthopsychiatry* 48 (October):593–607.

Newcomb, Theodore M.
1950 *Social Psychology*. New York: Dryden Press.

Newman, Donald J.
1966 *Conviction: The Determination of Guilt or Innocence Without Trial*. Boston: Little, Brown.

Newman, Graeme R.
1975 "A Theory of Deviance Removal." *British Journal of Sociology* 26 (June):203–217.

Newsweek
1973 "This Is Your Veep." October 22:25–36.
1977 "The Silent One." November 7:89–90.
1982a "Curbing Drunk Drivers." January 25:30.
1982b "Smoking More or Less." October 25:40.

New Times Weekly
1977   "From Drive-in Banking to Call-in Robbery."
        October 26–November 11:4.

New York Times
1983a   "Guide Dog Helps Blind Woman Work in
        Newspaper Route." October 27:15.
1983b   "For Homosexuals' Parents, Strength in Com-
        munity." October 10:16.

Nielsen Report
1984   *Nielsen Report on Television*. Northbrook, Ill.:
        A.C. Nielsen.

Norton, Nancy Lee and Geoffrey Stokes
1977   "Right-to-Life: Documents Reveal Improper
        Financing." *Village Voice*, November 28:12.

"Notes and Comment"
1961   "Corporate Crime." *Yale Law Journal* 71 (De-
        cember):280–306.

Nuehring, Elane and Gerald E. Markle
1974   "Nicotine and Norms: The Re-emergence
        of a Deviant Behavior." *Social Problems* 21
        (April):511–526.

Nunnally, Jum C.
1961   *Popular Conceptions of Mental Health; Their De-
        velopment and Change*. New York: Holt, Rine-
        hart and Winston.

Nye, F. Ivan
1958   *Family Relationships and Delinquent Behavior*.
        New York: Wiley and Sons.

Odgers, Sue
1978   "Sex on Wheels." *Paraplegia News* 31
        (April):38–39.

Packer, Herbert L.
1968   *The Limits of the Criminal Sanction*. Stanford:
        Stanford University Press.

Papachristou, Judith
1976   *Women Together*. New York: Alfred A. Knopf.

Paraplegia News
1977a   "Trolleys to be Partly Accessible." January:28.
1977b   "Barrier Busters Get Tax Break." January:35.
1978   "Crystal the Terrible Tumbleweed." April:24–
        25.

Parker, Jerry and Pat Lauderdale
1980   "Political Deviance in Courtroom Settings."
        Pp. 47–71 in Pat Lauderdale, ed., *A Political
        Analysis of Deviance*. Minneapolis: University of
        Minnesota Press.

Partridge, Eric
1970   *A Dictionary of Slang and Unconventional English*.
        7th ed. New York: Macmillan.

Payne, William D.
1973   "Negative Labels: Passageways and Prisons."
        Crime and Delinquency 19 (January):33–40.

People Weekly
1984a   "New Hope, Old Anguish." March 19:25–27.
1984b   "Haunted by Her Past." August 6:80–82.

Pepinsky, Harold E. and Paul Jesilow
1984   *Myths That Cause Crime*. Cabin John, Md.:
        Seven Locks Press.

Perry, Joseph B., Jr. and Erdwin H. Pfuhl, Jr.
1963   "Adjustment of Children in 'Solo' and 'Remar-
        riage' Homes." *Marriage and Family Living* 25
        (May):221–223.

Perry, Troy D.
1973   *The Lord Is My Shepherd and He Knows I'm Gay*.
        New York: Bantam Books.

Pfohl, Stephen J.
1977   "The 'Discovery' of Child Abuse." *Social Prob-
        lems* 24 (February):310–323.
1985   *Images of Deviance and Social Control, A Sociolog-
        ical History*. New York: McGraw-Hill.

Pfuhl, Erdwin H., Jr.
1978   "The Unwed Father: A 'Non-Deviant' Rule
        Breaker." *The Sociological Quarterly* 19 (Win-
        ter):113–128.
1983   "Police Strikes and Conventional Crime: A
        Look at the Data." *Criminology* 21 (Novem-
        ber):489–503.
1985   "Humanistic Criminology: Future Prospects."
        Forthcoming.

Phillips, Derek
1963   "Rejection: A Possible Consequence of Seeking
        Help for Mental Disorders." *American Sociologi-
        cal Review* 28 (December):963–973.

Phoenix Gazette
1984a   "Pedophilia: America's Dirty Little Secret."
        September 19:A-1.
1984b   "Sex Assaults on Youths Bring 58½ Year
        Term." September 13:C-1.

Pierson, Ransdell
1982   "Uptight on Gay News." *Columbia Journalism
        Review*, March/April:25–33.

Piliavin, Irving and Scott Briar
1964   "Police Encounters with Juveniles." *American
        Journal of Sociology* 70 (September):206–214.

Piven, Frances Fox
1981   "Deviant Behavior and the Remaking of the
        World." *Social Problems* 28 (June):489–508.

Piven, Frances Fox and Richard A. Cloward
1977   *Poor People's Movements, Why They Succeed,
        How They Fail*. New York: Pantheon Books.

Platt, Anthony
1969   *The Child Savers, The Invention of Delinquency*.
        Chicago: University of Chicago Press.

Playboy
1976 "Playboy Interview: Jimmy Carter." November:63–86.
1978 "Playboy Interview: Anita Bryant." May:73ff.
1980 "Forum Newsfront." July:59.

Polsky, Ned
1967 *Hustlers, Beats, and Others.* Chicago: Aldine.

Ponse, Barbara
1976 "Secrecy in the Lesbian World." *Urban Life* 5 (October):313–338.

Powell, Elwin H.
1958 "Occupation, Status, and Suicide: Toward a Redefinition of Anomie." *American Sociological Review* 23 (April):131–139.

Powell, Lyman P.
1940 *Mary Baker Eddy, A Life Size Portrait.* New York: L.P. Powell.

President's Commission on Law Enforcement and Administration of Justice
1967a *The Challenge of Crime in a Free Society.* Washington, D.C.: U.S. Government Printing Office.
1967b *Task Force Report: Organized Crime.* Washington, D.C.: U.S. Government Printing Office.

Quinney, Richard
1965 "A Conception of Man and Society for Criminology." *The Sociological Quarterly* 6 (Spring):119–127.
1969 *Crime and Justice in Society.* Ed. Boston: Little, Brown.
1970a *The Problem of Crime.* New York: Dodd, Mead.
1970b *The Social Reality of Crime.* Boston: Little, Brown.
1973 "There's a Lot of Folks Grateful to the Lone Ranger: With Some Notes on the Rise and Fall of American Criminology." *The Insurgent Sociologist* 4 (Fall):56–64.
1975 *Criminology, Analysis and Critique of Crime in America.* Boston: Little, Brown.

Radzinowicz, Leon
1966 *Ideology and Crime.* New York: Columbia University Press.

Rapoport, David C. and Yonah Alexander
1982 *The Morality of Terrorism, Religious and Secular Justifications.* New York: Pergamon Press.

Reasons, Charles E.
1970 "A Developmental Model for the Analysis of Social Problems: Prostitution and Moral Reform in Twentieth Century America." Pacific Sociological Association, Anaheim, Calif., April 1970.
1974 "The 'Dope' on the Bureau of Narcotics in Maintaining the Criminal Approach to the Drug Problem." Pp. 144–155 in Charles E. Reasons, ed., *The Criminologist: Crime and the Criminal.* Pacific Palisades, Calif.: Goodyear.

Reiss, Albert J., Jr., and David J. Bordua
1967 "Environment and Organization: A Perspective on the Police." Pp. 25–55 in David J. Bordua, ed., *The Police: Six Sociological Essays.* New York: Wiley and Sons.

Reitman, Ben L.
1975 *Sister of the Road, The Autobiography of Box-Car Bertha.* New York: Harper and Row.

Richards, Pamela, Richard A. Berk and Brenda Forster
1979 *Crime as Play: Delinquency in a Middle Class Suburb.* Cambridge, Mass.: Ballinger.

Ritzer, George
1975 *Sociology, A Multiple Paradigm Science.* Boston: Allyn and Bacon.

Robin, Gerald D.
1969 "Employees as Offenders." *Journal of Research in Crime and Delinquency* 6 (January):17–33.
1970 "The Corporate and Judicial Disposition of Employee Thieves." Pp. 119–142 in Erwin O. Smigel and H. Laurence Ross, eds., *Crimes Against Bureaucracy.* New York: Van Nostrand Reinhold.

Roby, Pamela A.
1969 "Politics and Criminal Law: Revision of the New York State Penal Law on Prostitution." *Social Problems* 17 (Summer):83–109.

Rodriguez, Octavio
1974 "Getting Straight: Reflections of a Former Addict." Pp. 83–89 in Jerry Jacobs, ed., *Deviance: Field Studies and Self-Disclosures.* Palo Alto, Calif.: National Press Books.

Romano, Mary D.
1982 "Sex and Disability, Are They Mutually Exclusive?" Pp. 64–75 in M. Eisenberg, C. Griggins, and R. Duval, eds., *Disabled People as Second Class Citizens.* New York: Springer.

Rose, Arnold M.
1965 *Sociology, The Study of Human Relations,* 2d ed. New York: Alfred A. Knopf.
1968 "Law and the Causation of Social Problems." *Social Problems* 16 (Summer):18–40.

Rosenberg, Morris
1979 *Conceiving the Self.* New York: Basic Books.

Rosenhan, D.L.
1973 "On Being Sane in Insane Places." *Science* 179 (January 19):250–258.

Rosett, Arthur and Donald R. Cressey
1976 *Justice by Consent: Plea Bargains in the American Courthouse.* Philadelphia: J.B. Lippincott.

214

Ross, Robert and Graham L. Staines
1972   "The Politics of Analyzing Social Problems."
        Social Problems 20 (Summer):18–40.

Rossi, Peter H., E. Waite, C.E. Bose and R.E. Berk
1974   "The Seriousness of Crime: Normative Struc-
        ture and Individual Differences." *American So-
        ciological Review* 39 (April):224–237.

Rossman, Parker
1973   "The Pederasts." *Society* 10 (March/April):29–
        35.
1976   *Sexual Experience Between Men and Boys: Explor-
        ing the Pederast Underground.* New York: Asso-
        ciation Press.

Rotenberg, Mordechai
1974   "Self-Labeling: A Missing Link in the 'Social
        Reaction' Theory of Deviance." *The Sociological
        Review* 22 (August):335–354.

Rubington, Earl
1975   "Top and Bottom: How Police Administrators
        and Public Inebriates View Decriminalization."
        Journal of Drug Issues 5 (Fall):412–425.

Rubington, Earl and Martin S. Weinberg
1973   *Deviance, The Interactionist Perspective.* 2d ed.
        New York: Macmillan.
1977   *The Study of Social Problems.* 2d ed. New York:
        Oxford University Press.
1981   *Deviance, The Interactionist Perspective.* 4th ed.
        New York: Macmillan.

Russell, Diana E.H.
1982   *Rape in Marriage.* New York: Macmillan.

Safilios-Rothschild, Constantina
1970   *The Sociology and Social Psychology of Disability
        and Rehabilitation.* New York: Random House.

Sagarin, Edward
1969   *Odd Man In, Societies of Deviants in America.*
        Chicago: Quandrangle Books.
1975   *Deviants and Deviance, An Introduction to the
        Study of Disvalued People and Behavior.* New
        York: Praeger.

Sagarin, Edward and Donal E.J. MacNamara
1975   "The Homosexual as a Crime Victim." *Inter-
        national Journal of Criminology and Penology* 3
        (February):13–25.

Sataloff, Joseph, Robert Thayer Sataloff and Lawrence A.
Vassallo
1980   *Hearing Loss.* 2d ed. Philadelphia: J.B. Lippin-
        cott.

Scheff, Thomas J.
1964   "The Societal Reaction to Deviance: Ascriptive
        Elements in the Psychiatric Screening of Mental
        Patients in a Midwestern State." *Social Problems*
        11 (Spring):401–413.
1966   *Being Mentally Ill: A Sociological Theory.* Chi-
        cago: Aldine.
1968   "Negotiating Reality: Notes on Power in the
        Assessment of Responsibility." *Social Problems*
        16 (Summer):3–17.

Schmid, Alex P. and Janny de Graaf
1982   *Violence as Communication, Insurgent Terrorism
        and the Western News Media.* Beverly Hills: Sage
        Publications.

Schmid, Calvin F.
1928   *Suicides in Seattle, 1914 to 1925.* Seattle: Univer-
        sity of Washington Publications in the Social
        Sciences.

Schonell, F.J. and B.H. Watts
1956   "A First Survey of the Effects of a Subnormal
        Child on the Family Unit." *American Journal of
        Mental Deficiency* 61 (July):210–219.

Schrag, Peter
1970   "America's Other Radicals." *Harper's Magazine,*
        August:35–46.

Schur, Edwin M.
1971   *Labeling Deviant Behavior, Its Sociological Impli-
        cations.* New York: Harper and Row.
1973   *Radical Nonintervention, Rethinking the Delin-
        quency Problem.* Englewood Cliffs, N.J.: Pren-
        tice-Hall.
1979   *Interpreting Deviance: A Sociological Introduction.*
        New York: Harper and Row.
1980   *The Politics of Deviance, Stigma Contests and the
        Uses of Power.* Englewood Cliffs, N.J.: Prentice-
        Hall.
1984   *Labeling Women Deviant: Gender, Stigma, and So-
        cial Control.* New York: Random House.

Schwab, John J. and Ruby B. Schwab
1973   "The Epidemiology of Mental Illness." Pp. 58–
        83 in Gene Usdin, ed., *Psychiatry: Education and
        Image.* New York: Bruner/Mazel.

Schwartz, Charlotte Green
1956   "The Stigma of Mental Illness." *Journal of Re-
        habilitation* 22 (July/August):7–29.

Schwartz, John L.
1976   "Officer Calls on Legislators to Examine Smut
        for a Day." *Arizona Republic,* April 26:A-1, 12.

Schwartz, Richard D. and Jerome H. Skolnick
1964   "Two Studies of Legal Stigma." Pp. 103–117 in
        Howard Becker, ed., *The Other Side, Perspec-
        tives on Deviance.* New York: The Free Press of
        Glencoe.

Scott, Marvin B. and Stanford M. Lyman
1968   "Accounts." *American Sociological Review* 33
        (February):46–62.

Scott, Robert A.
1965   "Comments About Interpersonal Processes of

Rehabilitation." Pp. 132–138 in Marvin B. Sussman, ed., *Sociology and Rehabiltation*. Washington, D.C.: American Sociological Association.

1969 *The Making of Blind Men*. New York: Russell Sage Foundation.

1970 "The Construction of Conceptions of Stigma by Professional Experts." Pp. 255–290 in Jack D. Douglas, ed., *Deviance and Respectability, The Social Construction of Moral Meanings*. New York: Basic Books.

1972 "A Proposed Framework for Analyzing Deviance as a Property of Social Order." Pp. 9–35 in Robert A. Scott and Jack D. Douglas, eds., *Theoretical Perspectives on Deviance*. New York: Basic Books.

Secord, Paul F. and Carl W. Backman
1964 *Social Psychology*. New York: McGraw-Hill.

Sellin, Thorsten
1951 "The Significance of Records of Crime." *Law Quarterly Review* 67 (October):489–504.

1962 "A Sociological Approach to the Study of Crime Causation." Pp. 3–9 in M. Wolfgang, L. Savitz, and N. Johnston, eds., *The Sociology of Crime and Delinquency*. New York: Wiley and Sons.

Shaskolsky, Leon
1973 "The Legal Institution: The Legitimizing Appendage." Pp. 294–337 in Larry T. Reynolds and James M. Henslin, eds., *American Society, A Critical Analysis*. New York: David McKay.

Shaw, Clifford R. and Henry D. McKay
1942 *Juvenile Delinquency and Urban Areas*. Chicago: University of Chicago Press.

Shaw, Colin
1969 "Television and Popular Morality: The Predicament of the Broadcasters." Pp. 117–127 in Paul Halmos, ed., *The Sociology of Mass Media Communicators*. Sociology Review Monograph No. 13. University of Keele, Great Britain.

Shilts, Randy
1982 *The Mayor of Castro Street, The Life and Times of Harvey Milk*. New York: St. Martin's Press.

Short, James F., Jr. and F. Ivan Nye
1958 "Extent of Unrecorded Juvenile Delinquency, Tentative Conclusions." *Journal of Criminal Law, Criminology, and Police Science* 49 (November/December):296–302.

Short, James F., Jr. and Fred L. Strodtbeck
1965 *Group Processes and Gang Delinquency*. Chicago: University of Chicago Press.

Shover, Neal
1984 "The Official Construction of Deviant Identi-

ties." Pp. 66–74 in Jack D. Douglas, ed., *The Sociology of Deviance*. Boston: Allyn and Bacon.

Shuey, Chris
1978 "The Nuke Fight Escalates." *New Times Weekly* 10 (December 6–13):3, 25.

Siegel, Harvey H.
1973 *Alcohol Detoxification Programs: Treatment Instead of Jail*. Springfield, Ill.: Charles C. Thomas.

Simmel, Georg
1950 *The Sociology of Georg Simmel*. Kurt H. Wolff, ed. and trans. New York: The Free Press.

Simmons, J.L.
1969 *Deviants*. Berkeley, Calif.: Glendessary Press.

Simpson, Ruth
1977 *From the Closet to the Courts, The Lesbian Transition*. New York: Penguin Books.

Singer, Max
1971 "The Vitality of Mythical Numbers." *The Public Interest* 23 (Spring):3–9.

Sklar, Ronald B.
1979 "The Criminal Law and the Incest Offender: A Case for Decriminalization?" *American Academy of Psychiatry and the Law Bulletin* 7(1):69–77.

Skolnick, Jerome H.
1966 *Justice Without Trial: Law Enforcement in a Democratic Society*. New York: Wiley and Sons.

Skolnick, Jerome H. and Richard Woodworth
1967 "Bureaucracy, Information, and Social Control: A Study of a Morals Detail." Pp. 99–136 in David J. Bordua, ed., *The Police: Six Sociological Essays*. New York: Wiley and Sons.

Smith, Dwight C., Jr.
1975 *The Mafia Mystique*. New York: Basic Books.

1976 "Mafia: The Prototypical Alien Conspiracy." *The Annals of the American Academy of Political and Social Science* 423 (January):75–88.

Smith, Philip M.
1955 "Broken Homes and Juvenile Delinquency." *Sociology and Social Research* 39 (May/June):307–311.

Smith, Richard Austin
1970 "The Incredible Electrical Conspiracy." Pp. 529–548 in Marvin E. Wolfgang, Leonard Savitz, and Norman Johnston, eds., *The Sociology of Crime and Delinquency*. 2d ed. New York: Wiley and Sons.

Smythe, Dallas W.
1954 "Reality as Presented by Television." *Public Opinion Quarterly* 18 (Summer):143–156.

Spector, Malcolm
1977 "Legitimizing Homosexuality." *Society* 14 (July/August):52–56.

216

Spector, Malcolm and John I. Kitsuse
1977   *Constructing Social Problems.* Menlo Park, Calif.: Cummings.

Spradley, James P.
1970   *You Owe Yourself a Drunk.* Boston: Little, Brown.

State Press (Arizona State University)
1980   " 'Alibi Service' Provides $20 Substitute Roommate." January 23:8.

Steinhoff, Patricia G., Roy G. Smith and Milton Diamond
1971   "The Characteristics and Motivations of Women Receiving Abortions." Unpublished.

Sudnow, David
1965   "Normal Crimes." Pp. 174–185 in Earl Rubington and Martin S. Weinberg, eds., *Deviance, The Interactionist Perspective.* 2d ed. New York: Macmillan.

Sutherland, Edwin H.
1937   *The Professional Thief, By a Professional Thief.* Chicago: University of Chicago Press.
1945   "Is 'White-Colar Crime' Crime?" Pp. 62–77 in Albert Cohen, Alfred Lindesmith, and Karl Schuessler, eds., *The Sutherland Papers.* Bloomington, Ind.: Indiana University Press.
1947   *Principles of Criminology.* 4th ed. Philadelphia: J.B. Lippincott.
1950a   "The Diffusion of Sexual Psychopath Laws." *American Journal of Sociology* 56 (September):142–148.
1950b   "The Sexual Psychopath Laws." *Journal of Criminal Law and Criminology* 40 (January/February):543–554.
1956   "Crime of Corporations." Pp. 78–96 in Albert Cohen, Alfred Lindesmith, and Karl Schuessler, eds., *The Sutherland Papers.* Bloomington, Ind.: Indiana University Press.

Sutherland, Edwin H. and Donald R. Cressey
1978   *Criminology.* 10th ed. Philadelphia: J.B. Lippincott.

Sykes, Gresham M.
1958   *The Society of Captives, A Study of a Maximum Security Prison.* Princeton: Princeton University Press.
1972   "The Future of Criminality." *American Behavioral Scientist* 15(3):403–419.

Sykes, Gresham M. and David Matza
1957   "Techniques of Neutralization: A Theory of Delinquency." *American Sociological Review* 22 (December):664–670.

Szasz, Thomas S.
1976a   "Some Call It Brainwashing." *The New Republic* 174 (March 6): 10–12.

1976b   "Mercenary Psychiatry." *The New Republic* 174 (March 13):10–12.

Taber, Merlin, Herbert C. Quay, Harold Mark and Vicki Nealey
1969   "Disease Ideology and Mental Health Research." *Social Problems* 16 (Winter):349–357.

Tannenbaum, Frank
1938   *Crime and the Community.* Boston: Ginn.

Taylor, Robert Lewis
1966   *Vessel of Wrath, The Life and Times of Carry Nation.* New York: New American Library.

Terry, W. Clinton, III, and David F. Luckenbill
1976   "Investigating Criminal Homicides: Police Work in Reporting and Solving Murders." Pp. 79–95 in William B. Sanders and Howard C. Daudistel, eds., *The Criminal Justice Process, A Reader.* New York: Praeger.

Thomlinson, Ralph
1965   *Sociological Concepts and Research, Acquisition, Analysis, and Interpretation of Social Information.* New York: Random House.

Thorsell, Bernard A. and Lloyd W. Klemke
1972   "The Labeling Process: Reinforcement and Deterrent." *Law and Society Review* 6 (February):393–403.

Thrasher, Frederic M.
1936   *The Gang.* Chicago: University of Chicago Press.
1963   *The Gang.* Abridged ed. Chicago: University of Chicago Press.

Time
1966   "The Supreme Court, Bad News for Smut Peddlers." April 1:56–57.
1974   "Lefty Liberation." January 7:85.
1975a   "Armed Forces: Homosexual Sergeant." June 9:18–19.
1975b   "Male and Female." June 16:73.
1977   "Let's Hear It for Stutterers' Lib!" October 31:98–101.
1982a   "Is the Party Finally Over?" April 26:58.
1982b   "How Toe-dully Max Is Their Valley." September 27:56.

Toby, Jackson
1957   "The Differential Impact of Family Disorganization." *American Sociological Review* 22 (October):505–512.

Toch, Hans
1965   *The Social Psychology of Social Movements.* Indianapolis: Bobbs-Merrill.

Toffler, Alvin
1970   *Future Shock.* New York: Bantam Books.

Tonge, Peter
1980   "$30,000 of 'Pilferware' Makes Its Way Back to

the Waldorf." *Christian Science Monitor*, December 2:17.

Truzzi, Marcello
1968 "Lilliputians in Gulliver's Land: The Social Role of the Dwarf." Pp. 197–211 in Marcello Truzzi, ed., *Sociology and Everyday Life*. Englewood Cliffs, N.J.: Prentice-Hall.

Turk, Austin T.
1976 "Law as a Weapon in Social Conflict." *Social Problems* 23 (February):276–291.

Turner, Henry A.
1958 "How Pressure Groups Operate." *Annals of the American Academy of Political and Social Science* 319 (September):63–72.

Turner, Ralph H.
1972 "Deviance Avowal as Neutralization of Commitment." *Social Problems* 19 (Winter):308–321.

Unitarian Universalist World
1976 "Coalition Opposes Anti-Abortion Plan." February 15:1–2.

U.S. Department of Justice
1975 *Criminal Victimization Surveys in 13 American Cities*. Washington, D.C.: U.S. Government Printing Office.
1981a "Addicts Commit Staggering Amount of Crime." *Justice Assistance News* 2 (May):5.
1981b *Criminal Victimization in the United States*. 1979.
1983 "Many Inmates Committed Crime While Abusing Drugs." *Justice Assistance News* 4 (April):3.

U.S. News and World Report
1978 "Uncle Sam's Computer Has Got You." April 10:44–48.
1983 "Pro and Con: Send All Drunk Drivers to Jail?" January 17:71–72.

Vago, Steven
1981 *Law and Society*. Englewood Cliffs, N.J.: Prentice-Hall.

Vander Zanden, James W.
1983 *American Minority Relations*. 4th ed. New York: Alfred A. Knopf.

Van Maanen, John
1978 "The Asshole." Pp. 221–238 in Peter K. Manning and John Van Maanen, eds., *Policing: A View From the Street*. Santa Monica, Calif.: Goodyear.

Varni, Charles A.
1972 "An Exploratory Study of Spouse-Swapping." *Pacific Sociological Review* 15 (October):507–522.

Vold, George B. and Thomas J. Bernard
1979 *Theoretical Criminology*. 2d ed. New York: Oxford University Press.

Vose, Clement E.
1958 "Litigation as a Form of Pressure Group Activity." *Annals* 319 (September):20–31.

Walker, Nigel and M. Argyle
1964 "Does the Law Affect Moral Judgments?" *British Journal of Criminology* 4 (October):570–581.

Wallace, Samuel E.
1965 *Skid Row as a Way of Life*. Totowa, N.J.: Bedminster Press.

Wallerstein, James S. and Clement J. Wyle
1947 "Our Law-Abiding Law-Breakers." *Probation* 25 (March/April):107–112.

Warren, Carol A.B.
1974a *Identity and Community in the Gay World*. New York: Wiley and Sons.
1974b "The Use of Stigmatizing Social Labels in Conventionalizing Deviant Behavior." *Sociology and Social Research* 58 (April):303–311.
1980 "Destigmatization of Identity: From Deviant to Charismatic." *Qualitative Sociology* 3 (Spring):59–72.

Warren, Carol A.B. and John M. Johnson
1972 "A Critique of Labeling Theory from the Phenomenological Perspective." Pp. 69–92 in Robert A. Scott and Jack D. Douglas, eds., *Theoretical Perspectives on Deviance*. New York: Basic Books.

Watson, Lyndon
1978 "Awakening of the New Minority." *Paraplegia News* 31 (May):20.

Weber, Max
1962 *Basic Concepts in Sociology*. New York: Philosophical Library.

Wegner, Dennis L. and C. Richard Fletcher
1969 "The Effect of Legal Counsel on Admissions to a State Mental Hospital: A Confrontation of Professions." *Journal of Health and Social Behavior* 10 (March):66–72.

Weinberg, Martin S.
1957 "Sexual Modesty, Social Meanings, and the Nudist Camp." *Social Problems* 11 (Winter):311–318.
1968 "The Problems of Midgets and Dwarfs and Organizational Remedies: A Study of the Little People of America." *Journal of Health and Social Behavior* 9 (March):65–71.
1981a "Becoming a Nudist." Pp. 291–304 in Earl Rubington and Martin S. Weinberg, eds., *Deviance, The Interactionist Perspective*. 4th ed. New York: Macmillan.
1981b "The Nudist Management of Respectability." Pp. 336–345 in Earl Rubington and Martin S. Weinberg, eds., *Deviance, The Interactionist Perspective*. 4th ed. New York: Macmillan.

Weinberg, Martin S. and Colin J. Williams
1974 *Male Homosexuals, Their Problems and Adaptations.* New York: Oxford University Press.

Weis, Kurt and Michael E. Milakovich
1974 "Political Misuses of Crime Rates." *Society* 11 (July/August):27–33.

Westley, William A.
1970 *Violence and the Police: A Sociological Study of Law, Custom, and Morality.* Cambridge, Mass.: The MIT Press.

Whitam, Frederick L.
1975 "Homosexuality as Emergent Behavior." Paper presented at the 46th annual meeting of the Pacific Sociological Association, Victoria, British Columbia, April 17–19.
1977a "The Homosexual Role: A Reconsideration." *The Journal of Sex Research* 13 (February):1–11.
1977b "Childhood Indicators of Male Homosexuality." *Archives of Sexual Behavior* 6 (2):89–96.

White, J.V.
1982 "Privacy in the Information Society." *Vital Speeches of the Day* 48 (March):313–315.

White, Ralph K., Beatrice A. Wright and Tamara Dembo
1948 "Studies in Adjustment to Visible Injuries: Evaluation of Curiosity by the Injured." *Journal of Abnormal and Social Psychology* 43 (January):13–28.

Whiting, Leila
1977 "The Central Registry for Child Abuse Cases: Rethinking Basic Assumptions." *Child Welfare* 56 January:761–767.

Wicker, Tom
1971 "The Harrisburg Story." *New York Times*, August 8. Cited in Robert Ross and Graham L. Staines, "The Politics of Analyzing Social Problems." *Social Problems* 20 (Summer 1972):24.

Wilde, William A.
1969 "Official News: Decision Making in a Metropolitan Newspaper." Unpublished Ph.D. dissertation. Northwestern University.

Wilkins, Leslie T.
1965 *Social Deviance: Social Policy, Action, and Research.* Englewood Cliffs, N.J.: Prentice-Hall.

Wilkinson, Karen
1974 "The Broken Family and Juvenile Delinquency." *Social Problems* 21 (June):726–739.

Wilkinson, Paul
1977 *Terrorism and the Liberal State.* New York: Wiley and Sons.

Williams, Colin J. and Martin S. Weinberg
1970 "Being Discovered: A Study of Homosexuals in the Military." *Social Problems* 18 (Fall):217–227.

Williams, Jay R. and Martin Gold
1972 "From Delinquent Behavior to Official Delinquency." *Social Problems* 20 (Fall):209–229.

Williams, Nancy
1974 "Sex for Money." Tempe, Arizona: The State Press (November 14).

Williams, Robin
1960 *American Society, A Sociological Interpretation.* 2d ed. Rev. New York: Alfred A. Knopf.

Winick, Charles
1964 "Physician Narcotic Addicts." Pp. 261–279 in Howard S. Becker, ed., *The Other Side, Perspectives on Deviance.* New York: The Free Press.
1978 *Deviance and Mass Media.* Ed. Beverly Hills, Calif.: Sage Publications.

Wiseman, Jacqueline P.
1970 *Stations of the Lost, The Treatment of Skid Row Alcoholics.* Englewood Cliffs, N.J.: Prentice-Hall.

World Almanac and Book of Facts
1983 New York: Newspaper Enterprise Association.

Wrong, Dennis H.
1961 "The Oversocialized Conception of Man in Modern Sociology." *American Sociological Review* 26 (April):183–193.
1968 "Some Problems in Defining Social Power." *American Journal of Sociology* 73 (May):673–681.
1979 *Power, Its Forms, Bases and Uses.* New York: Harper and Row.

Yankelovich, Daniel
1974 *The New Morality, A Profile of American Youth in the 70's.* New York: McGraw-Hill.
1981 "New Rules in American Life: Searching for Self-fulfillment in a World Turned Upside Down." *Psychology Today* 15 (April):35–91.

Yarrow, Marian Radke et al.
1955 "The Psychological Meaning of Mental Illness in the Family." *Journal of Social Issues* 11 (No. 4):12–24.

Yinger, J. Milton
1965 *Toward a Field Theory of Behavior, Personality and Social Structure.* New York: McGraw-Hill.

Young, Jock
1971 "The Role of Police as Amplifiers of Deviancy, Negotiators of Reality and Translators of Fantasy." Pp. 27–61 in Stanley Cohen, ed., *Images of Deviance.* Baltimore: Penguin Books.

Zukav, Gary
1979 *The Dancing Wu Li Masters, An Overview of the New Physics.* New York: Bantam Books.

Zwicker, Barrie
1982 "The Body Politic Acquittal." Pp. 5–6 in *Newsletter*, The Sex Information and Education Council of Canada, Vol. 17 (Fall):5–6.

Author Index

Subject Index

229